THE
LEGACY OF THE
MIDDLE AGES

LA DAME À LA LICORNE

About 1500. From a tapestry, Musée de Cluny, Paris

THE

LEGACY OF THE

MIDDLE AGES

EDITED BY

C. G. CRUMP & E. F. JACOB

OXFORD

AT THE CLARENDON PRESS

Oxford University Press, Walton Street, Oxford OX2 6DP

Oxford New York Toronto
Delhi Bombay Calcutta Madras Karachi
Petaling Jaya Singapore Hong Kong Tokyo
Nairobi Dar es Salaam Cape Town
Melbourne Auckland

and associated companies in
Beirut Berlin Ibadan Nicosia

Oxford is a trade mark of Oxford University Press

Published in the United States
by Oxford University Press, New York

ISBN 0 19 821907 5

First published 1926
Tenth impression

Printed in Great Britain
at the University Printing House, Oxford
by David Stanford
Printer to the University

PREFACE

THE legacies of Greece or Rome or Judaea come to us from men who owned a common language, a common civilization, and a common country. Those men left us gifts marked by signs easy to recognize and appreciate. But the legacy of the Middle Ages comes to us from men who lived in hard and dangerous times, in a society so chaotic and ill-defined that it is difficult to form any coherent picture of its mind and institutions. Greece, Rome, and Judaea are definite names, and it is not impossible to assign to their civilizations a definite place and time. But the Middle Ages have no clear beginning and can scarcely be said to have an end ; their chronological limits are as obscure as the frontiers of the nations which arose in those times of storm. Their legacy comes not from the citizens of one city, or the narrow limits of one country, cities and countries great because men of great genius and strong character lived together in narrow limits, but from all the many lands which may be defined as Western Europe. Within this area there were many intellectual centres whose importance altered with the changes and chances of the times. The difficulty of including in one volume all that was transmitted to us from this wide area and these many centuries need not be elaborated ; the success of the attempt can only be judged by the reader.

If any coherent picture of the intellectual and social life of that time was to be put together, there was but one way open, the way of selection. The most important subjects had to be chosen and those of less importance omitted. Science has been left to a succeeding volume, and some sides of medieval art are only partly described. For the same reason Scandinavian influences go practically untouched, and Spain, which transmitted the gifts of Islam in the twelfth century, is also neglected. But the chief contributions of the Middle Ages have been gathered together, and despite omissions the main lines and masses of the picture are all preserved.

The chapters fall into three divisions. The first five deal with the things of the mind and the spirit. In the centre and heart of the book come three upon law, the most fundamental and characteristic of medieval bequests ; the remainder are concerned with the fabric of society and government. There is no contributor who would not have desired to treat his subject at greater length, and there is none to whom the editors would not gladly have accorded it. For all restrictions we offer our apologies to contributors and readers alike.

We owe it to the memory of a great jurist to state that Sir Paul Vinogradoff did not live to see his article in proof. Our grateful thanks are due to Mrs. Crump, Mrs. Buckland, Miss Joan Evans, and Mr. S. Vesey-FitzGerald for translating the contributions of our French colleagues, and to Professor F. de Zulueta for useful advice and help. Limitations of space necessitated a slight reduction in the size of the palaeographical facsimiles, to which Dr. Lowe has kindly consented.

C. G. C.

E. F. J.

CONTENTS

LIST OF

ILLUSTRATIONS

ART—DECORATIVE AND INDUSTRIAL ARTS

LITERATURE—HANDWRITING

The illustrations in this article are slightly reduced

EDUCATION

INTRODUCTION

ON the 20th of February in the year 1641, while the House of Commons was preparing for the impeachment of the Earl of Strafford, there was a debate on the financial needs of the realm, arising from the war with Scotland and the distress of the northern counties. Mr. Pym proposed that for the safety of the Commonwealth the house should assume a legislative power and compel the city of London to lend the money. There were precedents, he thought, for this. The house seems to have misliked this suggestion and Sir Simonds D'Ewes was, *more suo*, very learned in opposing it; he gave a sketch of the history of Magna Charta, with an allusion to the 'subtle practice' of Hubert de Burgh, quoted the Memoranda Rolls of Henry III, and declared that he would evade any such demand by selling all his estate, except his books, at which the greater part of the house laughed. Those who have read the erudite utterances of Sir Simonds will share the incredulous and perhaps despairing amusement of his fellow members. But for the purpose of this paper the important point to notice is the common appeal to the practice of the past made by two men of diverse minds though of one aim. Pym is the radical desiring to establish the supremacy of the House of Commons, and ready to use that supremacy even for new purposes, but yet willing to use precedents, or even invent them, if men must have precedents to enable them to follow him; his antagonist is the other type of man, the man who believes that the things which he desires existed in the past, and that the careful study of books and parchments will result in the discovery of the truth of that belief.

B

Both types of mind can be found at all times, and both come to the front in times of rapid changes in social or political institutions. Against them may be set another type, the man who sees in the past the social and political forms which he desires to preserve and to which he desires to return, and appeals to history and research to support him in this attempt to return against the stream to the place in which he would be.

In the seventeenth century in England the men who stood for these types were lawyers, and their precedents and examples were cited in legal form and the dispute at least in its earlier stages was conducted in the courts of law. But if we turn to the next period of history, in which a similar appeal to medieval practice and authority was made, we shall find that then the appeal was made more passionately and yet more scientifically, and that those who made it were men interested in almost every department of human thought. It would, indeed, be possible to write a large part of the history of the nineteenth century under some such a title as ' The appeal to medieval times and its results '. It began as a reaction, a reaction from the system of thought upon which the French Revolution had been founded, a system which repudiated everything medieval and looked back to Greece and Rome or even to China for its inspiration. In literature this school produced the writings in prose and verse that have been grouped under the name of the romantic school, a term which comprises under one classification such varying minds as Walter Scott, Chateaubriand, Schiller, and Victor Hugo, and even more aberrant types. In the study of history medieval studies took on a new importance and spread into political thought. Resistance to the unification of Europe, which Napoleon desired to effect, produced and required a national spirit, and this spirit looked for its justification in the past and obtained it from the medieval historian. The same feeling can be discovered in the works of some nineteenth-century jurists; the whole conception of national law, of law as the expression of a particular social type produced by a particular race, derives from medieval studies. And if it is permissible to pursue the story down to less serious manifestations the existence in England of the type of thought known as 'young England', with its curious attempt to restore the glories of the medieval tournament, or the later attempt to establish 'guild' socialism on the lines of medieval craft organization, furnish a proof of the influence which the Middle Ages have exercised over different types of mind. Indeed it may be suggested that only the opposing current of scientific discovery and the schools of thought associated with it, prevented the influence of medieval studies playing an even more important part than they have done in the modern world. And if we add to these the utilitarian and economic doctrines which have acquired in continental Europe the name of the Manchester school of thought, we shall have almost exhausted the influences opposed to the power of the appeal to the Middle Ages. Enough has already been said to show that the force of this appeal was felt by men of very different aims and characters. Conservatives, Liberals, Socialists, theologians, and rationalists have drawn their arguments from the events and institutions of those times, have felt their attraction or been repelled by dislike for them. There are perhaps to-day signs that this influence is waning. Greater knowledge has produced its usual effect, and men are less inclined to praise or blame passionately the institutions and processes which they understand. But this change is not yet complete, and there is still need of knowledge, need to know what the Middle Ages were and what was the legacy they left behind. All we can expect to receive from posterity is the same treatment that we accord to those who have gone before us. We need not praise, nor need we blame overmuch, but certainly we must understand.

To understand the Middle Ages in Western Europe, for it is mainly with Western Europe that this book is concerned, we must begin with one important fact; the source of the food on which men lived. To know this we should have to know a good deal that is not yet known and perhaps is hardly knowable. But the main lines can be laid down and that is as much as need be attempted here. Over most of Western Europe there prevailed a type of agricultural settlement or estate known as the manor in England and by other names in other countries. Everywhere we find a group of dwellings in the middle of a cultivated area, surrounded by more or less waste or uncultivated land; there will be meadows meant to provide hay and pasture when the hay has been cut; each house in the village will have a share in the arable land and in the meadow, and rights over the waste and wood, rights of pasture and rights of taking timber and fuel and so on; and the whole thing will look like a compact settlement cutting out an area of cultivation from a new country. This is not the only form of agricultural life; it is easy to find others; it is only necessary to look at Wales or Brittany or almost any mountain country to find that the dwellings are less grouped and the farms more scattered; and it is not hard to find cases of such scattered settlements in most countries. But the grouped settlement is on the whole the most common, the 'heap village' as German scholars speak of it. In the times of which most is known, the village and its inhabitants are not indeed the only human element in the story. Among them and above them is the feudal lord who also has his share, and a large share, in the arable land and in the meadow, in the wood and in the waste. He is in some sense the ruler and the chief of the settlement ; the village officers are either his officers or answerable to him, and the court of the village is his court. More than this, most of the inhabitants of the village are not free men in relation to him ; they are his bondmen, they owe him payments in kind, in labour, and in money. Normally they cannot sue him in the king's court ; they cannot leave their holdings and go where they will ; and their daughters cannot marry without the manor, nor their sons leave it to better themselves in the church or in the towns. The lord and the lord's rights make the settlement a rigid body.

For a fuller description of this agricultural unit the reader should turn to the chapter on Customary Law. In this introduction it is only intended to describe the manor, by whatever name it may be called, in its function as the economic basis of society and to deal with the life led upon it. The difficulty of describing in any probable or reasonable way the life of the past is very great ; we cannot escape from our own feelings and prepossessions sufficiently to enable us to guess at the degree of happiness or well-being possessed by a dweller in a medieval manor. The only estimate that we can make of it must rest upon the evidence of discontent or resistance that we may be able to discover. Now it is pretty clear that no country organized on the system described escaped agrarian disturbances for very long. The strength of the system lay in its total self-sufficiency ; within limits the manor provided for its own subsistence, looked to the lord for its defence, and to its parish priest for its religious comforts. It is easy to over-rate this self-sufficiency. The manor was by no means independent of the surrounding country. The net of markets and fairs, weekly markets and yearly fairs, that grew up over England shows that the manor was a trading unit, exporting mainly grain and some hides and wool, and importing iron for their ploughs and other tools and cloth and so forth. But the bare necessities of life it could provide for itself and also support its lord and his officials, unless they became too expensive luxuries. The margin was, however, narrow; and if the burden on the inhabitants became too great, if the lord pushed his claims too far, if the seasons were too unkind, or if a general disaster such as a long war, a pestilence, or a general famine fell upon the country, there might be a riot, or a common desertion of the manor, or even a rising in rebellion over a large tract of country. These sudden attempts to escape from the system always ended in failure; the military power that could be brought against the un-organized villagers was too great to admit of the success even of their strongest efforts; but in many cases they were able to improve their positions slowly by putting continual pressure on the lords. Violent and general rebellion was of course rare; such risings took place, for instance, in Normandy in the eleventh century, and in England and France in the fourteenth and fifteenth centuries; and sporadic trouble in particular manors, chiefly on monastic manors, can be traced in the earlier part of the fourteenth century in England. How far similar troubles occurred on manors held by lay owners it is hard to say; the abbot was far more likely to appeal for help to the central government than the lay lord, and in consequence we know less about the lay lord and his troubles. One bit of evidence, however, we have: the continual applications at that date for exemplifications of passages from Doomsday book show how eagerly the tenants sought to prove that they were tenants on a manor which was ancient demesne of the crown, and so entitled to special remedies against what they held to be unreasonable demands from their lords.

If we look for a moment at the duties of the unfree or bond tenants or the villeins, who formed the bulk of the tenants of the manor, we shall see at once how onerous they were. The tenant had to make payments in money, in kind, and in labour. The payments in kind were usually chickens, eggs, honey, and other things of small value; though articles of greater cost, such as a ploughshare, might be given; in addition he had to grind his corn at the lord's mill and pay for doing so with money or a part of the flour. In France he had to bake his bread in the lord's oven, and pay for that also; to crush his grapes or his apples at the lord's press, and pay for that. The lord's oven existed in England also, but the lord's press seems unknown. But the most onerous charge on the villein was the labour exacted from him. He had to come with his own plough and cattle and plough the lord's land or demesne; he had to harrow, reap, and carry the crop, and do any other work required of him. The number of day's work he owed in the year was fixed but the lord could exact extra days in harvest or at other times, and could demand the performance of other duties from him. These tasks were incumbent not only on the tenant himself, but on his whole family; all were *nativi*, born bondmen of the lord.

This description applies to village life over most of Western Europe. It is true of England, France, Germany, and Italy, the countries where the institution can be most easily studied. It came to an end in each of these countries at different dates and in different ways. In Italy, at least in Northern Italy, the economic basis of the manor fell with the fall of the Holy Roman Empire and the growth of the Italian towns in power. The smaller lords, those who held fiefs from the great tenants in chief, were squeezed out by the joint pressure of the great men from above and the actual holders of the land from below by the beginning of the thirteenth century. And through that century a rapid process of the commutation of all labour-rents and other rights belonging to the lords for money payments was going on. Even in England it is difficult to draw the line between a manor and a borough. In Italy it is still more impossible. The desire of the lords, especially of the bishops and monastic houses, to come to terms with their resisting tenants, made them eager to recognize each unit of their property as consisting of individuals united by a joint responsibility, with whose representatives they could negotiate and contract. And in this way the *corte*, the lord's manor, or any other aggregate of persons rapidly grew into a commune, which in some cases can hardly, if at all, be distinguished except in size from a real municipality or great town. Nor did the resistance of the rural communes stop at that point ; they were more willing to enter into contracts with their lords than to keep them. And so gradually in the greater part of Northern Italy the feudal aristocracy threw in their lot with the great towns. These, in turn, gradually annexed by force or negotiation the country round them and took over the government of the rural communes, not always to the advantage of the latter. The rise of the rural communes in Italy was only possible because there was no strong central government to support the rights of the feudal lords. It was also easier for the communes to assume a modified self-government because agriculture in Italy seems not to have been organized on a communal system.

If we turn from Italy to England we shall find the earlier steps of the emancipation of the villagers occurring, but occurring two centuries later. But we shall find that even after the labour rents and some other of the lord's rights have been commuted for money payments that the manor still persisted. There is no growth of self-government, no substitution of the towns for the feudal lords. The manor remains as an agricultural unit, incapable of evolution because the system of agriculture is a rigid system, in which it is almost impossible for one man to cultivate his scattered strips in any other fashion than that used by his neighbours. In consequence any alteration or improvement in agriculture meant a profound change. In England the manor became an inconvenient legacy from the Middle Ages ; escape was only found through a fundamental change which, like all such changes, healed some old troubles and created some new ones. This is not the place in which to discuss the history of enclosures, which belongs to modern times; but it is necessary to emphasize the fact that the manorial system had its own evils, and that it sometimes bore even more hardly on the poorer classes than the system which succeeded it. The historian may at least congratulate himself on the fact that it is from the documents relating to enclosures that he obtains the best evidence as to what the manor really was ; had he to rely purely on medieval documents the task of reconstructing the manor would have been much harder.

Italy—Northern Italy, that is—and England are in fact at two opposite poles. In Italy there was no strong central government able and ready to enforce the law and keep order ; in England there was no freedom of agriculture, there were no varied crops, no vineyards or very few, and no olives. The two countries are alike in the one thing only, that both went through the stage of a feudalized agricultural unit. It is tempting to think that the community of the English village was the school which taught Englishmen to think ·politically. But it is well to remember that the medieval rural communes of Italy were far more organic than any English village, and that Italy has had a very different history from England. It was not only in the medieval manor court that the political habit of mind was fostered.

In France and Germany the manor had a longer life than in Italy. For Germany it would be possible to construct the history of its changes and final form. But it is not possible to do it here in a few pages. The literature is immense and controversial, and the manor in Germany is an institution which takes many forms and has a difficult history. In France the evidence for the nature of medieval agriculture seems to be scanty and the methods used vary far more widely than in England. The only clue seems to lie in the documents dealing with the attempts made by the Government in the eighteenth century, just before the revolution, to improve the system of agriculture. As in England it is only when the restrictions imposed by the communal methods of tillage begin to be inconvenient, that evidence of their real nature can easily be found. To a writer dealing only with medieval sources it is the feudal side of the story that is clear, the power of the lord and the burthen on the tenant ; he is apt to miss the details of the actual working of the institution. It is only in writing of the eighteenth century that he has to explain the hampering effect of the system of scattered holdings and of the common rights of pasture over hay-meadows when the hay has been cut and arable land when the crop has been gathered. But it is easy to see that in France as in England the manor, where [1] it existed in the English type, was an unfortunate legacy, a problem whose solution was difficult and uncomfortable. It was not solved before the revolution, and so far as the lay-out of the fields can be seen from the window of a railway carriage the strip system exists to-day over many miles of country.

[1] Roughly speaking, there were no manors of the English type in Normandy, Languedoc, Provence, or Dauphiné, i.e. there were no open fields, and no common cultivation and no rights of pasture. But see *Economic Journal*, vol. i, p. 59, for Seebohm's article on French Peasant Proprietorship.

In reading medieval history it is always necessary to keep in mind this agricultural foundation. It is the biggest factor in medieval life, the base on which rested all medieval trade and town life, all the splendour of medieval art and architecture, all the life lived in monasteries, all the curious learning of theologians and philosophers and lawyers, all the power of kings and statesmen. To move food from country to country on the modern scale was impossible, though it could be done if necessary to meet an emergency. It was not easy to move food from one part of a country to another. Normally each town subsisted on the food that could be brought to it by road for small distances, by sea or river for greater distances. The wonder is that the manor could and did produce sufficient surplus food beyond its own needs to supply the demands of the towns and the ruling classes. That this was done is its justification ; its failure came when other needs arose, needs for material that could be exported like wool, needs for a more rapid pro-duction of food for a growing population. But while they lasted the manors were in a way the living cells which formed the body politic ; and this is not less true even if it be admitted that their history is a history of rapid changes.

It is a common saying in medieval writers that society consists of those who work, those who guard, and those who pray. It is worth while to note in passing that these writers mean by the workers those who work on the land, and that the classification omits entirely the merchant and the dweller in the towns. In point of fact the merchant and the town fit with difficulty into the medieval scheme. The growth of a town economy is the mark of the beginning of a new form of society. Northern Italy, Southern Germany, and what we now call Belgium and Northern France are the seed-beds where the towns sprung up. There is a sense of modern times in those parts which one scarcely feels in

England or elsewhere. In England indeed, if we omit London, town life was unimportant, and even London is a small city compared with Florence, Venice, Nuremberg, Frankfort, Cologne, Bruges, and Ghent; and London is the only city or borough in England that ruled over a district without its own walls, and had within its walls or just without them the towers of nobles as an Italian town might have. But London is an exceptional city in England; the other cities and towns in that country were without her claims to distinction and lay outside the main line of development during that part of their history. They had their own importance, but their contribution to the legacy of the Middle Ages consisted principally in a series of problems which remained unsolved until the nineteenth century. But town history and town life is too large a subject for a passing note, and needs a separate chapter. Let us come back to the recognized classes of society, those that guard and those that pray.

The first of these comprises all the men who held their land by feudal tenures. There were other soldiers of course in medieval armies, archers, foot-soldiers, and the like, often of great military importance. But the warrior class was formed by the men who went to war on horseback and in armour, and held their lands by performing such services or paying for professional horsemen to serve for them. At first sight the system seems a simple one and originally it was no doubt as simple in practice as it was in theory. The feudal superior gave to his man a tract of land on condition that he should serve himself in the army and bring with him a specified number of other men properly equipped. The contract was made in a formal manner by a ceremonial oath of fidelity and a declaration that the recipient of the land was now the man of the donor; and both parties were bound, the lord to allow the tenant to hold the land and protect him against all attacks, the tenant to perform the service due. It is not necessary here to discuss the other incidents of the tenure, or to do more than note the fact that the relation of lord and tenant might be created by the action of the tenant, as well as by a gift from the lord. The point to be remembered is the personal relation established between the two parties. If the lord failed to discharge his obligation, the tenant was free to find another lord [1] from whom he might hold the land; if the tenant failed, the lord was entitled to take back the land into his own hands. The relation was not terminated by the death of either party, but continued from one generation to another, though it is clear that originally the contract was made for the life of the tenant only. Nor was the tenant bound to retain in his own hands the land held by him; he might grant out a part at any rate to others, to hold of him on similar terms, and in this way a sort of pyramid of relations might grow up with the lord 'paramount' at the apex, the tenants 'paravail' at the base, and the layers of 'mesne' tenants between. The weak point in the system was that the contract became meaningless as soon as the tenant held land from more than one lord. So far indeed as the legal relationship went it was not beyond the skill of feudal lawyers to devise means of apportioning to each lord his proper share of the tenant's allegiance, and of instructing the tenant in the way in which he should perform his possibly conflicting duties. But as a real relationship the feudal contract ceased to be of importance and necessarily declined into a legal form. It is not necessary to look far to find instances of the difficulties that arose; the best-known case in England is to be found in circumstances brought about by the loss of Normandy in the thirteenth century and the difficulty that arose when the same men found themselves

[1] This would be the chief lord of the lord from whom the tenant held.

holding of King John and of Philip of France at a time
when the two kings were at war. Nothing was possible in
that case but that the luckless tenants should abandon their
lands in one realm or the other. But the process was not
complete, and it was many years before the King of England
finally ceased to be the man of the King of France and to
owe him service for his duchy of Aquitaine. The King of
Naples after the fall of the Hohenstaufens was in an even
odder case. Charles of Anjou, the brother of St. Louis,
held Naples and Sicily of the Pope ; Provence, which came
to him with his wife, he held of the Emperor, a person who
was at the time rather shadowy ; Anjou he held of his
brother the King of France. And so we might go on to
the feudal difficulties of the King of Navarre. Nor, indeed,
were the positions of the greatest kings simple ; special
provisions had to be devised to deal with the case of a king
who by some accident should become the feudal inferior
of one of his own vassals. And if these accidents could occur
to kings, they might even more readily happen to smaller
men. It is pretty clear that by the end of the twelfth
century there was no considerable landholder in England
who did not owe service to several lords ; and the position
of the Earl of Oxford, who was an under-tenant of the
abbot of Ramsey, is in no way exceptional. In England,
indeed, the statute of Quia Emptores put an end to the
creation of new feudal superiorities and marks the point at
which the process of simplification in land tenure began.
But in other countries, such as Scotland and France, there
was no such legislation. Readers of St. Simon's memoirs
will remember that even in his day feudal superiorities were
not without interest in France ; and any one who wishes
to know why Campbell was a hated name in the Scotch
Highlands, and why so many of the clans supported the
Stuarts, will find a likely clue in the study of the feuda.

superiorities held by the Earl of Argyll and the use he made of them. It is not necessary to deny that originally feudalism had its good side ; undoubtedly it protected the weak and made for order. But as soon as it ceased to be a social form and became a system of law it left an awkward legacy to succeeding generations. That England escaped the worst effects of feudal law [1] is due to the statute Quia Emptores.

If we turn from the men who guard to the men who pray, we shall find ourselves in a wholly new society. It is not an easy thing to explain in a few words the separation between the medieval layman and the medieval clerk. One obvious material mark there was : the clerk was tonsured, that is to say he had a small round patch on his head from which all the hair was removed. The religious service used in making a clerk can be found in the *Pontificale Romanum,* or in any other similar collection of services. According to the strict rule a candidate for clergy must have been confirmed, must know how to read and write, and must understand the rudiments of faith. On the appointed day he must appear before the bishop carrying a surplice or gown, and a lighted candle. There is no canonical day or place or time for the making of clerks ; it can be done anywhere at any time. A pair of scissors must be provided for the bishop and a basin in which he may put the hair. The words of the service may be found in the sources mentioned above ; in this place only a few points need be noted. The bishop cuts with the scissors the hair of the candidate in four places, on the forehead, at the back of the head, and over each ear ; finally he cuts off some hairs from the middle of the head and puts them in the basin ; at a later stage in the service the bishop takes the gown and

[1] The common use of the word 'feudal' as a means of expressing disapproval of the English land system is more convenient than accurate.

puts it on the candidate ; and in his concluding address he tells him that on this day he has been made ' de foro ecclesie ' and has obtained the privileges of clergy, and warns him that he do nothing which may cause him to lose them. It is unnecessary to insist further on the words ' de foro ecclesie ' ; the claim was that the fact of clergy made the clerk as clerk subject only to ecclesiastical courts, at any rate in the eye of the Church, though the lay power might not always respect this point of view. Nor need we investigate further the subsequent career of the clerk who took orders, obtained benefices, and rose to high rank in the Church. It is enough here to point out that the tonsure, conferred as described above, is the first step which brings a man into the number of the people who pray ; it made him fit to hold a benefice, always on the condition that he proceeded to take the further steps required of him. There was, indeed, nothing irrevocable in the step he had taken ; the tonsure was not indelible ; a clerk could abandon his clergy ; indeed, if he chose, he might return to the lay world and even take up the profession of arms. An extreme case may show the possible eccentricities in a clerk's career. Philip of Savoy, the younger brother of Peter, count of Savoy and Lord of Richmond, was brought up as a clerk ; he never seems to have received any orders, but by dispensation he held benefices and was successively allowed to become bishop-elect of Valence, and archbishop-elect of Lyons. On his brother's death in 1268 Philip abandoned his clerical condition, resigned his benefices, and succeeded his brother as count of Savoy. He had in fact changed his life ; from a clerk he had become a layman ; and such a return was open to any clerk.

But if the clerk persevered there were many careers open to him even if he refused to take orders. He would, of course, begin his career at a school, the school of a great abbey, or in the house of a bishop or an archbishop. Thence he would go on to his university training, passing perhaps from one to another as the fame of the various teachers might attract him. He might become a notary or a lawyer or a learned doctor ; or he might enter into the service of the king or some other potentate or even into the service of the Roman court. In this latter case he would have been well advised to take orders, and so qualify himself to hold benefices whose revenues might provide him with a sufficient salary. But the main point to note is that among clerks equality was the rule ; rank and birth might count but character and ability counted also. The son of a peasant might become the first man in France under the king, as happened in the case of Suger, abbot of St. Denis. At the abbey school one of Suger's fellow scholars was the boy who was to reign over France as Louis VI ; and when the prince became king the son of the peasant had already become the abbot of the great monastery and was the most trusted councillor of the king ; when Louis VI died the abbot remained the most trusted councillor of his son. Suger is perhaps the finest example of his type, the ecclesiastical statesman. He was, indeed, neither saint nor theologian, but he was faithful to the rules of life to which his profession bound him. He neither enriched himself or his family nor neglected his abbey. He was well read, a good writer, and a great administrator. No one could have said of him, as was said of Robert Burnell, bishop of Bath, the great chancellor of Edward I, that he had too many illegitimate children to be an archbishop. No one could have found material in his career for the famous doubt as to the possible salvation of archdeacons, a doubt founded on the lives of the many archdeacons who had earned that preferment by serving the king. Not every clerk could be a Suger, or even an archdeacon. Fate might bring him to a humbler position ; he might be a teacher in a village school, an assistant to the parish priest ; he might earn his bread by writing deeds and letters for the unskilled laity. But one thing he had, unless he lost it, his membership of a great fellowship, bound together by the possession of a common language, Latin, and subject to one law, the canon law. All Christendom was, in theory at least, open to him, and in theory and to some extent in fact there was no position in the Church to which he might not attain, no place in any government which he might not hold, no university in which he might not teach. The only thing that could restrict him to his own country was the jealousy felt for the foreigner, the growing differentiation of language, the earliest signs of the conception of nationalism.

It appears, therefore, that a clerical and ecclesiastical career was the easiest means of escape for those who found themselves unfitted or unhappy as tillers of the soil or as holders of fiefs. It was not, indeed, the only way by which an active mind or a resolute character could travel. The story of the industrious apprentice who rises in his master's service and marries his master's daughter, the romance of the low-born warrior who wins his spurs and weds the daughter of the great lord, may hardly be paralleled in real life, but are not impossible. The great banking firms, which adorned the cities of Italy and made the name of Lombard almost a common equivalent for financier, sprang from many origins. Nor could any one venture to say what was the origin of the family of de la Pole, who rose from obscurity in Hull almost to the throne of England. The citizens of a medieval town came from all ranks and might rise to any estate. But the new man in a medieval town had a harder fight than the new man who entered on life as a clerk ; a harder fight, because in every town he would find an established aristocracy of wealth and position and an organization of the larger merchants and traders into which he would have to make his way. Even harder was the struggle which faced the new man who tried to make his way as a soldier. The military system of the Middle Ages was based on feudalism and knighthood. The reception of knighthood was a duty and a privilege ; it signified that the knight had performed the duty of mastering his profession of arms and that he was fit to command a body of troops ; it was a privilege because the holding of land as a feudal tenant gave the holder a right to receive knighthood as well as a duty to obtain it. The knight-bachelor in his profession is in a position corresponding to the clerk who has taken his bachelor's degree at a university. But the new man, who did not come from the feudal class, had no such claim. His chance of success lay in another direction ; he could only rise from the ranks in a mercenary army, that is in an army not organized on a feudal basis and not even drawing its commanders from the usual source. The new man got his chance in the periods when the armies raised by contending kings consisted of bands of *routiers*. No one for instance can guess where the great soldier Mercadier, who commanded the armies of Richard I in France, came from. In the wars of Edward III Duguesclin is almost as mysterious in his origin ; the story of his romantic youth makes him the son of a poor Breton noble family, but his whole career is typical of a time when armies were made up of hired bands. He fought with such bands and against them, and save as a soldier could hardly have risen to be the Constable of France and the principal figure in the French resistance to the English. Sir John Hawkwood is an even more striking instance. From an obscure position he became a leader of a great company of mercenaries, and when the treaty of Brétigny brought a temporary peace to France, he led his troops into Italy and won there fame and fortune and a memorial on the wall of the Cathedral of Florence. The wars of Edward III were the golden age of the mercenary bands, and even the great *condottieri* of Italy hardly match the fame and fortune of the leaders of the earlier companies. In cruelty and rapacity there is little to choose between the meaner leaders in either country. But the Italians had more scope to show any power of government, any desire to create order, that they might possess, than had the new men who fought in the French wars. If we except a few men like Sir John Chandos on the English side and Duguesclin on the French side, both of whom came from the lower rank of feudal tenants, we shall not find in the other new men made by the wars many ideas beyond the reach of mere bandits. They had, in fact, come through a bad school to a bad eminence. Medieval warfare was to a great extent founded upon plunder and ransoms ; and any period of long and desperate fighting quickly destroyed the ideal of chivalry, which was the only restraining element in it, an ideal always weak and always confined to a few minds. And over the men who formed the bands of *routiers* who fought with Richard I or the companies who served in the wars of Edward III, even that weak ideal had no influence.

But the main fact that emerges from this survey is that society in the Middle Ages was not a rigid form, in which every man had a place and a life fixed for him. There were many ways of escape. The son of a peasant could get learning and rise in or through the Church ; he could win a place in a town and rise by craft or trade ; he could turn soldier. The born townsman had the same possibilities open to him. Even the man who was the younger son of a feudal family could turn clerk. But for the elder son, the heir to his family lands, only the profession of arms was open. In a highly feudalized country, like France, the small feudal tenant was apt to slip into poverty, to drop into a condition

that made his life a misery to himself and a menace to his
neighbours. Nor did this condition end with the Middle
Ages. In France and Germany the robber baron was a
reality even in later times. He could neither live on his
estate nor escape from it. As long as there was war, he was
able to serve as a soldier ; when peace came he was useless,
without means of support. And it is largely to this fact
that the character and even the fact of civil war may often
be traced. In England the wars of the Roses are the result
of the Hundred years war; in France the wars of religion
follow on the French wars in Italy. Both are in a way the
results of demobilization, the work of a military caste
suddenly reduced to poverty and idleness.

It is hardly necessary to point out that there are in all
societies influences that make for permanence. At all times
sons are likely to follow their fathers' trades and professions.
There are many reasons why this is so, and in the Middle
Ages these reasons were certainly even stronger than they
are to-day. But it is useless to under-estimate or exaggerate
their force. The rigidity of the manorial system could not
prevent every villein's son from leaving the manor for the
church or the town. The guilds in the towns might become
the stronghold of the medieval capitalist ; they might even
become a serious obstacle to trade and industry ; but there
were still ways of escape from the rigidity imposed by them
on town life.

If we turn from the possible varieties of individual
experience to the general life of medieval man, we shall
find the same scourges of society with which the men of the
present day are familiar. War, famine, and pestilence are
not extinct, even if man's control over all three is greater
than it was. But medieval wars were even more unreasonable
than the wars of our own day, arose on even slighter occasions and lasted longer. It is not strictly true that the
Hundred years war between England and France lasted for

a century; and it is not entirely true that it was a wholly unreasonable war. It began because no reasonable frontier existed between the lands of the two kings, and because no statesman at that time thought in terms of frontiers at all any more than the citizens of a Balkan state think to-day. It is not true that medieval populations were always in danger of famine, though periods of scarcity were not infrequent and famine might occur as it may in Russia or India to-day. Medieval pestilences were certainly commoner and more severe than they are to-day and there was less power to control them, though no one who realizes the havoc wrought by influenza and its followers will claim a high immunity from pestilences for the present day. That on the whole modern man uses more soap than his ancestors few will deny; and most will admit that there is more comfort to-day than there was in medieval days and far less crime. But civilization still rests on slender foundations; and if men lose their control over the sources of energy it would not take very many years to bring men back to medieval conditions, to which indeed we are often nearer than we realize. The fields of France are still laid out on the old plan; an American fundamentalist is the spiritual descendant of St. Bernard, and every fresh shock to the industrial system of England produces a series of suggested remedies based upon medieval lines of thought. If any justification is needed for this book, such a plea must rest on this fact that we are not so different from our ancestors as we believe, and that we had better know something about them before we use their methods. The institutions they devised, the lives they led, the laws which ruled them, the arts they practised, the religion in which they believed, their ways of thought, make up the sum of what they had to bequeath to us.

C. G. CRUMP.

THE CHRISTIAN LIFE

THE legacy of medieval Christianity to later ages was the problem of authority. Christians, it is unnecessary to add, did not create the problem, which is involved in the art of conscious living, but they revealed it in all the bewildering amplitude of the conflict between order and freedom, between obedience to Christ and submission to His Church. They have never been proud of it, for it has been to them a tiresome perplexity, an unmanageable side-issue in a labour vastly more important. Organized Christianity came into existence, and exists, to preserve a treasure, a command to be executed, a promise to be repeated, a mission to be fulfilled. This treasure belongs to past, present, and future ; it is potential, yet active ; an object of contemplation, yet the inspiration of right conduct. An unfathomable mystery, it must be related to all knowledge. And in their endeavours to guard and transmit their trust, its guardians have raised the most perplexing issues. They have caused endless destruction of life in the name of universal peace. They have built up the most realistic of political systems in the effort to establish a kingdom not of this world. In the exploration of the recesses of the soul, they have developed the arts and sciences, and constructed theories of the universe. And, in their desire to satisfy the deepest needs of mankind, they have raised up against themselves the visions, prophecies, and extravagances of excitable and obstinate men, and the dislike of many sensible men.

The treasure which has caused all this activity was cast into the world with a few simple sentences. *Thou shalt love the Lord thy God and thy neighbour as thyself. What shall it profit a man if he shall gain the whole world and lose his own soul ?* And again, *God so loved the world that he gave his only begotten Son, that whosoever believeth in Him should not perish but have everlasting life. No one cometh to the Father, save by Me. Take, eat ; this is my body.* And again, *Go and preach the Kingdom of God. Feed my sheep. Thou art Peter, and upon this rock will I build my Church. Peace I leave with you, my peace I give unto you. I have come not to bring peace, but a sword.*

I

Only those who accept the dogma of the divinity of Christ as the central fact in a long process of divine revelation can escape bewilderment in the contemplation of the spread of Christianity, which has been so unlike other religions in its claim to penetrate and control the whole of life. The historian, who must discard dogmas, betrays his bewilderment at every step. He tends to explain the history of the Church by explaining it away. The absorption of Greek thought and the penetration of the traditions of Rome by the new life and teaching are regarded as causes rather than as effects of their success. The Word was not as leaven; it was an artificial result of the strange ferment of religious excitement, superstitions, philosophical mysticism, desperate aspirations which stirred among the peoples of the Levant. Even if the Gospel narratives are accepted as generally true, reason and imagination combine in our days to reject the claims of any body of men, living a fragile life in a world which is but a speck in an infinite universe, to interpret with infallible accuracy the significance of the life of Christ, both for every human soul and in the whole process of nature. Whatever welcome Christ might receive to-day it is inconceivable that the later history of his followers could in the remotest degree resemble the history of the Christian Church.

We have not to inquire whether, in the conditions of life which prevailed during the early centuries, the spread of Christianity was as remarkable as it would be to-day. Probably we under-estimate the extent to which the Gospel appealed then to the trained intellect, just as we over-estimate the extent to which modern science has altered the outlook of the average man. ' Never in the whole history of the world', it has been said, ' did so many people believe so firmly in so many things, the authority for which they could not test, as do Londoners to-day.' But, however this may be, in the history of the medieval church from the fifth century onwards, the distinction between the sophisticated and the ignorant, though very marked, had not the particular significance which it has to-day. The most acute, disinterested and sincere intellects were among the expositors of the Church. The issue did not lie between reason and faith. Rationalistic opposition to Christianity had by this time almost ceased to trouble the Church. Paganism abounded, but it was the literal paganism of the natural man, a force to be disciplined or an object of missionary enterprise, not an intellectual power capable of resistance and organized life. In the Middle Ages, apologetic writing, with the exception of the *Summa contra Gentiles* of St. Thomas Aquinas, has not the importance in ecclesiastical literature possessed by the writings of the great Christian apologists or of St. Augustine ; if we set on one side the numerous but subordinate tracts against Jews and Mohammedans, it was anything but defensive in character, it was rather an attempt to reach self-understanding. Civilized Europe was educated in a body of doctrine and enriched by a wealth of religious experience which were in conscious harmony with current conceptions of the universe. What resistance there was, so far as it was rooted in a life alien to Christianity, was ruthlessly suppressed. Like the plague, it was endemic, but, except for occasional epidemics of which the Albigensian heresy was the most severe, it was kept successfully out of sight, a monstrous unthinkable thing, abhorrent to the conscience of mankind. The few great heretics, such as Wycliffe, did not base their objections to orthodox practice on principles unintelligible to the medieval mind ; still less were they rationalists. They were extremists, urged by a strange medley of mood and circumstance to carry farther than others would a critical habit which was general in the great centres of learning. They went over the line which every man who thought for himself, and every man of ardent piety, was likely to approach, but from which all but they recoiled in horror.[1] Hence the problem of authority did not arise from a conflict between the faith of an organized Christendom and the reason of men outside the Church. It was not due, though this would be nearer the truth, to a conflict between reason within and faith without the Church. It was the problem of controlling the interplay within the Church of faith and reason, of religious experience and theology, the revelation and the interpretation of the purposes of God. Medieval theology was not stagnant ; it sprang from intense religious feeling,

[1] Marsiglio of Padua in the fourteenth century was probably a 'rationalist' in the modern sense ; but when the Pope compared Wycliffe's doctrines with his, he was concerned with results, not with moods and processes. The sophistical disputations of the thirteenth and fourteenth centuries were deliberate acts of 'playing with fire' and sometimes, notably in the case of the thoroughgoing Siger of Brabant, the disciple of Averroes, led to trouble ; but, although important as a step towards the recognition of separate domains of faith and reason, they were not regarded very seriously, and the disputants rarely imagined that their conclusions could possess real validity.

and its function was to assist authority in the definition
of dogma, as in the long discussions which preceded the
definite assertion in 1216 of the doctrine of transubstantia-
tion. It could even impose a long disputed dogma upon
the Church. The dogma of the Immaculate Conception
of the Virgin, though left an open question by the Council
of Trent and formally accepted by Pope Pius IX as late as
1854, was widely adopted after its reception by the English
Benedictines, and, later, by the Franciscan theologian,
Duns Scotus. On the other hand, theology might easily
cross the line beyond which the general conscience, warned
by tradition, refused to go. If there were few obstinate
heretics in the Middle Ages, there were a great many
persons who at one time or another were taxed with
heresy. Nobody could feel safe unless he was prepared
to rely in the last resort upon the judgement of the Church
expressed through its authorized head. A pope, if he
relied on his private judgement, could go astray and be
called to book. The philosophical teaching of St. Thomas
was watched with anxiety and was repudiated by many as
charged with doctrine hostile to the faith. Heresy might
assail the mystic as he sought to analyse the communion of
the soul with God. And if, within the inner stronghold
of the Church, apart from which life seemed incredible,
dangers could beset the doctor and the saint, in how much
greater danger was the multitude of ignorant men, undis-
ciplined in the moral life, of the fanatics who could see but
one ray of light at a time, of those immersed in social and
economic life, distracted by ambition or pleasure or the
precarious nature of their calling? Beyond the problem of
authority lay the still greater problem of discipline, the task
of finding some harmony between the Christian view of
things and the life of the ordinary man.

How did it come about that the authority of the Church

was so generally accepted as inseparable from the duties
and aspirations of the Christian life? We now know enough
about what used to be called the 'age of faith' to discount
the conception of an obedient society, orderly to a point of
unnatural self-suppression in everything relating to the
government, the doctrine, the worship, the artistic interests
of the Church. We no longer believe in that well-behaved
body of the faithful, which, though essentially barbarous
and ignorant, was always so sweetly submissive in its attitude
to the mysteries of the Christian faith. Paganism in the
Middle Ages was as endemic, speculation as bold, speech as
pungent, the varieties of religious experience as numerous
and as extravagant as at any time in the history of mankind.
The state system of modern Europe, its nationalism, traditions of foreign policy, and strangely mixed ideas of right,
force, utility can be traced back into the Middle Ages.
Scholars who work among the repellent remains of late
medieval scholasticism say that, hidden away in those
unreadable manuscripts, are the germs of the mighty ideas
of Leonardo da Vinci, Copernicus, Bruno, Spinoza. Luther
fed his spirit on the writings of the Brethren of the Common
Life; the intellectual ancestry of Hegel has been traced
to the mystical philosophy of Eckhart. Can medieval
Christianity, then, really have possessed the inner coherence
which we have allowed to it? Ought we not to regard it
as a complicated tyranny from which men were constantly
striving to free themselves?

The answer to the view implied in these questions is,
I think, twofold. In the first place the medieval Church
was composed of societies rather than of individuals.
Secondly, the sincerely religious person satisfied the needs
of his inner life by adjusting himself to the interpretation of
the world which the Church expounded.

1. Historically, the medieval Church, as distinct from the

primitive Church, was composed of societies. If we look at the history of the spread of Christianity from the days of Constantine, we find that Christianity spread by the addition of masses of men, not by the conversion of particular people. There were some striking exceptions, but, generally speaking, the acceptance of Christianity was, to use a modern phrase, an affair of state, in which kings and other leaders, moved no doubt by missionaries and, as time went on, acting under the influence of the Pope, carried their subjects with them or imposed their will upon alien social groups. The success of the great St. Boniface in the eighth, and of the Cistercian monk, Christian of Oliva, in the thirteenth century was mainly due to the adherence of the local magnates and to the backing of friendly or interested powers outside. Boniface, for example, was more rapidly and permanently successful than had been the Celtic missionaries who preceded him in Germany, because he could rely upon Charles Martel in his organization of Thuringia and Hesse, and upon Duke Odilo in his organization of Bavaria. Christian of Oliva, the first bishop in Prussia (1212), had the support of the neighbouring duke of Masovia. The ' conversion ' of Norway illustrates the drastic policy of a ruthless king. King Olaf Tryggvason proceeded methodically, province by province ; and the Heimskringla, the later history of the kings of Norway, tells some profoundly interesting stories of the devotion to the old gods which he had to overcome, sometimes with almost incredible cruelty.[1] A religious system which originated in this way was, as in a more refined expression it has remained, a part of the social structure. Its organization was inextricably involved with that of the community.

---

[1] Laing, *Chronicle of the Kings of Norway* (1844), i. 427 ff. Evidence from other sources on the conversion of northern peoples is collected in Th. de Cauzons, *Histoire de l'Inquisition en France*, i (1909), 72 ff.

The powerful men who took pride in their work fostered
and endowed it ; they regarded resistance to it as an affront
not only to God, but to society. The clergy had a recognized
status in the tribal or national life ; they sat in the courts,
took cognizance of public affairs and private conduct,
helped to shape the customs which they put into writing.
Christianity, in general regard, though full of mystery, was
not an alien or esoteric body of practice and belief ; it
rapidly became an inseparable element in men's lives, just
as the old religions had been before it. We moderns are
directly descended from these people, and our paganism,
so far as it is unsophisticated, is the paganism of our forefathers, less crude and violent, but equally natural, equally
consistent with a life of Christian conformity, which begins
with baptism and closes with the solemn commitment of
the body to the grave and the soul to the keeping of God.
By paganism I mean a state of acquiescence, or merely
professional activity, unaccompanied by sustained religious
experience and inward discipline. It is not a state of vacancy
and scepticism. It is confined to no class of persons, and is
not hostile to, though it is easily wearied by, religious observance. It accepts what is offered without any sense of responsibility, has no sense of sin, and easily recovers from twinges of
conscience. At the same time, it is full of curiosity and is
easily moved by what is now called the group-mind. It is
sensitive to the activities of the crowd, is often emotional, and
can be raised to those moods of passion, superstition, and love
of persecution into which religion, on its side, can degenerate.
A medieval, like a modern, man remained a Christian
because he was born a Christian, and most medieval Christians were probably men of this kind—not a few popes,
cardinals, bishops, monks, friars, and parish clergy, and
a large number of the clerks who had no cure of souls.
The medieval Christian was, according to his lights, respect-

able. He was generally far too much interested in life, had too much to do, and was too affectionate, to be habitually cruel or sensual or superstitious. His life was inseparable from that of the community to which his Church gave a variety of colour, here radiant, there distressing. Although in periods of crisis he suffered decadence—sometimes widespread and horrible—casual decadence is more likely to have affected, not the conventional Christian, but the truly religious man.[1]

The history of the Church is the record of the gradual and mutual adaptation of Christianity and paganism to each other. The complete victory of the former has always been a remote vision. St. Paul's Epistles to the Corinthians show how the attempt to persuade their converts to put away earthly things taxed the patience and energy of the earliest apostles. The task became impossible when every member of any political community which possessed an ecclesiastical organization was supposed to be a follower of Christ. The influence of the Church penetrated social relations through and through, and it is foolish to feel surprise if Christianity suffered in the process. St. Boniface found that the German converts instinctively regarded baptism and the rites of the Church as forms of magic or merely external acts;[2] and his experience has countless parallels throughout the history of the Church up to our own day. The situation within the borders of the Roman Empire was especially perplexing. The lands around the Mediterranean were not merely full of superstition, they were intensely sophisticated, so that it is impossible to draw a sharp line between their superstition and their sophistry,

---

[1] For this aspect of medieval life see Coulton, *Five Centuries of Religion*, vol. i (1923), and Huizinga, *The Waning of the Middle Ages* (1924).

[2] Hauck, *Kirchengeschichte Deutschlands*, i. 474 ff.

between tradition and artifice, sincere piety and exotic faith.[1] The strange excesses which shocked St. Augustine and other ecclesiastical leaders in some of their fellow-Christians were probably not very different from the psychical extravagance which had disgusted Cicero and Plutarch. Hence, as the Christian faith penetrated the society of the Roman world, it fell under the influence both of rustic traditions and of a variegated paganism which shaded off into those philosophical and mystical refinements so dear to the theologian. We are apt to forget that in the days of Christ the sea of Galilee was not like a silent Wast-water, lying solitary beneath the lonely hills, but was bordered by towns with temples and villas like the lakes of Geneva or Como. From the first the Church was the victim as well as the victor, and as it absorbed the peoples of the Mediterranean in the west and spread eastwards into Persia and India, its spiritual life was shot through and through with the glittering fancies, the antinomianism, the morbid extravagances and the endless subtleties of men. It tried to purify a great sluice into which all the religions, every kind of philosophy, every remedy for the troubles and ennui of life had passed. And from this ordeal it passed on to cope with the mental and spiritual traditions of the great northern peoples. If we imagine that the Church was able to work upon a *tabula rasa*, we cannot understand the development either of its theology, its ritual, or its religious experience.

All this has long been familiar to students of the history of the early Church, and it is fairly familiar to those who study the interplay of Christianity and other traditions in the life of to-day ; but it is still apt to puzzle us when we regard the Church in the Middle Ages. How did the

[1] See Dill, *Roman Society from Nero to Marcus Aurelius*, Book IV, c. 1, pp. 443 ff.

medieval Church maintain a hold so hardly won in early
times, so easily lost in our own ? We must begin by realizing
that, although its influence meant much more than this,
the Church was the systematic expression of a life which
had taken the place of the older religions. It was organized
in dioceses of Roman or tribal origin ; its ministers were
not foreign enthusiasts, but men drawn from feudal and
village society. The clergy, it is true, made claims upon the
allegiance of their people which had no roots in natural
ties and were independent of their personal worthiness.
They were based on the truth that the kingdom of Christ
is not of this world, and the really serious difficulties which
the Church had to face were due to that ever-present spirit
of anti-clericalism which was in part resistance to the
claims of Christ, in part a sense of the contrast between
Christ and his ministers. At the same time life on earth
would never be comfortable, or even tolerable, if men had
no way of grappling with its mysteries and terrors ; and if
they require protection against these, they must pay the
price. On the whole the medieval pagans paid the price
cheerfully. They paid tithes and dues. They allowed the
clergy to receive their children into society at baptism,
to define the limits within which marriage was permissible,
to punish their sexual irregularities, to supervise the disposition of their goods by will, to guide their souls at the
hour of death and to bury their bodies. They recognized
the obligations of confession, penance, communion. In one
form or another much of the discipline was as old as society ;
there must be initiation, regulation, and ceremonial in
human relations if men and women are to live together ;
and, on the other hand, it was not altogether as though the
wide-spreading, penetrating, exotic life of the Church was
not largely in their own keeping. It was their own brothers
and cousins who crowned and anointed kings, ruled bishop-

rics and monasteries, and celebrated in their churches—the
churches which they themselves had built or helped to
maintain. Strangers might bring in new fashions and new
knowledge, but their successors would be men drawn from
themselves. It was all very interesting : the Church gave
them very much, and yet they were at the same time inside
the Church. They were both spectators and actors. They
got wonderful buildings, pictures, plays, festivals, stories
full of apocryphal detail about Biblical heroes and saints ;
but they could themselves help to build, paint, perform,
repeat. They gibed incessantly at the clergy with their
hypocrisy, venality, immorality, yet they had a good deal
of sympathy with them, for they were of their own flesh.
The real enemies were the cranks and heretics who would
not play the game.

What we call abuses or superstition in the medieval Church
were part of the price paid for, not obstacles to, its universality. They were due to the attempt of pagans to appropriate a mystery. If the people paid, so did the Church.
We distort the facts if we try to separate clergy and laity
too sharply, for paganism was common to both. Medieval
thinkers and reformers saw this far more clearly than we can,
and were never tired of discussing the problem.   In the
eleventh century Cardinal Peter Damiani pointed out in
his lurid way that it was of no use to try to keep the clergy
apart from the laity unless strict evangelical poverty were
insisted upon for all clergy alike. But Damiani and all the
preachers of Apostolic poverty who came after him were
entangled on the horns of a dilemma. If it is the function
of the Church to drive out sin, it must separate itself from
sin ; if the Church separates itself from sin, it becomes
a clique. The Church took another course. Under the
guidance of austere pontiffs like Gregory VII and Innocent
III it embarked upon an intensive policy of discipline,

whose basis was the very claim to universality. To Innocent III the dilemma was clear enough—few men have been
so tortured by reflections upon the misery of mankind—
but he was a statesman and lawyer, prepared to deal with
realities as he found them. By his time (he was a contemporary of our King John) it was too late to go back. As an
ecclesiastical system the body of Christ was becoming the
most intricate administration which the world had yet seen ;
as a society the Church affected and was affected by every
form of human endeavour. From the one point of view
the distinction between lay and clerical is all important ;
from the other it is irrelevant. The secular influences which
played upon sacred things did not work through the laity
alone. Certainly the men of outstanding piety and wisdom
were generally to be found among the clergy, the militia of
Christ ; but the wind bloweth where it listeth : the pope
might be a pagan at heart, the beggar a saint.[1]

In the fifth century, Basil, the local bishop, described in
his book on the miracles of St. Thecla, the conversation
of the pilgrims who gathered for the feast of the saint at
Seleucia. The visitors, sitting around a table, exchange
their impressions. ' One is astonished by the magnificence
and splendour of the ceremonies, another by the vast crowds
which they have attracted, a third by the large concourse of
bishops. One praises the eloquence of the preachers,
another the beauty of the psalmody, another the endurance
of the public during the long night office, another the fine
arrangement of the services, another the fervour in prayer
of the assistants. One recalls the dust, another the stifling
heat, while yet another has observed the coming and going

[1] The documents collected by Finke from the Aragonese archives and
elsewhere show, for example, that the famous but curious person, Pope
Boniface VIII, who lived a hundred years after Innocent III, was a pagan
in the sense in which I have used the word.

during the holy mysteries, how so-and-so went out, and how another returned and went away again, the cries and disputes, the disorder of people getting into each others' way and refusing to give place, each eager to be the first to participate.' [1] In a few words this picture describes the attitude of the faithful during the history of the Church. Add to the feast of a saint or martyr, the pilgrimages and jubilees, the ceremonies of corporate life, the coronation of kings, the initiation into knighthood, the passion and miracle plays, the propaganda and conduct of a crusade, the passage at any time through the countryside of a popular preacher and we have the circumstances in which the ' group mind ' was affected in the Middle Ages. Add, again, the churches and cathedrals with their descriptive or symbolic ritual, sculpture, wall painting, and we have the material forms which, so to speak, ' fixed ' the belief and imagination of the medieval Christian. An excitement of the senses accompanied the appeal of the spirit. One need not look further than the clerical class. From the little boys in the bishop's household to the bishop himself they felt with an infinite variety of intensity that they were members of a great professional body, but the conditions of their life would make them partisans—attached to their particular ' use ', eager for the success of their patron saint, anxious about their revenues, ready to fight on behalf of the views of their favourite teachers. The mixture of motives which in the few was a source of shame was in the many a sanction of self-confidence and corporate feeling. In the particular form in which this natural expression of human nature affects our modern world, it is a legacy from the conditions under which the Church developed in the Middle Ages, under the spacious opportunities opened up by a universal society.

[1] See Delehaye, ' Les recueils antiques de miracles des saints,' in *Analecta Bollandiana*, 1925, xliii. 56–7.

The interaction of theological subtlety and popular credulity had cruder and more dangerous effects. Perhaps the most striking example is its effect upon the system of indulgences. In its purest form the theory underlying the indulgence was a fine one. It was inspired by the writings of St. Paul and was safeguarded by the maxim of the Fathers, *Quod homo non punit, Deus punit*. The system itself was a natural development of the penitential system and was related to the power of absolution. Its justification was found, in the climax of a long discussion among canonists and theologians, in the doctrine of the treasure stored up by saints and martyrs and all good Christians, who, a great body of friends, combine to help the erring. But it was extremely difficult to avoid misconception and abuse. Some of the theological terms, notably the term ' remission of sins ', were misleading, some of the preachers of indulgences were ignorant or headstrong or unscrupulous. Warfare had constantly to be waged by bishops and universities against the belief that not punishment, but sin itself, was remitted, or that indulgences could benefit the dead as well as the living. The system encouraged fantastic and heterodox views about the unlimited powers of the Pope, or profitless discussions on the nature of purgatory ; and in some directions popular pressure proved too strong for the theologians, so that later speculation far outran the cautious handling of the subject by the great scholastics.[1]

2. We have seen that the pagan paid homage to the faith. The Church coloured his whole life and did so very rightly, because, so men vaguely felt, it interpreted life. Its secret was not merely part of life, it gave meaning to life, and was the spring of that knowledge of the universe of which the Church was the vehicle. Profane knowledge, as it is so

[1] Paulus, *Geschichte des Ablasses im Mittelalter*, e. g. i. 288 ff. ; ii. 170 ff., 197 ff. ; iii. 376 ff.

strangely called, was certainly of value only in so far as it led men to understand higher truth, yet it was not alien, not the property of teachers outside the Church. Hence we can never be sure that the absurdities and abuses of Christendom were unmixed with fine emotion. Over against the brutal criticism at the expense of ecclesiastics and their agents we must set the fact that every activity fell in some degree under clerical influence, and in doing so could be touched to finer issues. The history of chivalry gives us many examples. Pilgrims on the way to Rome or Compostella stayed in churches and monasteries whose inmates repeated tales and legendary incidents which were worked up into the *chansons de geste*. At the end of the twelfth century the Arthurian legend was refined by the noble improvisation of the Holy Graal, so that a suggestion, drawn originally perhaps from the apocryphal gospel of Nicodemus, gave the story of Parsival to the literature of chivalry. The theme of ' courteous love ' was developed under the influence of mystical experience and even of the logical methods of the schools, for the poets who turned from the exaltation of brutal passion to praise unselfish devotion to woman had been affected, we are told, by the cult of the Virgin and by theological elaborations of the meaning of ' Charitas '. Many delicate filaments bound the new chivalry to the unseen world. And this being so, it would be unwise to deny the existence of an unselfish note in the response to all the inducements which were offered to men and women to abstain from sin ; and we should be rash to assume that those who adopted as a career the task of offering the inducements to their neighbours were unvisited by the sense of their high calling. However professional their attitude, even if they looked upon holy mysteries as things which could be bought and sold, this was only possible because they believed that their calling and their wares were part of a divine economy, interpreting the very nature of things. Had this belief not been general, there might have been a revolt, but never a Reformation.

There is no clear border-line in the region of religious experience between the swamps and jungle of paganism and the sunlit uplands of pure faith. St. Francis was not without a speck, and there was doubtless a glimmering of piety in the relic mongers who traded in pigs' bones. But we have no difficulty in distinguishing the pagan from the saint when we see them. We can recognize throughout the history of the Church, in all the ranges of society, the presence of men and women to whom Christianity, as interpreted by the Church, gave the highest satisfaction possible to human nature. In the Middle Ages the hold of the Church was due to the fact that it could satisfy the best cravings of the whole man, his love of beauty, his desire for goodness, his endeavour after truth. In these days the demand for certainty is distracted by conflicting claims. In the Middle Ages it was not so : the divine mystery was felt to inspire a divine order in which all knowledge and all emotion could be reconciled. Of course, if we insist with cold objectivity on drawing out the implications of the religious experience or of the philosophical systems of sincere men, they will rarely fit the mould. Regarded in this way St. Augustine, Dante, Eckhart, are probably as intractable as Spinoza or Milton or Goethe. St. Thomas himself helped to open a door which the Church has tried in vain to close. We can no more estimate the measure of acquiescence between the Church and its members in the lives of saints and theologians than we can in the secret moods of its humbler children. The Church is constantly hastening after the saints, so that in learning from them it may also control them. But these spiritual discrepancies are signs of healthy life so long as the vigorous souls, however restless and independent they may be, continue to find their satisfaction in the Church. In the Middle Ages nearly all men of this type gave themselves whole-heartedly. The teaching of the Church did no lasting violence to their experience, doubts, misgivings, for in communion with the Church they found their highest satisfaction. Dante says :

> ' Human longing is measured in this life by that degree of knowledge which it is here possible to possess ; and that point is never transgressed except by misapprehension which is beside the intention of nature. . . . And this is why the saints envy not one another, because each one attains the goal of his longing, which longing is commensurate with the nature of his excellence.' [1]

This satisfaction was possible because men felt that they and all their social and spiritual affinities were part of the divine order inspired by the unfathomable mystery. They appropriated a body of truth in which, if they adjusted themselves to it, they felt sure of harmony, and to rebellion from which they traced the sin and misery of mankind. Readers of this volume will find in subsequent pages a brief discussion of the principles of this order—in the physical structure of earth and heavens, in the harmony of all law, natural and social, in the dovetailing of the discon-nected learning, true or false, about men, beasts, birds, plants, minerals, into a scheme combined of Biblical and classical suggestion. Here it is enough to point out that although most of the medieval cosmology and chronology have gone, the medieval view of the universe lasted a very long time and has by no means altogether disappeared. The medieval philosophy of history has not ceased to influence us. It was deduced from three sources, the Biblical chronology harmonized with that of non-Jewish peoples by Eusebius,

---

[1] *Il Convito*, iii, c. 15, trans. Wicksteed.

the Augustinian theory of the city of God and its later developments, the idea of the ' preparatio evangelica ', which took its finest form in Dante's conception of the provision of the Roman Empire by the Father, with its universal peace as a cradle for His Son. The Eusebian chronology, revised by Archbishop Ussher in the seventeenth century, has indeed gone, but in its simplest expression the conception of the preparation for the gospel is a living part of Christian thought. The belief that the earth is the centre of the stellar system has gone, but the anthropo-centric ideas bound up with it are dying very hard. The zoology of the medieval mind was fantastic, but it was due not to lack of intelligence, but to lack of observation, and could not be regarded as absurd so long as distinct species were held to be the results of separate acts of creation. Underlying the strange parallels between the truths of revelation and the phenomena of the natural world was that sense of rhythm in the universe, whose philosophical expres-sion has a very respectable origin in Greek thought and a destiny which would seem to be increasing in grandeur. In a word, medieval thought was at bottom anything but absurd. It was pursued with an ability which would find no difficulty in coping with the problems of modern science and speculation. And it reached forward to a mystical reception of God, in whom is the ordered union of all the objects of knowledge, natural and revealed, human and divine. The great mystics, indeed, boldly urged that for this very reason the search after God under settled forms is futile. Eckhart once said :

> ' He who fondly imagines to get more of God in thoughts, prayers, pious offices and so forth, than by the fireside or in the stall : in sooth he does but take God, as it were, and swaddle his head in a cloak and hide him under the table. For he who seeks God under settled forms lays hold of the form while missing the God concealed in it.'

And the same Master Eckhart, the Dominican contemporary of Dante, also said :

> ' Man has to seek God in error and forgetfulness and foolish-
> ness. For deity has in it the power of all things and no thing
> has the like. The sovran light of the impartible essence illumines
> all things. St. Dionysius says that beauty is good order with
> pre-eminent lucidity. Thus God is an arrangement of three
> Persons. And the soul's lower power should be ordered to her
> higher, and her higher ones to God ; her outward senses to her
> inward and her inward ones to reason : thought to intuition
> and intuition to the will and all to unity, so that the soul may
> be alone with nothing flowing into her but sheer divinity,
> flowing here into itself.' [1]

Eckhart lived at a time when the best strength of the
Church was expended in the codification of law and discipline and doctrine, and, although he was suspect, as probing
too deep, and some of his teaching was condemned after
his death, he reminds us that the Church was more than
a pedagogue, that it was a school in which the ignorant
and the learned worked together at a common task. Stripped
of all accessories the task of the Church was the elucidation,
in thought and life, of the divine mystery as revealed in the
Bible, all other texts and tools being subsidiary. The Bible
has rightly been called the text-book of the Middle Ages.
It was studied, of course, in Latin, the version, partly
compiled but very largely made by St. Jerome, being the
standard text or Vulgate. The canons of its interpretation,
unfortunately not so good as those laid down by Jerome,
were defined by St. Augustine. The standard commentary,
drawn from the Fathers, and afterwards known as the Gloss,
was compiled by Walafrid Strabo, abbot of Reichenau,
in the ninth century. The Gloss underlies all later work
and influenced every medieval exposition, including that

[1] *Meister Eckhart*, Pfeiffer's edition trans. Evans (London, 1924),
pp. 39-40, 49.

in stone and on glass. The text of the Vulgate was revised by Alcuin, in the days of Charles the Great, and again by scholars of the University of Paris in the thirteenth century, shortly after it had been divided into chapters by Stephen Langton. Dominicans and others provided it with critical apparatus and concordances. The authority of the Bible was final—it was an isolated and unsuccessful vagary of St. Bernard that he regarded the *text* as subject to the decision of the Church—and no more damaging charge could be levelled against a group of theologians than that it gave too little attention to scriptural study. No more perplexing problem could present itself than an apparent inconsistency between the teaching of the Bible and the general consensus of the Church. When Pope John XXII, preaching, as he was careful to say, not as pope but as a simple priest, taught his heretical doctrine of the Beatific Vision, he based his case upon the supreme authority of Scripture.[1] He bowed before the opposition of the theologians, and it was reserved for Wycliffe to give reality to the great question whether the Church is or is not to be regarded as the final authority in interpretation.

Here we come to an issue even more intractable than that between property and evangelical poverty. The greatest danger to the Church lay neither in dogma, nor in the hierarchy, nor in the interpretation of the world ; it lay in the inner experience of men who received all these things as a matter of course, and in whom the Church had for centuries found its strength. They had felt the impact of Christ, and, as time wore on, they found their way to Christ more and more through the Scriptures. As it strained to understand the truth in its mysterious inheritance and to relate it to the rest of experience, the Church had encouraged

---

[1] See Noel Valois' life of John XXII in *Histoire littéraire de la France*, xxxiv, notably pp. 559–67, 606.

a strange variety of thought and self-conscious religious life. Both the thought and the spiritual experience of the Middle Ages were destined to have a great future, within and without the Church. As we draw nearer to modern times, we feel that they were gaining an independent strength, a sense of confidence, a sanction within themselves stronger than the sanctions by which they had previously been directed. Just as the problem of the power of the Church had been narrowed down to the issue of poverty, so the problem of authority was at bottom the issue whether goodness and sincerity were their own sanctions. The issue is logically insoluble and has shattered Christendom. In the interests of order and unity the Church had been able to control the zealots who urged that the guardians and teachers of the faith should have no worldly ties : it had found room for all kinds of communities, from the well ordered and tolerant Benedictines to the severest types of asceticism ; it had even rallied them all to its defence, so that its richly brocaded garments were as it were upheld by mendicants. If they were restless or developed anti-nomian tendencies, the teachers of poverty were suppressed. There is no more poignant symbol of the unequal conflict than the handful of spiritual Franciscans urging their cause at the magnificent court of the Popes at Avignon. But the issue raised by sane and well-balanced religious experience—the issue of conscience, so closely related to that of poverty—was a more difficult matter to deal with. The more orthodox it was, the more dangerous it was. Wycliffe was a truly portentous figure, but he was too solitary, too subtle and dogmatic, to be a lasting menace. The Hussites of Bohemia were prophetic of the national churches which were to come, but, hidden away in a corner, and distracted by social and political aspirations, they could be controlled or placated. The real danger lay in the quiet, active, mystical men and women who, in the face of evil around them, began to think and to experience for themselves the implications of fellowship with Christ. They were not concerned with vexed questions of interpretation, but with the immediate appeal of the Bible, and of the life of prayer. To them so much which, in the eyes of ecclesiastics and lawyers, was all important, seemed trivial, the basis of their faith so much more essential than the superstructure, the sense of fellowship in the sacraments and prayer more urgent than the explanation of the mysterious.[1] There is nothing heterodox in this, unless it be the tendency to insist that the validity of a spiritual act depends upon the fitness of him who performs it. Recent apologists have shown how the experiences of the later mystics can be linked with the teaching of the twelfth-century mystics, St. Bernard and the school of St. Victor. Yet, notably through the schools of the Brethren of the Common Life in the Rhineland, the movement was strong enough to influence the life, not only of Ignatius Loyola, the founder of the Jesuits, but of Calvin and indirectly of Luther.[2]

How the growth of ordered self-controlled piety, affecting clergy and laity in little nests of spiritual contentment, could have results so striking in their diversity is one of the most fascinating problems in history. The movement seemed so hopeful, yet was so devastating in its effects. It is no part of my task to try to explain this problem, except to point out that its solution is clearly connected with the contemporary growth of an equally ordered and self-controlled secularism. This spirit of secularism affected the organized

[1] Cf. the chapter in the *Imitatio Christi* on nice disputes regarding the Lord's Supper, Book IV, c. 18.

[2] See especially Albert Hyma, *The Christian Renaissance* (Michigan and The Hague, 1924). Like the Friends of God before them, Groote and his followers protested against anything over-subtle or antinomian.

Church hardly less than the ' national states '. Piety and paganism, so to speak, came to their own and tried to settle their differences in new ways. The dream of a united Christendom, in which paganism would be transformed under the beneficent guidance of the official disciples of Christ, was seen to have been a dream. The Church had tried to control and never ceased to influence the world, but it could not identify the world with the Church in one Kingdom of God. The world had its own claims—claims of nationality, of the interplay of capital and labour, of trade, of social expression. Perhaps the issue is best summed up in the words of a Florentine chronicler, who lived in the days of Boniface VIII and Philip the Fair, of Master Eckhart and Dante : ' Humility is of no avail against sheer evil.' [1]

Many historians have traced the gradual emergence into separate life in the fourteenth and fifteenth centuries of the forces, hitherto inextricably connected, of political self-direction and an elaborate ecclesiastical organism no longer able, in their struggle for existence, to control the life of the spirit. But they have written in the light of four centuries of later history. For the ordinary man, were he devout or pagan at heart, life in those times must still have been full of colour and adventure in a world which nothing could shake. If we go to-day into Winchester cathedral, we can still recapture the sense of that ordered, that magnificent stability. Sheltered by the massive Norman walls and the intricate Gothic roof, the effigies of the ecclesiastics lie—Edington, Wykeham, Beaufort, Waynflete, Fox, prelates and statesmen, each in his painted, delicately chiselled shrine. Those tombs are a symbol of security. Those men lived in times full of perplexity, but undisturbed by any feelings of

---

[1] The words are ' Niente vale l' humiltà contra alla grande malizia '. Dino Compagni is meditating on the futility of self-effacing moderation in the civil strife of the Italian cities.

catastrophe. In their world heresy and antinomianism could have no abiding place. We realize why the call of Master Eckhart, deep thinker though he was, to withdraw oneself to commune with God in the ground of the soul, died away in secret, why the visionary prophesies of the Joachimites passed like whispers in the undergrowth, why the Friends of God and the Brethren of the Common Life were half contemptuously welcomed as harmless pietists who performed a useful function, why Wycliffe's academic influence withered so quickly. The sense of reality was still to be found in the conventional ways so full of colour and movement. There were few times and places during the last centuries of the Middle Ages in which the adventurous soul could not find intimations of the great opportunities for mind and spirit made possible by organized Christianity. The awakening might come slowly, or be arrested in some career in which the sense of vocation was dormant. But we must not believe that all lingered in the outer courts.

> Expertus potest credere
> Quid sit Iesum diligere

II

Hitherto we have been trying to understand the atmosphere of medieval Christianity, how it worked in an undeveloped society, fundamentally pagan. Christianity was presented through the Church as an interpretation of the universe, but still more as the living operation of divine providence. It was established as an essential element in the social order, and yet it called men to the greatest of adventures, the service and contemplation of God. It could give excitement to the frivolous, occupation of every kind, physical or intellectual or contemplative, to the serious; and it could offer opportunities in high places as in low to the depraved. It engaged the highest faculties in co-operation with the purpose of God by satisfying their craving for an ordered and just interpretation of life. In the Church human self-esteem was gratified : *nam non ecclesia propter coelum, sed propter ecclesiam coelum.* Through the Church man could escape from his sense of frustration by dedicating himself to the glory of God.

Before I close, something should be said about the organization in which, as a self-protective and directing force, the ideals of Christian society expressed themselves. For here, and notably in the earlier history of the papacy, we may find the highest attempt to give concrete and permanent shape to the energy, the audacity, love of order and austerity which played with such bewildering freedom in the medieval world.

The centralization of the Western Church under one head satisfied in large measure the desire for unity, order, peace, righteousness. The most fruitful influence in expressing this desire was undoubtedly the great bishop of Hippo, St. Augustine, to whose thought the famous pope Gregory the Great did most to give currency.[1] St. Augustine was not concerned with the papal power. It is not easy, indeed, to say how far he was concerned to maintain that the organized Church was the only expression on earth of the City of God. Just as he hesitated in his analysis of the grounds of secular authority, so he hesitated to admit that the truth might not lie with faithful souls who had been forced to suffer in silence through the errors or mis-understanding of ecclesiastical authority. His writings were very various and when, like the *De Civitate Dei*, they were written over a period of many years, they are not

[1] For what follows I am indebted particularly to the writings of Bernheim and an article by Hauck, ' Die Rezeption und Umbildung der allgemeinen Synode im Mittelalter' (*Historische Vierteljahrschrift*, 1907).

perfectly coherent. The important matter is that Augustine's philosophy of history became the main source of papal apologetic. Its central thought is the harmony which exists in the society at peace with itself in the enjoyment of God. This harmony—so others drew out his meaning—affects the whole of nature. It is not a quality which is added, rather it is acquiescence in something eternally true and real. It is not like the ' pax Romana '. In one passage of his book (xxii. 6) St. Augustine discusses the view, set out by Cicero in his *De Republica*, that no good state will engage in war unless for the sake of safety or in order to keep faith ; and he shows that in the earthly state this view involves a possible contradiction, for Cicero regards permanence as the mark of the state, and in order to keep itself alive a state may have to sacrifice its good faith for the sake of safety. But the safety of the City of God is maintained or, rather, acquired with and through faith ; if faith is lost, salvation is impossible. This argument is not merely a play upon the words *salus, fides*, for in the City of God the faith and salvation of the individual are bound up with the order of a society which has its permanence and its understanding in God. The next stage in the argument is that the supreme active quality of a state of harmony is *iustitia* or righteousness, while the prime cause of resistance to it is pride, the vice which for this reason, that it breaks up the peace of communion in the enjoyment of God, came to be regarded in later days as the worst of the seven deadly sins. So, finally, we can understand the deep significance of the insistence upon justice in the political thought of the Middle Ages. The just ruler, whether he be pope or king, is not merely one who deals fairly ; he is the one whose righteousness proves his kingdom to be part of the harmony of things. The unjust ruler is a tyrant, the victim of pride which sets itself against this harmony. When a tyrant

holds sway, a touch of confusion disturbs the whole of
nature. A shiver runs through the world, as when the veil
of the Temple was rent in twain at the time of the Crucifixion. The medieval chroniclers who drew dire conclusions
from times of plague, famine, loss of crops and herds,
violent storms and sudden death, paid homage, by no means
always unconscious homage, to this conviction. Conversely,
if justice prevails, all is at peace. This belief became
a theme for high speculation, as in Dante's vision of the
Empire, and survived to inspire Milton's 'Ode on the
Morning of Christ's Nativity'.

What may seem to us poetic fancy was an incentive to
action. It gave a direction to policy as clearly as the teaching
of the Stoics did in earlier times or as the doctrine of Karl
Marx has done in our own day. And it influenced some
of the most powerful men who ever lived. We do wrong
to popes like Gregory the Great, and Gregory VII and
Innocent III, if we regard them only as statesmen or lawyers;
and it is quite beside the point to accuse them of inconsistency, to collect, for example, Gregory VII's letters about
peace and justice, and to set over against them the devastating
effects of his conflict with the Emperor Henry IV. By
Gregory VII's time the visible Church on earth, under the
guidance of the Pope, had become the accepted embodiment
of the City of God, carrying with it all the high responsibilities which the maintenance of the divine order involved.
Henceforth the Church set its face against any distinction
between the Church visible and invisible.[1] Righteousness
must be tempered with mercy and gentleness; it was
inconceivable without them ; but it must insist on obedience
to the rule of order and beat down the proud. The just
ruler must be humble, remembering that the inequalities of
man are due to sin and that all men are by nature equal,

[1] Cf. the decrees of the Council of Trent, session xxiii, c. 1.

yet he has a trust from God and must not shirk the responsibility of conflict, even if it means the use of force and the sword, against evil.

In the next place, the papacy satisfied the desire for guidance and certainty. The absence of contact in the second and third centuries between the adventurous theologian and the mass of believers has frequently been noted. There was no strong middle element, and the learned, whose profound religious experience was refined and made aware of itself by philosophical contemplation, tended to regard themselves as the guardians of the heavenly treasure, the message entrusted to the Church. The things hidden from the wise, by which God made foolish the wisdom of the world (1 Cor. i. 20), were now, in the opinion of many, the things hidden by the wise. That this tendency, which many leaders deplored, was checked in the West, and the speculations of the theologians put to the test of the experience of the simple, was largely due to the leadership of the bishops of Rome.[1] In their categorical expressions of witness to the faith, free from all dialectic and Biblical argument and erudition, the Popes began their spacious task of registering the growth of religious and ecclesiastical experience. It would be impossible to say how far they declared a general will, and out of place to try to estimate their authority in the days of the great councils. But the foundations of papal power were laid in these acts of authoritative testimony to the faith of the common man. One of the great poets of the Church, St. Paulinus of Nola (d. 431), the rich senator and landowner who gave up his wealth for Christ, spoke the mind of the West when he said, ' In omnem fidelem Spiritus Dei spirat '.

[1] See, for example, the remarks of J. Lebreton on the action of Dionysius of Rome, in a remarkable article, ' La foi populaire et la théologie savante,' *Revue d'Histoire ecclésiastique*, 1924, xx, p. 9 note ; and, generally, pp. 33–7.

To describe the growth of papal leadership would be to write the history of the Church during the next eleven hundred years. The ecclesiastical organization of Rome itself was followed by the gradual penetration, in the West, of the *ordo romanus*, that is to say, of Roman liturgical uses, &c. The inclusion in Christendom of new peoples and areas under the joint influence of papal and secular authority involved the development of a disciplinary system : violence and passion had to be curbed, and barbarian habits subdued to the moral law of Christ. The penitentials with their codes of offences and punishments were one of the bases of the great system of canon law which was elaborated in a long series of handbooks and culminated in the Decretum of Gratian and the later codifications of decretals. The growth of the canon law was made possible by the work of provincial councils, by papal decrees and schools of juris-prudence, most of all perhaps by the development of diocesan administration. The history of these movements was very uneven. Local authority, whether clerical or lay, did not acquiesce easily and uniformly in the tendency to refer difficult matters to Rome, while the moral authority of the Papacy was frequently disturbed by faction in Rome itself and by the depravity of the successors of St. Peter. But in course of time the issue became clear. Reformers, whose moral sense was shocked by the subjection of spiritual life to the accidents of local caprice or secular interests, at last threw their influence on the side of centralized authority. The local hierarchy, so jealous of its rights, found that its freedom was better secured by submission to the higher authority of Rome than by uneasy co-operation with princes. The organization at head-quarters of a college of cardinals as an electoral and advisory body, the increasing employment of papal legates who, like the *missi dominici* of Charles the Great, and the itinerant justices of our

English kings, distributed the authority of their master, gave coherence and uniformity to the exercise of papal power ; the swollen stream of appeals and references to Rome hastened the steady elaboration of a common administrative system. The climax came at the beginning of the thirteenth century, when Innocent III gave definite expression to the theory of the *plenitudo potestatis* of the Pope, and, consciously reverting to the age of the great councils of Nicaea and Chalcedon, summoned an oecumenical council in which he restated the faith, in some degree codified the practice of the Church, and expounded a policy for the future.

Historians in a one-sided way often deal with this development as though it were nothing but a striving after papal infallibility, or a victory of personal ambition working with the aid of forged documents. The traditions of Protestant controversy were reinforced by Döllinger's anonymous tract, 'The Pope and the Council' (1869), a powerful criticism of the ultramontane ideas which were so hotly debated before and during the Vatican Council of 1870. However effectively this famous tract may appeal to us as a discussion of an ecclesiastical problem, it was not altogether happy as an interpretation of the Middle Ages. It suggests a perpetual cleavage between the central court of Christendom and Christendom itself.[1] Other historians have been unduly impressed by the drastic criticism to which medieval writers subjected the Curia ; they forget that men do not attack so persistently the abuses of an unnecessary tribunal, and they do not always point out that the criticism was not accompanied by any hint of schism. The denunciation of the delays, extortions and venality of the papal court was an indirect tribute to its actuality. The work done by the

[1] I do not deny, of course, that the doctrine of the papal power became increasingly definite. Its history was made clear by Schulte in 1871.

Curia was enormous, ranging from arbitrations between kings to minute regulations about disputes in a parish. The Pope, needless to say, could not transact all this business unaided. His chancery became the most technical and also the most efficient administrative machine which had ever existed. Every stage in the preparation of a bull or mandate was carefully scrutinized to secure authenticity, prevent forgery and guarantee that each formality, from the acquiescence of the pontiff to the consideration of technical objections by the parties, had been observed. And the preparation of a papal bull was merely the culmination of judicial process or of deliberation in council. When papal attention was most deeply engaged, the Pope naturally had recourse to his advisers, and asked the opinion of theologians and canonists. As the unworthy exponent of divine justice, he was expected to purge his mind of caprice and prejudice. The medieval mind, indeed, was much perplexed by the possibility of error in the interpretation of the will of God. It spent much labour in the invention of expedients and rules for distinguishing between the true and the false. The subtle dialectic, the procedure of the inquisition, the process of canonization had at least one object in common, the circumvention of the powers of evil. The Devil and his agents were everywhere, waiting to take advantage of mankind, which since the Fall had been so exposed to the wiles of duplicity. The great mercy of God is necessary, said St. Augustine, to secure that he who thinks he has good angels for friends, has not evil spirits as false friends. If we consider the vast literature of miracles and visions which meet us in the lives of the saints we may well believe that tests were necessary, and cease to marvel that they were often so ineffective. And if we are amazed at the credulity which could accept the revelations of a casual epileptic and at the incredulity which could denounce as suggestions of demons the visions of Joan of Arc, we should remember that, in accordance with belief in the fundamental necessity of unity and order, tests would especially be applied to those crucial cases, which seemed to involve the safety of the community, to detect pride and disobedience. For every power was subject to law. The Pope himself was not secure, for he was bound by the decisions of the Fathers and the great councils. He might err ; he might be condemned for heresy. His moral lapses, his administrative errors, it is true, were matters for God alone, but the most unflinching papalists were agreed that his dogmatic errors were a matter for the Church. In one of his sermons Innocent III dealt with the possibility that he might err in the faith, and declared that in such a case he could be judged by the Church ; and his view was sustained by later canonists and theologians.

Lastly, the growth of the papal power permitted within a united Church the development of a richer life. The history of the Church between the fifth and the thirteenth centuries reveals two tendencies, opposed in their natural operation, yet reconciled to a remarkable degree under the guidance of the hierarchy. The appropriation of Christianity by the vigorous half-civilized peoples of Western Europe resulted in spiritual and intellectual ferment, in a luxuriant growth of spiritual experience which manifested itself in religious associations, in speculation, in various forms of piety and superstition. But, in contrast with these phenomena, the spread of Christianity was directed by men, leaders in an organized community, who were inspired by the ideas of Cyprian, Ambrose, and Augustine. Conversion, in this view, was not an opportunity for free thought, but a call to duty in an ordered world. The varieties of experience were not repressed, but they were disciplined, so that the life of the Church was enriched, and not distracted, by monastic experiments, by the reception of neo-platonic theology, by the impetus of Greek and Arabic learning. Scope was allowed for the awakened energies of mind and spirit which, if undirected, have in all ages retarded progress in one direction as much as they have advanced it in another.[1] The medieval methods of cultivation and restraint are not in favour nowadays, but if we reflect upon the magnitude of the task, the condition of society and the amazing energy of its life in the early Middle Ages, it cannot justly be said that they were unduly repressive. And, by maintaining as a practical guide in life the conception of an ordered universe, in which there is a fundamental harmony between moral and physical law, the Church turned the faces of the European peoples in the only direction along which social and scientific advance was possible.

New movements within the Church reacted upon the idea of the Church. During the early period there was an inevitable tendency in ordinary speech, if not in theological thought, to narrow the conception of the Church. ' Little man, why is your head shaved ? ' says a heathen champion to the Pope, in one of the *chansons de geste*. The contrast between the Church, represented by a handful of clergy, and the still reluctant world was still so striking. The same tendency may be seen in the great struggles between the lay and clerical powers. As late as the end of the twelfth century great popes like Alexander III and Innocent III speak at times as though episcopate and church were synonymous terms. But by this time the scriptural view, summed up by the Fathers and always maintained by theologians, had acquired renewed significance in the development of all kinds of ecclesiastical activity. It is

[1] A useful introduction to the chief types of medieval heresy will be found in Alphandéry's *Les Idées morales chez les hétérodoxes latins au début du XIII* *siècle* (1903).

often said that the conception of the Church was narrowed by the growth of a papal tyranny. This is not a correct analysis of the subsequent unrest. The idea of the Church as the whole body of the faithful could only acquire such measure of reality as it ever has acquired through the growth of organized life which accompanied the growth of papal influence. The Church as a body of clergy and laity conscious of their membership in Christ, and at the same time coincident with the whole of European society in the West, did in fact come nearer to realization in the days of the Crusades, of the revived Benedictine movements, of Abelard and St. Bernard, Gratian and Petrus Lombardus than in any other period in its history. The conception was developed with magnificent elaboration in the writings of Hugh of St. Victor.

How, borne down by the heavy weight of intricate, incessantly more intricate, machinery, torn asunder by the conflicting motion of its adventurous life, the Church failed to maintain agreement with this view of things, it would require an essay much longer than the present to explain. In the eyes of many the Church has seemed but to relax its hold in order to secure itself more firmly. To others its history in the Middle Ages is the record of the greatest of all human efforts to find that certainty, that something out of life, which ' while it is expected is already gone—has passed unseen, in a sigh, in a flash—together with the youth, with the strength, with the romance of illusions '.

F. M. POWICKE.

2

ART

i. MEDIEVAL ARCHITECTURE

ARCHITECTURE arose as a simple craft of building, and then expanding became the several crafts of building in association. From times so remote that they may be called primitive, building in a customary way would have embodied many folk-customs and ritual elements. Architecture was thus a compound of custom and experiment, of superstition and ceremony. From the first it had a physical side and a psychological side and these were carried forward in the long stream of progressing tradition. In speaking of the diverse strands which make up old arts it is not implied that an architectural factor can ever be separated from a residuum of mere building, for such ' mere building ' has never had an existence, and we might as well try to isolate the beauty of a bird's nest from its utility as the aesthetics of architecture from its building basis. Of other arts than ' architecture ' it is taken for granted that the design and style (that is the appearance of things made) are part of the works themselves. There are no aesthetic theories, fortunately, about the design of ships and carts and the thought of ' design ' has hardly been separated from the thought of making them. Only of architecture, and partly in consequence of the use of that long word, has it come to be supposed that there are mysteries which constitute the essence of the art of building although they are different from the body of building which conditions and contains them. When the ancient schools of building flourished everything

made was in its own rank of one artistic kind. A cathedral
or a cottage was a customary product and was built as
naturally as a basket or a bowl. The same kind of art was
made in every shop and sold over every counter. This art
was the expression of the Folk mind; the spirit and body
were inseparable. The difference between modern ' designs
in the Gothic style ' and the real thing is that one is a whim
of fashion, the other was a function of life.

The dates and details of medieval arts are dealt with in
hundreds of volumes. Here our concern will be with
questions of origin, character, and spirit, leading up to an
endeavour to estimate the legacy bequeathed to us by this
old culture. To obtain a full understanding of the art of
the Middle Ages is of course impossible, yet we criticize
and judge where we ought rather to examine and wonder.
Old architecture was found out by men working in stone,
a cathedral was, as it were, a natural growth from a quarry.
In looking back at accomplished results it is next to impossible to understand all that was in the process which
embodied mysteries of man and the nature of things. We
approve of this and design something like that, until many
have deluded themselves into trying to believe that medieval
architecture might be built to-day although it would be as
easy to become Egyptian by a similar method. All living
arts are folk customs with their roots in the soil; they
express the common will of the community. We know so
much about past schools of art that we have divided what
was a fast-flowing stream into sections to which the names
of ' styles ' have been given, but the names are ours, and
when the works were being done it was thought that each
one in turn was the natural way of building. In any of our
towns there will be modern buildings in the Classic, Byzantine, Romanesque, and Gothic styles, but it is nearly
impossible to get it understood that they are not of the

same kind as the ancient buildings ; the very fact that they were designed in a named style is evidence of the difference. In the long process of development there were doubtless periods of greater and less energy and perhaps our style names sometimes coincide with such epochs; that is all there is in them. Great epochs of art were times of adventure and discovery. History and criticism are our forms of originality.

What we call medieval architecture was the building art which was developed in Western Europe in the time between the Roman decline and the Renaissance. The mature phase of this art is also called Gothic, a name which was given by scholars of the Renaissance period in Italy to the art of the Lombards which they regarded as Germanic and barbaric. After closer study the later type of medieval architecture, which we now call Gothic, was divided from the earlier phases which came to be called Romanesque with various subsections like Carolingian, Saxon, and Norman. Common use of semicircular arches was the chief criterion of discrimination between it and ' the Pointed or Gothic style '. Traceried windows and ribbed vaults were also observed to be characteristic of pointed Gothic. ' Romanesque ' means an art derived from Rome as the Romance languages derived. ' Gothic ' to us is the art of a later generation in which new strains of blood had begun to tell. The name Gothic after all has an inner fitness, it stands for an infusion of northern blood and a new spirit. Essentially this spirit is not of Rome but from the North.

In the body of Gothic there is also, as has long been recognized, much of the East. Wren, with his fresh strong sight, called it Saracenic. With the fuller study of mechanical development the tendency has been to look on the process itself as self explanatory, raising no questions as to why and whither, although a general debt to the East is commonly admitted. The borrowing is usually attributed to the Crusaders but oriental art had already influenced late Classical or Hellenistic art. Eastward, Rome not only entered into the rich and various forms of Hellenistic art which had been developed in Egypt, Syria, and Asia Minor, but came in direct contact with Persia and Armenia, and by commerce, with India and China. The extraordinary fertility of Christian-Egyptian or Coptic art has only been made known to us by the researches of the last half-century. Christian Egypt was certainly one of the great reservoirs from which the parched arts of Rome were refreshed ; Mesopotamia, Syria, Armenia, and Asia Minor were others.

One of the greatest phenomena of the Middle Ages was the continuous absorption in the West of oriental thought and art. Christianity was of the East ; the early monastic diffusion brought new seeds ; the age of pilgrimage deepened the interest and the Crusades followed. Arab conquests of Eastern Christian lands forced large numbers of clergy and craftsmen westward. Then the East came to the West politically and commercially by many routes, through Byzantine rule in Italy, by relations with the German Empire, and by Saracenic occupation of Sicily and Spain. Our King Offa issued gold coins imitating an Arab Dinar of the year 774 with its inscription. The art of the early Christian Church had penetrated to the West while Rome was yet the ruling power. Celtic and Anglian schools were formed later which were to react again on the continent of Europe. Most precious monuments of this art are the sculptured crosses at Ruthwell, Bewcastle, Hexham, and elsewhere ; the Lindisfarne and Kells books ; and several pieces of metalwork including a marvellous plaque recently found at Whitby. The technique of the metalwork of this school derived much from a non-Christian source in the East which reached England through the Teutonic peoples.

Churches of the ' Central type '—that is on circular and polygonal plans—were well known here in the time of Bede, and simpler rectangular Saxon churches frequently had a tall central mass with low chancel and porch—these have been called Tower churches and are variants of the central type so common in the East. The school of culture which gathered at the Court of Charlemagne drew to itself the art traditions of all Christendom. The great Emperor in seeking to revive Roman culture refounded medieval art. In the Carolingian age vital traditions of art existed eastward in the Byzantine Empire and in derivative schools in Italy, westward in Ireland and England, and to the south in Spain. The most living and potent of all was the last, and indeed it seems to have been almost a possibility that we should have to name this age from the Caliphs instead of from Charlemagne. The literature of the time following witnesses to similar influences. Especially characteristic is the *Chanson de Roland*. If we look beyond the incidents to the background of the story we shall see that what filled the minds of makers and listeners were Caliphs and Emirs, Mahomet, Arabs, Turks, and Saracens ' who had nothing white but their teeth ' ; Spain, Africa, Egypt, Persia ; Cordova, Toledo, Seville, Palermo, Babylon, and Alexandria with its harbour and ships ; silk from Alexandria, gold of Arabia, embroideries, ' olifants ' and ivory chairs, helmets and swords ornamented with carbuncles, saddles covered with gold and gems, painted shields, bright gonfalons, camels and lions.

Not only does a similar regard for things oriental appear in many of the Romances, but they themselves seem to be largely of an eastern character. The Orient and Spain were lands of romance, riches and arts, but they were schools of learning too. ' The ancient learning that first trickled into the Latin West came almost entirely through Arabic channels and but seldom direct from Greek sources. The great reservoir of learning was in Spain and to a less extent in Sicily.' It was inevitable that with the 'Arabian revival of learning', the acquaintance with Arabic numerals, trigonometry, astrology and philosophy, that the arts would have had their share of influence, and it is noteworthy that it was during the reign of our Henry II that a new type of ornamentation which seems to be ultimately Moorish and Arabic in character appears in the carvings of English architecture. The South of France was affected much earlier and Toulouse became the centre of an orientalizing type of Romanesque art. At Le Puy there are some remarkable carved wooden doors bearing Cufic inscriptions applied in an ornamental way, and this use of Cufic decoration spread later even to England.

About the year 1000 a powerful and progressive school of building began to form in Normandy, and the great Abbey Church at Jumièges, built from *c.* 1048 to 1067, 'was superior to any contemporary structure in Europe'. Edward the Confessor, while living in Normandy, acquired knowledge of the building work there being done, and after his return and coronation he rebuilt the Abbey Church at Westminster with such close resemblance to that at Jumièges that, as excavation has shown, it was practically a copy, and it may not be doubted that a Norman master-mason was brought here for the work. The church was of great size and cruciform, with a tall central tower over the crossing, through the windows of which light entered the central space as through a dome. The Confessor's church was begun about 1050 and consecrated shortly before the Conquest, when the other Abbey buildings do not seem to have been begun. The earliest of these, the Dormitory, still exists and the manner of building shows it to have been erected about 1070 ; it was practically a continuation of

1. LE MANS CATHEDRAL, WESTERN PORTAL (see p. 67)

the Confessor's work. All the arches of the vaulting, windows, and doors are built with a light-coloured stone and dark tufa arranged alternately. This fashion is characteristic of south-east France rather than of Normandy, but such counterchanged masonry is represented in the Bayeux embroidery. That it was delighted in for its own sake is shown by the way in which it was taken over into painted decoration. For more than a century it was a common method of internal decoration to paint walls and arches with alternate bands and blocks of lighter and darker colour, as may still be seen at Winchester, St. Albans, and many other places.

We have been accustomed to think of the immense body of building done in England in the century following the Conquest as 'Norman', and so it was in its chief first impulse, but threads of many colours were soon woven into its texture. In this era of building activity direct experiments must have been made here as well as in Normandy. Foreign influences would have reached us as well as Normandy and in some cases independently of it. Further, the old English stock, from which the craftsmen would largely have been recruited, would have contributed something to the mind behind style manifestations. The cathedral of Durham, a work of remarkable power, appears to have something of Lombard character built in with the stones; there was doubtless some Germanic and Lombardic contribution in all Norman building customs, but here seems to be a specific if weak infusion of Lombard 'feeling'. At Durham *ribbed* vaulting, the type of vault which was to be characteristic of Gothic buildings, was used in work done soon after 1093. According to Mr. J. Bilson, the vaults of the choir aisles date from 1096 and high vaults over the choir were erected in 1104, while 'Every part of the church was covered with ribbed vaulting between 1093 and 1133'.

Such vaulting exists in Lombardy but the dates are disputed: a habit of forming domes with ribs on the surfaces was already common in Byzantine practice. The dome of St. Sophia, as rebuilt after an earthquake in the last quarter of the tenth century by Tirdates, an Armenian architect, had ribs on its lower surface and the dome of the church of St. Theodore, Tyrone, also has ribs. It is said that ribbed vaults of early date exist in Armenia and there is a probability that the idea came from the East, as experiments of a similar kind seem to have been made in Moslem Spain. The method quickly spread in England. The aisles of the nave of Old St. Paul's were vaulted in this way and the remote 'Norman' church on Holy Island had a ribbed vault over the central span of the nave.

In Durham Cathedral much is remarkable besides the early ribbed vaults. The vaulting arches of the Chapter House sprang from large corbels sculptured into human forms, which are of Lombardic style while early examples of 'Norman' sculpture. A similar character of style appears also in the fine doorways of the church. The most important of these, the north entrance, must have been a work of great beauty and refinement, but it is twelfth-century work and has been much injured. The shafts are modern, except for two remaining inside which are carved all over, and the arches have been pared down. Some capitals of simple primary form are delicately fluted and truly beautiful. By comparing the less injured parts of the interior with what is left outside we may gain a fairly complete idea of this remarkable doorway and three or four others of smaller size are of similar style. Durham Cathedral is a great European monument. It has been claimed that in the period after the Conquest 'the real centre of the Norman school was in England rather than in Normandy'.

An earlier type of plan had been followed at Durham

Cathedral, but the newer pilgrimage church plan with an ambulatory about the apse and a series of radiating chapels was early adopted at St. Augustine's, Canterbury. After the Conquest such foreign fashions were soon known and smaller works of art, like sculptured fonts and tombs, of black Tournay marble were frequently imported.

Another variety of what we call the Norman style might better be thought of as Angevin Romanesque. It is obvious that Henry II, Count of Anjou and Maine, son of the Empress Maud, would bring a new strain into English politics and culture. In such works as the west front of Rochester Cathedral, the south porch of Malmesbury Abbey, the church of St. Peter, Northampton, parts of Reading Abbey, the old cloister of Westminster Abbey, &c., there is not only advance but difference of outlook which implies a fresh infusion from the orientalized Romanesque of South France. The most noticeable characteristic is a new type of crisp foliage cut in low relief ' arabesque ' on capitals, mouldings, and surfaces. In the latter half of the twelfth century we get sure evidence of this influence in the ornament imitating Cufic writing which appears in the Winchester Bible, a book specially admired by Henry II. The temper of the time is suggested by the description, in the ' Tristan ' of Thomas, of the silks brought to the court of King Mark : ' opulentes ', ' ornées d'étranges couleurs ', ' une étoffe de couleur exotique '. Later, when Henry III received the relic of the Holy Blood at Westminster, Matthew Paris records that ' the King sat gloriously on his throne clad in a golden garment of the most precious brocade of Baghdad '. The sculptured west doorway of Rochester Cathedral is so similar to finer doorways at Angers and Le Mans that its derivation may not be doubted. On the jambs are tall figures of a king and queen who, as the prototypes in France show, were Solomon and Sheba.

Here at Rochester too some infusion of Lombardic style may be traced in the little beasts on which some of the small shafts of the front are based. Over the Chapter House door too was a carving (now decayed) of the Ascent of Alexander. As is well known, a master was called from Saintes in the time of King John to build London Bridge, and Henry II brought a mint master from Tours.

It is especially difficult for us to form mind-pictures of the interiors of great Romanesque churches. As we know them they are bare and stern and grey; as they once were the walls were pictured and patterned all over with bright colouring. The altars were superb works of silver or enamel, a tall seven-branched candlestick stood on the axis, and a great crucifix lifted high on the rood-beam dominated the whole space. Whoever has seen the painted apse at Nevers and large remains of decoration at Le Puy and in the churches of Poitiers, the superb nave ceiling at Hildesheim covered with the Bible story from Adam to Christ, our somewhat similar ceiling at Peterborough, and the many extensive painted surfaces which exist at Norwich, Winchester, St. Albans, Canterbury, &c., will be able to understand that these most noble churches had refinements and delicacies of their own. Even the exterior walls, and especially sculptures, received an illumination of colour.

The love of story and brightness appears in a passage of Theophilus, an artist of the Rhine or north-east France, working about 1150–1200. 'Having illuminated the vaults or the walls with divers works and colours thou hast shown forth a vision of God's Paradise bright as springtide with flowers of every hue, fresh as green grass and as mantles embroidered with spring flowers.'

Some recent writers have endeavoured to 'define' Gothic architecture by certain structural features. These criteria have doubtless been correctly observed but they are not all;

2. CHARTRES CATHEDRAL. WESTERN ENTRANCE (see p. 70)

there were geographical and historical conditions and mental states as well which have to be reckoned with. Gothic architecture was the branch of medieval art, thought, and life in Western Europe concerned with building. The vital centre of the development of medieval art was the north of France ; the time when the special qualities which make up Gothicness became obvious was the middle of the twelfth century, and in another hundred years full maturity had been attained. Gothic is the art of that region and radiating from it at that time. This art and the architecture which was a subsection had various characteristics, some of which early students observed and some which they did not notice ; we have now come to appreciate others, but many probably still remain hidden from our eyes. If anything is certain it is that these works were not seen by the builders in the way that we look at them. The Gothic manner of building answered to a stage in the historical development of European mind and society, it depended on the past up to its own point and embodied the spirit of its own time : adventurous, romantic, mystical, it was the architecture of chivalry, feudalism, the Guilds and religion. The form may be described and copied but only the spirit made it a live thing.

When the energy of life that was to form a new phase of art began to stir it drew sustenance from all available sources. The Île-de-France was the centre of the evolution but ideas were gathered from all surrounding regions. The triapsidal plan of some German Romanesque churches was adopted at Noyon and elsewhere. The ambulatory was taken from mid-France. Figure sculpture and much else was inspired by South-French advances. M. Marcel Aubert recognizes certain Norman influences ; Burgundy and Champagne made contributions. Antique art was not only carried forward by tradition but by new reference. Early

Christian and Carolingian ivories and Lombard stone carving had an influence on sculpture; Byzantine and Rhenish enamels suggested motives for stained glass and Eastern silks for wall paintings. Everything borrowed, however, was taken with a strong hand because it was needed and it was perfectly assimilated. Such absorption indeed is the converse of expansion.

A leading part in the transformation into Gothic architecture has long been assigned to Abbot Suger, who rebuilt the church at St. Denis, the choir of which was consecrated in 1144. 'We gladly admit', says Mâle in his recent study, 'that the art of the Middle Ages was collective, but it was more intensely incarnated in some men; crowds do not create but individuals. Suger was one of the great men who turned art into new ways; thanks to him, St. Denis was from 1145 the *foyer* of a rekindled art which was to shine on France and Europe.' The famous de-ambulatory with radiating chapels of a peculiar type made a school and there are imitations in a dozen places. The monumental sculpture of North France was born at St. Denis; the portals of Chartres displayed their statues and reliefs after the model set by Suger. The glass of St. Denis was imitated in England as well as in France. 'I am convinced', writes Mâle, 'that the iconography of the Middle Age owes to Suger as much as do architecture, sculpture, and glass-painting. In the domain of symbolism Suger was a creator; he proposed to artists new types and combinations which were generally adopted in the following century. He told the story of his work himself and at each page appears love of beauty and faith in the virtue of art. He wrote: 'Our poor spirit is so feeble that it is only through sensible realities that it raises itself to truth.' His new church seems to have been begun about 1133 and the west front to have been finished *c.* 1140. Here in the façade was a noble sculptured doorway—' So at St. Denis between 1133 and 1140 was found that marvel the Gothic portal.' According to Mâle, sculptors were brought from the south of France who already possessed skill in dealing with such a great subject as the Last Judgement which filled the arch above the central doorway. ' The sculptor of St. Denis was evidently a man of the Midi.' But the scheme was improved by the gifted Abbot.

The type of sculptured tympana, or arch fillings, of western portals, followed at St. Denis, Mâle traces to a great work at Moissac which he suggests rendered into stone a picture of the Majesty between the four symbols of the Evangelists as represented in a famous Commentary on the Apocalypse produced in Spain towards the end of the eighth century. I refer to this especially because our Western cycle of sculpture, from say 650 to 1050, may have made a contribution to European art not recognized by the French scholar. Already on the Ruthwell cross, *c.* 675, we find Christ the Judge sculptured as the chief subject, while above was the Lamb surrounded by the four symbols of the Evangelists. That Christ was here the Judge is shown by his treading on two beasts, emblems of death and hell. There are several other reliefs on the cross, including the Crucifixion. Another subject was the meeting of SS. Paul and Anthony ; that is, the foundation of monasticism. Sculptured Last Judgements were more fully worked out on the fronts of Irish crosses erected about 900. On the cross at Monasterboice are many sculptured subjects perfectly coordinated into a didactic series. Those of one side represent on the stem, the Fall, the Expulsion, David and Goliath ; then on the cross proper the Last Judgement with St. Michael weighing souls and their final separation ; at the top is carved the meeting of SS. Paul and Anthony. On the other side are panels of the arrest of Christ, the Journey to Emmaus, and Christ's delivery of the keys [1] to St. Peter and a book to St. Paul. The chief subject on this side is the Crucifixion: on either side are the soldiers, above are two attendant angels. Over this great subject, at the head of the cross, is a panel of Moses with his lifted arms supported by Aaron and Hur. This subject occurring prominently is a pronounced example of the use of an Old Testament type of the Crucifixion. On referring to accounts and illustrations of other Irish crosses it becomes plain that the system of associating types from the Old Law with New Law fulfil-ments was clearly understood and practised in the West in the tenth century. Mâle tells how the subject of St. Michael weighing souls appeared and spread in the south of France in the twelfth century. The sculptors, he thinks, received the motive from the East; an ancient fresco recently discovered in Cappadocia shows an angel with a balance near Christ the Judge; probably the motive came from Egypt, where, in the Book of the Dead, souls were weighed by Osiris. Now the French examples illustrated are very like the Irish type carved at Monasterboice soon after A.D. 900, and the probability seems to be that the West preserved it and handed it back to the Continent. The subject of SS. Paul and Anthony meeting is also found in South-French Romanesque sculpture.

When M. Mâle finds the correspondence between the Old and New Testaments at the base of Suger's scheme of teaching by pictures and sculpture at St. Denis he supposes it to be a reappearance after neglect for some centuries. It was known to Bede, as he points out, but then, he suggests, it passed into oblivion. 'The symbolic opposition of the Old and New Testaments reappears at St. Denis under the influence of Suger.'

Again figures of the Wise and Foolish Virgins are asso-

[1] Usually said to be a roll or rod, but I think it is a primitive key.

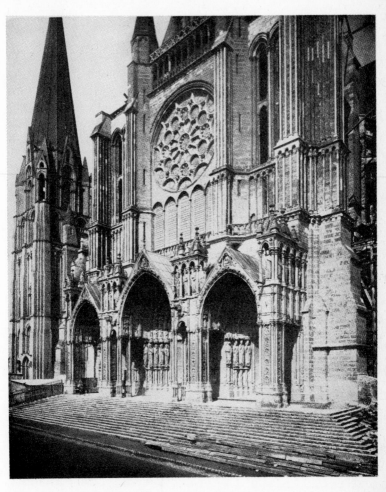

3. CHARTRES CATHEDRAL, SOUTHERN ENTRANCE (see p. 75)

ciated with the Last Judgement at St. Denis ; somewhat
earlier figures of the ten Virgins appear in South France,
but Mâle claims that again Suger made some new departure
in the treatment of the subject. 'At St. Denis it all at once
took a profound significance ; the ten Virgins became
symbols of the separated halves of humanity. It may be
that works of art now lost inspired Suger. Some verses of
Alcuin show that from the Carolingian epoch the Wise
Virgins had been associated with the Judgement, but Suger
applied the motive to monumental sculpture. However,
in the text of Alcuin only the Wise Virgins are mentioned.'
Now this association of the ten Virgins with the Judgement
had been made in the most significant way in Old Christian
Art. In a Coptic stuff (fifth century) lately shown at
South Kensington Museum the Judgement was represented
by a Throne with five Virgins carrying burning torches on
one side and five on the other having inverted torches.
That this scheme of representing the Judgement was known
to Alcuin suggests how continuity may have been maintained in other cases, and I have discussed the point because
it indicates that a far western contribution to Carolingian
culture may have been one of the formative germs of
Gothic art. Interlacing patterns of a 'Celtic' type persisted long in use for lead glazing in windows, and this too
was probably a contribution from the West through the
medium of illuminated manuscripts ; Theophilus speaks
of knot-work glazing.

Mature Gothic art was chiefly concerned in cathedral and
castle building, in town development, and Guild organization. The cathedrals of many of the cities of France were
now rebuilt on a general impulse and with energy and
power that are phenomenal. Perfecting of the Cathedral
type was carried forward by exploring all that could be done
to rear and balance the greatest structures that might be

made of the customary type required by the rites and common use. Gothic building depended not only on experimental construction but on expanding power in workmanship, and many peculiarities arose by delight in stone cutting. Undoubtedly intricacies of geometry and wonderments of craftsmanship came to be over-valued. Villars de Honnecourt, the thirteenth-century mason, tells how ' the art of geometry biddeth and teacheth ', and the fifteenth-century mason's book edited by J. O. Halliwell says, ' On this manner through good wit of geometry began first the art of masonry.' This geometry, however, included what we should now call mechanics.

Gothic building, as it was worked out by progression from antecedent data, produced high vaults, traceried windows, flying buttresses, spires and pinnacles, but essentially it was a manifestation of the life of an age. The art was vital, adventurous, energetic, organic. There was a marvellous development which can be likened to flowering, and with the release of activity came joy, wonder, rhythm. Thus it is that the more anxiously and learnedly we modern people copy or make variations of the forms wrought by exploring craftsmen in the past the less we resemble them. To be really like them we must turn about and look forward. Forms kill, but the inspiration might give life. All the once flourishing schools of art, Medieval, Greek, Oriental, worked out their own salvation, and we can only learn of them by facing the facts and finding our own way into the unknown.

From the middle of the twelfth century the movement forward into full Gothic was accomplished with great rapidity, and the result was achieved by transitions so gradual that all seems a natural process. It was a new spring-time in art. The vigorous cathedral at Noyon was begun about 1140, and its round-ended transepts were built *c.* 1170. Sens Cathedral was erected from about 1144 to 1168. Notre-Dame at Senlis was erected from *c.* 1155 to 1185. The great cathedral of Paris was begun *c.* 1162, and the altar was consecrated in 1182. Laon Cathedral was commenced about the same time. The vast cathedral at Bourges was begun *c.* 1172 and Chartres in 1194, excepting the west front, which is earlier. Reims Cathedral was commenced in 1211 ; Amiens, the crown of the group, about 1215, and Beauvais some ten years later.

In England the building of Canterbury Cathedral was undertaken in 1174 by a mason from Sens, who followed the style of the new cathedral in that city. The choir of St. Hugh at Lincoln was built before 1200. Many great abbeys were erected about the same time, and Salisbury Cathedral was begun in 1220. Notre-Dame at Paris and Amiens Cathedral were practically completed by the middle of the thirteenth century. 'About 1245 was the moment when Gothic architecture was at its apogee' (V.-le-Duc). The Sainte Chapelle at Paris was rapidly erected from 1245 to 1248. This wonderful little building at the very apex of the expanding process shows a certain self-consciousness : it appears to have been imagined as a colossal shrine for its relics. The speed with which these works were carried forward is evidence of the excitement with which they were wrought. Viollet-le-Duc more than once remarks on the rapidity of execution : 'There were interruptions, but always when they built they built quickly.' The effort was stupendous, the energy amazing, the beauty convincing and captivating. Thus the art of building climbed swiftly by exploration and adventure. In this springing Gothic is expressed health, vigour, rapture. A cathedral of the great time was a bursting out of power in construction and energy of workmanship. The joyful intimacy of men and works was well expressed by Richard Lionheart naming his fine new castle *Gaillard* and describing it as ' my beautiful one-year-old daughter '. Admiration for tenseness and poise is well brought out in a passage quoted by Dr. G. G. Coulton from an account in the Life of St. Hugh of the saint's work at Lincoln.

> ' With wondrous art he built the fabric of the Cathedral. In the structure the art equals the precious materials, for the vault may be compared to a bird stretching out its broad wings to fly ; planted on its firm columns it soars to the clouds . . . precious columns of swarthy stone close set in all its pores ; it may suspend the mind in doubt whether it be jasper or marble. Of this kind are formed those slender shafts which surround the great pillars as a bevy of maidens assembled for the dance.'

As the manner of building was pressed forward to its conclusions, piers became more slender, arches wider and more acute, and such mastery was attained over the possibilities of vaulting that stone might do no more. To provide counter-pressure to the expanding tendency of the vaults ' flying ' buttresses ramped up against the walls from lower levels, and larger churches had two tiers of these. Plain walls came near to being eliminated in the endeavour to gather up the structure into tense pier, branching vault, traceried windows, and resisting buttress. When the ' bays ' were entirely occupied by windows, which became screens between the flying buttresses, the structural end had been nearly reached. Tracery at first formed by grouping separate openings finally became a network of branching bars of stone. The mystery of mouldings is explained by the fact that their lines and shadows were a means of emphasis : rounds and fillets showing bright between deep hollows led the eye up the piers and arches in directions opposite to the accidental jointing of the separate stones.

Spires, pinnacles, tabernacles, gables, are all obviously

4. AMIENS CATHEDRAL, WEST FRONT (see p. 75)

congruous with the aspiring impulse; there is something joyous and triumphant about these high-lifted things which needs little further explanation. Tall spires were landmarks and beacons and from the belfries the bells called far.

> We travel the dusty road till the light of the day is dim
> And sunset shows us spires away on the world's rim.[1]

Doubtless too an instinctive memory was retained that the steeple was the special mark of a *Domus altaris*. It carried on the spirit of the old Saxon high crosses which in inscriptions are called ' Victory beacons '.

From one point of view the evolution of the cathedrals was a purely structural movement; all had to be organized for stability and the balancing of active ever-dangerous forces by meeting thrust with counter-thrust. The problem of sustaining these pavilions of stone high in the air was not easy and the builders solved it so as to obtain maximum results for their labour and material; no ounce of force was to be wasted. The masons elected to build dangerously; there was an inner energy forcing them on. Our way of talking about ' styles ' has obscured this mysterious element of energy in the art. The old builders themselves had wonder and wrought wonder into their structures; they had the ability which children have of being enchanted with their own doings, and hence they entrance us. In the high-poised vaults, windows of branching work holding glass bright as sunset sky, and the multitude of watching and worshipping images there was magic.

The largest churches frequently had towers at the transept ends as well as at the west front; and at times towers were placed on each side of the eastern limb. These masses were a stay against internal expanding forces. Some French cathedrals have double aisles on either side of the

---

[1] John Masefield, *The Seekers.*

central space. At Chartres these surround the east limb of the church, and chapels open still further. Notre-Dame at Paris has double aisles to the nave as well; here, too, chapels have been added all round, filling the spaces between the far-projecting buttresses, so that the interior has no less than seven divisions in its width. The triforium was some-times a wall passage, at others it extended over the aisles and was a second vaulted story with chapels corresponding to some of those on the ground floor. Many variations are found in the disposition of parts; transepts were unimpor-tant or prominent, apsidal chapels might be one or many and project little or far. Experiment was so constant that there is no sameness and every building has its own char-acter. In a group of churches in north-west France a scheme, originally Early Christian and Roman, of making the transepts round-ended was received from Germany. The noble twelfth-century cathedral of Tournay in Belgium is of this fashion, so is the cathedral of Noyon in France. A beautiful church once at Valenciennes, built about 1200, was, judging from its plan, the most perfect example of this type. The transepts had ambulatories entirely similar to the eastern termination except that it had three radiating chapels while each transept had only one projecting east-ward. These two chapels and the central one of the *chevet* rose two stories high, having altars in the triforium as well as below. The triforium sweeping round these hemi-cycles with chapels opening from it must have been extraordinarily beautiful; doubtless it was vaulted. There were two small towers in the north-east and south-east angles between the transepts and the eastern limb, but they did not rise much above the roof ridge.

Pointed arches and ribbed vaulting were used in buildings still Romanesque in character; it was the flying buttress which made the mature high Gothic possible. By springing these props from extended points of support at lower levels the high vaults were made secure. Seemingly inert walls now drew together and energetic pillars, bars, and ribs made up the construction in every part until all the members seemed active rather than static. As Professor C. H. Moore has said, ' The stiffness of a Gothic building resides in its supporting members, which owe their stability to a balance of active forces in contrast to the inert massiveness of an ancient building.' Villars de Honnecourt seems to have had this idea in mind when he wrote : ' If you would fain build altogether with columns and buttresses you must choose such as have enough projection. Take good heed how you work, and then you will do as wise and well instructed men should.'

Great windows now fully lighted the vast interiors through brilliantly coloured glass. In France the glass was deeply stained so as to temper the sunlight. It is a wonderful experience to pass from the heat and blazing sunshine of a summer day into Chartres Cathedral, where for a short time only the illuminated windows may be seen piercing through a general shadow. In England in such a church as Salisbury Cathedral, with its large windows (not yet traceried) and fair scheme of glazing, the interior became a cistern full flooded with light.

Traceried windows of the new type seem first to have been perfected at Reims Cathedral. Villars de Honnecourt says : ' I was on my way to obey a call to the land of Hungary when I drew this window because it pleased me best of all windows.' In setting two or more separate lights together in the arch-shaped space of a vaulting compartment a custom arose of piercing a circle or rose above the vertical lights ; then increasingly it seemed obvious that the whole wall-space beneath the containing arch might be perforated. So arose the idea of a composite window, which now became a mere screen of delicate work under a large and strong arch. In earlier tracery the forms still show their derivation from separate units and to the end a traceried window was conceived as being made up of vertical 'lights' under a main arch divided by stone bars in the form of sub-arches, the idea of a lattice of perforations filling a space is hardly ever formed. In a similar way Rose windows expanded until they filled great circles, and later square compartments, but the divisions almost always radiated from a centre as in early foliation. Cusping was used for single door and window openings long before it was applied to compound tracery.

'Tabernacle work' was a development of canopies over the recesses and niches in which images were set. From an early time they represented shelters and shrines. Paul the Silentiary, *c*. 560, describing the church of Santa Sofia, says that the figures of Christ and St. Peter wrought on the altar-curtains were under 'temples of gold'. A factor in the evolution of ornate later work was delight in seeing tracery set against blue sky. Dibdin, describing Strasbourg spire, noticed that 'through the interstices the bright blue sky appears with a lustre of which you have no conception in England'. This spire is still more amazing as I have seen it in dark silhouette against midnight lightning.

In rebuilding the Abbey Church of Westminster further inspiration was sought in France. The work was begun in 1245 and pressed forward feverishly by the eager King Henry III. The first portion, including the east-end, transepts, and Chapter-house, seems to have been practically completed in about ten years by the first master employed, Henry of Reyns. This part of the building shows close study of the cathedrals of Reims and Amiens. The treatment and workmanship are in the English tradition,

5. LE MANS CATHEDRAL, APSE

and what was gathered was so much subdued to our native way of craftsmanship that it is more probable that Master Henry of Reyns had his name from some such place as Raines in Essex than from Reims in France.

Most of the building work undertaken in England from the time when Canterbury Cathedral was built had been rather for monastic churches in country districts than for cathedrals, and in these country buildings modest measure and customary ways gave an exquisite charm, shy, yet graceful. Westminster Abbey, however, the great church attached to the King's Palace in a suburb of London, the special interest of the connoisseur King, was a more ambitious work designed after a study of the cathedral type in France. Here apparently for the first time in England double tiers of flying buttresses were used and bar-traceried windows. The plan was adapted from the cathedrals of Reims and Amiens, the apsidal chapels particularly from the former; the internal bay design and the transept front with its portals were imitated from Amiens. Here in the north porch the sculptures of Amiens were closely studied. In the great arch-space of the central doorway was represented the Last Judgement, a Majestic Christ in the midst with angels on either hand bearing instruments of the Passion, while others called the waking dead. On the jambs below were ranged tall single figures of Apostles. The side-doors probably had sculptures relating to the Virgin and St. Peter. All this would have been illuminated with bright colour and gilding. The octagonal Chapter-house, a traditional English form, had large four-light windows of advanced tracery worked with a knowledge of results recently attained in France. An inscription on the tiled floor which I have been able recently to read claimed that 'As the Rose is to other flowers so this House is among buildings'. The interior of the church was decorated, around and above the

High Altar, with so much gilding that there must have been a general glow of gold ; this treatment was doubtless taken from the Sainte Chapelle.

The new departure at Westminster was imitated and echoed in many later works all over the country ; developed bar-tracery became common and doubled flying-buttresses were erected at St. Albans. The Chapter-house and Cloister of Westminster were practically copied at Salisbury. The sculptured central porch and the Chapter-house windows were imitated at Lincoln Cathedral ; and the porch was again echoed at Lichfield. From the time of the consecration of Westminster Abbey Church in 1269 there was no further great transfusion of French art on the English stock ; there were influences and importations, but the arts as a whole went their own ways. It has even been thought that the late phase of English building known as ' Perpendicular ' may have influenced the French flamboyant fashion.

The English type of Gothic which followed the advances at Westminster has from the character of the tracery been called Geometrical. The circles and simple forms which composed this tracery were soon modified by more completely associating one form with another, branching the bars of stone so that the unit forms were more merged in an ' all-over ' pattern. This phase has been called Curvilinear from the flowing lines of the tracery-bars. Later again the tracery became a net-work largely made up of straight lines. The buildings in which such tracery appears have been called ' Perpendicular '. In this later work and especially in the latest medieval phase—the Tudor—the arches are extended and flattened so that in some cases they become almost horizontal in the central part of the span. One of the influences bringing about this change was the increasing estimation in later days of carpentry as the leading art in house-building. In constructing low-level stories with timbers shaped into curved forms, arch-shapes were naturally flattened and straightened ; hence the carpenters' need reacted on masons' craft, furnishing serviceable hints in house building which flowed forward as a fashion. This reaction of wooden forms on stone construction is an example not only of the obvious direct conditioning of constructive forms by material so that substance is always half the ' style ', but it shows how one material may legitimately influence the treatment of another by suggestion. The mason had to show that he could build well lighted, low-storied houses as well as the carpenter. Thus too in modern days construction in iron has followed the methods of framing and bracing used in carpentry.

As with Romanesque buildings so with Gothic, the stone-work was not completed until it had received a coating of white or ochre on which partial applications of bright colour and gilding made all fair, clear, and sharply defined. Sculpture especially was heightened by further decoration of painting, and this not only in the interiors of buildings but outside in the weather. What the great portals of French cathedrals, with their ranks of Saint figures, were when newly painted and gilt can hardly be guessed at ; such gay splendours may not now be seen on earth. In books these buildings are necessarily described as architectural corpses, 'we murder to dissect'. What they are, in the sun and moonlight as one wanders around them or sees them afar off, or again enters the still interiors under the different conditions of sunlight striking through the coloured glass, or at night when lights reveal only the lower part of piers which pass away upward into the immense volume of gloom, no pen may write. All that stained glass might be like in its glory can only be imagined in cathedrals like Chartres, Bourges, and Le Mans : we necessarily speak in terms of design, subject, and colour, but in fact, as the light filters through, ancient stained glass has fairy wonder in it.

In Gothic arts sculptured and painted figures of men and animals often seem exaggerated and quaint, but generally this came from the need for adapting the forms for special purposes ; these purposes were stained glass, wall painting, heraldry, and the like, not portraits in frames. Now figures photographically correct would not be effective in architectural sculpture or glass as seen from scores of yards away. Simple ways of arranging figures and typical modes of representing hands, feet, hair, and other details had to be found. A foot, for instance, properly foreshortened would appear at a distance as a shapeless lump, hence was maintained the convention of representing painted figures as lifted on their toes. Lions, stags and eagles represented heraldically on flags and shields had not only to be displayed in a simple summary manner, but their parts had to be so disposed that they would fill as much as possible of the available space in an even manner. 'The statue of a king placed fifty feet above the spectator's eye and involved in the intricacies of niche-work and buttress must be emphasized in its royalty ; hence those exaggerations of attitude which so admirably justify themselves in the West fronts of Exeter and Wells.' Notwithstanding these traditions there was a constant movement towards naturalism, and in the representation of vegetation by carving this had gone far in France even in the middle of the thirteenth century.

The Sainte Chapelle of Paris had the whole interior decorated after the model of goldsmiths' enamelled work. The wall-arcades had inlays of coloured glass, and mouldings were decorated with gilt gesso work in delicate patterns. There can be no doubt that it was thought of as a shrine for the precious relics it was to contain. Similar inlays of coloured glass are found on some fragments at Bourges and St. Denis.

6. REIMS CATHEDRAL, WEST FRONT (see p. 75)

The wooden altar-piece at Westminster is perhaps the most wonderful thing of this kind now existing, and in the Victoria and Albert Museum is a late thirteenth-century stone figure of the Virgin with little panels of decorated glass set in the robe. Mock Cufic inscriptions have been mentioned, they were still used in this period, and Oriental silks were eagerly collected. These are evidences for continued Oriental influence. To some extent conscious admiration of things Eastern may be discerned in Gothic works.

At times, especially in England, where dark grey Purbeck marble was a favourite material, shafts of columns and other select parts of masonry were highly polished, carvings and mouldings were gilt, and wall surfaces were whitened and covered with simple ' masonry ' patterns in red lines. The reclining figures of sculptured tombs were painted ' like to life ' with red lips, staring eyes, coloured or gilt hair and patterned garments. Pavements, in a few special cases as at Westminster, were a mosaic of precious materials, others were plain polished marble, some of large smooth white slabs having incised pictures filled with coloured mastics. There are examples of these three kinds in Canterbury Cathedral. Many pavements were of glazed tiles, either set in geometrical patterns like a fine pavement recently found at Byland Abbey, or of the sort called ' painted tiles ' in old documents. The several kinds of paving show a general desire that the surface should be polished and light-reflecting. Of course, these floors were unencumbered and streaks of light would strike along them. We must add in thought the furniture, the altars, shrines, roods, candlesticks. The frontal of the altar at Westminster was a marvellous piece of gold embroidery, set with precious stones, pearls and enamels. In other places were frontals wholly of gold and silver or enamel work. All this was but the setting for a never-ending drama broken up by entrances and exits accompanied by the music of 'the merry organ', solemn bells, and chanting men. A cathedral was the heart of its city, an embodiment of its life and thought in vital experimental craftsmanship ; it was a growth from the minds of the people which sprang up, reached high, expanded wide, then withered and died away.

Much is known of the master masons who built and 'designed', as we now should say, the cathedrals of France and England. The great Gothic was in large measure the work of the lay masters of the town guilds. One of the building masters, Villars de Honnecourt, has left a large book of drawings, recipes, and advice which is known as his 'Sketch Book'. It seems clear, however, from the method of composition and addresses to the reader that it must have been intended for 'publication'. He appears to have been of Picardy, to have built a fine church at Vaucelles, *c.* 1230, and then, about 1250, the remarkable choir of St. Quentin, destroyed in the war. It is much the same kind of book as an earlier work on Divers Arts by the monk Theophilus. Lately an artist's book, *c.* 1300, has been made known which is in the Pepys Library at Cambridge. Two or three books on the rules of Masons' Guilds exist. In these no word about 'compositions' or 'styles' is found, only much about work, geometry and structural mechanics and the brotherhood of craftsmen. Villars says that his book contains ' good advice for the great power of masonry, and engines of carpentry. You will find likewise the power of portraiture and drawing, even as the art of geometry biddeth and teacheth.'

Recent scientific observers of the ' Gothic style ' have been particularly interested in the exact course traced in the transformation from Romanesque. Every least change has been worked out so fully that all seems to have been an obvious movement in a structural and almost a mechanical advance in a sort of stone engineering. The question, how-

7. REIMS CATHEDRAL, LEFT PORTAL, WEST FRONT (see p. 75)

ever, arises, why was this development in a particular direction ? The way and the end were not foreknown, but looking back we can see that the whole was one indivisible progress, and there must have been an inner spirit informing the forms. Scholars who have laid down the curve of change would allow that religious, economic, and other causes must have profoundly affected the arts. Changes in society were always reshaping ideas and forms. Until the end of the eleventh century medieval art was mainly monastic, the fifteenth century was the age of merchant art.

All the time the craftsmen were feeling their way and possibly the medieval period was essentially the craftsman's age in history; craftsmen's culture has been little understood; the thirteenth century witnessed the culmination of a particular kind of life.

On the question, What is the essence of Gothic ? I may refer to four witnesses. Ruskin saw in it not only form but power and life ; there was a ' look of mountain brotherhood between the Cathedral and the Alp '. Morris saw ' freedom of hand and mind subordinated to the co-operative harmony', organic structure growth, commonness, ' every man who produces works of handicraft is an artist'. Dr. Salomon Reinach sees in it a Celtic element, ' the art of the Middle Ages may be characterized as *Northern*'. This thought is in perfect harmony with Ruskin's in discerning mind behind phenomena and in the ' barbaric temperament' of that mind. Again, Dr. Josef Strzygowski in *The Origins of Christian Church Art* points out how ' the northern spirit informed the art which we call Gothic . . . the creative force rose from the well springs of youth'.

There must have been some common psychological aggregate, which we call the mentality of peoples that directed the architectural process and shaped the result. For instance, as will be readily agreed, there was in the

Gothic system of building what a modern student of the Renaissance has called ' the western love of the vertical '. Sharpness, slenderness, springingness are traits ; in England some decorative arches ascend to three or four times their width.   A love of apertures is just as marked ; this was manifested not only in windows but by traceried parapets and intricate tabernacle work.   Delight is also evident in peaks and fringes of masonry seen against the sky in spires, sharp gables, ranks and bunches of pinnacles.   As the style worked itself out, it is easy to see that intricacy of every kind was an attraction to the workmen ; the tendency to multiply shafts and ribs, and to push out more and more crockets seems to have been inherent.   Cusps, foliation, much-ribbed mouldings, appear to have been of the essence of the inner idea which the masons were always, although unconsciously, trying to embody in building.

As is commonly known, carving became more naturalistic. This of course may be explained as the result of increasing skill, but there seems to have been another impulse.   The manner in which tufts of foliage jut out, as crockets and finials, from the edges of pinnacles and terminate them with a big bunch at the apex is significant of some liking.   In ornamental carving bud-like forms first appeared, then strong growths followed, and finally tangles of lax and wrinkled foliage were represented.   It has also been noticed that the capitals to columns, derived from Roman architecture, tended to disappear.   In earlier forms of medieval work the arch-section was markedly different from that of the pillar and one was divided off from the other by a bold capital ; steadily the capitals were diminished and arch mouldings approximated more closely to the form of the supporting pier.   Frequently the two parts became identical in form and the cap was contracted to a narrow band or it disappeared altogether ;   the piers were then like much furrowed tree-trunks from which arches branched without interruption. Again, it has been remarked that window tracery began as an association of separate apertures; these drew together and the masons seem thenceforth to have been more concerned with the branching bars of stone than with the openings left between them, large branches threw off smaller ones and those were again subdivided. The resulting effect of this elaborate tracery is curiously like crossing tree-branches as seen against the sky. Interlacing boughs and branches framing 'panes' of bright blue sky will explain this better than words to any one who is willing to go outside the ordinary bounds of archaeology.

It used indeed to be said that branching vaults rising from long avenues of pillars must have been directly imitated from the woods; now, however, that the development has been traced from the beginning we know that it was not so. But a hidden tendency of mind which gradually found its satisfaction still remains a true cause. In Gothic architecture we find up-springing, extension, branching, continuity, interlacing, sprouting, flowering. The forest mind seems to have been in the people and the forest romances were born of the same blood as the buildings. To overstate the point, the Gothic is Robin Hood architecture. Morris says, 'the German hero ballad-epics, the French Romances, the English forest-ballads, the Icelandic sagas represent its literature'.

Our last sight of Gothic before it disappeared is a fringe of much crocketed pinnacles like pine-trees ranged along a peaked horizon. The northern forests had nurtured a people who could do no other than build according to their ideals; not knowing but only doing. As the Greek expressed lucidity and serenity, so Northern Art had the mystery of the great forests behind it. It is even possible that the delight we experience under the vaults of a noble

cathedral is in some degree a far-off race memory of life
in forests and village 'greens'; W. H. Hudson, writing of
Salisbury Cathedral in *A Shepherd's Life*, noted ' the shock
of pleased wonder, at the sight of that immense interior,
that extending nave with pillars that stand like the tall
trunks of pines and beeches, and at the end the light screen
which allows the eye to travel on through the rich choir,
to see with fresh wonder and delight, high up and far off
that glory of coloured glass '.

The legacy of the Middle Ages is too great to be com-
puted, we are still living on the inheritance without realizing
what the world will be like when all is squandered. In regard
to any traditional art, we are now in the night following
that day, not knowing whether there will be another dawn.
The Middle Ages left us precious and vast individual buildings, the glory of stained glass, and the mighty music of
bells. Further, they gave the type and frame of our cities
as those were up to the day that living men can remember.
More than all, they left to us the thought-image of England
itself which we still hold in our hearts; towns, villages,
churches, bridges, houses, the whole organization and
economy of the country were until recently medieval in fact
or tradition. The Middle Ages bequeathed a testimony as
to the possibility of there being a progressive culture reaching
noble results ; they gave evidence that productive work
may be counted all joy, that the manual arts spring like
drama and music from the hearts of common people; they
revealed the tender beauty of that which comes fresh from
the folk mind. They proved that ' art ' is not a remote
luxury or fashionable futility, but rather it is the right
way of doing right things so that the human spirit shines
through the body of labour. Art is not free design which
may be imposed by a class remote from the craftsmen.

8. REIMS CATHEDRAL. STATUES IN THE LEFT PORTAL, WEST FRONT (see p. 75)

Scholars of design only arise when experimental art is dead. Paper flowers have not the fragrance of those growing from the soil. Gothic architecture was developed by craft-mastery fostered in the Guilds; it was found out in the nature of things by exploration; it was not a look of grandeur or correctness obtained by making a composition of borrowed ' features '.

This art teaches that the centre of the building arts must always be structure. As Professor Moore has said :

> ' The total structural system governs the character of every-thing in true Gothic building. . . . Viollet-le-Duc was the first to realize the significance of structure as the formative principle of every style. . . . Ruskin saw something of the meaning of the French master's work and once said to the writer, "Viollet-le-Duc has shown the skeleton of a Gothic building to be as wonderful as that of an animal ".'

This idea of the building art being an active organic thing carrying a renewing spirit within itself gives us a general philosophy of the art. A work of art is to be something found in materials and processes when used for worthy and significant purposes. Gothic architecture was discovered in doing, and workmanship itself was of the innermost essence of the style. Mastery of stone cutting and other wonders of craftsmanship were played with, and up to a point all art is the play spirit in labour. As saith Theophilus : ' Work therefore, good man, happy in this life before God's face and man's.'

W. R. LETHABY.

NOTE.—On the Norman Cathedral at Durham see Mr. J. Bilson's important article in the *Archaeological Journal*, vol. xxix, issued since this was in print.

ii. MEDIEVAL SCULPTURE

AMONG the manifestations of thought and art with which the Middle Ages have enriched the common inheritance of humanity sculpture would undoubtedly be placed in the first rank with medieval architecture, that marvellous architecture which has won the admiration of all subsequent ages for its boldness, its vigour, its essential *rightness*. Even in later days, when the dictums of classic art once more resumed their sway over the minds of men, luring them to the worship of Greece and Rome, every one, whether learned or ignorant, still marvelled at the splendour and the greatness of our cathedrals. On the other hand, the glorious sculpture which adorned them was universally despised. So much was this the case that Rousseau declared that their confused ornamentation only survived ' for the disgrace of those who had had the patience to fashion it '. To-day this sentiment is very far from being shared, and the plastic art of the Middle Ages is held by its richness, its variety, and its beauty to be almost on an equality with that of antiquity.

For some centuries the art of sculpture was almost wholly neglected, and such works as were produced were merely feeble copies of the antique. But at the end of the eleventh century a new and marvellous art suddenly appeared, almost simultaneously and everywhere alike. It enriched Romanesque architecture with a wealth of ornament whose originality was unquestionable and whose rudeness of workmanship slowly acquired a mastery over form and expression, a mastery which culminated, in the middle of the twelfth century, in veritable masterpieces of sculpture. After briefly tracing the rapid evolution of this new art from its earliest days, its full development in the thirteenth century, when medieval architecture reached the height of its glory, will be dealt with.

Stone was the true material for these masterpieces of sculpture; but the earlier craftsmen, of pre-Romanesque days, had already tried their hands at casting and carving in metal, ivory, and wood; their efforts, although rude, yet show either the influence of antique tradition or a new striving after originality. Romanesque and Gothic carvers made use of the same materials, endeavouring to express in them their ideals both of sculpture and Christianity.

Plastic art in the Middle Ages did, in truth, devote itself to the service of Christianity in its purest and loftiest form. Image-makers, always subservient to clerks and often re-cruited from their ranks, sought only to illustrate the teaching of the Church and to interpret in the most effective way its most essential types and dogmas. Their art, free in the details of its realization, more and more permeated with humanity, secular in execution, is before all things illustrative, didactic, and religious. The beauty which they strove to represent was almost always subservient to the highest and deepest thought. The Christian sentiment, the mystic meaning, the traditional grandeur of the figures and scenes of the Old and New Testaments inspired them; and if profane elements did intermingle, as in the representations of the glories of this world on tombs, it was still the Christian view of death which dominated them. Hence a moral value, a unity in the fundamental idea, a touching sincerity which magnify this art wherein are no weak pretences, no uncertainties, no emptiness of thought, such as are so often manifest in styles where skill and technical knowledge fail from lack of faith to compensate for the absence of moral support and power of expression.

This profound quality, this species of essential framework, which is apparent in all this plastic art, is almost invariably

rendered doubly strong by the sustaining power of architecture, with which it is always so intimately connected.
There are no works without moral significance and, for a long
period, none that are detached from architecture or without
their destined niche in a building. Art for art's sake did not
exist. What a lesson and what a contrast, if not to art in
the great days of antiquity yet, at least, to the Alexandrine
and Roman epochs as much as to our own ! We cling with
veneration, even with passion, to all that past indifference
and past destructiveness, whether purely wanton or due to
changes in religious or political faiths, have left us of the
plastic art of the Middle Ages. Too many complete works
have, alas ! been mutilated ; irreparable losses limit our
knowledge. But, on the one hand, profound and illuminating researches, such as Mâle's for instance, have enabled us
to pierce the hidden meaning of these ' poems in stone '.
On the other hand, our architects and archaeologists had
long begun to study them for their plastic, historical, and
monumental value, and to disentangle them from the ill-
considered restorations which disfigure them. Casts of all
the most notable examples of medieval sculpture have been
placed to-day in *musées documentaires*, created for the use of
students or for the preservation of the originals. Finally,
Art Museums have collected fragments, formerly scattered
and neglected, and placed them side by side with the most
celebrated examples of the art of all nations.

I. *Romanesque Art*

The later centuries of ancient Rome are marked by
a complete decadence in the art of sculpture. Roman art,
heir to the plastic art of Greece, had degenerated even before
the fall of the Western Empire, and it declined still more
rapidly after the Latin world fell a prey to the barbarians.
It did not, however, entirely disappear. In Italy and in

certain provinces of France, Provence, Auvergne, and along the Rhine for instance, traditions of ancient art found a refuge in workshops devoted to the fabrication of sarcophagi. These sarcophagi, which were pagan at first, were later on used for Christian burials and were decorated with Christian symbols. Such workshops were numerous all over the Empire, particularly in the lower Rhone valley, and their art gradually grew to be employed in the service of a triumphant Christianity.

During a prolonged period, both in Italy and Gaul, Christianity evinced a characteristic dislike to the use of images as being too closely linked with paganism ; it preferred to employ designs common to mosaic and decorative painting to beautify its temples and to illustrate its teaching. In the East the Christian metropolis of Byzantium remained in close contact with the culture and the art of Greece ; on the other hand, she also assimilated large Asiatic elements, and in spite of many disputes and many heated conflicts, men persisted in expressing their ideas in sculptural form and in retaining the use of images. And thus a rich and abundant art was established in highly favourable circumstances and developed, right up to the fifteenth century, in accordance with its own laws ; it was the earliest great Christian art which set itself to interpret the dogmas of faith and to construct a complete iconography. These laws as well as the style of the East reacted on the entire art of the West.

Naturally sculpture, and above all statues, played but a small part in Byzantine art. Nevertheless sarcophagi were made, very different from Latin ones, it is true, but yet decorated with figures in relief. An important number of these have been found in Ravenna and Venice, above all small ivory monuments which were widely distributed ; these ivories, in conjunction with paintings and fabrics woven in designs, furnished the barbarian image-makers, in search of ideas and new types, with delicate models wherein something of the spirit of Greece mingled with the strange fancies and sumptuous richness of the East. Workshops founded on Byzantine principles of art were widespread. One in the south-west of France, for instance, produced a certain type of sarcophagus in direct relation both with sculpture in low relief and with the ornamental and somewhat over-elaborated richness of Byzantine art.

The Merovingian period was wholly barbarous and only produced a few capitals, rough imitations of antique models like those in the crypt of St. Lawrence at Grenoble, a few lintels and a few friezes carved with geometrical or inter-laced designs, such as those of Jouarre in France and of Bradford-on-Avon in England. The Carolingian renaissance is essentially a Byzantine renaissance. Byzantium alone, in fact, was capable of giving Christendom examples of a living art and also of teaching it the wisdom of ancient tradition. The Palatine Chapel at Aix, the church of Germigny les Près are Byzantine buildings so far as structure and decora-tion is concerned (ninth century). Statuary, strictly speaking, plays no part in a Carolingian church. It is only at the end of the tenth and beginning of the eleventh centuries that the earliest attempts occur of the use of figures in decoration. We have a few images in high relief of this epoch still preserved, such as the statue in gold of Sainte Foy de Conques which is one of the oldest specimens of medieval statuary, heavy and rude enough, in spite of the traces of Byzantine art which it reveals. The development of plastic art in metal certainly seems in some parts of the Christianized world to have preceded that of stone images. It is this which enables us to assign to the beginning of the eleventh century the remarkable works in bronze, such as doors and columns in imitation of the column of Trajan, which the sainted Bishop Bernwardt set up at Hildesheim ; these works, undoubtedly of local craftsmanship but as undoubtedly inspired by the antique, were imitated in the doors of St. Zeno at Verona, although a number of bronze doors in Italy, as at Amalfi and Benevento, were executed by Byzantine workmen.

Decorative sculpture in the eleventh century still shows us nothing but rude and awkward attempts, where the early Romanesque carvers strive to reproduce in a relief, still very low, motives borrowed from Greco-Roman or Byzantine art. These may be acanthus leaves and scroll work more or less altered and adapted, or geometrical ornamentations, eastern in origin and probably barbarian ; or again certain compositions taken from illuminated manuscripts, like the figure of Christ seated ' in majesty ' surrounded by winged angels which was placed over the door of St. Genis des Fontaines in Rousillon about the year 1020. But little by little, at the end of the eleventh and beginning of the twelfth century, an art, far more skilful and far richer, arose with marvellous rapidity and so simultaneously that it is difficult to assert that any one place was influenced by any other ; this art strove, with greater seeking after expression if with less skill than that of the old sarcophagus-makers, to mould the human figure. On capitals and the tympana of doorways, in cloisters and churches, stories were portrayed which sought to interpret scenes from the Bible or allegories taken from the Fathers and preachers. These alternated with vaguer motives where the symbolic character of the representatiōns was often interwoven with the decorative fancies of the craftsman who interpreted, freely and without any very precise meaning, some fantastic idea suggested by an Oriental fabric or Byzantine ivory : a lion, a chimera, a bird, real or monstrous, conventional foliage or human figures more or less well proportioned and well balanced.

If we consider the various centres in France, so active at this epoch, Languedoc, Auvergne, Burgundy, Poitou, and Saintonge, or those in the region of the Rhine and Saxony, or in England, or again in Spain, the same effort is everywhere visible, in spite of slight differences; here in one place a leaning to the East, there in another to classical antiquity; here a prodigality of figures and there a restriction to linear decoration ; here an entire façade covered with an Oriental profusion of ornament, as in the schools of western France; there a certain vigorous sobriety as in those of Normandy and their English derivatives, where moreover Saxon and Irish influences accentuated the taste for combinations of curved lines and the barbaric interlacings which flourished in Scandinavia.

Some great scenes of monumental sculpture date from the first third of the twelfth century. The clumsy seated figure of Christ, in St. Sernin at Toulouse, surrounded by cherubim and in the act of blessing, probably belongs to the last years of the eleventh century. The Christ at St. Emeran at Ratisbon is of the same period. But at this date there also appeared in the tympana at Moissac, Souillac, and Beaulieu, and later at Autun and Vezelay, vast and tumultuous scenes from the Vision of the Apocalypse, the Last Judgement or Pentecost, dominated by grandiose figures of Christ giving his benediction or coming to judge the quick and the dead. Elsewhere, in the rough-hewn reliefs, like those at Extern in Westphalia, in the low reliefs, as those of Chichester Cathedral in England and in the cloisters of San Domingo de Silos in Spain, various scenes from the New Testament were depicted : the Descent from the Cross, the raising of Lazarus, the Crucifixion, or the holy women at the tomb of Christ. Imagination and a desire to animate the figures, to crowd the composition with innumerable accessories and with complicated episodes, all testify to a singularly vigorous intelligence. Human art seemed to have rediscovered a meaning and a secret which it had lost, and these image-carvers devoted themselves with enthusiasm to plastic representations which were veritable creations.

It was a new plastic art, varied, alive, youthful, and full of growth which came into being. Depending on Byzantine iconography for its compositions, it also made use of secular models and traditions, while at the same time endowing them with life. It was an art at once very young and very old, rich in fresh inspiration and in ancient tradition, and the rapidity of its growth, more startling than in any other archaic art whatsoever, can perhaps be rightly explained by this fact. It found in itself, however, its sources of expression and movement, enlarging to monumental size tiny models in ivory or translating into relief flat illuminations ; forcing itself to rediscover, without being conscious of it, the meaning of sculpture, of an image living and true, by studying in nature, as yet instinctively and haltingly and in defiance of conventions and formulas, the right treatment of faces, bodies, and drapery.

The truth that mere imitation was not enough to vivify these early efforts lies in the fact that Italy was far from being, at this moment, at the head of the creative movement. The Lombard art which flourished at Milan, Verona, Parma, and Modena, and the art of Bonnano and Gruamonte of Pisa is heavy and lifeless. We have to wait for the coming of Benedetto Antelami to the cathedral and baptistry of Parma to find any effort at original composition and living sculpture. If this Lombard art has any connexion with a French school, if it contributed in any way to its formation, it can only be with the school of Provence. It is certain that this latter school, as shown by the portals of St. Gilles du Gard and St. Trophime at Arles, is late in

9. TYMPANUM IN WESTERN DOORWAY

Chartres. XIIth century

development and lacking in originality and initiative. Other schools, particularly those in Languedoc, spread abroad their influence and their new discoveries, especially in the direction of Spain. If this influence is disputed, at least it must be admitted that from the twelfth century onwards workshops flourished on both slopes of the Pyrenees and on either side of the Rhine.

II. *Gothic Art*

One thing is at any rate incontrovertible. Just as in the twelfth century a new style of architecture, which we call ' Gothic ' and medieval authors more properly ' opus Francigenum ', arose in France, most probably northern France, so in the same way works in plastic art had made by the middle of the century such marked progress that we are entitled to consider them as the most perfect expression of Romanesque art. Yet they still retained the same *naïveté* and amplitude, the same aspect, at once decorative and monumental; but, undoubtedly, they constituted the starting-point of that subtler and more human art which blossomed forth in the thirteenth century.

The Royal portal at Chartres, which dates somewhere about 1145, is the perfect expression of the art of the epoch ; for the somewhat earlier portal of St. Denis is too mutilated and disfigured to be taken as an example. If we compare the grand figures of the tympana at Chartres with the scarcely older ones of Moissac and Vézelay, we find that the Christ of the Apocalyptic vision and the Virgin Mother seated in majesty show a restrained nobility, a perfection in the rendering of faces and gestures, a certainty of touch in the treatment of the drapery hitherto entirely unknown. Round these large figures a series of scenes and smaller figures are placed on the lintels of the tympana, on the archivolts, and on the capitals of the shafts which enrich the jambs of the doorways. These show a justness of proportion, a restraint and fitness of gesture which mark a similar remarkable progress. But it is the life-size figures standing on the supporting shafts which show the most incontestable and delightful freshness. Still lank and stiff, still an integral part of the building which they complete and vivify, they exhibit in all the details of position, dress, headgear, and type of face a search after exact truth and a quality in the workmanship which is truly amazing, when we remember that a bare half-century had elapsed since the newly revived plastic art could only express itself in the most archaic manner. The style and the way of placing these statues at Chartres won popularity not only in France, where similar portals were set up in the second half of the century, at Bourges, Angers, Le Mans, Corbeil, St. Loup de Naud, and elsewhere, but also in England in the cathedral of Rochester, in Saxony in the Golden Door at Freiberg, in Spain in the door of the ' Gloria ' at St. James of Compostella. In the case of this last example the style is in marked contrast to the earlier ' Toulousain ' style of the rest of the celebrated pilgrimage church. Between the west door at Chartres, which belongs to the cathedral which was burnt down in 1194, and the transepts, which were not built till about the beginning of the thirteenth century and which belong unquestionably to Gothic art, an intermediary series can be noted. In these the rules and conventionalities of Romanesque art disappear one by one ; the style is clearly simpler and less encumbered with those trammels of tradition which had served to sustain it in its early stages. In the style of decoration this simplification, this tendency towards naturalism, this transition to pure Gothic is easy to see ; but we can also clearly mark these changes in the carvings of the St. Anne door in Notre-Dame at Paris, in the statue of St. Étienne at Sens, and in the portal of Notre-Dame at

10. ST. FIRMIN BLESSING

Amiens. XIIIth century

Senlis. The change was hardly complete when the side-portals at Chartres were built and this is specially noticeable in the south door, where the upright Christ on the trumeau and the Apostles ranged along the shafts at the sides of the doorway are seen under an austere Last Judgement. A somewhat harsh regularity is still characteristic of this particular workshop, a certain constraint in gesture, a certain conventionality in the drapery. Perfect balance was not attained till between the years 1220 and 1230 when the Confessor's door, with its admirable figures of St. George and St. Theodore, was built at Chartres. To the same years belong the door with the Coronation of the Virgin at Notre-Dame in Paris and the entire portal at Amiens with its three incomparable statues on the trumeaux; these are the Christ as Teacher, known as the ' Beau Dieu ' of Amiens, the Virgin standing with the Child in her arms, and the bishop, St. Firmin, in the act of blessing. All the intricacies, all the awkwardnesses of the earlier art have gone; only a monumental grandeur remains, with the perfect adaptation of the figures to the architecture they adorn and from which they are scarcely emancipated. A certain austerity of style also remains tempered with a humanity, a truth, both psychological and plastic. The craftsman seems to be less interested in the imitation of mere details and the faces are possibly less individual, but the idealistic nobility of the type does not exclude a real contact with nature. The gestures are true without being over-accentuated, the draperies natural without being excessively complicated in their folds. It is the same with subjects less sublime than the large statues and supernatural scenes, such as the Coronation of the Virgin and the Last Judgement; in scenes depicting the lives of the saints, in representations of the cardinal virtues and vices or the monthly round of work, a homeliness and a justness of inspiration is combined with an austerity, terse and synthetic, which exclude all anecdote and mere picturesqueness.

This was undoubtedly the golden age of medieval sculpture, its classic period, because its development is serene and its mastery of its materials complete, while it seems to shun all movement and over-expression. As was natural, it was a brief moment in its never-ceasing evolution. This evolution, pursued in the decoration of the side-portals of Chartres Cathedral, especially the exterior porches built after 1235, was continued in the transept doors of Notre-Dame at Paris after 1250. It can also be seen in the varied and truly admirable carving in Notre-Dame at Reims which was in active course of construction from 1210 onwards. At Reims the statues were begun in the earliest style of Chartres, were continued in the severe style of Amiens, as may be seen in the Annunciation or the Presentation in the Temple, and towards the middle of the thirteenth century culminated in the marvellous masterpieces which typify the true art of Reims, an art full of vigour and life, of supple and delicate grace. This art is illustrated in the supernumerary figures of the Presentation, the attendant of Mary and the St. Joseph, in the St. Nicaise and his acolyte, the delicious smiling angel, so justly celebrated, to mention only the most typical of the larger figures in the west portal; also in the scenes from the life of St. Nicaise and the Last Judgement on the tympana of the north door; the Passion and the Apocalypse on the west archivolts; the Church and the Synagogue and Adam and Eve in the transept, and so on.

The statues stand almost completely detached from the column or from the background of the tympanum; they pulsate with their own individual life; they carry on veritable dialogues between themselves, quietly, without gesticulation or noise. Proud of his skill, the master-carver

11. THE SMILING ANGEL

Reims. XIIIth century

strives to make their faces, whether serious or smiling, really alive, to endow them with spiritual grace ; he aims at giving movement to the sculptural scenes, a sense of the confused animation of a crowd, or of the dramatic aspect of the Passion ; while in the little figures of the calendar, or in those which he carved on the pedestals of the big images he inclines to an anecdotal familiarity, after the manner of a genre picture. Elsewhere the decorative masks express by the play of their features the whole gamut of human feeling from perfect serenity to subtle irony or jovial conviviality. In these workshops there is shown an infinite amount of research and an extraordinary precocity. All the art of the following centuries, realistic, imaginative, emotional, can be here found in the germ. Nothing is lacking even to the intelligent and conscious imitation of antique beauty. In the famous group of the Visitation, and in other figures, whose inspiration is a mystery, the breadth, the suppleness, the thin and clinging draperies recall the Greek masterpieces of the fifth century B.C. and suggest those of a Renaissance where Christianity had survived in all its intensity.

Finally, in the second half of the thirteenth century such works as the Virgin of the Golden Door at Amiens, where the new ideal of the Virgin, tender and smiling Mother, graceful and exquisite Queen, or the Last Judgement at Bourges, crowded, fanciful, and full of amusing details, show the ever-increasing intricacies of this art ; the bas-reliefs of Rouen and Auxerre, where scenes from Genesis, lives of saints, figures of fantastical Bestiaries are represented, also indicate a less monumental tendency as well as a love of daintiness and variety. It was similar to the change at the end of the thirteenth century, when we enter into the purely ornamental type of sculpture with the mighty capitals ' à crochets ' of Notre-Dame, whose floral designs, mingled with or substituted for Romanesque motives, still show a magnificent simplicity and rhythm, and pass on to 'corbeilles' of unparalleled virtuosity, to flowers and leaves carved in undercut work, to friezes sculptured in high relief and almost too naturalistic in treatment.

These great works of the thirteenth century are almost all concentrated in the cathedrals of northern France, those sublime examples of Gothic art at its culminating point: Chartres, Laon, Paris, Amiens, Reims, Bourges. Each church has its own iconographic cycle, more or less complete and dominated at first by Christ the Teacher and the Last Judgement, and later by the Virgin Mother and her glorious apotheosis. In place of the styles of the provincial schools of Romanesque architecture, so varied in their originality, an almost uniform style was substituted derived from the builders of the Île-de-France; only slight differences in details mark the different centres. In the same way plastic art spread its influence on every side. Certain localities, Languedoc for instance, which was so active in the twelfth century, ceased to produce owing to the political conditions of the times; others followed the lead of the royal domain, as was the case in Burgundy, where in Notre-Dame at Dijon, at Semur and at St. Thibault, some important examples of decorative carving and figures were produced which were scarcely influenced by local feeling. In the cathedrals of Poitiers, Bordeaux, and Bayonne some fine pieces were also directly inspired by the northern statues and high reliefs but without attaining their perfection. At Lyons the portal of the cathedral is covered with a decoration of small bas-reliefs in quatrefoils, so like those of Rouen that we can scarcely distinguish one from the other.

It is well known how the glory of French Gothic art spread over the whole of Christendom in the days of St.

Louis. In many places outside France Romanesque lasted into the thirteenth century, here heavy and debased, there more alive and bearing an obvious local impress. But nowhere except in the north of France can we watch the slow evolution of Gothic art from the archaism of Chartres to the classicism of Paris. Characteristic imitations of French Gothic, as at Bamberg, or strong and individual works like those of Niccolo Pisano in Italy, which in a certain measure drew their inspiration from the same source, appeared quite suddenly in the second half of the thirteenth century. A little group of examples, which show a curious revival of antique art, had preceded these in Apulia and Campania, under Frederic II.

In Germany the survival of Romanesque is specially characteristic. It attained a perfection of style, easy, and elegant, which gives an impression of a rejuvenated Byzantine art. The most perfect examples of this can be seen in the bas-reliefs at Halberstadt and in St. Michael at Hildesheim. On the other hand, in the bas-reliefs in the choir of St. George at Bamberg there is an obvious striving after violent expression and extravagance of characterization. These are the same traits that we shall find a little later on in Germany; they first of all crept insidiously into the imitations of French Gothic in the portals of Bamberg, especially in the grinning faces in the Last Judgement and also in the celebrated statues of the Virgin and St. Elizabeth in the choir, which were undoubtedly suggested by the Visitation at Reims. At Magdeburg the wise and foolish Virgins, a subject repeated at Strasbourg, Nuremberg, and Erfurt, laugh, cry, and gesticulate with an exaggeration of sentiment which is slightly vulgar. At Naumburg the statues of the Saxon princes of past ages show an attempt at individuality and a power of expression rare at the date to which we must assign them (1260–75). Such were the characteristics which were to be met with at Strasbourg and Bâle and other places along the Rhine, half-way between Reims and Bamberg, characteristics which grew more pronounced farther east.

The French influence in Spain is still more typical. In the age of Gothic it was French architects who built the cathedrals of Burgos and Léon, and mainly French sculptors who decorated them. The Last Judgement in the cathedral of Léon bears a close relationship to that of Bourges and the dramatic or spiritual elements are here yet more complicated. If at Burgos the Sarmental door presents a somewhat dry and awkward version of the Apocalyptic Vision, the decoration of the doorway into the cloister is unequalled in its richness and breadth ; it seems almost in advance of the thirteenth century. The same can be said of the portrait statues of the kings of Castille which adorn the cloister.

English cathedrals of the thirteenth century also show an intimate relation with the movement in France, although the connexion between the one country and the other cannot always be traced. In England it is a question of small work, bas-reliefs, medallions, and spandrils rather than of large decorated surfaces, like the façade of Wells Cathedral. By the end of the twelfth century at Durham and by the middle of the thirteenth at Lincoln and Westminster Abbey, little scenes from the Bible or half figures of angels of great beauty are to be met with. But it is in the effigies on tombs carved in stone, wood, and Purbeck marble, or sometimes cast or beaten in metal, that the most original work was done. The oldest of these in England, a twelfth-century tomb, would seem to have been copied from the tombs at Tournay ; others at the beginning of the thirteenth century still have the finely folded drapery and other characteristics of purely Romanesque art. The fine bronze effigies, executed in 1291 by the London goldsmith William Torel for the

12. ADORATION OF THE MAGI

Bas-relief by Niccolo Pisano, from pulpit of Baptistery, Pisa. XIIIth century

tombs of Henry III and his daughter-in-law Eleanor of Castille, resemble in the severe dignity of their style the figures at St. Denis, carved in stone about 1250 to represent the long series of the ancestors of St. Louis. But we must not forget that the two undertakings were separated by forty years, and that by 1290 French art had already begun to abandon strict idealism in favour of real and strongly marked portraiture in effigies on tombs.

In Italy, although Gothic was not adopted in all its developments, yet buildings were erected in the French style at the end of the twelfth and in the thirteenth centuries. These buildings, monastic for the most part, had little carving of any sort and scarcely any of a purely ornamental nature. Émile Bertaux has, however, brought to light all that the first great exponent of Italian sculpture at the end of the thirteenth century, Niccolo Pisano, owes to France, possibly through his Apulian origin and his early contact with Norman workshops in Southern Italy. The decoration of the choir at Pisa by Niccolo dated from 1260. The composition of certain of Niccolo's bas-reliefs, the quite novel animation which he gives to the heavy and crowded carvings in high relief, which were in use before his time but whose Greco-Roman characteristics he exaggerated, are possibly partly due to Northern influence and to already existing examples of the style, partly to the artistic individualism, always common in Italy, of an original and master mind. Immediately following him, his son Giovanni repudiated all inspiration from the antique. In his share of the pulpit at Siena (1266), as in those of St. Andrew at Pistoja and the cathedral at Pisa, he shows himself as a realist given to an extreme of characterization, surpassing all the marked excesses of the Northern Gothic of his day, a precursor, in short, of Donatello and Mantegna. Certain Virgins with the Child, however, from the workshops of the two Pisani and their successors, show a striking resemblance to the French style, for example to the Golden Virgin of Amiens, which was copied far and wide throughout the fourteenth century. The art of Fra Guglielmo was simpler and quieter, and the same can be said of Tino da Camaino of Siena. It is to them that the canopied type of tomb placed against the wall is due. Examples of their work can be seen at Florence, Orvieto, and Naples. The style lasted in Italy for two hundred years. This particular style of sculpture was generally executed in marble or bronze and is rarely to be met with in any large architectural masses. When Andrea Pisano, and later on Ghiberti, made use again of small quatrefoils filled with biblical scenes in bas-relief with two or three figures in each analogous to the Gothic work at Rouen and Lyons, they only used them for folding doors in bronze. One of the few important pieces of decorative work in which sculpture plays an important part is the façade of Orvieto Cathedral, whose initial conception, due to Lorenzo Maïtani of Siena, recalls its French origin in some small measure. It shows, however, a difference of idea in the division of the bas-reliefs into friezes, representing the Tree of Jesse, the Last Judgement, and the Creation, an idea which is far from having the same value as that which appeared in the French tradition of the twelfth and thirteenth centuries.

III. *Sculpture in the Fourteenth and Fifteenth Centuries*

After the death of St. Louis and the building of the last of the great cathedrals, a marked change took place in the general type of French sculpture. A new ideal appeared, more graceful, finer, more sharply cut ; the skill of the carver increased, but his interest in style, in dignity, in adaptation of his work to buildings diminished. The age

13. MASSACRE OF THE INNOCENTS

Bas-relief by Giovanni Pisano, Museo Civico, Pisa. XIVth century

of vast monumental work was past. A single statue, or statuette, an altar reredos, took the place of the great works of yore, just as painted panels replaced huge decorative frescoes. Little by little the very virtuosity of the craftsmen created formulas ; a sort of preciosity appeared or an excessive striving after individuality and expression. A love of familiar scenes increased, joined with a striving after violent feeling, passion, suffering. Instead of Christ, lofty and serene, the Man of Sorrows is represented ; cheeks were hollowed, eyes laughed or were distorted with feeling, attitudes were contorted and subjects overloaded with picturesque details. It was the complex reality of life that they strove to seize ; it was the beginning of ' naturalism '. But the most typical change of all was the introduction of ' portraiture ', an art hitherto unknown. The recumbent figures on tombs at the end of the twelfth and throughout the thirteenth centuries were conventional idealized figures. There appeared, however, in the royal burial-place at St. Denis the first real portrait of a king that has been preserved, that of St. Louis's son, Philip III le Hardi, whose tomb was the joint production of Pierre de Chelles and Jean d'Arras. It is true that the figure of another of St. Louis's sons, buried at Royaumont before 1275, shows certain indications of an individual realism, while later on in the first half of the fourteenth century effigies are still to be found of fair ladies and brave knights carved in the old idealistic style. The change was neither sudden nor complete.

But it is in the figure of the Virgin Mother that the change was most speedily shown. The Golden Virgin of Amiens, which dates from 1288, has already been mentioned. In stone, marble, wood, and ivory, standing or sitting, multitudes of statues followed which all bear witness to the fervour of the worship of the Virgin, whose role of

Protectress became more and more a part of a religion less lofty but more tender than of old. They also bear witness to the imaginative ingenuity of the craftsmen who composed these groups of the Virgin and Child, often charming, often a little stereotyped, sometimes slipping into the insipid elegance of merely pious imagery. Taste deteriorated and the noble lady of the thirteenth century became a simple housewife in everyday clothes by the end of the fourteenth, or a peasant woman dandling or suckling her quite ordinary babe. Still of serious mien, sometimes scarcely smiling at the Child that she holds on her left arm, the Virgin, lightly veiled in many fine and supple folds, the outline of the hip strongly marked, is directly inspired by direct observation. At the same time the prophets and apostles bearded, smiling, or frowning, draped in many folded cloaks make a contrast to these gracious statues of the Virgin, of angels and youthful saints, from the figures of the Sainte Chapelle at Paris to those of the Chapelle de Rieux at Toulouse. By the end of the fourteenth century the saints lose their simple attributes and begin to be surrounded with a multitude of picturesque accessories borrowed either from everyday life or from the mystery plays. Again, the origin of many of the carvings on rood and choir screens, as well as on the reredoses of the family, mortuary, or guild chapels which clustered round the churches, can be traced to the love of these mystery plays. A sense of the picturesque developed, accompanied by a dramatic sense in depicting the scenes of the Passion. Especially this is noticeable in the representations of the Entombment, which was a more popular subject than any other throughout the fifteenth century. There was an effort to express every variety and intensity of human feeling on the faces of the actors combined with a very noble and impressive composition

The problem arises in relation to this striking transformation in Gothic art : What is the origin of this new feeling for realism which became so apparent in French, and indeed in European, art at this moment? It has often been explained by calling it *Franco-Flemish*, and though it is true that artists came from the north to France, especially to the court of the Valois kings, yet these were by no means always natives of Flanders. Quite as often they came from the Meuse country, or were Walloons, as were Pepin de Huy, André Beauneveu of Valenciennes, and Jean of Liége, who were all among the best-known masters of the period. But they did not bring with them ready made formulas. The Low Countries, both northern and southern, had been influenced either by the Rhine countries or by France during the twelfth and thirteenth centuries, and it cannot be safely asserted that they had founded a school of their own. The font at St. Bartholomew at Liége, the work of Renier de Huy, which is so astounding when its date (1112) is taken into account, undoubtedly ought to be associated with the early German work of the Romanesque period; while, on the other hand, carvings on buildings, such as those on the portal of the Hospital of St. John at Bruges, the statues in the porch of Tournay and even the St. Catherine of Courtray, fourteenth-century work attributed to Beauneveu, are in the purest French style.

The political development and economic activity of the Flemish towns, particularly from the fourteenth century onward, gave a special importance to the provinces along the Meuse and the Scheldt. They certainly supplied artists and craftsmen of a singularly vigorous temperament, but it is not so certain that they brought any difference of tradition with them to the court of France and later to that of Burgundy. The great workshops of the thirteenth century were undoubtedly the sources of their tradition ;

as for the new tendencies, which changed and debased the pure Gothic art of those workshops, these have already been dealt with.

It was during the first part of the fifteenth century that an art peculiar to the Low Countries arose in all its originality and power of expression. Examples of its products spread over the whole of Europe in the form of wood carvings of an exuberant virtuosity, enhanced by paint and gilding and accompanied by panels painted in oils. These were produced in great quantities by the artists of Ghent, Brussels, Bruges, and Antwerp. France also absorbed a large number of reredoses and retables of this sort which were sometimes copied by French workmen. This style of work penetrated into North Germany, Sweden, and Norway as well as into Spain. But whereas Spain scarcely used anything except imported works, Germany only employed Flemish models as a starting-point for work of her own. It is possible that masters from the Low Countries settled in Germany; at any rate it is certain that workshops flourished there and large quantities of carvings in wood were produced. The German tendency to movement and gesture, already noticed, exaggerated the Flemish taste for the picturesque, the dramatic, and the homely, as can be seen very clearly at Nuremberg, Würzburg, and Ulm. In German tombs, where the sculpture had always leaned towards over-accentuated feeling, portrait effigies of princes and bishops grew rapidly in number and were often too forcibly speaking likenesses.

But to return to France in the fourteenth century, it is clear that the inspiration of the new art was frequently counterbalanced by the strength of the Gothic tradition of the thirteenth century. This is seen most clearly when French productions are compared with those of other countries. The Virgins of the Île-de-France show an

14. CHARLES V OF FRANCE

from Church of the Celestins (Louvre). XIVth century

unconstrained dignity and a delicate grace truly remarkable.
In the matter of portraiture the works of the age are noticeable for their nobility and their wonderful poise, as can be
seen in the royal effigies in St. Denis, in the statues of
Charles V and his wife Jeanne de Bourbon from the
portal of the Celestins in Paris, now in the Louvre, in the
figures carved on the chimney-piece at Poitiers, and lastly
in those of the buttresses of Amiens Cathedral added in
the fourteenth century. Finally in exceptional examples,
such as the Coronation of the Virgin at La Ferté Milon,
there is a breadth of composition and a majesty of treatment to which no other European art attained in the
fourteenth century.

No doubt it was this living tradition united to the
individual work of men of genius which about 1400 created
a new art in Burgundy, fostered by favourable political
and economic conditions and by the wealth of Philip le
Hardi and Jean sans peur, but it is vain to seek the secret
of its origin in the nationality of its earliest craftsmen.
It is assuredly true, however, that the best examples of
Burgundian work, at the end of the fourteenth and the
beginning of the fifteenth centuries, were begun by an
artist who came from the Meuse country, Jean de Marville,
and were finished by two Dutchmen, Claus Sluter and
Claus van Werve : namely, the portal of the Charterhouse
of Champnol, the Well of Moses, and the Ducal tombs at
Dijon. But before the advent of these artists nothing in
their own country could account for the vigour and amplitude of these figures, whether great or small, whether
Virgins, saints, prophets, donors, effigies, or ' weepers ' ;
all alike with strongly marked features as alive and expressive
as nature herself, all clothed in gorgeous drapery falling in
majestically ample folds, and all obviously taken from actual
models. The court of Charles V at Paris and later the works

undertaken at Angers, Bourges, and Méhun sur Yèvre could very effectively furnish Claus Sluter with models by which he was well fitted to profit.

The style set by Sluter lasted for nearly a century and was practised both in Burgundy and in many parts of France. At Moulins, Avignon, Albi, and Toulouse a considerable quantity of carving inspired by it can be seen, tombs, Virgins, Holy Sepulchres, all of which exaggerate both his good qualities and his faults. Clumsiness, a certain grossness, and sometimes a vulgarity mingled with a spicy good humour are combined with an easy strength of execution and a happiness in composition, as for example in the tomb of Philippe Pot, where the antique theme of ' weepers ' is developed to a high degree of merit and reaches monumental size.

By Franche Comté, Switzerland and Alsace this Burgundian art invaded Germany and certainly made its influence felt. It is even open to question whether, up to a point, it did not also influence Italian masters of the fifteenth century : Ghiberti, Donatello, and Jacopo della Quercia. At this epoch northern art had certainly penetrated into Italy, a penetration to be repaid later on in ample measure. Written evidence survives to prove this in regard to Ghiberti, who praises a certain Maestro Tedesco who had known and influenced him in his youth. Some of Donatello's prophets forcibly recall those in the Chartreuse at Champnol, and there is a certain St. Louis of Toulouse by him which has the heaviness and the robust amplitude of a Burgundian statue. Trade and travel brought countries into relation with each other. In northern Italy at the end of the fourteenth and beginning of the fifteenth centuries, especially at Venice, Verona, and Milan, the works of the two brothers Massegna, the capitals of the Ducal Palace, the tombs of the Scaligers, and even the bas-reliefs of

15. VIRGIN, BY JEAN DE MARVILLE

from the Charterhouse, Dijon. XVth century

Orcagna at Florence, all seem to prove clearly the influence of Western art.

However this may be, it is an analogous phenomenon; it is a beginning of that realism which, tardily enough, renewed and revivified in Italy the Gothic art of Pisa and Florence. For Gothic art had here worn itself out in dull repetitions after Giotto's curiously learned and allegorical work on the Campanile of Florence in 1334 and Nino Pisano's charming if somewhat finicking compositions. The earliest and greatest of the Quattrocento artists, Ghiberti, Donatello, and Jacopo della Quercia, were above all things embued with realism and nature. But at the same time they were also under the influence of humanism. Humanism, which began with Petrarch in the fourteenth century, spread over the whole of Italy and, owing to the passionate love of Brunelleschi, Michelozzo, and Alberti for everything antique, speedily influenced all exterior decoration whether architectural or any other art. In other lands it did not spread beyond the realm of knowledge and erudition. Italy took the lead in this Renaissance of the classics from the beginning of the fifteenth century. When at its end, thanks to the Italian wars and to the prodigious fame won by Italian art by that time, the influence of humanism spread from Italy to northern Europe, the art it taught was an art saturated with Greek and Roman feeling. It was the Renaissance of the classics that it spread abroad.

During the fifteenth century Northern art had not ceased to be active. It would be an error even to think that it had become so entirely degenerate that a renaissance was essential. By the fatality of evolution it had doubtless deviated from the noble and pure ideal of the thirteenth century; it had even lost the almost too exquisite grace, the hard incisive strength of the fourteenth century. But it was still living, still as varied as possible. National schools had grown up, and these national schools were each subdivided into various vigorous secondary schools, similar and yet distinct from each other. Those of Germany and the Low Countries have already been mentioned. Spain, after following France, was overrun with Flemish artists and productions. But Frenchmen, Burgundians, and Italians also flocked to share in the hospitality and orders of Spain, and by the end of the century, thanks to the riches poured into the country after the discovery of America, these cosmopolitan studios worked with an intensity and an abundance of output which was truly prodigious. The churches, convents, and palaces they produced were the most sumptuous in all Christendom.

From the thirteenth century in England, the local schools, while accepting French and Flemish styles, developed along their own original lines with great activity. They largely contributed to the enrichment of the 'flamboyant' styles, and later to the 'perpendicular' which followed it so closely. Their work for the most part was represented by series of statues enshrined in their proper niches or forming mural decorations, or in the adornment of rood-lofts, of reredos and of stalls, all of exquisite workmanship but rarely attaining to anything truly impressive or living in either figures or scenes. Their general effect is, on the whole, cold and lacking in vitality. Tombs were an object of special luxury. That of Dame Eleanor Percy at Beverley Minster, with its highly ornamental canopy and little figures like those at Strasbourg, executed in the fourteenth century, or that of Richard Beauchamp at Warwick, in the fifteenth, with its mourning groups like the tombs at Dijon, are among the most characteristic examples. To these must be added a number of tombs in bronze, such as those of Edward III's at Westminster and of the Black Prince at Canterbury, two of the finest realistic portrait effigies of the century.

A special monumental and industrial art was developed in England in the fourteenth century and very largely practised in the fifteenth : that of alabaster tombs. The material was taken from the quarries of Chellaston in Derbyshire, and for the most part carved in the workshops of Nottingham. Sepulchral effigies in alabaster were exported to the Continent, and still more commonly small religious objects, often statuettes cut in relief and attached to panels destined sometimes for the bases of tombs, and sometimes for the construction of a detached reredos. Generally these represented the Passion or scenes from the life of the Virgin. This industrial art, whose success was assured in the fourteenth century, produced throughout the fifteenth pieces easily portable and executed in a style which, though a little fixed and monotonous, was not devoid of liveliness and expressiveness. Its products were spread over the whole of Europe, in France, Spain, the Low Countries, Germany, and even as far as Norway, rivalling the Flemish retables and reredoses to which they bore some resemblance in the multiplicity of the figures in their compositions, but marred by the wearisome repetition of thin and angular forms and faces lacking in expression.

In France at the end of the Hundred Years' War a new activity arose side by side with the style peculiar to the Burgundian workshops. This was particularly the case in the valley of the Loire, where the ruin and devastation of war had not penetrated and where the royal court had set up its abode. Bourges, in the days of Jean de Berry and Jacques Cœur, and Tours, where Charles VII and Louis XI lived when not residing in one or other of the neighbouring castles of Chinon, Loches, or Le Plessis, were important centres. In these two towns a very charming art came into existence, less grandiose and striking than that of Burgundy. It is very clearly illustrated by the rare examples which have survived to the present day, as for instance, by the recumbent effigies of the Bueil family in Touraine, by the sumptuous decorations of certain mansions like that of Jacques Cœur at Bourges, or by more simple houses in town or country where the carving is in wood, or again by statues in stone of the Virgin and Saints in the chapel of Dunois Castle at Chateaudun, or by other similar sacred carvings. All are simple, charming, delicate, realistic, and though fully draped yet entirely free from fatiguing details and virtuosity. Gracefulness, perception, and a sense of just proportion predominate in this art rather than mere size or any special style. Something of the style of French Gothic of the thirteenth and fourteenth centuries reappears here after a realism a trifle common and a little over-straining after dramatic effect. In short, it is both a return to traditional purity and a kind of calm after the forced and over-expressive style which had prevailed through several generations. Truly it was an exquisite and harmonious art, whether seen in the paintings of Jean Fouquet of Tours or in the sculpture of his fellow townsman, and almost contemporary, Michel Colombe. Born somewhere about 1430 and settled in Tours in his early manhood, Michel Colombe is known to us only by the work of his old age done at a date when Italian influences were already penetrating into France. It was inevitable that he should accept a certain amount of collaboration in the decorative parts of his work, and adopt certain ultra-montane iconographic themes in the composition of his statuary. Nevertheless he remained essentially French and Gothic in spirit. This fact is obvious even in the Virtues with which he engirdled the tomb of François II of Brittany at Nantes (1505–10), which was made after an Italianized design by his colleague Perréal.

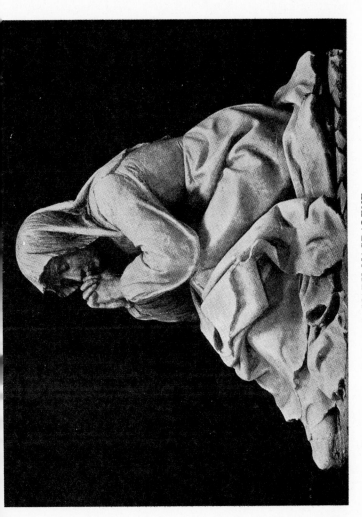

16. MARY MAGDALENE

from Abbey of Solesmes. Late XVth century

It is still more obvious in the quite Gothic and realistic St. George at Gaillon, although this was set between pilasters and arabesques in a purely Italian style. Some years earlier than the date of François of Brittany's tomb, a French master, probably a native of Tours and sometimes identified, though with less certainty, with Michel Colombe, carved the magnificent Easter Sepulchre at Solesmes. On either side of the monument he placed architectural and decorative ' motifs ' in the Italian style, which are closely allied to Gothic art in their graceful intricacies and their vigorous treatment of traditionally flamboyant foliage. But in the centre he installed the superb group of the Entombment, perhaps the most beautiful of all those which have already been described. This group, with its restrained and balanced composition, worthy of the great cathedral portals, with its strength and impressive truthfulness in the treatment of the figures, in the satisfying breadth of its draperies, all culminating in the weeping Magdalen seated and rapt in prayer, assuredly is the last of the great Gothic master-pieces, one of the most perfect, the most touching, the most human. In itself alone it proves the grandeur and the power, the underlying delicacy, the plastic and moral value, of medieval sculpture throughout four centuries. For if some works of outstanding genius surpass the rest, as does this sepulchre at Solesmes, yet it must not be forgotten that in every age on the eve of the Renaissance, just as in the cathedral and Romanesque epochs, these exceptional examples were always surrounded and supported by an abundant crop of lesser works. It is by such, grouped round greater masterpieces and embued with the qualities proper to their own particular age, that the greatness and the allurement of all art is made, whatever form it may take.

PAUL VITRY.

iii. DECORATIVE AND INDUSTRIAL ARTS

THE industrial arts of the Middle Ages do not hold their due place in the history of art ; they have, indeed, left nothing behind them that can be compared with the cathedral of Reims or the ' Beau Dieu ' of Amiens ; and the very materials which the craftsmen used, precious metals, copper, pottery, glass, linen, wool, or silk, are too tempting or too frail to survive the threatening hands of many generations. Inventories describe for us an immense quantity of goldsmiths' work ; such work was heaped up in the treasuries of churches, it lay on the tables of princes, lords, and citizens ; but the great dishes that were the pride of the Merovingian kings, the famous treasures that Charlemagne collected at Aix-la-Chapelle, the gold plate of the bankers of the Renaissance, have almost all vanished, stolen, plundered, or melted down in times of war or revolution. The Byzantine or Syrian silks, the English and French embroideries of the early Middle Ages, the innumerable tapestries of the fourteenth, fifteenth, and sixteenth centuries are described affectionately in·the old chronicles and in the old epics, in romances and in inventories ; all that remain are a few precious fragments that cover the relics of a saint, or some rare specimen the pride of a collection or a museum. Stained-glass windows, though more fragile, have shown more power to survive ; but they have often undergone addition and restoration, and must be studied with the utmost caution. I hope to show that these arts played a considerable part in the social life of the Middle Ages, and that even to-day the study of them will profit the artist as well as the archaeologist and the historian.

The goldwork of the early Middle Ages springs directly

from the art of the barbarians. The jewels found in Merovingian, Frankish, and Burgundian tombs are made of cast metal, decorated with interlaced patterns, with curved lines inextricably knotted together, and with conventionalized representations of men and animals, in the style of the barbarian peoples, a style suited to the mind of the native Celts, who had never really accepted the art of high-relief, which the Greek and Roman artists, who followed Caesar's armies into Gaul, had tried to teach them. The most beautiful specimens are decorated in ' cloisonné ', a process whose origin must be looked for in the East, in Egypt, Persia, and on the shores of the Black Sea. The Byzantine artists used the method successfully, and the barbarians carried it with them to the countries through which they passed in their wanderings. Garnets, precious stones, and sliced pastes were set into little cells marked out by thin bands of metal fixed on their edge to the foundation plate. From the fifth to the eighth century this method was used to decorate the most precious objects, such as the scabbard of Childeric found at Tournay in 1653, and the beautiful crowns which Receswinth, King of the Goths in Spain in the third quarter of the seventh century, dedicated to some famous sanctuary in Toledo. The Franks showed themselves particularly skilful in this craft ; and St. Éloi, the minister of Dagobert, won fame by his cloisonné work, of which at least one example is known to us by drawings, namely the chalice of Chelles.

The Carolingian renaissance, due to the direct impulse of the Emperor, who understood how much the development of letters and arts could enhance the majesty of the ruler and the greatness of his empire, took its inspiration from the civilization of Rome seen through the medium of Ravenna and Byzantium. These Byzantine influences were mingled with others taken directly from the East ; inter-

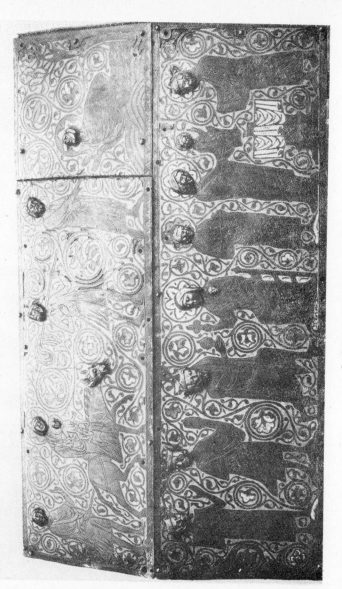

17. CASKET, LIMOGES WORK

XIIIth century. Musée de Cluny

laced ornament and geometric designs became enriched by figures set face to face, decorations based upon the form of palm-leaves and hunting scenes, and were enlivened by the introduction of panels of work in relief forming real little pictures. These are sometimes wrought with great skill as on the famous ' paliotto ' of St. Ambrose of Milan, the work of Master Volvinus, which was finished in 835.

About the same time, as the result of Byzantine influence, enamel gradually took the place of garnets and sliced paste in cloisonné work ; the little cells were filled with a paste of glass, coloured by means of metallic oxides, which were then fused and polished. This becomes opaque when on a copper or iron base, but remains translucent over gold or silver, as on the beautiful reliquary of Althaeus at Sion, on the ewer of Charlemagne at St. Maurice d'Agaune, and on the delicate reliquary of the Holy Cross in Ste Radegonde at Poitiers. Soon, in order to simplify the work, grooves were hollowed out of the metal base, which were then filled with enamel, thus leaving thin lines of metal to mark out the pattern on the surface ; in this way plaques of champlevé enamel were made, imitating cloisonné but produced more quickly.

During the Romanesque period the goldsmiths' art was carried on in two districts, in Aquitaine and in the country of the Meuse and Rhine, where the tradition of the Carolingian renaissance still survived. Shrines and plaques of cloisonné and champlevé enamel, like those preserved in the treasury of Conques, objects in bronze, cast and chiselled like those made for St. Bernwardt, bishop of Hildesheim at the beginning of the eleventh century, golden retables like that given by the Emperor Henry II to the cathedral of Bâle and now in Musée de Cluny at Paris, all show us the goldsmiths' skill. Their craft is also fully known to us through the treatise written by the monk Theophilus, who may

certainly be identified with Rogker of the abbey of Helmers-
hausen near Paderborn, who lived at the beginning of the
twelfth century.   In Lorraine during that century the
famous goldsmiths Godfrey de Claire, Nicolas de Verdun,
the monks Gilbert and Frederick of the workshop of St.
Pantaleon of Cologne carved and enamelled great shrines
shaped like churches, sometimes with aisles and transepts,
about which little statues in the round, beautiful as the great
contemporary statues of wood and stone, keep watch.

In the middle of the twelfth century the art of champlevé
enamel is centred at Limoges, where during two centuries
the goldsmiths living round St. Martial produced a considerable number of small shrines, crosses, altar vessels,
pyxes, croziers, gemellions, busts made to hold relics, and
sepulchral images often of great size like that of William of
Valence at Westminster.   These and other objects, made
for civil and ecclesiastical use, are ornamented in champlevé
enamel with designs, repeated from generation to generation.
Only with great difficulty did fresh influences renew and
modify the traditions of these workshops, which produced
their works on an industrial scale for the whole of Christendom.   The figures used were at first enamelled on a background of metal, but in the thirteenth century they were
cast and chiselled and applied to a background enamelled
with bands, flowers, or scroll patterns.   In the fourteenth
century they are reserved in metal on a background of
enamel, and have their details first engraved and then filled
in with enamel.   Besides such enamels, the twelfth and
thirteenth centuries produced goldsmiths' work soberly
decorated, depending for effect upon grace and elegance of
outline, such as the ciborium of Reims and the reliquary of
the Holy Thorn at St. Maurice d'Agaune.

Towards the middle of the thirteenth century the masterpieces of Gothic architecture were dominant in art and

18. ENAMEL PLAQUE, LIMOGES WORK

XIIth century. Musée de Cluny

the other arts became merely echoes of it, and the gold-smiths strove to model their shrines on the great cathedrals, as in the shrines of St. Eleutherius at Tournay, of St. Taurin at Evreux, and of St. Gertrude at Nivelle, fashioned with nave, aisles, choir, and transepts, decorated with buttresses and flying-buttresses and delicate pinnacles. In the four-teenth century, however, the influence of sculpture prevails over that of architecture ; reliquaries are borne by angels or priests ; the saint himself is often represented ; and such figures as the Virgin of Roncevaux or that of Jeanne d'Evreux in the Louvre will bear comparison with the finest works of sculpture on a large scale. In the fifteenth century as wealth and the taste for luxury increased, an excess of decoration replaced the former simplicity and elegance. Complicated lines became common ; design was no longer restrained by the recollection of the great models of the past ; and monstrances and sacred vessels, drinking-cups and salt-cellars, were made in contorted and often heavy shapes.

By the middle of the fourteenth century the increase in wealth and in the supply of the precious metals gradually caused the work produced at Limoges to fall into disuse. It was replaced by translucent enamel placed upon gold, produced first in Italy and afterwards almost everywhere. This remained the fashion until the middle of the fifteenth century, when Limoges invented a new technique, and relighted its furnaces, which had been cold for more than a century ; this was the art of painting with enamel on copper. Until the seventeenth century this craft was practised by many artists, the so-called Monvaerhl, the Pénicauds, Pierre Reymond, Léonard Limousin, the artist who made the great plaques of the Sainte Chapelle and of the apostles of Anet, now at St. Père at Chartres, the splendid portraits of Francis I, of Queen Eleanor, and of the

Constable Anne de Montmorency. To the same school belong the Nouailhers, the Courts and the Courteys, who painted on plates, dinner-services, and plaques in bright colours or in grisaille, taking from antiquity and pagan mythology the subjects which the Italian Renaissance had made known to all.

The art of carving in ivory followed a course parallel to that of sculpture ; and I should not have to speak of it here, were it not that its evolution throws light on certain points in the history of the industrial arts which are not illustrated by the story of the art of the goldsmiths. Ivories furnish us with some of the most valuable evidence of the Carolingian renaissance. Workshops of ivory-carvers were established near the great Rhenish monasteries at Trèves, at Lorsch, at Cologne and at Aix-la-Chapelle, while others were set up at Reims and yet a third group at Metz. These craftsmen had relearnt the technique of the ivory-carvers of Rome, Byzantium, and Alexandria, and translated into low relief the miniatures painted in the monasteries which sheltered them. Those who worked in the Rhineland drew from Byzantine ivories something of that nobility of pose, that beauty of proportion and majesty of calm, which come from Greece. The school of Reims took its chief inspiration from Alexandrian ivories, aiming chiefly at producing the picturesque and lively style of pose and gesture which the miniaturists of that district portray with so much truth, especially in the famous Utrecht Psalter. In the Romanesque period sculpture in stone, which during the eleventh century had had to relearn its technique from the goldsmiths and the ivory-carvers, rapidly gained a complete mastery of its craft. In consequence ivories almost disappeared in the West. In the East and in the Moorish parts of Spain remarkable work was still produced ; and this was one of the chief ways by which the West received the forms and

19. IVORY COVER TO PSALTER OF CHARLES THE BOLD

IXth century. Bibliothèque Nationale

subjects of oriental iconography. The thirteenth century saw a renaissance in the art of the ivory-carvers, who then came under the influence of the sculptors in stone, and imitated or even copied the masterpieces of the great cathedrals. Every one feels the charm of these Virgins of the late thirteenth or early fourteenth centuries, leaning a little to one side, slender, delicate, lovable, full of a slightly affected grace ; the most beautiful being the Virgin of the Sainte Chapelle, now in the Louvre. By the end of the fourteenth century we find the same subjects continually repeated ; there is a continual production of little tabernacles sheltering a virgin between angels, or of scenes from the childhood of Christ, triptychs and diptychs intended for domestic oratories and private chapels, on which are crowded the same scenes of the Passion or of the life of the Virgin which cover the great retables ; and the work soon became complicated, overloaded and rather uninteresting. Such tendencies were exaggerated by the spirit of relentless realism which ruled in the late fourteenth and in the fifteenth centuries. The secular ivories of the fourteenth century keep a certain grace and charm ; mirrors, caskets, and women's toilet services are adorned with pretty scenes, where knights talk with their ladies, play dice, crown their heads with roses, or joust together ; sometimes there are episodes from fashionable romances, such as the Roman de la Rose, Tristan et Yseult, or La Chatelaine de Vergy.

The development of furniture follows in the same way that of sculpture ; and the history of wood-carving can be studied in the choir-stalls of churches. Their type became fixed in the thirteenth century, and has not altered since that period ; between the sides (*parcloses*) of the stalls there is a seat which can be raised ; and underneath it is a small ledge called a misericorde, against which the clerk, who had to stand during long services, could rest. The sides carry elbow-rests, slightly sloping backwards; the back of the stall is crowned by a canopy, which becomes more and more projecting in the course of the fourteenth and fifteenth centuries, and which is supported on the scroll-work (*volutes*) forming the upper part of the stall ends (*jouées terminales*). At first, as in Notre-Dame de la Roche near Chevreuse and in the Cathedral of Poitiers, the ornament is simple, the back fairly low, and the canopy projects but little. In the fourteenth and fifteenth centuries, at Lisieux and Toul, at La Chaise Dieu and at Rodez, and also in the great English cathedrals, the back is heightened, the canopy projects farther, pendants hang from it, and ornament is so rich as to become exuberant. Little figures, grimacing masks, figures of prophets and saints decorate the sides; comic scenes from proverbs and morality-plays are carved on the misericordes. During the first half of the sixteenth century most choir-stalls are still Gothic; those of Amiens, Brou, and Auch are some of the richest that were ever made. But here and there decorative details in the style of the Renaissance begin to appear; and sometimes, as in the beautiful choir-stalls of Gaillon, carved early in the sixteenth century for the Cardinal of Amboise, and now at St. Denis, the whole decoration is based upon classical subjects. But the thing that persisted and continued to persist during the classic period was the form of the stall, which remained what it had been made in the twelfth and thirteenth centuries.

Of domestic furniture few specimens have survived, yet enough remains to enable us to understand the changes which took place in that craft during the Middle Ages. The earliest pieces, chests or cupboards of the twelfth, thirteenth or fourteenth centuries are built on posts, which form the feet; and between these posts planks are fixed lengthwise to form the sides; they are carpenter's work.

In spite of iron bindings, in spite of linen and leather glued inside and sometimes outside, the planks crack, split and come out of joint. In the fifteenth century, instead of using long and wide planks, the joiner makes a series of frames formed of upright and cross pieces tenoned and morticed together and sets within them light panels held in rebates formed in the frame. The wood may warp, or swell; no break or crack will result. Modern furniture was therefore born in the fifteenth century. During the whole of the sixteenth century it continued to be made by the joiner; only its ornament varied and followed the fashion. But the veneered and painted furniture of the Italian type does not penetrate into France. It is only at the end of this century and during the seventeenth century that there is a reaction against the excessive use of figures and mouldings; the form is simplified, and the wood of the frame, which up to then had itself been ornamented, disappears under veneers, veneers of precious woods, veneers of ebony, or a covering of marquetry; while the joiner disappeared to make way for the cabinet-maker.

The arts which I have dealt with, briefly, are intended for the decoration of buildings, churches or houses, but they have a definite purpose of their own, and a special use; there are other arts, which are essentially and purely decorative, such as wall-paintings, stuffs, embroideries and tapestries, and stained glass. These I wish to discuss at greater length, since their influence on modern decorative art is very clear.

In the first Christian churches narrow windows admitted a scanty light, and the wide stretches of wall were decorated by mosaics and paintings; and these were used also on the floor and the vaulting. Mosaics ask for time and patience from the artist; they endure longer, and many have come down to us in good condition. Paintings, whether in fresco or encaustic, where the work is in closer relationship with the craftsman and at the same time more perishable, have nearly everywhere disappeared. Both commonly represented stories from the Old and New Testaments, martyrdoms, portraits of the bishops of the place, landscapes, seascapes, hunting scenes and victories symbolized by emperors. They are essentially didactic, as is affirmed by councils and synods: at Constantinople in 892, and at Arras in 1025. Charlemagne decrees in his Capitularies of 807 that all the interior surfaces of the churches should be painted for the instruction of the faithful. Sidonius Apollinarius, Fortunatus, and Gregory of Tours all relate that in Gaul, from the time of the Merovingians, the bishops interested themselves in the decoration of their churches. Patient, archbishop of Lyons, rebuilt his cathedral and enriched it with mosaics. Bishop Namatius had the walls of his church of St. Étienne at Clermont covered with paintings from the Old and New Testaments, and Gregory of Tours describes how the bishop's wife selected the subjects from among the miniatures of a manuscript. Childebert I built St. Vincent and Sainte-Croix at Paris and adorned the floor with mosaics, the walls with paintings, and the ceilings with gilding. The whole story of St. Martin can be seen on the walls of the cathedral of Tours, the famous miracles he wrought and his battles with idolatry. Fortunatus cites many other instances of such decoration, and he describes the piety of the Franks, who had these paintings and mosaics made by men of their own nation without invoking the aid of the Italians. Under Charlemagne and his successors the interior decoration of churches remained equally rich. We know the subject of the paintings in Charlemagne's palace at Aix as well as in that of Louis the Pious at Ingelheim. Side by side with the story of David and Solomon, the founding of Constantinople by Constantine, Charles Martel

20. EMBROIDERED CROSS (*opus Anglicanum*)

About 1400. Collection Martin Le Roy

vanquishing the Frisians, Pepin conquering Aquitaine, Charlemagne overthrowing the Saxons and the victorious battles of the Emperor and his ancestors were all to be seen. In Reims Cathedral, which was rebuilt by Ebbo, his successor Hincmar had the walls decorated with paintings and the floor with mosaics, representing saints and angels. In the monasteries not only the churches but also the dormitories and the refectories were decorated with paintings.

In the tenth century, this art in France suffered an eclipse; the never-ending wars of the great barons, the absence of all sense of security, impeded the progress of civilization. In Italy, in Switzerland, and in Germany there were flourishing centres where the old traditions were preserved. There were workshops of renown at Monte Cassino, at Salerno, and at Farfa, where the church is painted within and without as in the Roumanian churches of to-day; at St. Gall and Reichenau this was also the case. The names of some of the artists who worked there have come down to us, though their works have almost entirely disappeared. During both the tenth and the eleventh centuries in France and England it was the usual practice to whitewash the walls and to hang them on feast-days with embroideries and precious stuffs, while the timbers of the structure were painted.

The German monk Theophilus in his *Diversarum artium schedula* describes the technique of the painters of his day in the following manner. On a wall covered with mortar the painter traced the main lines of his picture, and marked in the outlines of his figures; he then laid a wash of fine lime over as much of the surface as he could paint in one day, and while the lime was still wet he painted the outlines in fresco and laid on his colours in a flat wash. Modelling was got by means of hatching, white lines in the high-lights and dark lines in the shadows. For the light tints a paint was used with a white-lead base; there was a dark tint which Theophilus calls 'posch', made up of a dark green mixed with a little red; feet, hands, and faces were painted in a flesh colour made of a mixture of white, cinnabar, and ochre. The tints used were few: red and yellow ochres, and green and white. Blue was expensive, and difficult to use in fresco; it was applied with size on the wash when dry, and often flaked off; it was only used to produce an effect of dignity, for the nimbus of Christ or on the edging of his robe.

This technique was employed in the few paintings of the twelfth century which have come down to us. At St. Savin in Poitou all the histories of the Old and New Testaments are painted, and with them are also represented scenes of the Last Judgement and the latter end of man. In the same style are the surviving paintings in the churches in the valley of the Loire, in Touraine, and in the Sarthe. But while Theophilus recommends the dark-blue ground beloved by Byzantine and Oriental artists, in the paintings of the North of France the figures stand out against a light background, and it is not until we reach Central France and Burgundy, at Le Puy and Charlieu and Cluny, that we find Romanesque frescoes on a blue ground.

In the Gothic period the size of the windows increased so much that the walls became only the supports for the intersecting arches of the vaulting, the thrust of which was taken by the flying buttresses; a method of construction which allowed full play to the daring of the architect. In consequence general schemes of painting were replaced by detached pictures in fresco or encaustic filling up a spandrel or a segment of the vault. In chapels or little churches painters still decorated the walls with sacred scenes, while in the rooms of houses or the halls of castles they used scenes from romances; in both cases the pictures form a long band painted to resemble tapestry hung on the wall and enriched with embroidered borders. Italy accepted from Gothic architecture only its main principle, the inter-secting arches of the vault ; the large windows were rejected, since they would have admitted too much sun ; and thus Italian churches continued to offer the painter large surfaces to decorate. By the end of the thirteenth century the Italian painters were accustomed to work in fresco, and were thus able to express their thoughts with freedom and rapidity. In the lower church at Assisi the artists still retain some of the dryness and harshness of their Byzantine masters, but in the upper church, at the beginning of the fourteenth century, Giotto and his pupils, while still pre-serving the unalterable design of the sacred iconography, paint the scenes from the Gospel with freedom, and endow their figures with an expression, a sense of life, an ease of gesture and pose, which then first appear in all their delight-ful freshness and which continue to increase all through the fourteenth and fifteenth centuries. In other countries, in France and England, embroidered hangings and tapestries took the place of paintings ; these were hung out only on the great feast-days to enrich the splendour of the building with their glowing colour.

From the beginning of the Romanesque period work-shops of embroiderers in the Empire produced such remark-able works as the mantles preserved in the treasuries of Bamberg and Ratisbon, and the famous cope used at the coronations of the kings of Hungary, which was made for St. Stephen, the king, and his wife Gisela of Bavaria, and given by them in 1031 to the church of Stuhlweissenburg. In England, from the tenth century, there were famous workshops of embroiderers, and Durham Cathedral still preserves the stole and maniple of its bishop, St. Cuthbert, embroidered by Queen Aelflaed, the wife of Edward the Elder, who died before 916. English embroiderers kept their reputation through all the Middle Ages, and their work, known as *opus Anglicanum*, was exported to the whole of Christendom, notably to Italy, where it was especially appreciated by the Popes and Princes of the Church. From these workshops must have come that long band of linen embroidered in coloured wools which is usually called ' The Bayeux Tapestry ' and attributed to Queen Matilda. The whole tragedy of Harold and William, the broken oath, the building of the fleet, the invasion of England, the battle of Hastings, is there unfolded in scenes full of vivid and picturesque detail. The style, the details of dress and armour, the lettering of the legends, all suggest that this hanging must have been made by English embroiderers at the end of the eleventh century under the direction of some English clerk, attached to the Norman cause, and that it was made for William's half-brother Eudes de Courteville, whose figure continually appears in the foreground.

In the thirteenth century there were many embroiderers in Paris. The *Livre des Métiers* of Étienne Boileau, provost of the Merchants of Paris from 1258 to 1268, mentions them repeatedly. Many examples of later thirteenth and four-teenth-century work remain showing most admirable skill in execution and grace in design. Such pieces as the Passion cope at St. Bertrand de Comminges or the altar frontal of the hospital of Château-Thierry, on which the coronation of the Virgin, the adoration of the Magi, the presentation in the Temple, and St. John and St. Paul are shown beneath a trefoiled arch, are compositions of real charm, possessing as true a claim to rank as an art as the sculpture which they imitate.

From the fourteenth century tapestry almost completely takes the place of embroidery, and in many cases even of

21. TAPESTRY OF THE APOCALYPSE, CATHEDRAL OF ANGERS

Late XIVth century

Et datus est mihi calamus similis virgae, et dictum est mihi: Surge et metire Templum (xi. 1)

painting in the decoration of churches and castles. Tapestries are mentioned as early as the tenth century, for instance as in use at the church of St. Florent, Saumur, and at the court of Queen Adelaide, the wife of Hugh Capet. Fragments of tapestries which may be as old as the eleventh and twelfth centuries are still preserved in the treasuries of Halberstadt, of St. Geryon of Cologne, and at Quedlinburg, but it is not until the beginning of the fourteenth century that we hear of workshops equipped with looms set vertically (*haute lisse*). This term is found for the first time in 1303, in an addition to Étienne Boileau's statutes of guilds. At that time Arras and Paris were the two chief centres of the art; under the stimulating patronage of Mahaut, Countess of Artois (1302–27), the tapestries of Arras became famous for their delicacy and the quality of their yarn. King Jean and his sons, Charles V and the Dukes of Anjou, Berri, Orleans, and Burgundy, had a great liking for tapestries; and we know by the inventories of their possessions that many were woven for them. We hear of scenes from the Old and New Testaments, and from the lives of the saints, trees and foliage, scenes from romances of chivalry and epic poems, such as Gérard de Nevers, William of Aquitaine, the Saint-Graal, representations of allegories and moralities like the *Procès de Souper et de Banquet*, actually found in the tent of Charles the Bold; there were also scenes of country life, pastorals, hunting scenes, and scenes taken from contemporary history, battles, tournaments, and knightly feasts. We know for instance that the Parisian weaver, Nicholas Bataille, with the help of Jacques Dourdin and Pierre Baumetz wove the history of Bertrand Duguesclin; and that Bataille and Dourdin carried out in less than three years, between 1397 and 1400, the famous set of hangings of the Jousts of St. Denis, which included six panels covering nearly 350 square metres. It was taken away by the Duke of Bedford, and the remains of it may perhaps exist even to-day in some English collection.

One such set of hangings has come down to us almost complete, the Apocalypse now preserved in the Cathedral of Angers. It is the more precious in that the history of its weaving is completely known, thanks to the work of Léopold Delisle, Jules Guiffrey, and Louis de Farcy. The Duke of Anjou borrowed from the rich library of his brother Charles V a manuscript of the Apocalypse. In the inventory of the king's manuscripts, drawn up in 1380, by the librarian Jean Blanchet, there is a note on the margin of the description of the Apocalypse, ' The king has lent it to M. d'Anjou, for the making of a beautiful tapestry.' From the miniatures in the manuscript the painter Jean de Bruges made large cartoons, which were paid for in 1378. Nicholas Bataille then began the weaving, which was not finished before the middle of the fifteenth century. The whole consists of seven large pieces five metres high and twenty to twenty-four metres wide, and is thus more than a hundred and fifty metres long, and covers a surface of seven hundred and twenty square metres. Each piece contains fifteen pictures arranged in two rows. In the earlier pieces the background is plain, but as the work went on, the backgrounds became covered with trellis with a powdering of flowers, butterflies, birds, and vines. Thus the whole evolution of the art of tapestry, composition, design, and technique can be followed in this incomparable set covering, as it does, the whole period from 1378 until 1450 or thereabouts.

During the fifteenth century tapestries were still produced in the looms of Arras ; but they were somewhat confused in composition, and so crowded with scenes and figures that the background is completely hidden. The drawing, however, is good and the colouring rich. From these workshops came most of those pieces in the collection of the Dukes of Bur-

gundy which were taken by the Swiss from Charles the
Bold at Granson and Morat, and are now in the Museum
of Berne. In 1477 Arras was destroyed by Louis XI, and
its flourishing industry never revived. The Arras weavers
migrated to Tournay, Valenciennes, Bruges, and especially
to Brussels. There weavers were already numerous and the
new-comers gave a fresh stimulus to their work. The
magnificent pieces woven for Joanna of Castille and Margaret of Austria, for Charles V and Philip II, are famous
everywhere, and are the pride of the collections of Vienna
and Madrid. Jean de Bruxelles, Bernard van Orley, Peter
Coeck of Alost, Michael Coxcie, these last working under the
influence of Raphael and the great masters of the Italian
renaissance, all produced fine compositions, allegorical,
didactic, and religious, depicting triumphal processions and
stories of the gods and heroes drawn from classic mythology.
The earlier of these compositions were very crowded and
somewhat overweighted; the later ones are simpler in
style and better composed, uniting the elegance of the
Italian renaissance with the realistic genius of the Flemish
artists. In France at the end of the fifteenth century and
the beginning of the sixteenth Gothic art was still a living
influence in tapestry; an influence clearly to be seen in
such hangings as the Life of the Virgin and the Life of
St. Remy at Reims, the history of the Virgin at Notre-
Dame de Beaune and the history of the New Testament at
La Chaise Dieu. Moral scenes, like those which accompany
this last example, were made known to all by the circulation
of the *Speculum Humanæ Salvationis* and the *Biblia Pau-
perum.*

In the valley of the Loire a school of tapestry arose whose
spirit seemed in keeping with the pleasant country of its
birth and where Gothic art lost something of its hold long
before the triumph of the Italian renaissance. This school

specialized in the fabrication of charming tapestries of rare grace and freshness, where lovers, musicians, and allegorical figures stand out against a flowery background; as for instance in 'The Concert de Rohan' in the church of St. Florent at Saumur, and in the charming panels of 'La Dame à la Licorne', now exhibited in the Cluny Museum at Paris. This last piece was possibly made in Central France by weavers trained in the School of the Loire.

Francis I and Henry II tried to establish, under the direction of Primaticcio and Philibert de l'Orme his successor, at Fontainebleau and afterwards at Paris, workshops which might hold their own against the weavers of Brussels. Some of their productions, for example that in the Gallerie François I designed by Rosso and Primaticcio, are admirable alike in composition and execution. But these royal workshops rapidly declined during the disturbances and wars of the sixteenth century; and at the beginning of the seventeenth century Henry IV in order to revive the industry was forced to attract to Paris Flemish artists like the Coomans and the De la Planche. These he established under his special protection and with very considerable privileges in the hope of freeing France from the tribute she had paid for over a century to the weavers of Brussels.

The large number of tapestries woven during the Middle Ages is easily explained; they were in frequent use. In churches they were hung round the choir and behind the choir stalls as a screen against draughts; and on feast-days they were used to decorate the arches between the nave and aisles and those of the triforium above. In the cities the streets were hung with them in honour of a procession, a state entry, or solemn ceremony. In castles they were hung along the walls and used as door curtains, or were fixed on rods for bed testers or behind armchairs in the chimney-corner. They served as screens and made the cold

22. TAPESTRIES OF THE APOCALYPSE. CATHEDRAL OF ANGERS

End of XIVth century

The Beast and the False Prophet driven into the marsh of sulphurous fire (xix. 20)
The Angel leading St. John to the Heavenly Jerusalem (xxi. 10–11)

and bare halls of strong castles more habitable. The hooks meant to support tapestry have often been found still in place. They were also used as partitions to divide the great halls into smaller rooms. Sometimes they were spread on floors. This fashion of carpets came from the east and was still unknown in France, England, and Northern Europe in the middle of the thirteenth century ; but when Eleanor of Castile, the bride of Prince Edward, the future Edward I, reached Westminster, she found her apartments furnished by her own servants and the floors covered with carpets after the Spanish custom ; and the court then adopted this fashion.

Kings and lords carried these tapestries with them, wherever they went ; and in this way Charles the Bold lost at Granson and Morat the finest tapestries of the house of Burgundy, which were carried off by the Swiss when they captured his camp and his tent.

Medieval tapestries are admirably fitted to their purpose ; they make no attempt to rival painting, but are primarily decorative. Tapestry must be essentially movable and flexible ; and the composition of the scenes represented must be full, quiet, and dignified, as befits all ornament meant to express and complete the lines of architecture ; it must be full because its task is to fill up and fill in, and therefore it must not show empty spaces, which would, as it were, leave holes in the wall to be covered ; so figures, accessories, and details must be numerous, the backgrounds must be covered with foliage and flowers, the horizon line must be set high so that the scenes depicted should cover the space and the sky be reduced to small importance. On the other hand, since the technique of tapestry requires that it be seen from a distance, it is useless to model the figures too carefully ; the colouring must be simple, limited in scale, without those half-tones and broken colours which

alter quickly in the light and lose their relative values.
Tapestry must give an impression of gaiety and joy, so grey
and neutral tones must be avoided. It is by brilliance and
directness of colouring and not by a manifold scheme of
tints that tapestry achieves its effects. Such are the rules
of the great art of tapestry in the Middle Ages and the
Renaissance ; and it is the infringement of these rules which
makes the tapestries of the nineteenth century seem to us
so poor and mean.

With the history of the art of stained glass I shall bring
to an end this rapid survey of the industrial and decorative
arts of the Middle Ages. Here too we find the same complete harmony between composition and technique and
purpose, the same break at the Renaissance due to the
failure to understand this fundamental rule, and in the end
the modern return to the old technique. The purpose of
stained glass is to fill in the window-spaces ; it is also meant
to instruct, and to give to the interior of church or hall
a warm and luminous atmosphere, delighting the eye and
uplifting the spirit. At the same time it must be a mosaic
of glass, a truth thoroughly understood by the medieval
artist. The glass itself is stained right through its substance ;
the pieces are rough and irregularly shaped, cut with a hot
iron and trimmed with a grozing-iron [1] to follow the lines
of the cartoon ; they are set in leads, which are themselves
stiffened by an iron tracery, to which, after the twelfth
century, stone bars were added. The colours are simple :
a cobalt blue, a copper red, a green got from copper, purple
from manganese, and a yellow ; they are separated by the
thick leads, which allow to each colour its own value ; and
their arrangement shows an admirable understanding of the
laws of translucent colours, laws very different from those

---

[1] A species of pincers or nippers used to crush the rough edges of
the pieces of glass.

applying to colours laid on an opaque surface. The lines of the figures, the folds of the drapery and details generally are painted in *grisaille*, strongly defined since they are meant to be seen against the light and from a distance. The subjects are simple ; when the windows are lofty the figures are few and on a large scale, and often isolated; in other cases they are filled with small pictures easily understood by the people of the Middle Ages, who knew every incident in the lives of the Saints. Such windows set forth the story of the Deity, of the Virgin, and of the Saints with all that luxury of detail which lives for us in the text of the Golden Legend. Such are the windows in the choir of St. Denis, which were made between 1140 and 1144 under the supervision of Suger himself. These windows, unhappily much restored, represent the history of the Virgin, that of Moses, the tree of Jesse, and parallel scenes from the Old and New Testaments. Such again are the windows in the west front of Chartres Cathedral, where the tree of Jesse once more is the subject chosen ; a subject repeated in the Sainte Chapelle at Paris, at York, at Canterbury, and later on at Autun, at Beauvais, and in many other churches in France, England, and Germany from the thirteenth to the sixteenth century. A little of the glass in the cathedrals of Le Mans and Angers, the great painting of the Crucifixion in the window at the end of the choir at Poitiers, and a certain amount of stained glass at Chalons sur Marne, Strasbourg, and Augsburg date from the twelfth century. In the thirteenth century the size of windows was increased as if for the purpose of giving more space to the glasspainters, so great was the love of our forefathers for the beauty of glass through which the sun seemed for ever to shine, and where the whole story of the Golden Legend was unfolded amid the blue of heaven. At Chartres, Poitiers, Bourges, Le Mans, Reims, Soissons, Angers, and

Tours there are magnificent windows, as also in the choirs of Sens, Laon, and Lyons. These are all filled either with scenes arranged in a series of medallions or with large figures of saints, apostles, and prophets; and when we enter these great cathedrals of the thirteenth century the iridescent light which passes through these windows falls upon us and straightway transports us to a higher world. Who is there who has not felt the sudden thrill which seizes on the visitor to the Sainte Chapelle at Paris as he suddenly enters the upper chapel from the dark staircase and meets the blaze of colour which bursts upon him from a thousand medallions in the fifteen great windows, with their story of the Bible told in its entirety?

During the fourteenth and fifteenth centuries the technique of stained glass remained unchanged; composition was lightened and simplified and large figures almost everywhere took the place of narratives. A silver stain, which could be melted into the glass, and a flesh colour were added to the glass-worker's palette without overloading it; diapered backgrounds gave a new brilliance and the windows in the choir of Evreux and in the chapels along the nave of Strasbourg are as beautiful as any of the twelfth and thirteenth centuries. In the sixteenth century the technique of glass painting became more scientific but remained obedient to the laws which govern the true art of stained glass. The glass was in larger pieces, smoother, and less thick; it was often composed of two layers of different colour to give greater variety and intensity. Sometimes portions of the upper layer were removed with a small tool and in this way pretty effects of colour could be obtained. Compositions usually remained clear and simple, often copied from engravings or drawings and adapted to the limitations of glass. One of the most flourishing workshops was that of Engrand Leprince at Beauvais, where early in

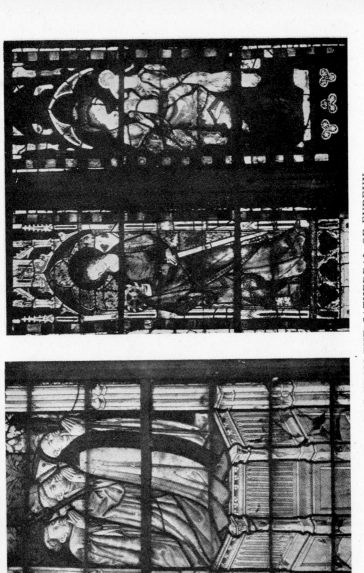

23. WINDOWS FROM THE CATHEDRAL OF EVREUX

XIVth and XVth centuries

the sixteenth century magnificent windows were produced; for example, the famous Tree of Jesse on a blue ground in St. Étienne at Beauvais and the Chariot window in St. Vincent at Rouen. The churches of Montmorency and Ecouen both possess series of stained-glass windows of the same date, which clearly show the influence of the Île-de-France school; the technique is as excellent as the compositions are beautiful. Several churches in Paris have preserved some of this glass, which was so abundant before the fashion of the eighteenth century and the Revolution brought about its disappearance; instances are St. Étienne du Mont, St. Merry, St. Gervais, St. Germain l'Auxerrois, and La Sainte-Chapelle at Vincennes. The Norman school also produced a considerable quantity of stained glass, and the churches of Rouen can still show splendid examples; others can be found at Louviers, Pont-Audemer, Conches, and in many other churches of the departments of the Eure and the Seine-Inférieure. In Champagne also there was a great industry, especially at Troyes and round that town; this glass is perhaps less beautiful, less rich than that of Normandy and the Île-de-France, but the makers of it had a perfect understanding of their art. Their colours are simple and fresh, the tones are clearly separated, the figures few and sharply outlined; all the glass is stained throughout its thickness, and the colour enhanced by the use of silver stain and *grisaille*.

In other parts of France there are noteworthy windows, such as the window with the story of St. Louis at Champigny-sur-Veude near Chinon, the Tree of Jesse with its clear white background in the Cathedral at Autun; and above all the magnificent windows made for Margaret of Austria in 1528 in her chapel of Brou. The most beautiful of these is the window in which she has had herself shown as the donor kneeling opposite to her husband Philibert le

       L

Beau. Between them is shown the Assumption of the Virgin, crowned by a fine frieze after Titian representing the triumph of Faith. The Italian Renaissance had given to stained glass a new iconography with new details, magnificent models to use, but its technique remained that of the Middle Ages. In the middle of the sixteenth century a new technique appeared, the art of painting in enamel on glass. It was an easy art, and won its way with the artists, but it led them into an absurdity, the folly of imitating in glass paintings on canvas, and this course brought about the ruin of the art of stained glass. It was only by returning to the technique of the Middle Ages that nineteenth-century artists were able to recapture the true beauty and glory of stained glass.

In the course of this brief study we have seen how closely the industrial arts follow the evolution of art in general, and how intimately they are connected with the decorative portions of the building, for which they provide the ornament. We have also seen that the ornament they give is a function of their technique, which in turn depends on the use made of it. This freedom in the use of ornament is the foundation of medieval art ; it is this freedom that once more inspires modern ornament, and has given back to us the art of tapestry and of stained glass.

Marcel Aubert.

24. WINDOW OF GUY DE LAVAL

Church of Montmorency. 1523–1533

3
LITERATURE

i. SOME ASPECTS OF MEDIEVAL LATIN LITERATURE

THE modern student who sits down to write of medieval literature in any of its many aspects may well bethink himself of a story from the early days of the coming of the Friars. It is related in a Franciscan sermon that a certain priest was wont, year by year, to keep the feast of St. Nicholas (our Santa Claus). And, lo, it chanced that he became so poor that he was unable to celebrate the wonted festivity (*convivium*). As he lay in his bed thinking what to do, there sounded in his ear the bells ringing to Matins. The refrain of the first expressed his own perplexity. 'What shall I do ? What shall I do ? ' (*Ieo ke fray ; Ieo ke fray.*) The second answered it : ' Borrow away, Borrow away ' (*A crey ; A crey*). While he was cogitating where the money was to come from for repayment, they both sounded together, and it seemed to him that they said : ' Something from one, something from him ' (*Ke de un, ke de el ; ke de un, ke de el*). And he rose and kept the feast with borrowed money. The sermon, we are told, was approved by the Chapter. If our own borrowings do not meet with the same approval we may console ourselves with the reflection that this story at any rate has in it something of the music of the Middle Ages as well as an illustration of the mingling of languages which made the thirteenth century pregnant with wonderful possibilities for the future of literature.

Fastidious Roman ears of Jerome's time disliked the

'sacred but barbarous language' of the Scriptures with more reason, it must be admitted, than an earlier critic had for finding 'Patavinity' in Livy. But the austere classicist of a later day has extended less toleration still to the Latin of the Middle Ages. Certainly it belongs neither to the Golden nor the Silver Age as those are ordinarily discriminated ; and there are many who would scoff at the suggestion that it is not, therefore, to be condemned. The language of the New Testament lay under a similar cloud of disparagement so long as it was regarded as merely a debased form of classical Greek. A label is at best an incomplete description : a false, or misinterpreted, label may be not merely misleading but the instrument of a great wrong, more especially when it extends to six folio volumes with four more of appendix or supplement, as is the case with the monumental work of Charles du Fresne du Cange with its damning title *Glossarium Mediae et Infimae Latinitatis.* Yet it is probable that what scoffers have rendered as 'Infamous Latin' will share in days to come something like the same rehabilitation as has been granted to the *Koine,* when it is recognized as the living organ of expression of an age and of people whose heirs and debtors are the critics themselves.

We shall remind ourselves of the dangers of exaggeration on the other side. Regarded as in any strict sense a succession to that of classical writers, the Latinity of many of the medieval composers in prose or verse would justify most of the hard things that have been said against it. It was inevitable that it should show some change when the works of the great stylists had fallen into oblivion or disrepute. Cicero wrote verse (of a kind) as well as prose ; but no voice was heard in the Middle Ages to say ' Vates Tulli gentilium Da Christo testimonium ', and as for his prose men remembered rather Jerome's awful warning of celestial condemnation 'Ciceronianus es !' Virgil escaped, less hardly, to win from Dante the most glorious of vindications. But Virgil could be credited with a theological and an ethical interest, and if this could hardly be said of Horace or of Ovid except by those who were prepared to believe anything to be profitable to edification, if properly understood, such minds were not wanting in theological circles—at least in the Middle Ages. But any one who takes the trouble to examine the character of the classical quotations to be found in works or letters from the twelfth to the fourteenth centuries will be astonished at their limited range, and the more when he compares them with the not after all very extensive collections of works found in catalogues of monastic libraries.[1] And if the time came when authors were content or obliged to impart to their writings an appearance of learning or of wit by a classical 'tag' or two borrowed through Aulus Gellius or Jerome or Macrobius or some lesser light, there were many to whom (to all appearance) even so much was unknown or unesteemed. Yet never always nor to all, for the classical tradition did not wholly die at any time; nor is it wise to assume that it did so, in order to glorify the Renaissance. But still less shall we understand the Middle Ages if we seek to defend them by pointing to such evidences as relics surviving in a scene of universal ruin. It is along other lines, if at all, that we shall find the clue to what we are seeking, namely in a new trend of language and in some ways a new development of literature.

A return to Jerome may seem to need apology, save to those who read him ; but to draw from that fount of learning

---

[1] The present writer had made some tentative efforts towards a study of their range, when the appearance of the fascinating *History of Classical Scholarship from the Sixth Century B.C. to the End of the Middle Ages* (vol. i, Cambridge University Press, 1903) by Dr. J. E. Sandys provided the enduring delight which outweighs all temporary disappointments.

once is to return many times. There is a curiously interesting passage, however, which may serve as excuse here :
' The Galatians,' he says, ' except for the Greek speech,
which is that of all the Orient, have almost the same tongue
of their own as the people of Trèves : it does not matter
if some corruptions have crept in thence, for the Africans
have to some extent changed the tongue of the Phoenicians,
and Latin itself is daily being changed by time and place.'
We are not concerned with the Galatians, though we
remember that as to Trèves Jerome is speaking from personal
knowledge.   But the modification of Latin to which he
thus points at the opening of the fifth century made startling
progress in the centuries that followed.   Nor was it without
ostensible defenders in unexpected quarters.   The less
carefully guarded utterances of great men are the most
interesting and therefore have the best chance of remem-
brance.   There are few students of such matters who have
not either hailed or deplored the protest of Gregory the
Great against subjecting the Divine Oracles to the rules of
Donatus, even if they do not follow John of Salisbury in
attributing to him the crime of burning the Palatine
Library.   But the great Pope was not a mere 'Philistine';
and while ' nugae et seculares litterae ', which he deemed
unworthy of a religious layman and still more of a bishop,
included much that we should deem valuable, his censure
is not an excuse for barbarism, though it has often been
thus interpreted.   His plea is for something else in comparison with which, by the irony of history, not the bodies
of Christians but the books of pagan Romans seemed *vile
damnum*.   It is curious, however, that his apprehensions
have not more often been noticed as a testimony to the still
powerful influence of the Classics at a time when it has been
regarded as well-nigh dead.   However, it is more certain
that barbarism came than that its course could have been

sensibly affected by any conceivable action of the rulers of the Church.

The problem of the future, as Jerome has shown us, was not entirely new. None but the unreflecting suppose that the ordinary Roman citizen of Northern Italy, or of Rome itself, in the last days of the Republic, talked to his neighbour, still less in his family, in the style of Cicero's *Orations* or Caesar's *Commentaries*, or in the early days of the Empire wrote to his friends in the manner of the younger Pliny. And already loan-words are coming into use in quite respectable circles for other things besides means of conveyance. After all the use of appropriate ' neologisms ' is far from being a sign of linguistic or even of literary decadence, and the best writers of most ages and countries have provided ' exceptions ' to the rules of grammarians as well as of prosodists. But we are witnesses, as we study, of a marvellous phenomenon—the making of two of the great languages of the modern world, French and English ; and in the process many streams converge. In this, as in all study really scientific, observation must precede criticism. Let us look at some of the most startling examples that we can find. Jordanes, a Gothic ecclesiastic of the sixth century, writes history and avails himself liberally of existing materials : they are in Latin, and he too would write in Latin, though it is to him a foreign language and his grammar and syntax are shaky : ' scito,' he says, ' me maiorum secutum scriptis ex eorum latissima prata paucos flores legisse.' Let us move on five hundred years or more to the greatest of the ' Chansons de Geste '. Roland is enumerating the duties of the vassal to his lord :

> Por son signor deit hom sofrir granz mals
> E endurer e forz freiz e granz calz.
> Si'n deit hom perdre del sanc e de la carn.

It is Latin without mixture, if not pure. An eminent French critic has amused himself and us by writing out the Latin which it represents :

> Pro suum seniorem debet homo sufferire grandes malos
> Et indurare et fortes frigidos et grandes calidos.
> Sic inde debet homo perdere de illum sanguinem et de illam carnem.[1]

The maieutic process is horrible, but it is a fine vigorous child that is born. Or we may look at an intermediate stage of ' progress ' or decay. The student who has not made the acquaintance of the *Historia Francorum* of Gregory of Tours has still an unforgettable joy in store. The great classicist in Sir John Sandys regards its Latinity with grave disapprobation ; but in the sympathetic hands of M. Bonnet it yields nearly 800 pages of a study as fascinating as it is illuminative.[2] There we may see something of the way in which things came to be, the sources of confusion of sound and of form, and the curious vagaries of sixth-century syntax, of which Gregory's fondness for a nominative or accusative absolute are but two among many.

We cannot enter into the hotly disputed question of the relative proportions of Latin and indigenous elements in the production of ' French '. It was not perhaps without malice that M. Bonnet placed on the title-page of his book the words of Gregory : ' Per meam rusticitatem uestram prudentiam exercebo.' It is the wildest absurdity, however, to suppose that all medieval writers who wrote Latin wrote ' dog Latin '. It could never be wholly so while Jerome and Augustine and Gregory the Great were studied, even if we depreciate unduly Orosius, John Cassian, Cassiodorus,

---

[1] Ferdinand Brunot in Petit de Julleville, *Histoire de la Langue et de la Littérature française*, II. ii, p. 471.

[2] *Le Latin de Grégoire de Tours* (Paris, Hachette, 1890).

Boethius, or Isidore of Seville. And in the hands of the Schoolmen, Latin as a living language became a dialectical instrument of marvellous flexibility as well as cogent force, certainly without producing any impression of 'rusticity' upon the reader. By the thirteenth century Grosseteste could write that there were in England two languages— Latin for the clergy, French for the ignorant, for English had not as yet come once more into its own in general esteem. But 'Latin for the clergy' in days when, as it has been said, 'the Church was the common shelter for all who held the pen' meant a certain bias as well as a certain limitation in the mode of literary development. It would be instructive, but it is for our present purpose strictly irrelevant, to discuss the number of ignorant 'clergy' even among those in sacred orders at any period. The priest who shocked St. Boniface in the eighth century by administering baptism 'in nomine Patria et Filia et Spiritu sancta' was certainly not unique in his ignorance, but scarcely more typical than the schoolboy who wrote 'intelligere dor' for 'I am given to understand' in the nineteenth. Our concern is with the formative influences which moulded the language no less than the thought of the Middle Ages as well as with the ignorant or uninstructed who made strange use of materials, the history and meaning of which they very imperfectly understood.

Foremost among such influences must be placed the Latin Scriptures in the Vulgate version. If any demonstration were necessary it might be found in the difficulty experienced by modern scholars in getting behind the Vulgate. But again we must beware of exaggeration. One of the first and hardest lessons for the medievalist is to learn not to accept general statements on whatever authority without examination of their meaning and validity. Not every child of well-to-do parents in the Middle Ages saw in a vision of the night at the age of eight a grave commanding figure which inquired 'Hast thou read the Book of Joshua, the son of Nun?' and another that demanded 'Dost thou know the Book of Tobit?' And Gregory answered, of Joshua that he had never heard of it, that he was having great difficulty in learning to read at all, and of Tobit that he had not read it. And many eminent persons, including Henry Beauclerc, would probably have been incapable of doing so at any age. Again, there is strong reason for thinking not merely that Gregory knew and used other versions, or at least another version, besides the Vulgate, but that it is the Latin of some of these rude older versions which lies behind some of the word-forms in Old French. It must be remembered, too, that the influence of the Scripture language might be very large even among people who could not read. It is harder to trace literary or linguistic influence of Missal or of Breviary, though the latter provided stories for sermons which were helped out by other 'Pulpit aids' often of greater length than variety. But the modern student may be grateful for an inheritance in prayers and hymns of the riches of which he is too often unconscious. We cannot resist the temptation to transcribe three out of many which every reader will recognize as already known in English dress:

'Deus, auctor pacis et amator, quem nosse vivere, cui servire regnare est, protege ab omnibus impugnationibus supplices tuos: ut qui defensione tua fidimus, nullius hostilitatis arma timeamus.'[1]

'Deus, qui fidelium mentes unius efficis voluntatis, da populis tuis, id amare quod praecipis, id desiderare quod promittis, ut inter mundanas varietates ibi nostra fixa sint corda ubi vera sunt gaudia.'[2]

---

[1] Cf. Second Collect, for Peace, Morning Prayer.
[2] Cf. Collect of Fourth Sunday after Easter.

' Deus, in te sperantium fortitudo, adesto propitius invoca-
tionibus nostris ; et quia sine te nihil potest mortalis
infirmitas, praesta auxilium gratiae tuae, ut in exequendis
mandatis tuis et voluntate tibi et actione placeamus.' [1]

This is great Latin, whether it be of the seventh or of
any century, and will remain so whatever criticism may be
offered of language or syntax. And the same may be held,
if with a difference, yet also an added attractiveness, of the
hymns. The Christian Church, it has been finely said,
started on its way singing.[2] Ambrose had to meet the
Arian charge that his hymns were to the people as magic
spells ; and for us too ' Aeterne rerum conditor' or
' Splendor paternae gloriae' have the same attraction, if
for a different reason. In course of time each Hour service
came to have its hymn, and no less the Seasons and the
Saints' days. The iambic tetrameters of Ambrose were
paralleled by other classical metres but also by systems of
scansion by accent, of elision and of rhymed verses which
had no strictly classical ancestry. Under musical influences
perhaps as early as the eighth century came the ' tropes '
or added melodies, for glory rather than for sense, and the
sequences or ' proses ' which from the ninth century
onwards came to supply rhythmical verses to fit the added
melody, ' Prose' because at first not metrical, ' Sequentia'
because supplying words for the trope *following after* e.g.
the Alleluia of the Mass. Most famous among such compositions are ' Veni sancte Spiritus', perhaps by Innocent III
in the thirteenth century and the ' Stola regni laureatus '
or the ' Heri mundus exultavit ' of Adam of St. Victor some
fifty years earlier. Of favourite hymns we can name but
a few. Who does not love the ' Cultor Dei memento ' of

[1] Cf. Collect of First Sunday after Trinity.

[2] W. H. Frere, *Hymns Ancient and Modern : Historical Edition*
(Clowes, 1909), a work to which this section is deeply indebted.

Prudentius or the 'Pange lingua' and 'Vexilla Regis'
of Fortunatus or the great hymn for Prime by an unknown
author, 'Iam lucis orto sidere'? If we can no longer
assign to Bernard of Clairvaux 'Iesu, dulcis memoria', nor
even perhaps 'Salve, cuius dulcis vultus' as we can the
'Hic breve vivitur' and 'Hora novissima' to Bernard of
Morlas, that need not lessen our appreciation of any of
them; and the 'Alleluia, dulce carmen', 'Alleluia piis
edite laudibus', or 'Urbs Sion aurea, patria lactea', though
anonymous have as secure a place as the 'O quanta qualia
sunt illa sabbata' of Abailard, the 'Stabat mater dolorosa'
of Jacopone, the 'Dies irae' of Thomas of Celano, or the
'Quisquis valet numerare' and 'Jerusalem luminosa' of
Thomas à Kempis. Our list is becoming a catalogue; but
that is itself a striking tribute to the capacity of these
hymns for expressing the hopes and fears and longings of
the human spirit, as well as its deepest devotion in 'Sancti
venite, Christi corpus sumite'—the wonderful Irish hymn
of the seventh century—or its reasonable faith, in the
'Adoro te devote', the 'Bone pastor, panis vere', and the
'Verbum supernum prodiens' of Thomas Aquinas. It has
been said of some of the later hymns that they have a devotional rather than a literary value, and it may be so, nor
need we greatly deplore that they should have been not
less loved when we remember that the 'Hymnum canentes
martyrum' and 'Praecursor altus luminis' of the Venerable
Bede failed to win affection because they lacked the inspiration
which others could give.

We learn from a modern writer on the Middle Ages that
'all life was saturated with religion to such an extent
that the people were in constant danger of losing sight of
the distinction between things spiritual and things temporal'.[1] The inference that he draws is misleading, for the
human impulse to parody is as independent of saturation

[1] J. Huizinga, *The Waning of the Middle Ages* (Arnold, 1924), p. 140.

with religion as it is essentially of malice or profanity. The austerity and difficulty of classical metres might or might not provoke the product of an *Otium didascali*, the solemn jesting of the gravely frivolous ; but accentual scansion, the lure of rhythm and of rhyme, and a catchy tune proved to many as irresistible as they are still found to be to unregenerate minds. Youth because it is young would slay a giant (which after all is one of the glories of youth) ; and Golias whether represented by Education or one of the powers that be, even (*horresco referens !*) a Bishop, may be slain perhaps by a set of derisive verses as well as by a stone from a sling. And students in all civilized lands in all ages have their songs, of which the refrain will remain when the rest is forgotten. We wonder how many but for that would remember more than the first line of ' Heus, Rogere ! ' Some will be grave, some gay, flippant, amorous, irreverent, sometimes obscene ; the Goliardic verse or ' Carmina Burana ' achieved a popularity from the twelfth century onwards at which it is quite useless and even, some may think, quite unnecessary to be shocked. All metres, all methods of composition, were fair game or natural instruments, and in the *Confessio Goliae*, it has been said, ' nests that one medieval Latin verse which everybody still knows by heart: "Meum est propositum in taberna mori . . ." ' [1] That is the lighter side ; but satire could be alike fierce and almost diabolically ingenious as any one may see for himself who cares to turn to poems attributed to Walter Map which were first published by the Camden Society or the *jeux d'esprit* of the Anglo-Latin satirists of the twelfth century issued under the grave auspices of the Master of the Rolls.

The spirit of the Middle Ages is impatient of capture, insusceptible of analysis, though many have essayed the task, and we may derive instruction, if also amusement,

---

[1] H. O. Taylor, *The Mediaeval Mind* (Macmillan, 1911), ii. 218.

from watching them. 'The men of the Middle **Age**', a critic will tell us, 'were big children, credulous, and *naïfs*, who in history preferred anecdotes, in sermons *exempla*, and in science the fantastical and the marvellous. Men who saw God and the devil everywhere could possess neither the critical spirit nor the gift of observation.'[1] *Distinguamus, O sodales !* The *ewig weibliche* is everywhere the mother of the eternal child, but grown men were grown men even if they kept that spirit, and even though ' their astronomers are astrologers, their chemists alchemists, their mathematicians sorcerers'. If the four chief attributes of man at his highest be Love, Reason, Faith, and the sense of Wonder, they at least had them all : which does not mean that they always used them well. It is quite true that they loved stories in their histories, especially stories of marvel or of portent. Yet we are not really sorry to find Matthew Paris, greatest of medieval chroniclers, turning aside to describe and to paint that wonderful elephant which is his joy (and ours). But he did not see in it the devil as Philippe de Thaon had called the ' cocodrille ' (crocodile) in ' the oldest and for that reason in itself the most interesting of French Bestiaries ', written in England about a century earlier. De Thaon tells us that his work is translated from Latin, but he introduces Latin into it. We see the same influence at work in sermons in what is known as the ' macaronic style ', with its strange mixture of Latin and French, a mixing of languages which reacted on the language of the people and which survived even when sermons preached *in vulgari*, whether French or English, became common. Giraldus Cambrensis, so he himself relates, once reduced a Welsh congregation to tears by preaching to them in Latin of which they understood not a word ; but some priests could not understand the Latin of their texts so well as their hearers, if we may

[1] A. Piaget in Petit de Julleville, *op. cit.*, II. ii, p. 165.

credit his account of one who, preaching on St. Luke vii. 41, treated ' quingentos ' and ' quinquaginta ' as the same, and being pressed by the *praepositus villae* : ' Then he did not give either more than the other,' extricated himself with the explanation : ' The one lot were Angevin pennies, the others sterling.' The story, and there are many like it, may tempt some readers to turn for themselves to the *Gemma Ecclesiastica* from which it is taken. It was written for the instruction of clergy by a man who knew their difficulties and is full of things which they would remember. Of the same kind, but with lay-hearers in view, are the enormous collections of ' exempla ' which the reader will find in the works of men like Bromyard or Brumton or other authors of a ' Summa Praedicantium '.

Truth embodied in a tale has proverbial efficiency, but it certainly received illustration by strange means and in strange quarters. To England and to the fourteenth century belong the ' Contes Moralisés ' of the Franciscan, Nicolas Bozon. But of even greater influence is the celebrated ' Gesta Romanorum ', belonging also perhaps originally to England in the end of the thirteenth century, but famous throughout Europe and exercising in its Latin or its English form an attraction which those who read it will readily acknowledge. ' Either directly or indirectly [it] furnished to Boccaccio the ground-work of his tale of the *Two Friends* ; to Lydgate of his *Tale of Two Merchants* ; to Gower and Chaucer of their *History of Constance*; to Shakspere of his *Merchant of Venice*, *Lear*, and *Pericles* (?) ; to Parnell of his *Hermit* ; to Walpole of his *Mysterious Mother* ; and to Schiller of his tale of *Fridolin*.' [1] The claim perhaps goes too far ; but it was certainly one of the most popular of all medieval books ; and if it is stronger in morals than in

---

[1] S. J. Herrtage, *The Early English Versions of the Gesta Romanorum* (Early English Text Society, Extra Series, xxxiii), p. xxvi. The moral is on p. 41.

history, 'ther be many of us that woll rathir put her lyf
and trust in to the help of the world þan to the help of god,
þe which is not oonly myghti but almyghty; and þerfore
seith oure saviour *Si habueritis fidem ut granum synapis,
poteritis dicere huic monti transi, et transiet,* That is to say,
if ye have feith, as moche as hath þe corn of synewey, ye
shull mow sey to a mounten, passe, and hit passeth at a word
of you',—and that is what the medieval writer wished his
readers chiefly to understand.

It has been made a reproach to the Middle Ages that
they brought into prominence Latin authors of the second
or third rank or of no rank at all in preference to most of the
Great Ones. Yet if we look for the manuscripts of one
author who is usually adduced as an example, we shall find,
strange to say, only one complete manuscript of Phaedrus
in existence. That the Roman fabulists enjoyed popularity
may be as true as that in the *Gesta* or the Fabulists of the
thirteenth century we find traces of eastern influence.
In the case of the 'Directorium Humanae Vitae' of John of
Capua in the thirteenth or the 'Liber Kalilae et Dimnae'
of Raymond of Béziers in the following century this cannot
be doubted. When the latter translated a work which he
had found in Spanish into Latin 'que lingua communior
est et intelligibilior ceteris' to the glory of the Divine
Name, the utility of the state, and the honour, among
others, of Philip of France and Margaret of England, he
disclosed the history so far as he knew it, of this 'liber
regius'. But in less clear cases caution is necessary, for
there are many stories which are, or seem to be, part of the
common stock of most of the races of the world. Again the
'fabulae' may be in prose or verse, of considerable length
like the work of 'Raimondus de Biterris' or as short as the
'parable' of Odo of Cheriton (d. 1247), 'Vnde Archita
Tarentinus offensus servienti ait : Quantum te afflictarem,

nisi iratus essem!' or the fourteen lines of 'Johannes de Schepeya' on the birds choosing a king, with its conclusion ' Ideo necessarium est ut praelatus sciat pascere, sciat picare et quandoque percutere subiectos, ne lasciuiant, et teneat medium inter nimiam simplicitatem et nimiam seueritatem '—reflections which have an additional interest since John of Sheppey (d. 1360) was himself a bishop.

Equally or even more fruitful for purposes of ' edification ' or warning were stories from the Lives of the Saints, whether taken from the Breviary or scattered in separate compositions or preserved in oral tradition. They are almost innumerable, and if the reader thinks, as he will, that he observes a great sameness of treatment and of incident in many of them, one of the most illustrious of the Bollandists will show him how this came to be.[1] But it was no accident that the compiler of the most famous of all popular collections, the *Legenda Aurea*, the thirteenth-century Archbishop of Genoa, James of Varaggio, whom we call Jacobus de (*or* a) Voragine, was a Dominican, and therefore *ex professo* a preacher. No work of its kind can compare with it in its influence alike before and after the discovery of printing. Early printers did not produce what would not sell, and Wynkyn de Worde chose even better, when he selected the *Gesta Romanorum* and the *Legenda Aurea*, than Caxton with *Le Jeu d'Echecs moralisé* or the *Treatise of Hawkyng*. To the modern student of folk-lore and the marvellous and also of linguistic ' development ' we would commend too the great collection of Irish Lives,[2] and if he desire something of a different type the Lives of St. Bernard of Clairvaux and St. Catherine of Siena.

We live in towns, but are often ' pagan ' none the less; and in a critical age, without wholly escaping from illusion

---

[1] H. Delehaye, *Les Légendes Hagiographiques* (Brussels, 1905).
[2] C. Plummer, *Vitae Sanctorum Hiberniae* (Clarendon Press, 1910).

But it is only in Herefordshire, perhaps, or other rural counties that simple folk still see the oxen bend the knee on Christmas night when Christ is born. In the Middle Ages even men who could not read might learn by sight as well as ear. And therefore there grew up a type of 'literature', at first unwritten and in consequence hard to trace in its historical development—the Mystery Plays in 'France' and England and 'Germany' with their strange minglings of vulgar and Latin speech. 'Le culte chrétien', it has been said, 'est essentiellement dramatique.' And after all it was but a step from the 'prose' or sequence of the Christmas Mass 'Quem quaeritis in praesepe, pastores, dicite?' with its answer 'Salvatorem Christum Dominum . . .'[1] or the 'Victimae paschali laudes', which told of the joy of Easter, to dramatic representation, from the tenth or eleventh century onwards. An extension to other subjects, e. g. 'The Ten Virgins' or 'The Raising of Lazarus', 'Adam' or 'Daniel' or 'The Magi', was natural enough. First come the simple words of the Latin gospels, then the text rendered in verse still Latin, then dialogue is amplified and the vernacular inevitably and quite naturally introduced. So we have in an eleventh-century play :

> Amen dico
> Vos ignosco,
> Nam caretis lumine;
> Quo qui ⟨perdunt⟩
> Procul pergunt
> Huius aulae limine

or again in the 'Daniel' played by the clerks or students at Beauvais in the twelfth :

> Vir propheta Dei, Daniel, *vien al Roi,*
> Veni, desiderat *parler à toi.*
> Pavet et turbatur, Daniel; *vien al Roi*
> Vellet quod nos latet *savoir par toi.*

[1] For this and what follows, see L. Petit de Julleville; *Les Mystères* (Paris, Hachette, 1880), vol. i, pp. 25 ff.

or the speech of Martha in the *Suscitatio Lazari* of the same
century :

> Si venisses primitus,
> *Dol en ai,*
> Non esset hic gemitus.
> *Bais frere, perdu vos ai.*

The words have a haunting ring : it is vernacular speech,
a little heightened perhaps now and then but still the
language of every day. It would be easy to multiply
illustrations where the 'Langue d'oc' or the 'Langue
d'oil' take their places side by side with Latin, and the
English student will be hard to please if he does not find
interest also in the York and Chester Plays published by the
Early English Text Society.

Few of us speak exactly as we write, except perhaps the
youthful Macaulay with his 'I thank you, Madam, the
agony is abated'. Fewer still write as they speak either in
vocabulary or style. But there are certain classes of medieval
writings into which the vernacular makes its way, even
if the main language is Latin, and does so almost of necessity.
The development of a science of economics has led to an
extension of the term 'literature' which may warrant the
inclusion of a 'compotus' roll or of household accounts.
Nor is it reasonable to complain if in such a case a dialect
dictionary will often be more useful than a Latin lexicon.
We may doubt whether the modern student who laboriously
expands contractions into Latin terminations is not often
doing more than the original writer could have done without
an effort or would have thought it worth while to do at all.
But the fifteenth-century clerk in an episcopal registry who
transcribed an indictment of a certain Thomas who assaulted
(*fecit insultum*) a certain Robert ' et cum uno cultello vocat.
" a London knyffe " pret. 4d. . . . felonice percussit . . . et
ibidem felonice interfecit et murderauit,'[1] certainly did

[1] Cardinal Morton's Register, i, f. 196 b.

not marvel at the Latinity of his brother who wrote the
original document in the interests of the peace of our
Lord the King. It said what had to be said, and said it in
a way that could be understood. He wished no more.
And, after all, friars like Thomas of Eccleston or Roger
Bacon and great lawyers like Bracton equally with the
writers in the Year Books use a vocabulary which has as
necessarily been enlarged as that of Scotus or Aquinas ;
and the medieval physicians have indeed drunk strange
waters, as any one may see for himself who is attracted by
curious titles, in latinized or unlatinized Arabic or Greek,
found in catalogues of manuscripts to read their works for
himself. And if the learning of the East enriched the Latin
language as well as Latin literature by way of Salerno or of
Spain, so in many other quarters did tales of travellers and
chronicles of the Crusades.

Let us turn for a moment to expositions of political
theory, remembering since we are in the Middle Ages that
we shall never separate it wholly from the ethical motive
or the soul's unceasing quest. ' Omnia cedunt in usum
sapientis, habentque materiam virtutis exercendae quae-
cunque dicuntur aut fiunt ' : so says John of Salisbury in
the *Policraticus*, which we may venture to consider one of
the greatest political treatises of the Middle Ages, while
at the same time reflecting upon the admirable Latin which
some men at least could write in the twelfth century.
' The purpose of society is not merely that man should live
virtuously, but that by virtue he should come to the enjoyment of God ' : thus teaches St. Thomas of Aquino in the
thirteenth. ' O frater Leo, pecorella Dei, quamvis frater
Minor loquatur lingua angelica, et sciat stellarum cursus
et virtutes herbarum, et sciat revelationes thesauri terrarum,
et si cognoscat virtutes et proprietates avium et piscium,
animalium, hominum, radicum, arborum, lapidum et

aquarum, scribe bene et nota diligenter quia non est ibi
perfecta laetitia ' : so with many like words Frater Hugo-
linus records the judgement of the Blessed Francis. ' Ah,
Domine Deus, quando ero tecum totus unitus et absorptus
meique totaliter oblitus ? ' such is the aspiration of Thomas
à Kempis in the *Imitatio Christi*—the one medieval work
besides the *Summa* of Aquinas which is without question
or reserve a possession for ever. *E contra* Gregory VII sees
in kingly power an operation of the devil, and Walter Map
a century later begins his *De Nugis Curialium* with a description of Hell, while the fourteenth-century author of the
Somnium Viridarii tells us that ' Roma a praedonibus et
latronibus fuit constructa : unde adhuc retinet primor-
dium. Nam " Romanus rodit: quos rodere non valet odit ".'
There are many phases of medieval thinking here, as there
are many styles of writing, yet more remain than any single
mind can compass, as may presently appear.

He who saw ' perfecta laetitia ' in rejection by men
while in the service of God, sang too the Song of the Sun ;
and the extract we have given from the teaching of St.
Francis with its lovely Latin—why should we not say it ?—
has a further interest. For just that encyclopaedic knowledge, in which for him true joy did not consist, was what
with painful care the systematic minds of the Middle Ages,
at least those of a certain type, strove hardest to achieve.
There may be one or two men living now who have read
the whole of the *Speculum Maius* of Vincent of Beauvais :
there will scarcely be three. It is stupendous alike in its
variety, its scope, and its limitations, but parts at least are
of singular interest. And it did not stand alone. We have
often wondered whether the thirteenth century was not the
real testing time of Latin as a vehicle for the expression of
thought. Certainly when the Florentine Brunetto Latini
compiled his great ' Trésor des Choses ' a few years before

Vincent's death in 1264 he chose to write in ' French ', and he tells us why : ' Et se aucuns demandoit pourcoi chius livres est escris en roumanch, selonc le patois de Franche, puis ke nous sommes Ytalijen, je diroie que ch'est pour deus raisons : l'une que nous sommes en Franche ; l'autre pour chou que la parleure est plus délitable, et plus kemune a tous langages.'[1] It is the supreme triumph of the genius of the Latin language that it survived the test. But admittedly it sometimes took strange forms. Fra Ugolino, the reputed author of the *Floretum*, was a contemporary of Dante who had shown in the *Divina Commedia* and the *De Monarchia* what new and old might be and in the *De Vulgari Eloquentia* what the future might hope. But Ugolino can write ' Tu non es unus pulcher homo ' for the old, if he can also join the two languages in ' Sed quando dicet tibi : Tu es damnatus, et tu secure respondeas : *Apri la bocca et mote cecato*, id est, aperi os tuum et ibi pone cacum.' It is not really to the point to urge that his very simplicity is more attractive than all the luxuriance of St. Bernard's expositions of the Song of Songs or St. Bonaventure's seraphic commentaries on the Master of Sentences, though it may be true. Perhaps the Latin of Fra Ugolino, the Latin of Monte Giorgio, was like the French of Marlborough, the medieval rival of Stratford atte Bow.[2] There is malice, though not venom, in the

---

[1] It is a curious foil to ' Lingua romana coram clericis saporem suavitatis non habet '.

[2] If the story be, as Matthew Paris feared, *offendiculum amicorum*, it is Walter Map's, not ours. Geoffrey, son of Henry II, was ordered by the Pope, after seven years' tenure of the bishopric of Lincoln, either to resign or seek consecration. ' Diu tergiversans neutrum et utrumque voluit et noluit. Rex igitur qui sollicite considerabat multam terram occupatam a ficu tali, coegit eum ad alterutrum. Is autem elegit cedere. Cessit igitur apud Merleburgam, ubi fons est quem si quis, ut aiunt, gustaverit, Gallice barbarizat, unde cum vitiose quis illa lingua loquitur, dicimus

story which the reference recalls, but the *Nugae Curialium*, like other collections of anecdotes, sometimes at any rate embody history and we do not doubt that this is true. *Le style c'est l'homme même* : yet we wonder a little as we read the twelfth-century poet of Pisa quoted by Mr. H. O. Taylor :

> Inclytorum Pisanorum scripturus historiam
> Antiquorum Romanorum renovo memoriam,
> Nam ostendit modo Pisa laudem admirabilem,
> Quam olim recepit Roma vincendo Carthaginem.[1]

What sort of a man was he who could write like that ? The last line must be one of the worst in Latin literature. We feel as if the steed refusing the fence had shot its owner through the air. However, he recovers himself and writes quite a great deal more : and that also is the medieval spirit. It must be admitted that the numbers in which some of these writers lisped were their misfortune rather than their merit. But we must not suppose that he was exceptional in his attitude or his courage. We will wend our way back a century or so to Gandersheim and find in the pages of Hrosvitha ' illustris et clarissima virgo et monialis ', one of the most interesting of the learned ladies of the Middle Ages,[2] another specimen, if in curious verse :

> Non me plus licito tantae sophiae fore iacto
> Vt sperem plene verbis me dicere posse.

eum loqui Gallicum Merleburgae : unde Map, cum audisset eum verba resignationis domino Ricardo Cantuariensi dicere, et quaesisset dominus archiepiscopus ab eo "Quid loqueris?" volens eum iterare quod dixerat, ut omnes audirent, et ipso tacente quaereret item " Quid loqueris ? " respondit pro eo Map " Gallicum Merleburgae ". Ridentibus igitur aliis, ipse recessit iratus.' (*De Nugis Curialium*, Dist. v, c. 6, ed. Wright, pp. 235–6.)

[1] Cf. H. O. Taylor, *The Mediaeval Mind*, i. 252.

[2] Mr. Taylor (*op. cit.* ii. 215) hardly atones for calling her ' tiresome ' by adding that she is ' unquestionably immortal '.

She has brought the great Otto in her narrative to the imperial throne :

> Hactenus Oddonis famosi denique regis
> Gesta (licet tenui musa) cecini modulando.

Now she sends Bérenger into exile with his wife Villa, deposes the Pope and returning to Saxony creates his son 'infantem in cunis', King at Aachen; but these are matters,

> Tangere quae vereor, quia foemineo prohibebor
> Sexu : nec vili debent sermone reuolui
>
> . . . .
>
> Haec igitur nostris nequeunt exponier orsis :
> Sed quaerunt seriem longe sibi nobiliorem.
> Hinc ego tantarum prohibente grauedine rerum
> Vltra non tendo : finem sed prouide pono.

O admirable Hrosvitha! Even on the technical side these leonine hexameters repay examination, and we can only long for space in which to show her also as writer of plays. It is a long stretch from Gandersheim to the Birmingham Oratory, from Hrosvitha to Cardinal Newman, but she in her age could show how Terence could be made quite *convenable* by an adjustment of characters and a *dénouement* which exhibits the triumph of Virtue. The modern reader will be foolish if he does not smile rather than criticize, and though he may regret that her discernment did not extend to the fact that Terence wrote in verse, she would not mind : 'Si enim alicui placet mea devotio, gaudebo. Si autem vel pro mea abiectione vel pro vitiosi sermonis rusticitate nulli placet, memet ipsam placet quod feci.'

Memet ipsam placet quod feci! It accounts for much. But we must turn to look at history in another mode. A medieval French translator of a Latin chronicle once observed that he wrote in prose rather than in verse because

rhyme led to the addition of words not in the Latin.[1]
Verse chroniclers like the author of the ' Ligurinus ' had no
such scruple. At any rate he describes at great length events
which he says that he has not been worthy to witness. Otto
of Freising, on whom he based himself, had done better when
he wrote *inter alia* a chronicle stretching in the medieval
manner from Adam to A.D. 1152, and *De Gestis Friderici I.*
If we can take nothing else from the latter famous book it
shall be a description of his hero, of whom, justifying himself
by the description given by Sidonius Apollinaris of Theodoric
the Goth, he says that ' et moribus et forma talis est ut et
illis dignus sit agnosci qui eum minus familiariter intuentur '.
And as we look, the picture grows before us.

> ' Forma corporis decenter exacta : statura longissimis breuior,
> procerior eminentiorque mediocribus : flaua caesaries, paululum
> a vertice frontis crispata. Aures vix superiacentibus crinibus
> operiuntur, tonsore pro reuerentia Imperii pilos capitis et
> genarum assidua succisione curtante. Orbes oculorum acuti et
> perspicaces, nasus venustus, barba subrufa, labra subtilia, nec
> dilatati oris angulis ampliata, totaque facies laeta et hilaris.
> Dentium series ordinata niueum colorem repraesentant. Gut-
> turis et colli non obesi, sed parumper succulenti, lactea cutis, et
> quae iuuenili rubore suffundatur. Eumque illi crebro colorem
> non ira sed verecundia facit. Humeri paulisper prominentes.
> In succinctis ilibus vigor. Crura suris fulta turgentibus hono-
> rabilia et bene mascula. Incessus firmus et constans, vox clara,
> totaque corporis habitudo virilis. Tali corporis forma plurima et
> dignitas et auctoritas tam stanti quam sedenti acquiritur.'

Certainly Barbarossa is every inch an Emperor, and who
shall deny that a medieval writer can be an artist in words?
His younger contemporary, Lambert of Hersfeld, though
inferior as a stylist, can draw a striking picture too, as in the
scene of the affray between the Bishop of Bamberg and the

---

[1] The translator of the chronicle of the pseudo-Turpin. Cf. C. V.
Langlois in Petit de Julleville, *Histoire de la Lang. et Litt. Franç.*, II. ii,
p. 282.

'Dux Arabum'. In a quieter manner is the charmingly simple description of London and the Becket family in the anonymous Life of St. Thomas ; in one more sprightly the vivid little scene of King and Chancellor and poor man wherein the Chancellor loses his cloak by involuntary beneficence as told by William FitzStephen, most graphic of biographers. Or if we are in a different mood we may turn from the chroniclers to the fine passage of stately rhetoric in which Peter Damiani solemnly throws overboard and abandons to their fate Plato and Pythagoras, Nicomachus and Euclid, bent-backed with complicated studies of geometrical figures, the rhetors with their syllogisms and the Peripatetics looking for truth at the bottom of a well, the tragic and the comic poets, Cicero and Demosthenes, in comparison with the simplicity of Christ, and seeks counsel on a liturgical question of Leo the hermit ! This, too, is medieval.

We might add many other studies in the use of words, each of which would have an interest of its own. Let us choose one in the grand style—William of Malmesbury's introduction to his *Gesta Pontificum* :

'Erat certe plenum segnitiei et ignominiae nescire saltem nomina principum nostrae provinciae, cum pertendat alias cognitio nostra ad tractus usque Indiae, et si quid ultra iacet quod infinito Oceano patet. His adductus rationibus, et hic et alibi, traxi stilum per latebrosissimas historias, quanquam mihi non hic affluat eadem copia scientiae quae in Gestis Regum. Siquidem ibi aliquid de cronicis quae prae me habebam mutuatus, velut e sublimi specula fulgente facula, quo gressum sine errore tenderem, ammonebar. Hic autem pene omni destitutus solatio, crassas ignorantiae tenebras palpo, nec ulla lucerna historiae praevia semitam dirigo. Aderit tamen, ut spero, lux mentium, ut et integra non vacillet veritas et instituta conservetur brevitas.'

Our last example shall be one which shows as vividly as anything that we know both the development of vocabulary and

the extraordinary effectiveness of medieval Latin in capable
hands. It is taken from Nicholas of Butrinto's account of his
experiences during the journey of the Emperor Henry VII
in Italy :

> ' Mane fecimus equos parari et somas ligari. Et dum essemus
> in mensa expectantes nuncium nostrum et responsionem Pote-
> statis, audivimus quod campana cum martello pulsabatur. In
> continenti vidimus totam stratam plenam armatorum peditum
> et equitum. Tunc domum nostram giraverunt. Postea ad
> scalam quidam de Maguelotis popularis, pulcher homo valde
> volens ascendere incepit clamare : *Moriantur tales !* Hospes diu
> gladio evaginato in gradibus non dimittebat aliquem ascendere.
>   In illo tumultu somarii nostri et equi fere omnes per praedictos
> ducti sunt. Tunc per diversa loca gradus ascenderunt, et ad
> cameram nostram venerunt cultellis evaginatis. De nostris
> familiaribus tunc aliqui fugerunt dimittentes se per fenestras
> cadere ad unum hortum ; inter quos fuit socius meus frater
> Praedicator. Alii se pre timore mortis abscondentes sub lectis.
> Pauci tunc nobiscum remanserunt. Sed Deus . . . sic nos . . .
> confortavit quod in mea conscientia nunquam timui, licet magis
> essem in periculo quam alius. Dum hec fierent, in civitate
> Florentina fuit tumultus. Quidam dicebant quod male erat
> factum sic nos banniendo.'

We have not preserved the ' instituta brevitas ' ourselves,
and can only suggest by reference the quaint interest of
works like Gascoigne's *Liber Veritatum*, the charm of letters
like those of Peter of Blois or of Pecham or the more formal
style of the Papal Chancery seen, for example, among those
of Gregory VII, or the character of the letter which becomes a moral treatise in the hands of Henry of Huntingdon,
or of some other writer ' De Contemptu Mundi '. We
have said nothing of works of moral theology in which
some would have us see *le moyen âge intime*, though seldom
because ' legentibus necnon audientibus ad meritum pro-
ficiunt '. But this is not a survey of medieval literature,
else must much have been said of Roger Bacon and of

Grosseteste and more of the English chroniclers, whom to know is to love, and of Bede, in some ways greater than them all. It is but a note of some stages in a great development where some have heedlessly seen nothing but decay. The Middle Ages are neither a sordid tragedy of ecclesiasticism nor a splendid interlude, but the testing ground wherein many seeds were sown, some good, some bad. We boast ourselves far better than our fathers, but if we dub them barbarians we are still their children. Nor shall we grumble at our inheritance if while some dispute of the origin of the modern state we hold in our hearts the idea of the 'pecorella Dei', in our hands some of the greatest literature of the world.

Claude Jenkins.

ii. VERNACULAR LITERATURE

FASTIDIOUS travellers often acquire a feeling of their own national superiority over races which have attained a lesser degree of civilization, mechanical or intellectual or both. If they roam far afield enough they are given to affect an attachment to some particular race, with which they have come into touch, not far removed in kind from the attachment which is felt for a pet animal. The Romans possessed a good share of such fastidiousness, and with some reason considered themselves superior to most races of the ancient world. There came a day when some of these races overran the Roman Empire and from the very outset broke up the complex organization of civilized life. Let us imagine that a similar disaster befell the modern world. Think of unkempt hordes camping in the squares of our cities, pulling up the rails of the railways, cutting down the wires of telegraphs and telephones, setting fire to palaces, factories, and churches. One must try, however imperfectly, to visualize the colossal upheaval which brought the ancient world to an end. It is easy to say now that the ancient world was corrupt ; the modern world is perhaps little better ; and the barbaric invasions had the relentlessness of a cataclysm. The invaders were more backward than some of the races which our fastidious travellers either spurn or patronize and it took Europe almost a thousand years to recover from that deadly blow. But nothing is absolute in life ; the destruction was not complete and, though rapid, it was far from being sudden. There were edifices which did not collapse ; there were forces, old forces and new forces, which worked for the salvage of some of the most treasured possessions; in their turn the invaders often gloried in frenzied destruction but at times chose to preserve some of their newly acquired properties. And it is from those debris of the ancient world and from the effects of those unconcerted efforts that something has come down to the modern world which it can claim as its legacy from the Middle Ages. Those thousand years must here be considered together; we must see what they left behind them without analysing the complex process by which such results were achieved. Three principal elements were in conflict, the ancient world as embodied in the Roman Empire, Christianity which transformed and sub-verted the principles on which the Roman Empire was based, and the barbarians who came on to the scene as predestined forces of destruction.

Marks of decline were traceable in Latin culture long before the western empire collapsed, but the bulk of classical learning, in some parts of Europe at least, was almost intact at the beginning of the Middle Ages; in regions more distant from the natural centre the process of disintegration and re-elaboration had already commenced. Where the bulk of learning was intact it had altered its character; it was intact, but not truly alive, and such life as it preserved was drawn from new sources. The races which were destroying the ancient empire were stepping forward at the same time as its heirs, and they were the destroyers and the heirs of ancient culture as well as of political power.

In a way destruction meant rejuvenation, for it may be a paradox, but not so absurd a paradox as a bigoted classicist would think it, to affirm that one of the principal benefits which the Middle Ages bestowed upon the modern era was the colossal destruction of monuments and books; their integral survival would have forced the new peoples into the conscious position of pupils and their conquering energies would have been deadened.

But the lifelessness of ancient culture at the end of the classical period was produced by other causes than age and decay. It was Christianity which sapped the vitality of ancient learning and ancient institutions. Ancient learning was heathen and could not survive in its original form when the ancient beliefs were discarded. Greek and Latin became the languages of the Church and culture took refuge within the precincts of ecclesiastical buildings, Cassiodorus pointing the way; but the Christian Church soon became aware of the need officially to wage war against classical culture. Such a contradiction was not to be avoided, for the Christian Church on the one hand was forced to antagonize all that was the product of false belief, and on the other hand it was impelled to make use in this war of the weapons that classical learning provided. No one seemed to discern at first that the right direction for a victorious attack was to christianize rather than to destroy classical culture, and thus its suppression was aimed at. Much was destroyed but much also was christianized, so much in fact that it has been asserted that the function of the Middle Ages was the christianization of classical culture.

It was a period of crisis and thus a period full of crying contrasts. It saw the rise of the new world and it was fully dominated by ancient thought and traditions. Medieval men aimed in politics at a universal empire and brought about the rise of modern nations ; the languages of learning and of the Church, almost two names for the same thing at this age, was Latin, and it was at this age that a multitude of vernaculars broke through the Latin shell or took the place of Latin and stood forth as literary languages. Whether classical models were ignored, antagonized, or imitated, the result was the same. The glamour of classicism was too great to prove ineffective. To the people who hated and despised all things Latin, Rome became the centre of thought because of their hatred ; to others the glory of imperial Rome was a source of undying regret or passionate envy ; and legends arose about her. Rome loomed greater in this misty period of ignorance than she had shone in the hey-day of her glory ; but it was as different a Rome as those envious, regretful, and ambitious men were different from the rulers of the ancient world.

Everything seems so confusing and perplexing at a first glance that one well understands how the adjective ' dark ' readily occurred to those who wrote about the Middle Ages. But if one looks beyond the printed, or even the written page, and strives to call forth in one's imagination the events of those days, looking at them with the same close attention and interested uncertainty with which one needs must look upon contemporary events, things cease to be puzzling and strange. For the Middle Ages appear to possess the perplexing character of things living ; change or if one prefers a more ambitious if less accurate word, progress, did not follow then and never follows a straight course.

In literature there was an inevitable division. There was on one side the official literature, Latin, which pre-tended to continue the Latin tradition, and did continue it to a certain extent despite the intrusion of all sorts of new elements ; and on the other side there was vernacular literature, a literature which had some claim to be considered the spontaneous production of the new peoples and which truly voiced their feelings despite an increasing tendency to conform to classical models. It is precisely this twofold characteristic of vernacular literature which reveals the complexity of this epoch and gave rise to momentous movements and developments lasting well beyond the accepted boundaries of the Middle Ages.

But literature is conditioned by language, and conversely any effective statement of facts or needs or sentiments potentially is literature. It only needs a man endowed with special powers of expression to transform everyday language into a means of artistic creation. The Romans did not consider other nations their equals ; out of snobbery their intellectual classes may have learnt Greek, but as a people they carried their native language with them. Neighbours of kindred racial stock seem readily to have accepted their conqueror's tongue. Later, Etruscans and Celts yielded in the same way, and it is no wonder therefore that, when the power and glamour of Rome became greater and extended beyond the Alps and the sea, peoples more backward in civilization should offer little resistance to accepting Latin as their only or their second language when submitting to the political rule of the Romans. Even so English is now spoken by British subjects in different latitudes and of different races. But each race brings peculiarities of its own in the pronunciation and in the construction of English ; and it could be admitted *a priori* even if direct proofs were lacking, and they are not, that Latin was spoken with different inflexions by provincials, and that at a later age it was written by provincials who were unable entirely to suppress their native habits of thought. Conversely when the Roman hold upon the provinces began to slacken, this linguistic uniformity ceased to exist. Where the Roman domination had lasted longer, local Romanized dialects gradually worked themselves up to the dignity of written languages (Romance languages) ; and where the Roman mark had been stamped less deeply and new barbarians had settled in large numbers, the local languages, ancient or new, asserted their pre-eminence by consciously antagonizing the language which their previous masters or foes had spoken, while at the same time they endeavoured to adapt their own speech to the requirements of written languages on the model of Latin.

With a few exceptions, notably in Saxon England, the language used in the schools, where schools existed, was still Latin, but people used their own language in ordinary intercourse; and the number of children who were sent to school, in course of time and in most places, grew steadily less, until in most countries education became restricted to such as aimed at pursuing an ecclesiastical career. Even if able to write and speak Latin in a fashion, they were not ignorant of their own vernacular; and their own proficiency in the language of 'grammar' reacted upon their usage of vernacular, particularly when they attempted to write it.

To the tyrannical sway of Latin there succeeded a multiplicity of dialects, for there was no logical reason why one or the other of the dialects spoken by any group of individuals should be preferred, when writing, to the dialects of kindred groups. There began a struggle for pre-eminence and the ultimate victory of one or two dialects in each racial association was due to cultural as much as to linguistic and political causes.

By degrees most of these dialects crept into written records, in the form of glosses to Latin texts and legal documents, when an oath was administered to people who were ignorant of Latin or their evidence taken; but there is no proof that the earliest-written records of each single vernacular or dialect are contemporary with its earliest literary usage. The circumstances of such a usage at its inception can only be inferred. Dante in his youthful *Vita nova* faced this problem for Italian and Provençal and ventured upon a guess, which cannot now be substantiated, when he wrote: ' of these (poets) the first was moved to the writing of such verses by the wish to make himself understood of a certain lady unto whom Latin poetry was difficult.' Dante was thinking of the conditions prevailing under the later years of the feudal régime and, so far as one is able to see, he erred in the particular no less than in the general case. Who could lay down a rule as to the emotion which a man, gifted with some versifying ability, would be first prompted to express in a poem written in everyday language?

Individual peculiarities must have had as much influence as racial and group tendencies and customs. Very little is known about the earliest *winileodos* of the Germans; and the earliest specimens of love poetry in France are of so polished a type as to postulate an antecedent period of development. Above every other consideration it is necessary to bear in mind that, after the fifth century, there is no ground for assuming such uniform conditions in western Europe as had prevailed, during the period of centralized rule. Teutons and Latins lived under different conditions; and Teutons differed from Teutons, as Latins or latinized peoples differed from other groups of the same races. No doubt men were men, whether fair skinned or swarthy, but in dealing with intellectual and artistic activities one dares not to press a parallel down to the bedrock of common instincts. A rough division must be made between Teutons and Latins. The first literary attempts in the Teutonic languages need not be parallel to and due to the same process of development as the earliest attempts in the Romance languages.

The Teutons were rapidly passing from a lower to a higher stage of civilization, and they believed that their triumph was due to their valour alone; for centuries they had fought amid forests, mountains, and moors, and they had worshipped their gods; some clans had prospered, others had suffered defeat; at this time they seemed to hold the wealth and the destiny of the world in their grasp. In such conditions it is to be supposed that religious zeal, heathen at first and later Christian, clannish pride, memories of war must have gone to the creation of myths and epics, and must have found poetic expression no later than the milder passion of love.

The Romance peoples had other interests and a different fate; their culture was declining rather than developing; in Italy the new settlers kept aloof from or were rapidly assimilated by the natives, in Spain the Goths were not many and they were also assimilated, while the Arabs had a creed and a culture of their own and proved impervious to the attractions of Latin and Christian civilization. Only in Gaul the latinized inhabitants freely mixed with the conquerors. In Britain the latinization had been comparatively superficial and the invaders drove the inhabitants westwards.

On the whole the Teutonic vernaculars reached literary rank sooner than the Romance vernaculars which had no clear ground but had to conquer the competition of Latin; and thus one could assert that the medieval literature in the vernacular was, during the earlier centuries, Teutonic, that, later, the people of France added their voices to it, and that Spaniards and Italians were last into the field. Nor can one overlook the different incidence of the process of christianization. It is obvious that the advent of Christianity hastened, to say the least, the disintegration of the Roman Empire, and thus caused the Latin and latinized peoples to suffer a loss of dignity and power. On the contrary it was the conversion to Christianity which fitted the Teutons for political pre-eminence. Christian literature was mainly Latin and Greek in the old imperial lands, but among the Germanic peoples, who had but recently been converted to Christianity, it is conceivable that some of the earliest written works must have dealt with religion. Works on religion had a twofold importance: they satisfied the requirements of piety and Apostolicism, and they constituted an unconscious record of the recent evolution towards a higher civilization. Even before the Goths were urged on their westward migration their bishop Wulfila had translated the Bible for them (fourth century).

The Roman Empire was still in being, but, in the light of later events, one could scarcely imagine a more significant and menacing fact than this first introduction of a barbaric people to Christianity coinciding with the introduction of their language into the world of literature. For centuries still other Teutonic groups lived in ignorance of Christianity or resisted the efforts directed to their conversion. It is only in the days of Charlemagne that one can speak of a christianized western Europe. But meanwhile there had been a push of migration which had brought Teutonic settlers into Gaul, Britain, Scandinavia, Italy, Iberia, and North Africa; hustling the previous occupiers, intermingling and intermarrying with them, practically suppressing them or keeping them in a state of political subjection as the case may have been in the different countries. Of course, the nearer the invaders reached to the more civilized centres, and the longer their residence lasted, the quicker were their strides towards a more cultured condition. In Gaul, Iberia, Italy, the Alpine region and Dacia they were unable to withstand the powerful attraction of the Romance languages which were locally spoken and soon the new settlers lost every recollection of their original tongues. So little is known about these wordless races that it is impossible to set down definite information about the manner in which the change took place in each country. But some guess may be risked with the perilous aid of analogy. One learns from the daily press about the impressions of African potentates who visit the capitals of Europe;

if one makes some allowance for the professional picturesqueness of the recorders' style, that gives one something to go upon. But a further step is required. One must still try to imagine how such impressions would vary and be modified if these potentates were coming as conquerors. For it was precisely as restive and ambitious allies, and more often as conquerors, that the Germans came upon the glory of civilized life. They were leaving behind their old camps in the forests of central Europe, and found themselves in large cities with marble palaces, temples, monumental bridges; in their home they had depended for food upon hunting, fishing, cattle grazing, and primitive agriculture, and they were brought into contact with the amenities and comfort arising from intensive cultivation of land and organized trade. This was puzzling enough, but the contact with Rome must have required another and more arduous effort from the Germans; for they had to be inserted into the network of civilized life and to settle down among people who were vanquished, it is true, and crushed into political subjection, but who still towered above their conquerors from the height of an incomparably superior culture and of glorious traditions.

In so far as Gaul, Iberia, and Italy are concerned, ' Roma victa vicit Germaniam,' but there were degrees in the extent of this victory. Rome had produced no popular epics. The Romans were little inclined to poetic amplifications; these undaunted builders were wont to construct their epics in stone; miles and miles of paved roads, cutting straight across hills and forests, must have possessed an almost emotional appeal such as the long sequences of single rhymed lines may have had for the French. When one comes upon some conspicuous remains of Roman work, one seldom fails to be impressed by it as by something massive and almost repulsive in its single-minded forcefulness. But however this be, the Romans would sooner do things than sit around camp-fires singing the praises of their mythical heroes. They were satisfied to leave the recording to more or less partial historians. It was not so with most of the Germans. With them, on the evidence of Tacitus, epic songs were a national habit even before they began to use the Runic alphabet; theirs was probably a hero-worship strongly admixed with primitive mythology. But these songs were not written, and the later works which have been preserved were either written or modified under the influence of Christianity, as *Beowulf* or the *Hildebrandslied*. The Scop or gleeman was unknown to Roman days and could only be compared to early Greek poets. The northern myths, however disguised, penetrated into European literature and with them a new taste for epics which was to find expression in different countries : epics of war such as *Beowulf*, epics based on Germanic myths such as the *Edda* or much later the *Niebelungenlied* (end of twelfth century), and epics in some way connected with conflicts between Heathens and Christians such as the *Chanson de Roland* and to a certain extent the *Cantar de mio Cid*. And side by side with these representative poets there were epic ballads, *chansons*, *cantares*, some of which are still extant and many of which have been lost; and also historical accounts in prose and in verse in which at times the epic prevails over the historical element, such as the Anglo-Saxon *Chronicle*, the *Kaiserkronik*, or the *Cronica general* of Alphonse ' el Sabio '. Some of these legends either had from the beginning or were to receive in the distant future such poetic expression as would endow them with the gift of eternity. The *Chanson de Roland* is a thing beautiful in itself, and beautiful are *Parzival* and the *Cantar de mio Cid*, but other legends had to wait for the master touch of Ariosto and Wagner.

But not the Germanic race alone added to the store of

poetical traditions which had come down from the classical days. The medieval invaders pushed westwards but did not destroy the Celts in Britain and France, and thus they came into touch with the Breton *lais* about King Arthur and the Round Table ; *lais* which originally were or soon became differentiated from epics and stood for the essential virtues which belong to chivalry. This romantic literature, wherever it originated, became widely known in the manner in which it was elaborated in France ; for it was in France that the Latin and the barbaric elements mixed more freely, so that from the tenth to the thirteenth century France became the crucible in which the old stuff was remodelled and the new stuff shaped for the use of the contemporary world. The medieval French conception of chivalry gave the world the courtly lyrics of Provence and the passionate romances of Britain. It matters little whether or not this romantic stuff found its most perfect expression in France or elsewhere, at the beginning of the thirteenth or at the end of the fifteenth century, in Wolfram's *Parzival* or in the book of Sir Thomas Malory.

The fascination and the fashion of Arthurian romances were all-conquering during the later Middle Ages ; in France and in French and Anglo-Norman speaking countries the note of passionate love and knightly devotion was touched upon with so refined a delicacy that it is little wonder that the names of Tristram, Lancelot, Yseult, and the others became acclimatized almost everywhere. The wealth of French productions was so great that even such little jewels as *Aucassin et Nicolette* and the *lais* of Marie de France comparatively received little attention.

But Teutons and Celts were not alone in contributing fresh sources of inspiration to the new vernacular literatures. In Spain and Portugal the contact with Arabs and Orientals was immediate and lasting and their influence greatest and most widely diffused; elsewhere, in Sicily and southern Italy and on merchants, crusaders and pilgrims, it was less profound. It would be easy to emphasize unduly the importance of this element, but in Spain at any rate the century-long conflict against the Moors and their residence in the country had a good deal to do in laying the lines along which the vernacular literature developed: they may have contributed lyrical elements, according to some scholars they may also have suggested epic cycles; they certainly stamped a taste for oriental gorgeousness and complication upon language and literature such as the Alhambra realizes in stone. And when the political power of Spain was at its zenith and other literatures had become barren, this taste was accepted or arose also in other countries in the days of Baroque. Thus the earlier Middle Ages saw the glory of Teutonic literature: the rise of Teutonic epic, of Celtic romance and the fierce religious zeal of the neophites. Charlemagne, who was so important a factor in shaping the political ideals of the later Middle Ages, may be taken as a symbol. It was he who fostered the revival of classical learning and collected at the same time the old Teutonic sagas, he, a German-speaking sovereign, who was destined to become the national hero of France, he who forced the reluctant Saxons into the Christian fold and battled against the Moors of Spain. Thus he towered up in the culminating period of the earlier Middle Ages, for he summed up in himself the characteristic traits of his Teuton ancestors, strength, zeal, valour, and pride; and yet he was drawn into the sphere of classical civilization to the extent of being proud to be styled ' Roman Emperor ', and by every means in his power to foster the study of ancient culture. His object in doing so was religious as well as political, but he seems instinctively to have felt the approaching eclipse of the old Teutonic star; and just as

Boethius, on the threshold of the Middle Ages, endeavoured to save classicism from total destruction, Charlemagne, feeling that the heathen glory of the Teutons was waning, ordered that their ancient songs should be saved from impending oblivion. In a way he belonged to the Spanish as well as to the French epic cycle, and considering his leaning towards Latin culture it seems fitting that he should have been celebrated in the full glory of the Renaissance by the most classical of Italian poets, Lodovico Ariosto.

Again, as a relentless persecutor of heathendom, Charlemagne is significant. As such he won favour with the clergy. Religious literature took many forms during the Middle Ages, from the simple exposition of the *Weissenburger Katechismus* and Cædmon's *Paraphrase* to the old Saxon epic of which *Der Heliand* is a fragment (about 830) and the countless legends of Saints, translations and adaptations from Latin texts. It would be too much to credit the Middle Ages with having created and bestowed upon later periods all that is Christian in modern literature, but a good deal of it would not have been written but for the intervention of the new peoples who then acquired political importance.

The enthusiasm of neophytes was not satisfied with a direct appeal to reason ; hero-worship such as gave rise to epic, gave also rise to the legends of Saints. Brief data of Latin texts were amplified by the imagination of poets, more enthusiastic than logical, who felt the need of providing their ignorant audiences with the right kind of material ; the realistic misinterpretation of metaphoric expression, in the earlier lives of Saints, became a source of extraordinary errors and of a number of preposterous miracles ; every exuberant suggestion was translated into an exaggerated reality ; the giant Christopher became a common decoration of churches. This legendary literature left few traces in later ages, and inspired only one or two works of permanent value. From the fourth century there had existed the *Visio Sancti Pauli*, a legend describing St. Paul's rapture in the afterworld. A few centuries later the monks, and particularly the ascetic and enthusiastic Irish monks, seized upon this theme and produced a series of legends of the afterworld, from the legend of St. Patrick to that of the monk St. Brendan. These visions made a complete appeal. The realistic description of harrowing penalties inflicted upon the spirits in Hell was intended as a deterrent from sin, strong enough to impress the mind of Christians whose sensibility had been blunted by the hardships of medieval life; moreover these descriptions, horrifying as they were, answered to that strain of self-martyrization which became so common during periods of mystical emotion and brought about fastings, hermitic penances, self-fustigations, such as were practised by anchorites in the East, and by Irish monks and their continental pupils who strove after a reform in monasticism. The Last Judgement with its terrors was kept ever present to the mind of the potential sinner just as the gallows was kept in evidence in the eyes of potential criminals. Carvings and frescoes on churches were ever recalling the impending menace. The faithful, on turning to leave the churches, were forced to look upon the Last Judgement frescoed above the portals. On the other hand the people often had a hard lot to bear, men and women alike; wars, sieges, piratical invasions, famines, plagues, poverty, and sickness were more frequent and deadly than in our days. It would be absurd to describe the Middle Ages as a series of bleak years uninterrupted by a ray of sunshine; there must have been happy, gentle, tender people no doubt, but happiness was sought in the afterworld more often than it is now. The ancients had imagined a joyous period in a mythical golden age of the past; the men of the Middle Ages replied to this by their legends of the earthly Paradise and better still by their conception of the afterworld, of a Paradise and a Purgatory, so much more rich in spiritual content than the Elysian Fields of the Romans. In our days one occasionally reads of perfect happiness based on some Utopian constitution, but at best these are intellectual opinions, vague hopes, and seldom become creeds. In the Middle Ages men sought a refuge from reality in their unshakable belief in heavenly reward, and thus it became as obvious that visions should describe realistically this happy state, as that other legends should represent the horrors of damnation. In primitive days, among simple and primitive men, it was but natural that the joys of Paradise should be realistically represented so as to render the descriptions of the Christian heaven an echo of the dreams of the hungry; but there is little doubt that the world owes some of the features of two of its literary masterpieces, the *Divine Comedy* and *Paradise Lost*, to the medieval output of transcendental visions. These visions had been among the tools used by the monks who were engaged in bringing about the conversion of such among the Germans as still adhered to heathen practices, but the enjoyment of visionary works did not cease when those monks had completed their task and the unsettling migration of peoples had stopped. There were always men whose instincts turned to mysticism and who required the aid of transcendental literature. Unhappiness and ignorance were perhaps never worse than during the tenth century, and destitute and ignorant men were to be found in plenty throughout the Middle Ages. The visions describing almost materialistic heavens had a particular appeal for such sections of the population as felt keenly the desire to escape from their surrounding reality. As if to satisfy such a requirement there appeared tales about happy islands in distant seas where no rain fell, no winter existed, and food was abundant. These tales were indirectly related to the earlier transcendental visions and were not immune from oriental influence; in their literary form they seemed at times to be based on certain classical data and they constituted a parallel and a precedent for the pastoral poetry of the later Middle Ages and of the Renaissance. For pastoral poets obeyed a similar wish to escape from reality and to create for themselves a world of fancy in which peace and happiness reigned and imagination was free from the restrictions and the checks of truth. One might even argue that there are stories written in our days about distant islands in the Southern Pacific which bear some resemblance in their origin and development to these medieval prototypes.

To religious literature also the drama was due; out of the Roman liturgy, particularly of Easter Sunday, dramatic actions were developed which were transferred from the churches into the churchyards on acquiring lay elements. *Miracle Plays, Mystères, Geistliche Schauspiele, Autos Sacramentales, Sacre Rappresentazioni,* are but different names for the same thing. Until the Renaissance the drama owed nothing to the classics, and even then the influence of the Greek drama was exercised rather through dramatic theory than through direct imitation, if one ignores the painfully pedantic adaptations from Terence and Plautus. The religious drama appealed perhaps to the common people more than to the gentry; the gentry found their amusements in their castles; in court epics and lyrics. It was in lyric poetry perhaps that France showed her later medieval pre-eminence most. Classical lyrics had become stereotyped but religious lyrics acquired an ease and sincerity of sentiment which cannot be overlooked in the study of medieval psychology; particularly the cult of the Virgin Mary called forth impassioned and entrancing hymns, but all were written in Latin. In the vernacular there must have been some lyrics of a sort at all times ; Charlemagne thought it necessary to forbid nuns from receiving *winileodos*, love poems most likely, but very little is known about these primitive lyrics. Then, suddenly, about the twelfth century, when the Feudal system in some countries had become well established, there broke out in France a stream of lyric poetry so profuse, so perfect, and so varied in form that it postulates a long period of pre-paration.

Love poetry had been common among the Arabs. It had evidently existed among the Teutons, but nothing could be compared to the grandiose poetic activity of Provence. From William of Poitiers onward, for about 150 years, there was a constant output of lyrics, conventional as the Feudal civilization was conventional, which imposed itself as a model to poets in all vernaculars ; poets of Spain, of northern ·France, of England, the Minnesingers of Germany, and lastly the poets of ' stil nuovo ' in Italy. It was a fashion, a craze almost comparable to the craze for modern dances in our days ; and it was not courtly poetry alone, for there is evidence that it was far from being restricted to the halls of the gentry. The fashion spread and its diffusion was helped by the stupendous event of the Crusades with their intermingling of peoples for objects which were not only of this world.

There may be traces of oriental poetry in a love lyric of the twelfth and thirteenth centuries ; there may be realism in the poems of the Minnesinger ; there may be some new shade of naturalism in the *Owl and the Nightingale* ; there may be a new philosophic strain in the poetry of ' stil nuovo ' ; but all modern lyrics owe their origin to the extraordinary success of the Troubadours. Dante and

Petrarch set their lady loves on an altar and Goethe went back to the same idea in another form. Ronsard's, Wyatt's, and even Shakespeare's lyrics would have been different if the troubadours had not set a fashion.

All this was taking place in an atmosphere saturated with Latin traditions and habits which by degrees were also affecting the non-Latin nations. In the days of Charlemagne the French sovereign with the help of Anglo-Saxon and Irish scholars endeavoured to revive classical learning, and from the eleventh century onward a persistent effort was made in this direction. Such classical traditions were too alive and effective to be as readily christianized in the same way as the waning Teuton myths had been. A compromise was found in the Middle Ages by allegorically interpreting the works of literature and thus exploiting a device which the Alexandrine Fathers, as early as the third century, had applied to sacred texts. All that could not otherwise be explained from a Christian standpoint was interpreted allegorically; allegory became an obsession, for classical and exegetical precedents were easily found in justification of its use. Again it was France which showed the way; one simple example must suffice. It could scarcely be asserted that Ovid's *Metamorphoseon libri* has any claim to teach Christian virtues, but in France there appeared an *Ovide Moralisé* in which the allegorical device rendered easy what would have been impossible otherwise. And allegory did not spend and exhaust itself in the Middle Ages; Dante stood on the threshold of the Renaissance and was much closer to the Renaissance than is generally believed, but his poem is allegorical; Spenser was one of the leaders of the Renaissance in England, but the *Faerie Queene* is permeated with allegoricism. But allegory satisfied an intellectual habit and could only find favour with people of learning, just as the complexities of the Arthurian romances and the refinements of the later troubadours delighted the gentry. And after the earlier centuries of the Middle Ages another class began to assert itself, the 'bourgeoisie'. This middle class owed its revival in part to the strong individualism of the Germans, but still more to the advance in industry and trade; it was formed of busy and practical people who may have enjoyed, on occasions, religious and transcendental works, but who, as a rule, desired to be entertained. The routine of their daily task made them long for something different. Pilgrims and crusaders back from the East, merchants resting after distant journeys had many adventures to tell and the account of these adventures enjoyed great favour with the middle classes. Stories of adventure and travel, however, seem to spring from every soil and in every age. Homer had pointed the way, *Widsith* and the Icelandic tales and Marco Polo's *Milione* answered to the same need. But travellers, pilgrims, and crusaders interspersed their accounts with anecdotes and tales; East and West were ransacked for anything that could arouse pathos, interest, curiosity, and wonder, or excite ribald laughter. Those who stayed at home searched in classical books for that which travellers found in hearsay reports of oriental tales. A vast literature was formed of which the sources are strangely intertwined.

So long as Rome ruled, the massive uniformity of Latin had been little accessible to external influences apart from the Greek. The vernacular literatures, on the contrary, had no traditions and were readily receptive. Here again it was France which led the way, for the French, as may be seen in the *Fabliaux*, added a licence, which was not necessarily coarse, to their tales, and thus the floodgates of later medieval story-telling were opened. Finally Boccaccio and Chaucer became the models for the ages to come; they loved a good story, whatever its kind, and knew how to tell it.

There is no masterpiece in the French literature of the Middle Ages, not even the *Chanson de Roland*, which ranks with the few great masterpieces of literature; the *Roman de la Rose* is stiff compared to Dante's *Comedy*, the Arthurian romances are overshadowed by Wolfram von Eschenbach's *Parzival*; but yet it is in France that all the materials, both lasting materials and less enduring materials, for European literature were elaborated during the later part of the Middle Ages, precisely as during the first part the Teutonic strain had prevailed.

We have seen that oriental tales seem to have penetrated Europe through France or to have become acceptable to Europe after they had been touched upon in France. And the whole time from the earlier to the later Middle Ages a new national consciousness became noticeable in writers; the reign of Latin ceased when the feeling of universality had become obsolete. With the disappearance of that feeling vernacular literatures gained strength; the audiences to which poets appealed was no longer the wide world, but a comparatively restricted group of men with which each poet had a language in common. The pre-eminence of French literature was such for a time that French threatened to become a universal means of literary expression, but men rapidly turned to a more promising course; a symphony took the place of unison. Towards the end of this age the slow process of the rediscovery of classical learning ceased to be instinctive; it became conscious of its purpose. Thus the Renaissance proper began to dawn. The pendulum was swinging back. Centuries of destruction and renovation had at last provoked a reaction; and the scholars of the Renaissance became its agents and champions. Their services to learning were immense, but, as was almost inevitable, they went to the other extreme. At an earlier date an attempt had been made to destroy what was ancient;

the scholars of the Renaissance wished to suppress what was recent and insanely tried to exclude the local vernaculars from literature. They only succeeded in stunting in some countries and in disturbing in most others the normal process of literary creation in the vernacular. It was a just retribution that the works of the masters of the Renaissance, from Ariosto to Spenser and Rabelais, should be steeped in medievalism. Long before then modern literature had begun; Petrarch's lyrics were models which needed no altering to be attuned to the climate of different countries and later centuries.

Thus in the Middle Ages much was destroyed of their classical heritage, while what was not destroyed was transformed and adapted; but while destruction and adaptation went on new voices were heard; the fierce voices of the Teuton race first, then more faintly the voices of Celts and Orientals which were echoed in France and from France through the rest of Europe. Ancient lore was passed on to the modern age in a form which was almost unrecognizable, but while this heritage was rejected and suppressed by the Renaissance, the voices which were new the Renaissance was powerless to suppress.

Part of the same heritage is revealed by changes in poetic technique among which one is so representative and precious that it cannot be passed over in silence. Classical poetry had been quantitative; during the decadence of Rome the feeling for quantities gradually became weaker; in the Latin hymns of the Church quantitative and accentual verses are found for a period side by side; and then quantity disappears. The Romance vernaculars knew no quantities. Germanic verses were also based on stressed syllables, but mere numbers of syllables and sequences of stresses seemed unsatisfying to the ear; the Teutons had a liking for alliteration which has not entirely disappeared as a subsidiary adornment. Latin had known rhyme as an occasional adornment, and thus medieval writers added rhymes to quantitative verse with a grating effect.

In the end it was rhyme that triumphed. Long *laisses* of monorhymic verses at first and later the fascinating jingle of cunningly disposed rhymes, fleet as the feet of dancing youths, tinkling as silver bells, thundering as the tread of an army. More cultured ages tried to rebel against this imposition, just as the Renaissance rebelled against medievalism. But the rhyme is still with us, just as the heritage of the Middle Ages, romantic and lyrical, is still with us and together with it the countless variations and groupings of lines, from the solemn *chanso* of the Provençals, to the faceted sonnet, Ariosto's *ottava* and the Spenserian stanza, all this that we have and ancients had not, this music so soft and penetrating, many voiced and harmonious in all languages ; with which no one would like to dispense, and which is a reminder of all that is less conspicuous but not less important in the heritage that the Middle Ages have bestowed upon the literature of later days.

CESARE FOLIGNO.

iii. HANDWRITING

THE impulse to fashion signs and symbols to express ideas came late in man's development. Compared with his long sojourn on earth, his engraved and written records are things of yesterday. Yet, though his pictographs and early alphabets are of relatively recent date, they are thousands of years older than the characters with which we deal in this essay. They belong to alien civilizations, and do not concern us here. Our own letters, as is well known, go back to the Latins, who got them from the Greek colonists in Italy; who in turn borrowed them from the Phoenicians. But the particular forms of letters employed to-day both in writing and printing are not a direct inheritance from Rome; they are rather the creation of the centuries which transmitted, and in transmitting modified, that inheritance. They are, in short, the legacy of the Middle Ages.

While writing was establishing itself in the economy of man's life as the normal vehicle by which religious, legal, political, or literary traditions could be handed on, various questions of form inevitably arose. The answers to those questions became the laws of a new art. It is only by realizing that writing was an art, subject to rules and regulations and not a thing at the mercy of individual whim, that one can properly understand the history of writing. Calligraphy is distinguished by harmony of style. It is conscious of the methods by which it gets its results. Its forms are definite. If the art of writing was one of the latest of man's achievements, it was also one of the slowest in developing. Being itself an instrument of conservation, it was in the nature of things extremely conservative. Painting, sculpture, literature, and even architecture change more from age to age than does writing. Once a type had found favour, it was apt to last for centuries. Thus we know that uncial and half-uncial scripts—the scripts in use when St. Jerome was revising and translating the Bible for Pope Damasus, the script in which our oldest texts of the Bible were written—lasted for five whole centuries; and the same long life may be surmised for Capitalis Rustica, the script with which Tacitus, Trajan, Pliny, must have been familiar, the script of our oldest extant manuscripts of Plautus, Terence, Virgil, Sallust, Cicero, Persius, Juvenal; the script too which engravers of the second century had begun using for inscriptions alongside of the older and more suitable Capitalis Quadrata. Other scripts, which came into being after the barbarian invasions, like the Beneventan in South Italy, the Visigothic in Spain, also lasted five hundred years each. The Irish script lasted even longer. If other minuscule scripts were cut short in their career, like the cursive types of north Italy, the Merovingian types in France, and the Anglo-Saxon script, there were in each case extraordinary historic events to account for the fact. For, though scripts seem to move down the ages with the majestic slowness of glaciers, they are not mere carriers or external instruments, but genuine manifestations of their age, bearing the marks of its vicissitudes. Thus writing, which is primarily but the humble medium for recording the deeds, thoughts, and interests of an age, by dint of being itself an art, becomes at once an expression and a register of the spirit which informs that age. Herein lies the peculiar interest that writing has for the student of culture in general.

The history of writing is so intimately bound up with the history of the book as to be inseparable from it. It was in the copying of books that handwriting found its main expression as an art. It is with the writing found in books, then, that we are chiefly concerned in what follows.

If we examine our legacy in the matter of writing, we notice that, with the exception of Greece, Armenia, and the lands of orthodox Slavs, the Latin alphabet is used in all the countries of western civilization, and wherever that civilization penetrates beyond the Occident. The various forms of the Latin letters used to-day in printing and writing are, broadly speaking, of two kinds : the round or Roman, like the type of this page, and the pointed or so-called Gothic, which we call black-letter type. The Roman type is the normal one everywhere outside of Germany and Austria, where Gothic characters are still used extensively, though by no means exclusively. In still using the Gothic type the Germans are merely showing themselves more conservative than we are. They are preserving a tradition that has lived for over eight centuries. If we, on the other hand, read and write the clear, round, Roman type we have the Italian humanists of the fifteenth century to thank for it. For it was they who first broke with a venerable tradition by discarding the Gothic script which all Europe had been writing since the thirteenth century. Italy's example was soon followed by France, Holland, and then by England, all during the sixteenth century. It was only in the nine-teenth century that the Scandinavian countries and Den-mark gave up the use of the Gothic script. To-day Germany and German Austria are alone in clinging to the pointed black-letter style, though they use it mainly in their text-books and books of belles-lettres and devotion.

The script the Italian humanists introduced was not a creation of their own. It was not a new script at all. It was only a revival. Their passion for the classics brought in its wake an abhorrence of everything Gothic, which came to be a synonym for barbaric. A substitute for the Gothic script had to be found. It was indeed found, as if made to order, in those very manuscripts of the classics for which the libraries of Europe were then being eagerly and diligently ransacked. It so happens that the great majority of the classics are written in the Carolingian minuscule of the ninth and tenth centuries. The clear, round, and comely characters of this script were to the humanist's eye the very antithesis of the Gothic. They fitted in admirably with his notion of a *scriptura antiqua*, a *scriptura Romana*. Thus the humanistic minuscule came into being. It was a conscious work of resuscitation achieved by a small band of men like Poggio, Niccolò Niccoli, Traversari, and their zealous followers. Petrarch was still Gothic-bound, though his hand is one of the clearest, for Italian Gothic never lost all the good features of its Caroline progenitor. Once launched the success of the humanistic script was assured. History repeated itself. The fitter script survived. Just as in the ninth century the Caroline minuscule drove many rivals from the field, so the humanistic minuscule was destined to triumph over its competitors. The countries with a strongly established Latin culture, Italy, France, Spain, were naturally the first to succumb to the fascination of the type which had such manifest beauty of form, and which purported to go back to the Romans. The northern countries, especially those that were never properly Romanized, and as a result of the Reformation came to feel a natural antagonism to things Roman, were slowest to adopt the new, so-called 'Roman' script, despite its obvious advantages. In Germany the process of Romanization was still further retarded by the false doctrine that Gothic was her national script, to cherish which was an act of patriotism. In reality, as we shall see, Gothic, which had been the script of all Europe, is nothing but a later development of the Caroline minuscule.

What is this Caroline minuscule which the Humanists

revived, and which became the basis of our script? How ancient is it? Where did it arise? What are its antecedents? Is it a unique phenomenon or part of a general movement? Did it originate in Rome, as some claim, or in France? Perhaps the best way of answering these questions would be to look back and examine the period immediately preceding the birth of minuscule, and follow its rise in the various centres of Europe. It is indispensable to take this rather extensive survey, for only by understanding the history of minuscule script can we gain an understanding of what was distinctive in the legacy of the Middle Ages.

For several centuries after the break-up of the Roman Empire scribes had been content to copy their Bibles, Missals, Jeromes, and Augustines, as well as their Livys, Ovids, and Juvenals, in uncial and half-uncial letters, that is, in those two book scripts, whose obscure origins go back to the fourth or even third centuries, and whose period of greatness falls in the fifth century for uncials and in the sixth for half-uncials. The notaries, public or private, no longer used the cursive formed by straight strokes, the everyday script known to Cicero, Seneca, or Suetonius, whose tablets would have been unintelligible to men of the fifth century; but a new cursive composed of curved strokes and of a new type of ligature; the beginnings of which we can trace back to the fourth century, and the importance of which lies in the fact that it became in time the basis of several calligraphic scripts. After the sixth century we become aware of a gradual deterioration. No real works of art, no literature to speak of, appears for several generations. Spelling begins to grow corrupt, the old scripts become more artificial. The old discipline is going. Traditions are breaking down or altogether dying out. But the torpor consequent upon the bankruptcy of the old

world, and confusion resulting from the migration of the
Germanic nations and incessant wars, were not to last for
ever. New life-forces begin to stir by the beginning of the
eighth century. The foundations of a new Europe are to
be laid in that century. It is during this period that new
scripts begin to make their shy appearance. This is noticeable, not in one country only, but in nearly all, in Greek- as
well as in Latin-writing countries—a clear indication that
it was the result of a general condition.

By then the book trade, it must be remembered, had been
dead for centuries. The scribes were no longer hired men,
paid by author or publisher, but clerics and monks, who
worked for the Church, whether they copied books for
choir, parish school, or monastic library. Not only was
there a distinct change in the kind of book copied, there
was as great a change in the conditions of work, in its motives
and rewards. This was already the case in the sixth century,
as we gather from Cassiodorus' avowal that he feels ' of all
bodily tasks a perhaps not unjust preference for the work
of scribes (provided they copy accurately), since by reading
and re-reading Holy Scripture they gain wholesome mental
instruction, and by copying the precepts of the Lord they
help to disseminate them far and wide '. Here the scribes'
rewards, we see, are intellectual and spiritual ; the books
to be copied are religious. Cassiodorus loves this theme of
the scribe, and continues characteristically thus : ' What
happy application, what praiseworthy industry, to preach
unto men by means of the hand, to untie the tongues by
means of the fingers, to bring quiet and salvation to mortals,
and fight the Devil's insidious wiles with pen and ink ! For
every word of the Lord which is copied deals Satan a wound.
Thus, though seated in one spot, the scribe traverses diverse
lands through the dissemination of what he has written.'
These words describe an atmosphere and attitude utterly

foreign to the old Roman spirit. We are moving in a new world. And who would suspect these words of coming from a veteran politician ? It was after a busy public career, as Chancellor of Theodoric and his successors that Cassiodorus retired, in his ripe old age, to his estate in Squillace in the extreme end of Italy, there to pass the end of his days in reading and writing. Although his interest, as we have seen, was mainly religious and his concern with Holy Scripture, he had many books of secular learning in his library, of which we are unusually well informed, and he explicitly recommends his monks to use them and copy them. From the rules of orthography and grammar which he lays down we can measure how low learning had already sunk by that time. Although he stands with his face averted from the ancient Roman past, the first man of letters, as it were, to step into the Middle Ages, as Petrarch may be said to be the first to step out of them—he is justly praised as the man whose zeal in the cause of letters has been largely responsible for the preservation of learning. For Cassiodorus lived and wrote at a critical moment, and it is safe to say that but for him, Petrarch and his fellow humanists would have had far fewer classics to revive, and the history of writing might have been very different from what it is. But the renaissance of the fourteenth and fifteenth centuries was preceded by another renaissance which, though less brilliant, is of the greatest importance for classical learning and all-important, as we shall see, for the future of handwriting—I mean the Carolingian renaissance, when learning and the arts were once more pursued with vigour and zeal. Stir and movement were in fact evident for many decades before the reign of Charlemagne, as our manuscripts amply attest. During the whole of the eighth century we encounter on all sides earnest attempts at new forms of writing.

The old scripts evidently no longer answered to the needs of the times. The conditions for forming a new script, however, and the necessity for doing so, were not everywhere the same. It may be presumed that conditions were least propitious in Rome, the stronghold of the ancient majuscules. They must have been most favourable in those centres where the force of ancient traditions was felt least, where new experiments would receive the greatest encouragement.

The reasons why the old majuscule scripts had outlived their usefulness were varied and complex. For one thing, economic causes must have contributed to the disappearance of the more stately rustic, uncial and half-uncial scripts. The times of a plentiful supply of papyrus were no more. By the eighth century, a papyrus codex was the exception. Vellum and parchment were the rule. But animal skins were at all times expensive, and they must have been doubly difficult to procure after the disorganization resulting from devastating wars. Thus the supply of membranes could hardly keep pace with the demand, especially in centres where many books were copied. The exercise of economy became a necessity, and necessity is the mother of invention. The obvious way of saving vellum was to write more on a page. One way of getting more on a page was to make narrow instead of broad letters, to write a smaller script, in short, to use minuscule. It is this forced economy which made the Irish, probably an impecunious race even in the seventh and eighth centuries, squeeze more writing into a page than a decent regard for the reader's convenience would warrant, or good taste dictate. By writing a tiny, crowded script, by using subscript letters, and above all by abbreviating nearly every second word, they managed to get all that was humanly possible out of the available skins. And it is perhaps not a mere coincidence that the two centres from whence come most of our Latin palimpsests

AVIDEVSILLIXIALISHOMINVMMITESCERIDISCAT
IAMNEQ·AAIMDATADESPRVSVAINECCXAMINABIS
IPSAETIACENTIPSAERVASVSAICONCIDITESILVAE
NONILLVMNOSTAIPOSSVNTAIVIARELABORES·

PETRVSAPOSTOIVSIHV XPI
ELECTISADVENISDISPER
SIONIS·PONTICALATIAE
CAPPADOCIAE·ASIAEETBY
THYNIAE· SECVNDVM
PRAESCIENTIADI·PATRIS
INSCIFICATIONEMSPS··

quiapopuliuelleadōest
arbitriuoluntasquodadōsit
quodcumiran ·atidisimusc iar aliberati
Inamdiexconsuetudinelocua
dictaintellexi

TVNCTVADICTVADFVTVRE
SEPTIANELIOESPPRECAI
NEQVIORESSECTIN
TRANITETHABITANT
IBICTSIVNTNOVISSI
MAHOMINIRILLIVSPE
IORAPRIORIBVSSIC
ERITCGENERATIONI

25. *a.* Capitalis Rustica; *b.* Uncial; *c.* Half-uncial; *d.* Quarter-uncial

are both Irish foundations. How thoroughly the lesson of thrift had been inculcated in the followers of St. Columban and St. Gall, and how badly in need they were of writing material in the seventh and eighth centuries, may be surmised from the frequency with which the monks of St. Gall and Bobbio made use of membranes that had already been written upon. It was not out of contempt for the classics that Cicero's *De Republica*, Fronto's letters, Lucan and Juvenal were erased—for biblical and patristic texts suffered a similar fate—but out of sheer need of writing material.

Another reason why new book-scripts were emerging was the gradual dying off of the scribes who knew how to write the old ones. For one person capable of writing good uncial or half-uncial there must have been half a dozen who could write the everyday hand, the cursive of the notary. And if the single scribe of a community failed to train and educate a successor, calligraphic tradition naturally died out in that locality. This doubtless happened in many places during the invasions and other disturbances so fatal to the continuity of tradition, and thus generations grew up ignorant of the methods and manners of the old calligraphy. Yet communities which could not boast of a scribe might still have a notary, or some one who knew how to write down wills, conveyances, or other contracts. Wherever the Roman legions went there Rome's legal and administrative institutions followed. And the normal medium for recording legal transactions was the cursive script. Thus cursive was the *scriptura franca*, as it were, of the Roman Empire. Cursive remained even where calligraphy was lost. Cursive script is to calligraphy what dialect is to literary diction. It has a rank vigour and protean potentiality denied to calligraphy. It was out of the dialects of the Roman soldier and the peasant that the Romance tongues were evolved. Similarly it was out of the cursive hand that new book-scripts sprang up in many districts. New life was needed in calligraphy. It came, as it usually does, from lower forms. For scripts, like populations, recruit chiefly from below.

There was one other important source out of which a new and economical script could be extracted. The best-known script of the early Middle Ages, next to cursive, must have been the half-uncial. It is itself an example of a calligraphic script formed by promoting cursive elements to a higher state. Conscious of its lowlier origin this script was less pretentious than the uncial, and having less dignity to maintain could without incongruity be written quite small and thus be used to make cheaper books. The small-type of half-uncial, thus produced, to which Traube (I dare say jestingly) gave the name of ' quarter-uncial ', has the size and almost the form of minuscule, and, like minuscule, is written on the four-line principle, with the descending and ascending letters touching the first and fourth lines respectively. It differs from minuscule, to be sure, in the general effect, in that indescribable something, that bloom, which separates a fifth-century manuscript from an eighth. When the majuscule scripts no longer managed to hold their own, this small type of half-uncial, which existed in France as well as Italy, became, after slight modification due to the impact of cursive and uncial models, an obvious candidate for their place. How very successful a candidate it was one sees when one considers the fate of the Caroline minuscule. But it must not be thought that medieval scribes failed to realize, as some modern scholars do, that minuscule and half-uncial were two different scripts. To a ninth-century calligrapher a half-uncial manuscript, like the Basilican Hilary of the year 509, was written in majuscule characters and, as such, belonged to another and higher category than the script in which he was accustomed to

26. IRISH AND ENGLISH MAJUSCULE SCRIPTS

a. The Book of Kells;   *b.* Lindisfarne Gospels

copy books. The ninth-century manuscripts written by
the scribes of Tours prove that conclusively. And no one
in that century can be said to be more conscious of the
correct 'hierarchy' of scripts than the monks of St. Martin's
at Tours.

The half-uncial and cursive scripts, then, must have been
the common material everywhere ready to hand to serve
as the basis of new scripts. How variously the basic ingredients were combined is seen from the divergent types which
arose in the early Middle Ages.

The medieval contribution to writing, *par excellence*, is the
minuscule. It took different forms in different countries,
the most unusual developments coming from the outlying
lands. Nations situated remote from Rome, and consequently less bound by her traditions, could give free play
to native bent and strike out on lines of their own. This
happened in the British Isles. The centuries between
Gregory the Great and Charlemagne, which on the Continent were the darkest of the Middle Ages, were for Ireland
a period of brilliant activity. Left to herself undisturbed
for generations, she developed a monasticism and a liturgy
of her own, with distinct Gallican traces, but very unlike
Rome's ; and being outside the general current she retained
the antiquated mode of fixing Easter Sunday. What is of
importance to us here, she developed a variety of Latin
script, all her own, and her own characteristic system of
abbreviation. The efforts of her missionaries in time
extended beyond her own shores to Gaul, to the Alps,
Italy, Germany, as the Irish foundations of Luxeuil, St. Gall,
Bobbio, St. Kilian's testify. By way of Iona Irish teachers
reach England and penetrate as far east as Jarrow. Willibrord, Aldhelm, Bede, sit at the feet of Celtic masters. These
facts are in our histories. But they are also writ large on

the face of our manuscripts. ' Show me how you write and I'll tell you who your teacher was,' was profoundly true of the early Middle Ages. The oldest manuscripts of England are so like the Irish as to seem identical. This fact speaks volumes. To realize the fundamental character of England's indebtedness to Ireland in educational matters in the early period, we need only consider these simple facts : the manuscripts read and copied during the four centuries of Roman occupation, assuming that they were not lost or destroyed after the Germanic conquerors settled the island, must have been in ' capitalis rustica ', or in uncials. The books England received with the great missions from Rome under St. Augustine and under Hadrian and Theodore, and those sent by Pope Gregory in 601, must have been mainly in ' littera Romana ', or uncials. For the copy of the Gospels which tradition connects with St. Augustine's mission—it is now preserved at Corpus Christi College, Cambridge—is in uncial script, and the script justifies the tradition in point of age. Some of England's oldest charters (from south England) and her earliest dated biblical manuscripts (from north England)—I refer to the Cotton charters in the British Museum and to Ceolfrid's Bible now known as the Codex Amiatinus, and the Stonyhurst Gospel of St. John—are in the uncial hand. For all that, Rome's example was not strong enough to counteract the nearer influence of the Celtic teachers. For the predominant script of England, that which became her national script, is the script she learned from Ireland and not from Rome. At the Council of Whitby, the conflict between the Roman and the Celtic liturgy ended in a victory for Rome. The less dramatic conflict, however, between the two scripts, ended in a victory for the Celts.

To Ireland belongs the credit of having been the first to develop a minuscule in the true sense of the word. In the

27. BANGOR ANTIPHONARY. IRISH MINUSCULE

et nobis nat̄ ap̄os simonis cannane & simonis zelotur qui a
templorum portantibus occisi sunt insuanis cruт̃ p̄b·sarum

A 1 Ianuarius d̄ ḡpax

urbis praefec̄ cum dicaret hodie octauiae dic̄ caeli sunt
cessare usupб· sacionb: idolonum & sacruficis pullurs a
gladiatonibus hac dicaasa occisus est· Inonibиs stefani
in bononia τau ісta h̄cach· Inaffni uiconir pelicis narcissi
airgini & dationū iiii· papa priman̄ sacau̇rnini E sacau̇rnini uicto
honorata leuis h̄smcas   E militē xxx·
flaubt d̄b̄os scr̄ faubu cum p̄b· suis· agustoduno d̄poratsruprrani ḡfi

28. MARTYROLOGY OF ST. WILLIBRORD. ANGLO-SAXON MINUSCULE

Bangor Antiphonary, written between 680 and 691 (it is now in the Ambrosiana at Milan), we have an example of fully developed minuscule, with punctuation, separation of words and initials—all that we associate with minuscule. We are probably not far from the truth if we assume that the beginnings of this script go still farther back. But before developing a minuscule Irish calligraphers had created a majuscule, the Irish half-uncial as it is styled, of which the Book of Kells, a work of unsurpassed skill and artistry, is the most eminent example. We are still in the dark as to the appearance of the first Bibles and books of devotion which taught the Irish their letters and Christianity. We infer that they were not written in uncial characters, since Irish scribes seem utterly ignorant of this ancient type; but there is good ground for thinking that they were written in half-uncials, since Irish œ and ꞩ could only have come from a half-uncial alphabet. The particular type of half-uncial which served as a model must have come by way of Gaul. It has certain uncial admixtures not found in the canonical half-uncial of Italy, which, to judge by its early dated examples, must have attained its full development during the fifth century. As the province lagged behind the mother-land, there is nothing inherently improbable in the supposition that a half-uncial type, with numerous uncial adhesions, was still largely in vogue in Gaul in the first half of the fifth century. The evidence of palaeography would seem to confirm the testimony of hagiography, both as to the period and the instrument of Ireland's conversion.

The English were apt pupils. In fact they improved upon their masters. For all its similarity to the Irish the English script is different. It is less bizarre, clearer and less crowded. Like the Irish, the English had both a majuscule and minuscule script. The Lindisfarne Gospels is the

English calligraphic counterpart to the Book of Kells. It is a book of rare beauty and superb craftsmanship. And in St. Willibrord's Calendar and Martyrology, which was written between 703 and 721, we possess an early example of English minuscule to match the Bangor Antiphonary. The high degree of excellence attained in this manuscript presupposes earlier stages and less perfect attempts, so that the beginnings of the Anglo-Saxon minuscule must go back well into the seventh ceutury. Wherever the English and Irish went, there their books went with them. Their manuscripts are to be seen to this day at Saint Gall, Fulda, and Würzburg; and were to be seen at Bobbio, Corbie, Tours, Epternach, and elsewhere, before the monastic libraries were dispersed. But the English and Irish took not only their books but also their script with them. They teach it wherever they settle, and many are the books written by their continental pupils. Yet after a few generations, the Insular scripts yield to the influence of continental scripts, which finally supplant them. The Insular scripts, though first in the minuscule race, did not possess the cardinal virtue of clearness which distinguished the minuscule that eventually won the day.

Another country which early evolved a successful minuscule was Spain. And again, geographical position was largely responsible for the fact; the enormous vogue enjoyed by the works of Isidore Bishop of Seville must, however, have been an important contributing cause. During the whole of the seventh century, until Bede's writings began to circulate, Isidore's primacy was undisputed. His Etymologies was the most studied text-book of Europe, until it was supplanted in the ninth century by the encyclopaedia of Rabanus Maurus. The Saracen invasion indirectly helped the spread of Spanish learning. Spanish scholars migrated, and examples of the Spanish

29. VISIGOTHIC SCRIPT

script reached Italy and Gaul. The Orationale Mozara-
bicum, now at Verona, must have reached Italy before 732.
It is written in fully developed Visigothic minuscule, with
perhaps a greater mixture of cursive elements than is permitted later. Scribes of Vercelli, Pisa, Lucca, Monte
Cassino, of Fleury, Autun, Lyons, and Corbie, and scribes
of centres which we cannot fix, came into contact with
Visigothic scribes and methods, as chronicles and extant
manuscripts attest. The Visigothic minuscule derives in
the main from the half-uncial, supplemented by a few
cursive elements (chiefly ligatures with *t*). The half-
uncial which served as model was the one that has the
uncial form of *g*; which may have been the prevalent type
in Spain. This uncial *g* in the midst of minuscule letters,
which is a Visigothic peculiarity, could hardly have come
from any other source. Visigothic minuscule is neat, self-
possessed, restrained, but not easy to read. The similarity
between *a* and *u* is confusing. The form of *t*, as in the
Beneventan, is a stumbling-block. Like the Beneventan,
it follows the even tenor of its way for five centuries,
undisturbed. It took an ecclesiastical council to suppress it.
It is noteworthy that the script which was to supersede the
' Littera Toletana ', as Spanish minuscule was called, was
designated at the council as Gallic, not as Roman ; just as
in South Italy scripts not Beneventan were described as
Gallic or French—showing that in the late Middle Ages the
ordinary minuscule of Europe was regarded as French.

The first calligraphic minuscule frankly derived from
local cursive was a French achievement—the minuscule
now known rightly or wrongly as the ' Luxeuil ' type.
In saying this I have not forgotten early Italian attempts
like the Josephus on papyrus, of the Ambrosiana, or Saint
Jerome's *De viris illustribus*, of Vercelli, or their French
counterpart represented by the St. Avitus on papyrus.

These are worthy efforts marking a stage between cursive and minuscule, but they do not attain to the level of calligraphy. St. Columban, who founded the monastery of Luxeuil, did not stay there long, and he probably took his best teachers with him when he was expelled from France. For it is a curious fact that Irish manuscripts have not reached us by way of Luxeuil, and the earliest extant manuscript from Luxeuil shows no trace of Irish influence. The Homilies of St. Augustine, written in the year 669, in French uncials (it is now at the Pierpont Morgan library) contains not a single Irish abbreviation, nor any other Insular 'symptom'. The same is true of the eighth-century manuscripts in the so-called Luxeuil minuscule. But it is not improbable that contact with the Irish, who, as we have seen, must have been in possession of a minuscule as early as the first half of the seventh century, first familiarized the French calligrapher with the idea of a minuscule script. At any rate, the ' Luxeuil ' type is not merely an amateur attempt at writing Merovingian cursive in more or less orderly fashion. It is not one of those abortive efforts of which the eighth century witnessed many, especially in Italy. It has the expert flow of line, the finish and distinction, of a perfectly well-defined type, with a style of capitals for colophon quite its own, and characteristic initials possessing a grace of form and gaiety of colour hitherto unknown in Latin calligraphy. Although short-lived, it found favour far and wide in France and even beyond the Alps. Examples of this type exist to this day at Ivrea and Verona. North Italian scribes were manifestly charmed by the type, for they try to imitate it. It is quite possible that French scribes acted as teachers in Italy. In any case, the compliment paid the type in the attempted imitations is significant. It indicates the direction of the literary and artistic currents of the time, and is thus not without some

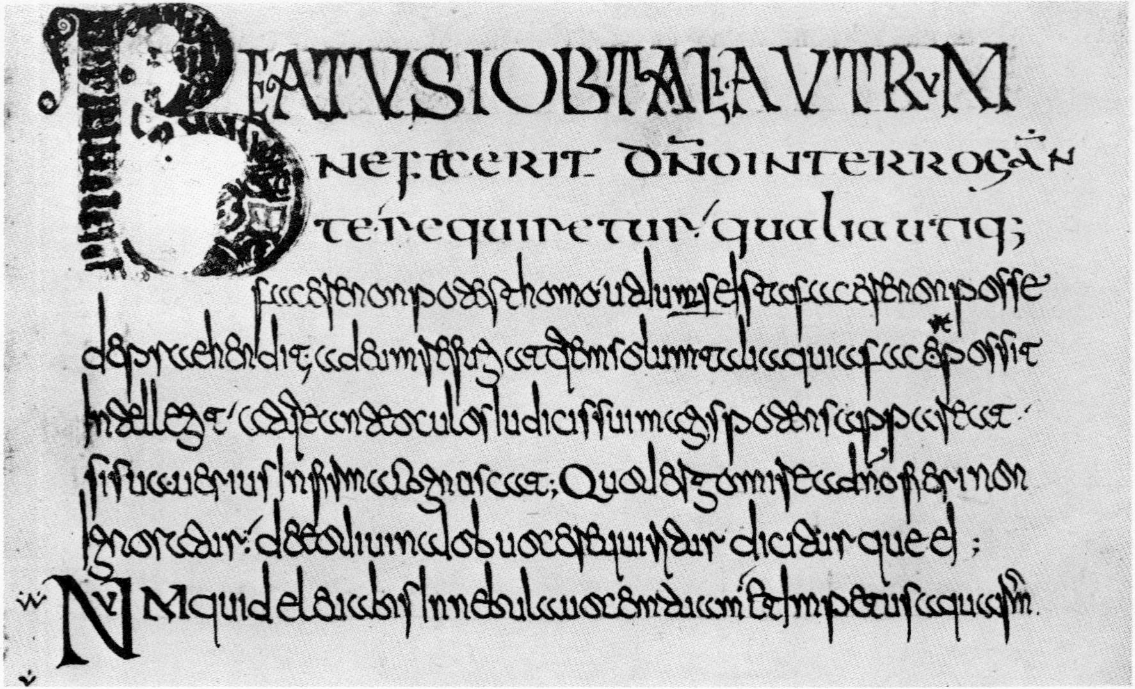

30. 'LUXEUIL' TYPE

31. 'CORBIE' *a–b* type

bearing on the general question of the origin of the Caroline minuscule.

At Bobbio, St. Columban's Italian foundation, we find a totally different state of things. Irish tradition survived into the eighth century. The old manuscripts brought from Ireland are preserved, and later generations imitate them in both script and abbreviations. But in time native traditions reassert themselves, and during the eighth century numerous attempts are made to form a minuscule, out of local cursive, or out of half-uncial, or out of mixed material, the most successful of which are the types based on cursive. By the middle of the eighth century no distinctive type had been achieved. So that when Abbot Anastasius (*c.* 750) ordered a copy of Gregory's *Moralia*, it was written for him not in minuscule but in uncial. The uncials are of an awkward, debased type, and the initials, in which the human head and hands play a large part, are not works of art. It is a far cry from the expert writing and charming initials found in manuscripts of the so-called Luxeuil type written some decades earlier. Owing to the ancient manuscripts which Bobbio has preserved for posterity, there is a tendency to exaggerate its importance as a school of writing. In the eighth century its influence must have been negligible : as a matter of fact, there are clear indications that it was somewhat under the influence of French schools. Unimportant too must have been the position of the more ancient centre of Verona. It had had a glorious past. It still has incomparably the richest collection of ancient uncial and half-uncial manuscripts, written in its own scriptoria. But it did not manage to hammer out a minuscule of its own. It tried and tried. But the attempts based on cursive, as well as those based on half-uncial, remained mere essays. Its scribes possessed so little originality that they attempted to imitate French models, which had probably reached them either from Reichenau or by way of Bobbio. When finally, in the ninth century, they succeeded in developing a minuscule, it was of the Caroline type, recalling vaguely the St. Gall and Reichenau variety. We know that their bishops Egino (†799) and Rothaldus (†840) had close relations with Reichenau. Archdeacon Pacificus (†840), through whom many new books came to Verona, was in touch with Corbie. Less well-known centres, like Vercelli and Novara, are far more successful than Verona. By the end of the eighth or in the early ninth century they are in possession of a well-developed minuscule based entirely on cursive, like the Beneventan. Their career, however, was cut short by the Caroline minuscule during the first half of the ninth century.

In central Italy, long after beautiful minuscule was being written in French centres, we encounter a pathetic example of scribal incompetence in the celebrated *Liber Pontificalis* of Lucca, written about the year 800. A scriptorium which countenanced such a hodge-podge of scripts, with uncial, half-uncial, and imitation Visigothic jostling elbows, had no standards, and was too backward to influence the course of writing. If Rome is the mother of the Caroline minuscule, as some palaeographers would have it, it is hard to reconcile the recalcitrant calligraphy of near-by Lucca with the exemplary performances of Corbie and Tours. But of the part played by Rome more will be said presently. In South Italy we have the great abbey of Monte Cassino, the mother house of western monasticism, and ancient centres like Capua and Naples. There too the universal need of a minuscule was felt, and by the middle of the eighth century a tentative script was formed out of the cursive. For a generation or two there existed some uncertainty and indecision, but after that we find strict conformity to a con-

leuauit bum oftenfignaur · coppuf maxty ēcessu ̄ auellana
moritur
Nungaauiq; claudio epulaucy pedyste messer
liner̄ · ̄ndistincato suar orialienar manui · nte
ille quessiuiar · popoferaq; poculu ̄ explicar con
uiuio celebraenar · uestuacts qpēdieb; adii ·
gaudii ·lge ·ayistage· ulliusderaq; humani
oessecaus signardedicar · ̄ncu ̄leaumaes arceusar
oxpes oessicespa · ̄ncufilios messeuaes· Juuiaq;
oblsuione ̄ t ̄stractus · ceasendo nom ̄ oeffsgus
ptyuacus oepubliesf loens demonstrandes · deestaar niath
nxepessdqueestopx lnsigniar · leaussimi fexshdysty·
Cuis pellauiar ̄ steaullystar oxgepe ·honestargde ·
ab;
sed oxegs deaptmar ouepenar aystyeps muleas· :,

Corneli: atreicy Liber
VnDecim; EXP. Incip.XII
EDE MESSALINE.

conuulsa pncipis dom; opaoerpud
ybeaaos ceparmine qsdelygepe·
uxore claudio celibis uiae lnaonaenar ·steluoui

sciously adopted style: the South Italian schools had found the type which suited them; and for half a thousand years their peculiar script which we call Beneventan reigned practically supreme in the lower half of the Italian peninsula. It is the one medieval script of purely cursive origin that boasted a long life. Its success in holding its own against the Caroline minuscule shows that the reform emanating from beyond the Alps did not have sufficient force to counteract the predominant influence of Monte Cassino. It is a script difficult to read; but for all that it is one of the remarkable achievements of the Middle Ages—both as to calligraphy and ornamentation. By the end of the thirteenth century it yielded to the ordinary minuscule of the rest of Europe.

Having mentioned Luxeuil and Bobbio, the foundations of St. Columban, one must not quite pass over St. Gall, the Irish foundation named after Gallus, one of St. Columban's followers. It became a great centre of learning; and as at Bobbio, we find here a considerable number of ancient Irish manuscripts and some palimpsests. Very little is known of what happened there during the seventh century, but by the middle of the eighth we have a definite attempt at a local minuscule, not based on cursive. Winithar, notary and scribe, and expert at neither job, has left us a number of his performances. The advantage of their Irish tradition may account for the fact that the monks of St. Gall were in advance of other Teuton centres. They cannot be said to have attained a successful minuscule of their own before the ninth century. It is not unlike the Caroline, except that it has a certain characteristic breadth and weightiness, allows the use of the *ri*-ligature, and shows a characteristic weakness for the *nt*-ligature, even in the middle of a word. The same type of minuscule was practised at Reichenau, the celebrated abbey on the Lake of Constance, with which

St. Gall had the very closest relations; and the influence of the St. Gall-Reichenau school extended beyond its immediate vicinity. But there were other Teutonic centres which ventured upon different lines; and many of these show as their common feature a dependence upon Insular models. The Germanic peoples as such made no new contribution to handwriting.

This survey of the critical period in the formation of minuscule scripts will fitly close with mention of the particular type which was destined to play the important role in the subsequent history of writing. I mean, of course, the Caroline minuscule. The origin of this script is still in dispute; it is my belief that its home was not Italy, but yet a land whose ties with Rome and ancient Italian traditions had never been severed. Manuscripts still exist which show that in centres like Lyons, Autun, Tours, Luxeuil, Corbie, and Fleury, the ancient Italian scripts—uncial and half-uncial—had been practised with signal success at the very time when Italy was at its lowest. We have already seen that France was the first country on the Continent to develop a minuscule based on cursive, and that this script which goes by the name of Luxeuil (but which was probably at home in quite other centres) possessed such charm and originality that it influenced Italian scribes—a significant fact which suggests the superiority of Gallic over Italian scribes of that period. The Luxeuil type was the ancestor of the so-called Corbie type—a bolder, more rigid, and more legible minuscule which still bore traces of cursive. This strongly conventionalized script, which also goes by the name of the *ab* type, soon won favour with various centres of north France and lasted into the ninth century. It was at the same monastery of Corbie, and while the *ab* type was being successfully practised in that region, that scribes were trying to evolve a minuscule, based in the main on

33. MAURDRAMNUS BIBLE (CORBIE). EARLY CAROLINE MINUSCULE

racione x̄i ducet.
X̄pī autem gene
racio sic erat
Cum ess& desponsata
mater eius maria
ioseph. Antequam
conuenirent inuen
ta est inutero ha
bens despu sc̄o.
Ioseph autem uir
eius cum ess& iustus
et noll& eam tra

cam et ad̄no per
prophetam dicente
Ecce uirgo inutero
habebit & pari&
filium. & uocabunt
nomen eius emma
nuel. quod est in
terpretatum
nobiscum d̄r.,
Exsurgens autem
ioseph asomno. fec&
sicut precepit ei

34. ADA GOSPELS. EARLY CAROLINE MINUSCULE

half-uncial and free from cursive elements. Similar efforts were doubtless made in other French centres, but the first dated example of the new minuscule we call Caroline comes in fact from Corbie. I refer to the famous Bible written for Abbot Maurdramnus (†778), which is preserved in several volumes at Amiens. The next very early example is the still more famous Lectionary of Charlemagne, of the year 781. The manuscript itself is written on purple parchment, in large uncial letters; but its scribe, Godesscalc, added a page of dedicatory verses, not in uncials, but in minuscule characters which we are accustomed to regard as Caroline. We do not know the exact atelier whence issued this beautiful volume. It is generally assumed to be the work of the 'Palace school'. Wherever it came from, it demonstrates that as early as 781 a beautifully formed minuscule existed, and that a specimen of it was considered worthy of being included in a book meant for the Emperor. Closely allied to this script of Godesscalc is that of the Ada Bible, another book of the period destined for royalty. This new type based on half-uncial, whose distinctive feature was the elimination of cursive elements, must have won the warm approval of Charlemagne and Alcuin. For the school in which it was to reach its greatest perfection— a level of calligraphic art unsurpassed, to my mind, in the annals of writing—was the school directly under the Emperor's patronage, in the Abbey where Alcuin was Abbot—the school of St. Martin at Tours. It is hard to say how large a part Tours played in the early evolution of this minuscule. It was, if we may judge by the rather mediocre essays made during the eighth century, probably a secondary part. Alcuin himself, we know, never got to France until after the birth of the Caroline minuscule.

The orderliness, simplicity, clarity, and dignity of the new script were virtues that made a special appeal to a man

like Charlemagne, who, as we know, was not above taking
a profound interest in the labours of scribes. To the
imperial approbation was added that of Alcuin. He too
was in a position to appreciate the new minuscule, whose
special quality of legibility contrasted so favourably with the
difficulty of his native Anglo-Saxon hand. This double
sanction gave to the script the greatest possible prestige.
Among his other reforms Charlemagne had ordered a new
and standard text of the Benedictine Rule, and a revision
of the Vulgate and the liturgy; and these revised versions,
everywhere in demand, became as it were the apostles and
propagators of the new script. This, then, is the meaning
of the so-called Caroline ' reform '. It was not, as has
sometimes been naïvely pictured, the invention of a script
by a single scholar and its propagation by order of an emperor.
Scripts that survive have sturdier roots than that. It was
rather the achievement, after manifold endeavours, of a type,
the creation of which is a standing monument to the genius
for form possessed in so eminent a degree by the peoples of
Gaul, a type the intrinsic merits of which made its success
certain. That it became, with such extraordinary rapidity,
the dominant script of Europe, was due to a happy combination of political and literary circumstances attending
its birth.

It did not take much more than a generation to win over
all of the French schools to the Caroline minuscule. This
conquest could not have been accomplished without much
opposition and some heart-burning in those centres in
which the new script meant the death of the old *ab*-type
that had been practised with such great éclat throughout
the reign of Charlemagne. But, almost as soon as in France,
the new minuscule won adherents beyond the Alps. As if
by miracle, the scribes of northern and central Italy cease
writing their own local style and adopt the Caroline. Only

35. MAJUSCULE TYPES. Tours School

torum manu praeessis. longa linea
copiosi lactis effluere. puer. sur
rexit incolomis. Nos obstupefacti
tantae rei miraculo. Idquod ipsa
cogebat ueritas fatebamur. Non
ee subcaelo. qui martinum possit
Imitari.

¶¶¶ CONSEQUENTI ITIDEM
TEMPORE · ITER CUM EODē
dum dioceses uisitat, agebamus
nobis nescio qua necessitate remo
rantib; aliquantulum ille pro
cesserat. Interim per aggerē
publicum plena militantib; uiris

36. CAROLINE MINUSCULE. Tours School

Spain, South Italy, Ireland, and England withstood the new influence. But, in the course of the tenth century, thanks to close contact with the Continent, the new script has won its way into England, where before long it assumes the predominant position, the Anglo-Saxon type having been relegated to the copying of vernacular. As for Spain and South Italy, as we have seen, they did not give up their own scripts until the twelfth and thirteenth centuries respectively.

It has been argued with great learning that Rome took a leading part in the evolution of the Caroline minuscule; that she was in the forefront of the movement, as befitted her position as ' caput ecclesiae '. It is pointed out that Rome had for centuries been an unfailing source for supplying the transalpine churches and monasteries with books; that as the centre of Christendom she required a large body of copyists, and, furthermore, the very existence of a book like the ' Liber Diurnus ', the papal formulary, written in good minuscule of the ninth century, furnishes irrefragable evidence that the new minuscule was cultivated at Rome, and strong presumption that it started its career there. It is true that Rome had always been a great repository of books, especially of the older books ; that it had been a great exchange centre, a book mart. But that is not the same thing as being an important centre for producing books. It has great works of art now, supremely great, but they are not Roman works. They are the performances of men from elsewhere, specially summoned to produce those works. Fra Angelico, Ghirlandaio, Raphael, and Michael Angelo were pressed into service to the greater glory of Rome. It was never during the Middle Ages, nor has it been since, a literary or artistic centre, although artists and litterateurs in great numbers have always flocked thither. We know for a fact that the copyists of Rome in the time

of Nicholas V were mostly Germans and Frenchmen.
That was in the heyday of the Renaissance. Perhaps it was
the same during the renaissance in Charlemagne's time.
Rome, the centre of Christendom, the seat of ecclesiastical
authority and administration, had of course a huge staff
of officials ; but hardly of book-scribes. The documents
issued by the Curia, the papal bulls sent to the four corners
of the earth, were not written by calligraphers, in a script
which every one could read. The notaries of the Curia used
a very singular and difficult script, which was unintelligible
even to high prelates of the Middle Ages, as witness the
predicament of Archbishop Ralph of Tours in 1075, who
could make neither head nor tail of a privilege because it
was written in 'littera romana'. This curial script is
Rome's unique medieval contribution to handwriting.
When it came to calligraphy she lagged sadly behind. It is
impossible to point to any great school of writing at Rome
during the Middle Ages, nor to Roman manuscripts of the
eighth, ninth, or tenth centuries, remarkable either for
beauty of script or illumination. This cannot all be due to
the medieval habit of anonymity. For we have scores of
beautiful manuscripts of the same period coming from
known schools to the north and south of Rome. The true
reason, however, is not far to seek. The Roman milieu
was not favourable to the development of great schools of
writing. Art does not flourish in an atmosphere of bureaucracy. But Rome's bureaucracy was cosmopolitan. Clerics
from all over Christendom took part in the administration ;
so that a book like the 'Liber Diurnus', now in the Vatican
Archives, if it was written at Rome, might none the less have
been the work of a northern scribe. But this book came to
Rome from Nonantola ; another ninth-century copy, now
at the Ambrosiana, came from Bobbio, and a third (known
as the Claromontanus, and now lost) was preserved in

France ; so that it looks as if this book had an interest for places outside of Rome, and as if every copy need not be of necessity considered a Roman product.

There are other reasons which tell against Rome. During the seventh and eighth centuries—the critical period for minuscule—she shows no signs of literary activity, and her intellectual life is said to have sunk to a very low level. These are not the conditions which produce new scripts. Moreover, Rome, the mother of the old majuscule scripts, was not likely to abandon them earlier than other centres. She was far more likely to cling to them longest of all. Extant uncial manuscripts suggest that this was the case. Again, it was in France and not in Rome that the new minuscule soonest reached its height of perfection. Finally, it has been argued that the extraordinarily rapid spread of the new minuscule cannot be satisfactorily explained unless on the hypothesis that it originated in the most influential centre of Christendom, where the fashion was set for the rest of the world to follow. But, had this been the case, we should expect cities to the south of Rome, and very close to it, to be at least as much affected by Rome's influence and example as the distant cities of northern Italy, Switzerland, and France. But Veroli, and Sulmona, not to mention places farther south, wrote Beneventan and not Caroline minuscule. Is it conceivable that the whole of Southern Italy succumbed to Beneventan influence, when powerful and ubiquitous Rome pulled in the contrary direction? Why should Lucca, Verona, Bobbio, Saint Gall, Tours, Corbie, and Orleans write in accordance with the alleged Roman pattern, while Capua, Naples, Benevento, and towns on both shores of the Adriatic follow the model of Monte Cassino? The more reasonable explanation is that the Caroline minuscule had its origin in France, and that French influence did not penetrate as far as Southern Italy, so that the influence of Monte Cassino remained predominant there. Our extant eighth-century manuscripts indicate that the course of the literary current, in Charlemagne's time and for a generation or two before, was from Gaul to Italy, and not vice versa. Lastly, the testimony of the ancients is on the side of France. By 'littera Romana' men of the Middle Ages understood two distinct scripts : the uncial characters of the book-hand and the curial cursive of papal charters. They did not use it to signify Caroline minuscule. On the other hand, 'littera Gallica,' or 'scriptura Francesca' was used to denote the ordinary or Caroline minuscule, as distinguished, say, from the Beneventan or Visigothic. It must be admitted, then, that Rome's part in the development of the new minuscule was that of a follower, not an initiator.

The second great contribution of the Middle Ages is the Gothic script. It may seem a far cry from the round Caroline minuscule of Charlemagne's time to this angular script ; yet the one is the legitimate child of the other, in direct line of descent. For four centuries generation after generation transmitted the Caroline heritage substantially unaltered, yet never quite the same ; and the accretion of these small variations produced in time a script astonishingly unlike the stock it sprang from. Owing to favourable conditions the Caroline script developed quickly and early attained its zenith. Perfection of form bred, as it usually does, artificial and adventitious elements : hairlines, hooks, and flourishes. Once this fluid mass of mannerisms got set, as it were, and its innovations codified, a new style was at hand. The natural movement away from a round script like the Caroline was in the direction of an angular script like the Gothic ; the reaction from a script whose letters are clear, well-defined, and unattached, was

37. GOTHIC SCRIPT

patrem nostrum: daturum se nobis

osine timore de manu inimicorum
nostrorum liberati: serviamus illi

in sanctitate et iustitiam coram ipso: om
nibus diebus nostris.

Et tu puer propheta altissimi vocaberis: pre
ibis enim ante faciem domini parare vi
as eius.

Ad dandam scientiam saluti plebi eius: in
remissionem peccatorum eorum.

Per viscera misericordie dei nostri: in qui
bus visitavit nos oriens ex alto.

Illuminare hijs qui in tenebris et in
umbra mortis sedent: ad dirigen
dos pedes nostros in viam pacis.

Magnificat anima mea dominum.
Et exultavit spiritus meus: in
deo salutari meo.

38. GOTHIC SCRIPT

a script in which the individuality of single letters is sunk in the harmony of the whole.

These general tendencies begin to take shape by the end of the twelfth century. It is the period when Gothic architecture comes into being. The spirit that informs that architecture is the self-same one that breathes new life into the degraded Caroline script. And the new style which the Gothic builders immortalize in stone is shaping also the appearance of the written letter. Open one of the many thirteenth-century Psalters or Books of Hours, and you seem to be looking at the text as through a series of Gothic windows—an effect produced by emphasizing the vertical and pointed and eliminating the round strokes, the prevalence of the heavily shaded upright strokes endowing the page with the mysterious semi-darkness of a Gothic chapel, in which all the elements are blended into a harmonious whole. The Gothic script is difficult to read. It has the serious faults of ambiguity, artificiality, and overloading. It is the child of an age that was not bent on achieving the practical, the age of St. Louis and St. Francis. It is as if the written page was to be looked at and not read. Instead of legibility its objective seems to be a certain effect of art and beauty, which it accomplishes by loving care bestowed upon each stroke and by the unerring consistency of its style. It is a product of the north, with the mysticism of the north, lacking Italian clarity as northern skies lack it. It never took a real hold in Italy. The finest examples come from France, Flanders, and England. In their way they are as perfect examples of Gothic art as is the Sainte Chapelle. The spirit of the Middle Ages lives nowhere more than in such Gothic manuscripts.

Roughly speaking, the Gothic script lived from 1200 to 1500. During these three centuries it was the script of all Europe, as no script had ever been before. This is not to say that regional differences did not exist. The Gothic script in Italy tends to be roundish, in France and England it is angular. Everywhere, however, it follows certain curious rules of its own. The cardinal rule is, that if a letter ends with a bow and the following letter begins with one, the two letters are written conjoint. Other rules are the use of 2 for *r* after a letter ending in a bow, the use of uncial *d* (δ), and of *s* (not ʃ) at the end of words. The joining of bows gave the line a look of compactness, a look already noticeable in Beneventan manuscripts as far back as the end of the eleventh century.

A script like the Gothic was bound to be repugnant to the taste of the Renaissance. The humanistic minuscule (the revived Caroline) was certain to drive it from the field. But this might have taken centuries had not the invention of printing hastened the process. If it is true that ' the Gothic sun set behind the colossal press of Mayence ', it was not because the first printers were unfriendly to Gothic. The earliest-printed books were exact reproductions of Gothic manuscripts. They owed their success to the closeness of the imitation. They took over bodily all the difficult conjoint letters and even all the numerous abbreviations. Only initials and rubrics were left blank for the miniator to fill in by hand. Very soon types were also cut in exact imitation of the humanistic script, and many are the beautiful incunabula in this roman type. At first the Roman was used in Italy for all sorts of books, as the Gothic was in Germany. Gradually there was a tendency to reserve the Roman for editions of the classics, to use a plain Gothic for other books in Latin and a sloping Gothic for books in the vernacular. For legal books in Anglo-French a special type was used. As was to be expected, the local variety of handwriting influenced at first the form of type. The German printers who settled in Italy used a roundish type

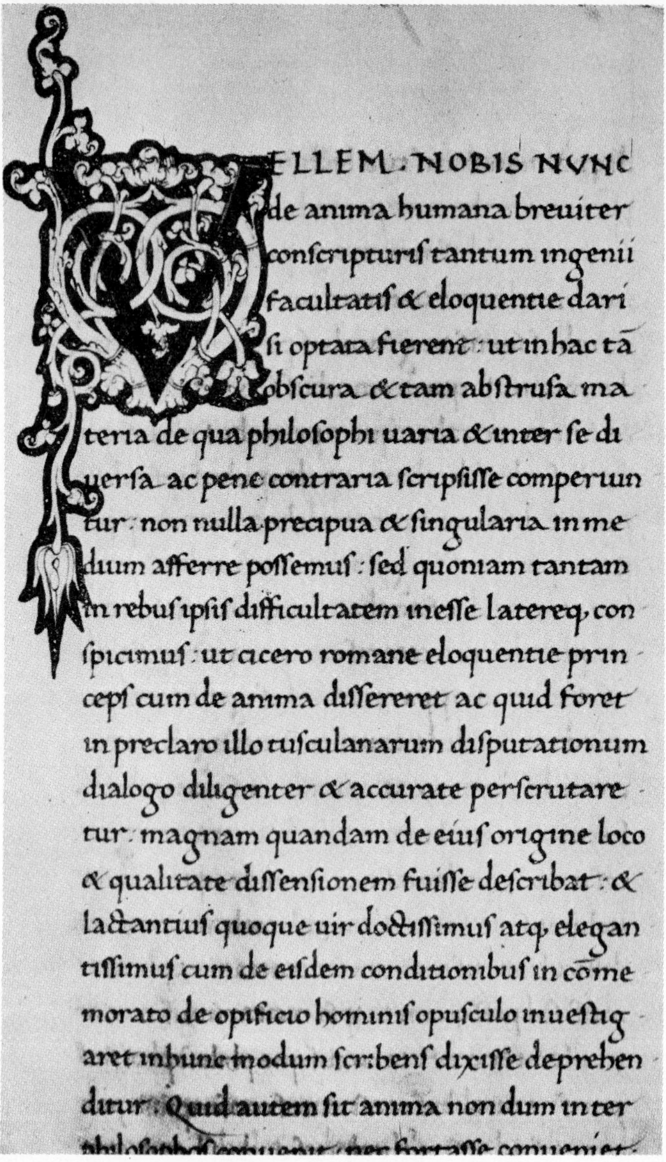

VELLEM : NOBIS NUNC
de anima humana breuiter
conscripturis tantum ingenii
facultatis & eloquentie dari
si optata fierent : ut in hac tã
obscura & tam abstrusa ma
teria de qua philosophi uaria & inter se di
uersa ac pene contraria scripsisse comperiun
tur : non nulla precipua & singularia in me
dium afferre possemus : sed quoniam tantam
in rebus ipsis difficultatem inesse latereq; con
spicimus : ut cicero romane eloquentie prin
ceps cum de anima dissereret ac quid foret
in preclaro illo tusculanarum disputationum
dialogo diligenter & accurate perscrutare
tur : magnam quandam de eius origine loco
& qualitate dissensionem fuisse describat : &
lactantius quoque uir doctissimus atq; elegan
tissimus cum de eisdem conditionibus in cõme
morato de opificio hominis opusculo inuestig
aret in hunc modum scr:bens dixisse deprehen
ditur : Quid autem sit anima non dum inter
philosophos conuenit : nec fortasse conueniet

39. HUMANISTIC SCRIPT

Cessi & sublato montem genitore petiui :

PVB: VERGILII MARONIS

AENEIDOS LIBER III :

OSTQVAM RES
ASIAE PRIA
MIQVE EVER
TEREGENTIM

IMMERITAMVISVM SVPE

RIS CECIDITQVE SVPERBVM

Ilui et omnis humo fumat Neptunia troia

Diuersa exilia : et desertas querere terras

Auguriis agimur diui : classemqz subipa

Antandro : et phrigiqz molimur moñbus Ide

Incerti quo fata ferant ubi sistere detur

Contrahimusqz uiros uix prima ieceperat estas

Et pr Anchises dare uentis uela iubebat

Littora tu pre, Lachrimas portuqz relinquo

Et campos ubi troia fuit feror exul ī altum

Cū socijs natoqz penatibus et magnis Dijs

Terra procul uastis colitur mauortia campis

of Gothic to meet the taste of their public. After 1480 many printers began to buy their punches and matrices instead of making their own type, with the result that the same type is found in many places. The Roman type came to dominate the romance lands, Gothic continued to flourish in Teutonic countries—as we know, it is still the predominant script of Germany and German Austria. Only in the last century was it abandoned in Scandinavia. Its hold upon England may be seen from the fact that to the end of the eighteenth century 'English face' was the designation for black face or Gothic. It survives with us to-day only as an ornamental script, to be used where legibility is a matter of indifference, as in church windows, tombstones, wood carving, portals, and, for some inscrutable reason, in the word 𝔚𝔥𝔢𝔯𝔢𝔞𝔰 at the beginning of clauses in a legal instrument. Before the close of the fifteenth century Aldus Manutius had a type cut for him, modelled on cursive, which gave us our italic characters. To the Roman, Gothic, and italic types were added the majestic characters of the 'capitalis quadrata' to use as capitals. The printer's equipment was complete. It is substantially his equipment to this day.

The hand we use in writing to-day has had in the main the same history as the book hand; except that the written characters have been even more conservative than the printed. In England the humanistic cursive became known in the Renaissance, but 'the sweet Roman hand' had a long struggle. Gothic characters persist into the eighteenth century. In Germany the Gothic script is the one still commonly taught in the schools.

The Legacy of the Middle Ages, then, is the legacy of Rome, with modifications developed in the course of transmission. The generic name we give to the modified legacy is minuscule. We have seen that when the majuscule scripts became obsolete, scribes everywhere tried to evolve a script to take their place. It was based on cursive, or on half-uncial, or on mixed material. Of the various attempts, the most successful was the type which was evolved in Gaul in the time of Charlemagne, and which we call Caroline minuscule. It became rapidly the predominant script in all lands save Spain, South Italy, and these islands. The Caroline script gradually developed into Gothic, which became the script of all Europe before the Renaissance, but which the humanists discarded for a revived Caroline. This humanistic minuscule and the Gothic were the scripts practised when printing was invented. And these two types were taken over by the printers, and survive to this day. Of the two, the type in general use is the one that originated in France and was brought to light again in Italy—the type we call Roman. Thus it is to France and Italy, the two lands in which the roots of Roman civilization went deepest down, that we owe the particular forms of the letters we write and read to this day.

E. A. LOWE.

4

PHILOSOPHY

THE Frankish successors of the Roman Empire were scarcely conscious that they were laying the foundations of a new epoch. To the contemporaries of Charlemagne it seemed as if the ancient dominion of the Caesars had once more received a legitimate successor. To them Rome was immortal, the mother of civilization outside whose sway lay only the darkness of barbarism, and the Church was the soul of the still living Empire. It was the Church and the Church only which through the confusion of the sixth, seventh, and eighth centuries had kept alight, albeit feebly, the torch of learning. She had been the sole transmitter of all that was left of the heritage of the classical age, and alone had saved mankind not only from hell, but from savagery. It was the realization of this fact, however vaguely and half-consciously apprehended, which gave to the medieval mind its unity and its distinguishing character.

The thought of the Middle Ages was thus essentially theocentric and the great medieval thinkers were one and all of them theologians : as soon as this ceased to be the case the Renaissance may be said to have begun. There were thus two factors which at each stage of its development determined the course of the scholastic philosophy. One of these, the dogmatic teaching of the Church, was permanent, and inelastic, the other varied from age to age, as the knowledge of the writings of the ancient philosophers gradually increased. From the ninth to the twelfth centuries direct acquaintance with the two greatest thinkers of antiquity was astonishingly small. Of Plato only the *Timaeus* in the translation of Chalchidius had survived, of Aristotle only the *Categories* and the *De interpretatione*, and though before the end of the twelfth century the whole of his logic had been rediscovered, it was not till the beginning of the thirteenth century that the contents of his principal writings were generally known. The earlier medieval period was entirely dominated by the writings of Augustine, who more than any of the Latin fathers had incorporated in his teaching the philosophical spirit of the later platonists, and who continued to exercise the profoundest and most enduring influence on the medieval mind, even at the time when the authority of Aristotle was at its strongest. And though in the later period Aristotelianism becomes the fashionable philosophy of the schools, its influence neverthe-less remains comparatively superficial. The theology of the Church in patristic times had been so deeply imbued with Platonism that to the end it remained Platonist rather than Aristotelian.

The task of the medieval thinker was thus one of recon-ciliation, of synthesis rather than creation. For at a time when men were beginning to learn once more the rudiments of civilization, the written word was surrounded with a halo of veneration. Not only did piety require an implicit belief in the literal accuracy of all sacred writings scriptural and even patristic, a similar consideration was extended also to the great secular writings of the past. Were they not the perfected triumphs of the purely human reason which in their own sphere no generation could hope to surpass? The scholastic problem was therefore the reconciliation of the Revelation of the Church with the philosophical speculation of ancient Greece. That such a reconciliation was possible was a basic conviction, for man the rational animal was created in the image of God. Yet human reason was corrupted in the sin of Adam, and where it came in conflict with the letter of Revelation, instant abdication was demanded: investigation itself became a deadly sin. That there was anything improper in such a submission never for an instant occurred to the medieval mind. To disbelieve in the teaching of the Church was regarded as something monstrous, a spiritual disease. It was equivalent to denying the rationality of the universe altogether. For reason and revelation alike had their ultimate ground in a single and unique source, the unfathomable nature of God. Failure to arrive at a satisfactory synthesis was therefore attributed to the corruption of man's intellect, the integrity of which could only be maintained by the grace of faith. The history of medieval thought is thus the unfolding of successive attempts to reconcile Christian dogma first with the Platonic and later with the Aristotelian philosophy.

John Scotus Erigena, the first and the most profound philosopher of the Middle Ages, came over from Ireland to the court of Charles the Bald about the middle of the ninth century. At once the last of the fathers and the first of the scholastics, he occupies a unique position in the history of medieval thought. While his contemporaries were acquainted only with the Latin fathers and the meagre fragments of the Greek philosophers which had survived in Latin translations, he possessed a competent knowledge of the Greek language and had read deeply in the Greek fathers and the writings of platonizing Christians like the so-called Dionysius the Areopagite, whose works he translated into Latin. The whole spirit of his philosophy is thus widely different from that of any other medieval writer. He is almost more neoplatonist than Christian, and the freedom with which he reinterprets the traditional dogmas of the Church is wholly without parallel in an age of literalism and blind adhesion to authority.

To sketch an outline of Erigena's system is by no means easy, for his thought abounds in abstruse half-mystical metaphysics which renders it very difficult to understand. In his chief work *De divisione naturae* he classifies ' Nature ' or, as we should say, Reality, into four kinds: that which creates and is not created; that which is created and creates; that which is created and does not create; that which neither creates nor is created. By these divisions he does not mean to specify four different things or classes, they are rather four aspects or stages of the one world process. The first deals with God as essence, the ultimate ground of the universe, the second with the Divine Ideas or first causes, the third with the created world, and the last with God as the consummation of all things. God alone has true being: He is without beginning or end, and is the beginning, middle, and end of all things, for all things which have being participate in His essence, subsist in and through Him and are moved towards Him as their last end. When, therefore, we say that God created all things we mean that He is in all things and underlies their essence; they are, to use the modern idealist's language, ' adjectival' to Him, for God alone has ' substantive' being. John, however, was no pantheist. Though God is in all things, He must not be confused with them; He is not merely the sum of things; in His own private being He transcends them all. Following the negative theology of the Areopagite we may even say, by a somewhat violent metaphor, that He is nothing, for His essense transcends all determinations and is inexpressible. For though reason arguing from the finite creation concludes that God is, that He is good, wise, living, &c., and though the revelation of the Church teaches that He is one Essence in three Substances or Persons, none of these definitions or attributes belong to Him in their literal sense; they are all more or less symbolic. The divine being transcends all possible conceptions.

From the first ' nature ' proceeds the second, created and creating, the ' intelligible world ' of the divine ideas, which form a system hierarchically arranged in Platonic fashion from the highest idea, the Good, through all the various *genera* and *species* down to the lowest idea, matter. This intelligible world is created eternally by the Father in the Son and nourished in the bosom of the Holy Ghost, by whose operation the primordial causes or ideas unfold themselves into the visible and sensible world. For like a true Platonist Erigena regards the divine ideas not only as prototypes but also as the causes of the world of sense. Creation is thus the procession of the divine being through the primordial causes into the visible and invisible creatures. And this procession is eternal. For God does not first conceive and then make, *Videt enim operando et videndo operatur*. By this eternal act God creates not only the created world, He also creates Himself. ' For the creature subsists in Him and He in creating is after a marvellous and ineffable manner created, invisible making Himself visible, unknown making Himself known, formless giving Himself form, superessential giving Himself being, maker of all things being in all things made.'

Passing to the third division, the nature that is created but not creative, John expounds his cosmology in the form of a commentary on the first chapters of Genesis, which he regards not as a statement of historical fact, but as a highly symbolical allegory. The centre of the created universe is man, who unites in his nature the spiritual and corporeal worlds. He is the microcosm, the workshop of creation, and in him the Divine Trinity creates itself. Erigena is, in fact, an uncompromising idealist. Thought is the only ultimate reality and the corporeal sensations are mere illusions.

To be and to be thought is one. Thought is not the image of things, it is their actual essence. Just as the divine thought creates eternally the divine ideas or causes of things, so human thought creates the essences of the things of the created world, and in it the unfolding of the divine nature is accomplished. The human soul is thus the image of the Trinity with its three faculties, understanding, reason, and sense. For as the Father creates the eternal ideas in the Son, so the understanding creates the highest concepts in the reason, and as the Holy Ghost distributes the effects of the primordial causes in the multiplicity of the created world, so sense divides and distributes the pure concepts into the *genera* and *species* of the visible world. But the image is not a perfect one. For in the fall of Adam the nature of man was corrupted and his soul submitted to the illusions of the physical senses. The physical qualities which make up corporeal things are mere appearances; they are a congeries of ' accidents ' which come into being and pass away, whereas the real essence of things is eternal. If we could but see things as they really are, their sensible qualities would vanish, they would wholly be resolved into their ideal elements. The story of the garden of Eden and the temptation is a symbol. There was no actual time when man existed in innocence; he fell as soon as he was created. Instead of turning his soul to God he turned towards himself; and this before he was tempted of the devil. Thus fallen he was no longer able to fulfil the function for which he was created, namely the bringing back of all things to their primordial causes, the involution of the divine essence into itself.

The last division, the Nature which neither creates nor is created, represents the final stage of the world process, when all things have returned into their first causes and rest in them ; when the distinction between creator and creature has been obliterated, and God is all in all. After the fall, man was no longer capable of performing this consummation. He had entered into the entanglement of the physical body and incurred the penalty of death. But the divine mercy had prepared a plan for his redemption ; the Word became flesh assuming the nature of man, and through the Incarnation human nature is restored to its original purity and brought back into its first causes. This restoration is accomplished in four stages, the death of the body, the resurrection of the dead, the transformation of the physical body into a spiritual body, and the final return of human nature into its primordial causes. In the resurrection the whole of the sensible creation will rise again transformed, transmuted, and eternalized, reassumed into the divine being, yet without absolute annihilation preserved eternally as a moment of the divine life ; *movebitur in Deum sicut aer movetur in lucem.* But this doctrine of the mystical return of all things into God, which was no new invention (we find it in Clement of Alexandria, Origen, Gregory of Nyssa), has to be adapted to the severer teaching of the Church, which makes an all-important distinction between the fate of the saved and of the damned. A place has to be found for eternal tortures. It cannot be human nature that suffers, for humanity was restored by the Incarnation, and true to his Platonic realism Erigena insists that humanity is one and indivisible. Even the diabolic nature will share in this abstract redemption. But the accidents of this perfected substance do not of necessity participate in this glorification. The evil of mankind is accidental, for evil has no positive essence, and evil shall be punished eternally by its own frustration. The wicked will find no realization of their wickedness in the future life, and fires of hell are the fires of an eternal conscience. The elect, on the other hand, will become united with God, they will be deified, and the condition of their deification is the knowledge and love of the Incarnate Word as revealed by the teaching of the Church.

The philosophy of Erigena was conceived on too grand a scale to appeal to the ecclesiastical intelligence of the ninth century. It was condemned as heretical, and the master left no disciples worthy of his name. In the troublous times of the tenth century darkness once more descended on the land, and when in the eleventh century philosophical speculation began once more to reappear, it was from far humbler sources that the main stream of medieval thought drew its origin. Scholasticism may be said to have been generated out of theology by the disputes of the logicians. First and foremost of these controversies was that between the ' realists ' and the ' nominalists ' concerning the nature of general concepts or ' universals '. Is ' humanity ', e.g. a real substance, one and the same in all human beings whose individuality consists in a mere congeries of ' accidents ', or is it merely a class name arbitrarily chosen to designate a plurality of particular men ? The former opinion was that of the so-called ' realists ', the latter, that of the so-called ' nominalists '. It might seem at first sight that such a controversy was both absurd and sterile, but in fact its consequences were of the greatest importance to the development of medieval thought, not so much because the issue itself was of such vast gravity, but on account of the theological implications which were deduced from it. Thus Roscellinus, the protagonist of the nominalist party, did not hesitate to apply his logical doctrine to the elucidation of the mysteries of the Trinity. If, he argued, the real is the universal, then the Three Persons are not three things but one thing, and the Father and the Holy Ghost became incarnate with the Son. If, on the other hand, the real is the singular, we should properly speak not of one God but of three Gods, and this horn of the dilemma he himself embraced. At this abominable tritheism the whole of Christendom stood aghast. The more conservative church-men, who like Peter Damian had long been distrustful of the study of logic, redoubled their protest against any attempt to understand the mysteries of the faith. But even among the most orthodox there were those who took a larger view. Anselm, afterwards Archbishop of Canter-bury, saw that heresy must be countered by its own weapon. The task he set himself was to give a philosophical explana-tion of Christian dogma which should at the same time be perfectly orthodox, and to co-ordinate the somewhat loosely connected tradition of the Latin Church. Starting from the basis of implicit faith, he yet sought, as far as was possible for the enfeebled and vitiated intellect, to arrive at some understanding of the holy mysteries, and to discover, if that might be permitted to him, the 'necessary reasons' underlying the principal tenets of the Church concerning the existence and nature of God and his relation to his creatures. For the first time since Augustine the great dogmas of the Trinity, the Incarnation, the Redemption, and the ever-pressing problem of free will and predestination received a systematic treatment which deserves to be called both philosophical and orthodox. It was a great advance, and its consequences were decisive. Whatever flaws we may discover in the famous ontological argument for the existence of God which Anselm was the first to formulate, its signi-ficance is incontestable; it marks the beginning of a new effort to place theology once more upon a rational basis.

Meanwhile the strife between nominalists and realists, hotly contested throughout the eleventh century, acted as a powerful stimulus on the growing activities of the medieval mind. Schools of dialectic began to multiply, and in spite of all the efforts of the most conservative theologians, the dialectical spirit began to invade the teaching of theology itself. An important stage of this development is marked by the career of Peter Abelard (d. 1142), the most renowned dialectician of the twelfth century. In logic he attempted to discover a middle way between the absurdities of the orthodox realists and the blasphemies of the nominalists. Universals are neither things nor names, they are concepts which are predicated of particulars. Thus when we say that Plato and Socrates are both men, we do not mean that there is a mysterious essence ' humanity ' which, one and the same, gives being to both, but we mean that both have similar essences. The humanity of Plato is numerically distinct from the humanity of Socrates, but it is of the same kind. Elementary as such considerations may appear, they were not without importance, and Abelard may be reckoned as one of the precursors of the logical theory of the thirteenth century, the so-called moderate or Aristotelian realism. But it was not as a mere logician that Abelard made his greatest impression on the speculation of his age. Like Anselm, he too set out to discover the necessary reasons which underlay the dogmas of the faith. But whereas Anselm's was a faith that inquires, Abelard's was a faith which begins by doubting. For it is only by doubting that we can come to the investigation of the truth—a dangerous doctrine in the eyes of twelfth-century churchmen ! In a treatise entitled *Sic et non*, he collected together all the contradictory statements he could find in the Scriptures and the fathers concerning various points of Christian doctrine, and though he laid down the principles on which the reconciliation should be effected, he did not venture to offer any solutions himself. Thus by borrowing the method of contemporary canonists, who had already begun to systematize and classify the conflicting rulings of ecclesiastical law, he laid the foundations of the scholastic method which was afterwards to govern the discussion of theological and philosophical questions. In his philosophical speculations Abelard was less fortunate. An ardent admirer of Plato, whose metaphysic he would embrace, even where he rejected his logic, he attributed to the pagan philosophers an anticipation of the Christian doctrine of the Trinity which seemed to trespass on the unique privileges of ecclesiastical revelation. Did not the One of the platonists typify the Father, the νοῦς the Son and the world-Soul the Holy Ghost? And though under pressure he afterwards withdrew this detestable opinion, his explanations of the mystery were incautious; he reduced the Trinity of Persons to a mere trinity of attributes, power, wisdom, and love, and his comparison of the triune unity to a seal, the bronze of which it is made, and the character incised on it, savoured too much of Sabellianism to escape the implacable fanaticism of the redoubtable St. Bernard, who had long been waiting for the opportunity of silencing the pernicious heretic.[1] The inspired ignorance and unscrupulous astuteness of the saint procured a condemnation at the Council of Sens, which did not even listen to a defence, and silenced for ever the peripatetic of Pallet. But the fulminations of the orthodox were unable to prevent the evolution of theological speculation. The twelfth century was an age of rapid development. Everywhere theology was being transformed by the philosophical spirit. In the Abbey of St. Victor, Hugo and Richard were developing the mystical side of the teaching of St. Augustine, on lines which were afterwards to be perfected by the Franciscan St. Bonaven-

---

[1] Cf. *Ep.* cxcii: 'Cum de Trinitate loquitur [Abaelardus] sapit Arium : cum de gratia, sapit Pelagium ; cum de persona Christi, sapit Nestorium.' Of Abelard's attempt to reconcile Platonism and Christianity he writes (*Tractatus de erroribus Abaelardi*, c. iv), ' ubi dum multum sudat quomodo Platonem faciat Christianum, se probat ethnicum.'

tura, while at Chartres there sprang up a realist school of Platonists who attempted to harmonize the teaching of the *Timaeus* with that of the Catholic Church. Indeed Chartres at this period was the centre of a humanist revival which has scarcely received from historians (Dr. R. L. Poole excepted [1]) the attention which it deserves. Not only were the classical authors Ovid, Virgil, Horace, Seneca, Cicero, carefully studied and the art of composition sedulously cultivated ; the natural sciences also received a due measure of attention, as is shown by the works of William of Conches, who attempted to reconcile the atomic theory of Democritus and the Epicureans with the physical theories of the *Timaeus.*

The development of this Platonic realism is of particular interest. To the realist, as we have already seen, general ideas were endowed with a mysterious metaphysical significance ; they were the reality (*res*) of which the particular was only the appearance. The world of ideas or ' forms ', which had first been described by Plato as the intelligible world, had long been identified by Christian thought with the divine ideas, the unity of which was the divine word or λόγος, through whom the world was created. These ideas are generated eternally by the Father in the Son before all worlds ; they are the archetypes or moulds from which the created world was cast. But ideas are universals, and the things of the created universe are particulars ; how then are the two related ? There must be some other principle to mediate between them, and this the scholastics found in ' matter '. The ' matter ' of the medieval philosophers must not, however, be conceived in terms of the

---

[1] Cf. his *Illustrations of the History of Mediaeval Thought and Learning*, 2nd ed. 1920 ; and his article ' The Masters of the Schools at Paris and Chartres in John of Salisbury's time ', *English Historical Review*, xxxv. 321 et seq. See also M. Clerval, *Les écoles de Chartres* (1895).

modern physicists. It was rather the Greek ὕλη, an absolutely indeterminate something, which was regarded as the principle of plurality and change. The created world was thus produced by the outflowing of the divine ideas or forms into matter, and all created things are *composita* or *conjuncta*, compounds of ' form ' and ' matter '. And though particular individual things pass away and come into being the world itself is imperishable, for the forms and matter are alike everlasting. The bond which unites form and matter and holds them together is the final cause of the world, the world-soul which is the Holy Ghost. The universe is thus a great organism animated by one life which lives in all creatures, in brutes and men and stones, and sustains it through all its manifold changes, the *spiritus vivificans* of the Nicene Creed. This theory, which approaches in some respects very closely to pantheism, is expounded in a quaintly characteristic mathematical symbolism by Theodoric of Chartres in his book *De sex dierum operibus*, and also by Bernard Silvestris in a picturesque allegorical dialogue *De universitate mundi*. But it would be a mistake to interpret it as a thorough-going monism ; for both writers, while maintaining that all things partake in the divine unity and are derived from it, are careful not to confuse the creator with the creature, and both insist equally upon the transcendence as well as the immanence of the divine being.

Meanwhile another powerful influence was beginning to pervade medieval thought. From the beginning of the twelfth century the ' new logic ' of Aristotle began to make its way into the schools, thus adding a new ingredient to their composite teaching. Much intellectual ingenuity was expended in endeavouring to form a synthesis between the logical doctrine of ' Plato ' and ' Aristotle ', which developed eventually into the typical scholastic doctrine of ' universals '.

The ' universal ' has a threefold existence. As ' idea ' it is
an eternal moment of the divine mind (*ante rem*), as
' essence ' it is individualized in the numerically different
real objects of the concrete world (*in re*), while as ' concept '
(*genus* or *species*) it is ' abstracted ' by the mind from the
particulars of sense-experience (*post rem*). Thus was ended
the second phase of the controversy between nominalism
and realism.

But the influence of Aristotle was by no means confined
to logic. Round about 1200 the great philosophical works
of the peripatetic philosopher made their way to the newly
founded university of Paris, the great metropolis of medieval
thought, in Latin translations made in Spain from the
Arabic text, together with the numerous commentaries of
the Arabian and Jewish philosophers. The *Physics*, *Metaphysics*, *De Anima*, *Ethics*, and *Naturalia*, which had been
lost for centuries became once more the property of Latin
Christendom. This rediscovery of the Aristotelian philosophy had a profound and sudden effect. Medieval thought
was confronted with a completed system which was worked
out with a scientific thoroughness and breadth of view,
wholly different from the fragmentary Platonism which had
been the inspiration of the previous centuries. Aristotle,
who had been known merely as a ' dialectian ', became at
once ' the Philosopher ', and his authority came to be
regarded as almost that of another Bible. Papal prohibitions
against ' reading ' the new treatises in the universities and
schools were quietly disregarded and afterwards withdrawn,
and from henceforward the chief, if not the only requirement
for the degree of Master of Arts, was an intimate and detailed
knowledge of the Aristotelian writings.

The medieval churchman was thus compelled to undertake
a task of synthesis far more complicated than any he had yet
attempted. Aristotelianism and Christianity had somehow

to be welded into a unity which embraced the totality of truth, human and divine. The first great effort in this direction was the *Summa Theologica* of the Franciscan Alexander of Hales, who attempted to graft on to the traditional theology the doctrines of the new philosophy. But the spirit of his work remained predominatingly ' Augustinian ' in its characteristic confusion of theological and philosophical speculation, and he was unable to bring the newer and the older elements into any coherent unity. A different method was adopted by the Dominican School of Albertus Magnus and his pupil St. Thomas Aquinas. The unity of philosophy and theology was definitely abandoned, and they became wholly separate sciences, the one the product of natural reason, the other that of divine revelation. The decisive factor in this division was the Aristotelian empiricist theory of knowledge. The older ' Augustinian ' theory of cognition which reached its highest expression in the Philosophy of St. Bonaventura, was essentially mystical in tendency. Knowledge is an intuition in which we catch some reflection of the eternal ideas of the divine mind, and the objects of sensual experience are in the last resort only the guise or symbol under which these eternal ideas are revealed. The ultimate object of knowledge is thus always God himself, and all knowing is dependent upon the illumination of the uncreated light which reveals itself to the soul of man by progressive stages rising from ordinary sense-experience to mystical contemplation. The distinction between faith and reason was thus blurred, for what is faith but a higher reason, and reason but an imperfect faith ? A complete separation of philosophy and theology was therefore theoretically impossible. The Aristotelian theory of knowledge, on the other hand, was naturalistic and empiricist. The mind is, of its own right, so to speak, endowed with certain basic principles of thought, and, for the rest, knowledge comes wholly from without through the experience of the senses which reflect or copy a really existing external world. *Nihil est in intellectu quod non prius fuerit in sensu.* This profound difference rendered the separation of natural reason from revelation inevitable. By making each supreme in its own sphere, it was hoped that conflict would be avoided. Theological truths could not indeed be proved, but it could be shown that they did not contradict the fundamental postulates of reason, and that was enough.

This divorce, while it appeared to make for harmony, was in fact intellectually disastrous. It was found impossible to avoid border-line conflicts, for the principles of the Aristotelian philosophy were really wholly incompatible with the Catholic faith, which both in its content and in its traditions was more closely allied to Platonism. The latent contradictions one by one revealed themselves beneath the cloak of compromise, and the ultimate result was a form of scepticism which expressed itself in the convenient theory of the two truths.

The great champion of Aristotelianism was St. Thomas Aquinas, who, breaking away from the older tradition of the schools, attempted to purify the Aristotelian doctrine from Arabian accretions and to use it as a philosophical foundation for Catholic theology. His amazing success was due to his unrivalled powers of systematization—a marvellous grasp of detail, and a faculty for lucid presentation which no medieval thinker could equal. But he attempted no less than the impossible, and the subsequent collapse of scholasticism was the direct result of the discovery of his failure.

A few illustrations may serve to show the typical difficulties of the Thomist Aristotelianism, which lead either to a complete distortion of the original system, or else to an impasse from which the only refuge was an act of faith. According to Aristotle's theory the universe is composed of two correlative principles, form and matter, both of which are eternal. The one is the principle of actuality, the other of potentiality. Matter of itself has no real existence, but only potential being : it is the principle of all change being for ever capable of assuming new forms. At the opposite pole is God, who is pure actuality, the form of forms and the final cause of the world. Between matter, the lowest term, and God, the highest, the real world of concrete ' substances ' composed of form and matter is arranged hierarchically in an ascending scale from the corruptible bodies of the sublunary world to the incorruptible spheres, revolving with an eternal motion, and though in the case of the terrestrial substances the individuals may come to birth and perish, yet the form or type is eternal, for ever realizing itself in the mutability of eternal matter.

The doctrine of the older scholastics with its Augustinian tradition was far different. For them matter was a sort of metaphysical world-stuff out of which the universe was created, a stuff which, while without any positive qualities, yet had some real existence of its own, even though it had never actually existed in isolation apart from form. Thomas, however, follows Aristotle in maintaining the correlativity of matter to form and in denying to it any real existence, but he is forced to reject the presupposition which is essentially implied in this theory, namely the eternity of the universe, and his *materia prima* is left in the awkward position of a sort of created nothing which has no representative idea in the divine mind and yet is somehow known by God. The problem of creation was one which caused him no little trouble. Too good a Christian to deny creation in time, he was nevertheless too good an Aristotelian to admit its demonstrability, with the result that he has to

take refuge ultimately in an act of faith, which is philosophically a very desperate expedient.

In his doctrine of the soul and its relation to the body
St. Thomas's Aristotelianism leads him into even greater
difficulties.   According to the 'Augustinian' school as
represented by Alexander of Hales and Bonaventura, body
and soul are each in a sense substances, each being composed
of form and matter.   But the body of itself is not a complete substance—it is a mere chemico-physical structure
which is not alive.   The soul, even though it is itself composite, acts as a 'perfective form' towards the body and
gives it its living functions.   At their dissolution in death,
each still is substantially itself, though the form of the body
being 'corruptible' the latter quickly disintegrates, while
the soul continues its substantial existence.   This ingenious
doctrine of the plurality of forms was naturally abhorrent
to the strict Aristotelianism of St. Thomas.   Form and
matter are essentially correlative, and one substance can
therefore only have one substantial form.   The soul is, as
Aristotle taught, the substantial form of the body, and soul
and body are not two substances but one substance.   But
here an awkward dilemma arises, and once more the implications of the Aristotelian doctrine have to be avoided.
At death the union of form and matter is dissolved and the
individual destroyed.   What then of immortality ?   The
soul, says St. Thomas, is a 'separable form ', it can continue
to exist as an individual without matter, surely a very
strange conclusion, and one which directly contradicts the
fundamental thesis of Aristotelianism, namely, that the
individual, which is the real, is the compound of form and
matter.   In fact St. Thomas's *anima separata* is a philosophical monstrosity.   For a 'form ' is universal and on his
own teaching the universal can only be 'individualized' in
matter.   A plurality of 'forms' of the same 'species ', e.g.

a plurality of departed spirits, is a logical absurdity which illustrates admirably the complete incompatibility of the Aristotelian and the Christian doctrines.

The same contradiction meets us also in his ethics. Here again St. Thomas attempts to reconcile Aristotle with Christianity, and though his treatment of ethical problems is unique among the scholastic philosophers both for its thoroughness and for its dialectical skill, a satisfactory synthesis was not really attainable. For the Church had long worked out in intimate detail a system of morality the character of which was wholly different from the ethics of ancient Greece. And while St. Thomas borrows the phraseology and the formal principles of the Aristotelian system, he entirely changes their original meaning by constructing with them a ' natural' morality which is to serve merely as a basis for the supernatural morality of the world of grace, the very conception of which is fundamentally irreconcilable with Aristotle's basic idea of the nature of ethics. It would in fact be difficult to find two ethical ideals which are so wholly disparate as those of the good Christian man and the μεγαλόψυχος.

And yet this curious patchwork of irreconcilable ideas was somehow made to work. It suited exactly the genius of the medieval mind which expressed itself in the synthesis of traditional authorities. The greater the variety and even the contrariety of elements, the subtler the ingenuity necessary to reconcile them and the more satisfactory the product, as reproducing more perfectly the accumulated wisdom of the past. Plato and Aristotle, were they not the great patriarchs of human reason ? To conceive that they could have been wholly in error would be inordinate presumption. The first demand of the spirit of the age was for inclusiveness rather than for real consistency. That philosophy and theology could be unified, that they were both somehow true was a postulate that could not be questioned, and in formal logic there was the instrument ready to hand : the syllogism was a tool that was all but omnipotent. The scholastic, in fact, was far too clever a logician to feel the need for real consistency.

The success of St. Thomas's teaching was immediate and startling—in spite of the bitter opposition of the more conservative theologians, even within his own order, and the condemnation of his doctrines both at Paris and at Oxford. Never before had the medieval schools witnessed any system which could be compared with Thomism for the completeness of its articulation and thoroughness of application. It became at once the 'system of reference' of subsequent scholasticism. But its weaknesses and inconsistencies did not escape the criticism of the adherents of the older type of doctrine, especially within the rival Franciscan order, which lost little time in publishing a 'Correctory of brother Thomas' by William Lamarre, and raised for itself a doctor as famous as the 'Angelic' in the person of Duns Scotus. The Philosophy of Scotus, which, owing to his early death, never reached the same completeness of expression as that of Thomas, is a critical reconstruction of the older Augustinian scholasticism, deeply influenced by the Thomist system. It also is a synthesis between philosophy and theology, but less strictly Aristotelian, for where St. Thomas followed the peripatetic philosopher almost blindly, Duns is far more discriminating in his selection, and chooses only those elements which could be made to harmonize more easily with the teaching of the Church. On several fundamental points he is in complete agreement with the Angelic Doctor. He accepts without reserve the empiricist Aristotelian theory of knowledge, and also the formal separation of Philosophy and Theology. But the basic principles of his metaphysic are far different. His theory of form and

matter is a restatement of the older doctrine. While
agreeing with the generally accepted teaching of his order,
that matter has real being and that all created things are
composed of form and matter, Duns goes one step farther,
and maintains the fundamental unity of matter in all
creation, a doctrine which is derived from the platonizing
Jewish philosopher, Salaman ben Gabirol (Avicebron).
Matter thus becomes the principle of 'Creatursein' : it is
the metaphysical stuff from which the whole created world,
spiritual as well as physical, was formed. This doctrine of
the unity of the created universe is expressed in a beautiful
symbol. The world is a gigantic tree planted and tended
by God, whose root is matter and whose trunk is divided
into two main branches representing the physical and the
spiritual creation. The twigs represent the perishable
substances, the falling leaves their 'accidents', while the
flowers represent the human soul and the fruit the Angels.[1]
He is thus saved from the strange dilemmas of the Thomist
Aristotelianism, but the doctrine of creation in time also
causes him discomfort, and he is compelled to admit that
while probable it is not strictly demonstrable. At the same
time his conception of form and matter enables him to
avoid the Thomist confusion of the relation of the soul
to the body, and the curious theory of the separate forms.
Scotus agrees with Alexander of Hales and Bonaventura in
maintaining that both soul and body are composed of form
and matter, while also admitting the Thomist contention
that the soul stands to the body as its substantial form.
The survival of the soul as a substance in its own right is
therefore not a palpable absurdity, yet he will not concede
that it can strictly be demonstrated, though again he

---

[1] This passage occurs in the *De rerum principio*, a treatise the authenticity of which has recently been doubted, but there is no reason to regard
the evidence against its genuineness as conclusive.

concedes that balance of probability is strongly in its favour.

The most interesting of Duns's contributions to the history of thought is his doctrine of the will, which is worked out with great minuteness and psychological penetration. Whereas Thomas inclines to an intellectualistic determinism, because he adheres to the Aristotelian formulae, and Aristotle had never succeeded in arriving at a conception of the will at all, Scotus comes forward as the champion of libertarianism, upholding the primacy of the will over the intellect. The will, though it may be, and indeed is, influenced by the intellect, is not, however, ' determined ' by it : in the last resort it determines itself, and thus it is that a man can act even against his better judgement ; for the will holds the power of attention, and is to a large extent the controller of man's thoughts, for it can turn the contemplation of the intellect from one object to another, and thus accomplish its purpose, behind the back, as it were, of the still small voice of reason. But this interesting theory of freedom leads at once to difficulties. The freedom of man and the freedom of God come into collision, and Duns exercises all his subtlety in vain when he attempts to grapple with the great theological problems of the Reformation, of Grace and free will, and the divine responsibility for evil. In the sphere of ethics also this voluntaristic doctrine leads to difficulties and contradictions, and he is forced somewhat unwillingly to base the whole moral law not on the necessities of reason but on the inscrutable determinations of the divine will.

In spite of the constructive elements in his philosophy, the chief results of Scotism were rather critical and destructive. Duns had laid bare with merciless acuteness the latent contradictions in the Thomist system, and he had criticized as invalid many of the arguments by which

Thomas had attempted to establish a 'natural' theology. Creationism, Immortality, the Divine Omnipotence, &c., these and many other dogmas of the Church were shown to be undemonstrable by natural reason, and though Scotus introduced no new principle of scepticism and only applied more rigorously the distinction invented by Thomas, the psychological effect of the transfer of one doctrine after another from the province of reason to the province of faith, was enormous. The pre-established harmony between reason and revelation, which was the fundamental postulate of medieval thought, was collapsing with alarming rapidity.

There was yet another disintegrating influence which grew more and more powerful at the beginning of the fourteenth century. The works of the Arabian physician and commentator on Aristotle had been widely studied, and a school of 'Averroists' grew up at Paris and also in the universities of Northern Italy, e.g. Padua, where medicine was eagerly studied. The most important articles in the Averroist creed were the eternity of the world, and the denial of the individual immortality of the soul. According to the latter theory, there is only one 'reason' which is eternal and which thinks in each of us by coming into temporary contact with the mortal sensitive soul which disintegrates with the death of the body. Both doctrines reproduced far more accurately the real teaching of Aristotle than the Christianized version of St. Thomas, and they appealed to the more rationalistic scientific temperament, but unfortunately they were irreconcilable with the fundamental teaching of the Church. This awkward circumstance was therefore explained away by the ingenious and comfortable hypothesis of the 'two truths', according to which a proposition could be philosophically true and theologically false or vice versa. Was not the reconciliation

of contradictions an edifying proof of the divine omnipotence? But the reconciliation of contradictions was the
one task which even the subtlety of the scholastic was unable
to accomplish, and the result of this disastrous teaching was
a polite but scarcely disguised scepticism which heralded the
philosophy of the Renaissance.

The final breakdown of the scholastic attempt to combine
Aristotelianism with Christianity is clearly apparent in the
last great medieval thinker, the anti-papalist William of
Ockham, the reviver of 'Nominalism', who attacked the
so-called 'moderate' realism which had ruled the schools
for about a century. Ockham rejects the conception of the
universal as immanent in particulars (*in re*). Only the
singular exists and the 'universal' is a fiction of the mind,
a 'term' or natural sign which stands for a plurality of
singulars. The immediate object of all forms of knowledge
(*scientiae*) is the proposition whose terms are 'universals'
which somehow represent real things, though they are not
the things themselves but only 'signs' of them. This
apparently commonplace doctrine really struck at the roots
of the whole Aristotelian theory of knowledge as understood
by the Middle Ages, and opened the way to a scepticism
which Ockham himself would have been the first to repudi-
ate. For it was argued that if all knowledge is of proposi-
tions and not of 'things', then logic is the only science and
physics and metaphysics are impossible, and, what is more,
if there is no universal immanent in things-in-themselves,
how is any knowledge of them possible? how do we know
that our 'signs' represent them as they really are? For
have you not already admitted that 'signs' are 'universals',
and there are no 'universals' in things? The difficulties
of the correspondence theory of truth are thus raised in the
most acute form. Once the *universale in re* was abolished,
the bridge between logic and metaphysic was broken down

by the destruction of the real identity of 'form' and essence.

Nor were the results of Ockham's teaching any less destructive in the wider realm of metaphysics and theology. Not content with maintaining as indemonstrable the immortality of the soul, he went even farther and denied the validity of the arguments proving the existence of God and His attributes, such as unity, goodness, omnipotence, and so forth, and though he maintained that on purely rational grounds the balance lay in favour of the assumption that there is a God, he insisted that the dogmas of the Church such as the Trinity and the Incarnation were not only indemonstrable but highly improbable, in the sense that to most of the wise men of the world who relied on natural reason they appeared to be false. He developed also to an exaggerated degree the voluntarism of Scotus. The will of God is absolutely arbitrary and bound by no laws, the physical and the moral order are alike contingent, the nature of the world and the distinction between right and wrong rest solely on the absolutely arbitrary decision of the divine will. The same applies to the order of Grace: God could if He wished save the wicked and damn the righteous, just as He might have become incarnate in an ox or a stone.

Scepticism could scarcely be carried farther without relapsing into downright infidelity. Medieval thought had exhausted its power of growth, and a further synthetic development was no longer possible. The history of philosophy in the later Middle Ages is a story of decay. The three main schools, Thomism, Scotism, and Terminism continued, it is true, for two centuries and more reproducing and commenting on the doctrines of their founders, growing generation by generation more futilely academic and elaborately sterile, until scholasticism became the laughingstock of the humanists of the Renaissance, a chimera bombinating in a vacuum of fatuity. The great dream of St. Anselm, the building up of a Christian philosophy, which had seemed so near to fulfilment in the *Summa* of St. Thomas Aquinas, gradually faded and passed away, and with it passed that fascinating form of the human spirit, the medieval mind.

It is, of course, a comparatively easy thing to criticize thought of a past age from a modern standpoint, and to lay bare its inconsistencies and inadequacies. But to discover post-mortem the cause of death is not to solve the mystery of life. The written word is, after all, little more than the skeleton or fossil of the living thought, and our histories of philosophy are rather anatomies than physiologies. And so with the philosophy of the Middle Ages, whose outlook on the world and whose problems were so different from ours, it is hard to realize that it was once a living thing, and to grasp, beneath the inadequate logic of its expression, the profounder unity of the life which gave it birth. The medieval spirit was dominated throughout by the conception of a supreme harmony subordinating the natural to the supernatural order, a harmony in which all the activities of the soul, religion, philosophy, art, science, and conduct were united in the realization of the ideal of the City of God. The Christian thus had, in the last analysis, little need for a philosophy—the questions which really interested him and the problems which were of supreme importance to his destiny were all answered, and his needs all satisfied, by his theology and its concrete manifestation in his personal religious life. The achievement of the Middle Ages lay therefore not so much in the intellectual construction of a philosophic system as in the mysticism of the devout life, and the more imaginative synthesis of art, which in the Divine Comedy of Dante expressed itself in the creation of purest poetry. Fixing his gaze upon the Divine Essence, Dante, at the end of the *Paradiso*, exclaims :

> Nel suo profondo vidi che s'interna,
>   Legato con amore in un volume,
>   Ciò che per l'universo si squaderna ;
> Sustanzia ed accidenti e lor costume,
>   Quasi conflati insieme per tal modo
>   Che ciò ch'io dico è un semplice lume.[1]

All arts and all sciences, to use the noble conception of St. Bonaventura, were but roads which lead back to the supreme *sapientia*, theology. The Catholic faith rounded and embraced the life of the medieval thinker, just as in his cosmology the *primum mobile* contained in itself the totality of space and created by its divinely sustained movement the totality of time. But this self-contained completeness was inadequate to satisfy the growing needs, scientific and philosophical, of the advancing spirit ; and just as the abandonment of the Ptolemaic system rendered obsolete the medieval conceptions of astronomical science, so the ' Copernican revolution ' of the idealism of the eighteenth century has rendered obsolete the philosophical ' Weltanschauung ' of the Middle Ages. But even if there is little in modern thought which can be regarded as a direct legacy of the Middle Age, except perhaps the doubtful blessing of formal logic, it must always be remembered that it was scholasticism which transmitted to European culture its first acquaintance with the philosophical heritage of Greece and Rome, and founded the academic tradition of our universities which has continued unbroken to the present time.

C. R. S. HARRIS.

---

[1] xxxiii. 85–90 :

> I saw that in its depth far down is lying,
>   Bound up with love together in one volume,
>   What through the universe in leaves is scattered ;
> Substance, and accident, and their operations
>   All interfused together in such wise
>   That what I speak of is one simple light.   (tr. Longfellow.)

5

EDUCATION

THE Chief Justice, ruling in 1410 that the education of children was a 'spiritual' matter, that is, one beyond the cognizance of the King's Bench, was asserting history as well as law; from the earliest to the latest Middle Ages public education throughout the West was a function of the Church. The pre-Christian Empire gave rank and privilege to distinguished *rhetors*, professors of rhetoric, and in the first century of our era State salaries were paid to those who practised in Rome, and perhaps to others who taught elsewhere. No such encouragement was given to the *grammatici* and *literatores* of the secondary and primary schools. Yet such schools existed and in many places were supported from public funds and by private enterprise.

The definitely local control of education combined with a central general oversight was the creation of the Church, which in due course evolved an organization comprising schools, universities, colleges. The unit was the diocesan bishop's household and its 'clerks', who there taught the Faith, prepared men for holy orders, and conducted the services of the cathedral and diocesan business generally. As instructors of the clergy-school the chief aim of these clerks was to teach 'divine letters', that is, the Scriptures and the patristic writings. In essentials this instruction and the Roman rhetorical training occupied common ground; both taught 'grammar', that is, language and literature, both aimed at persuasion by training speakers and writers. The thorough understanding of a literature which was involved in grammar demanded the mastery of a considerable body of miscellaneous knowledge without which classical works remained obscure. The 'liberal arts' were therefore as necessary to the Church as the ἐγκύκλιος παιδεία, the circle of arts and sciences, had been to pre-Christian culture. 'For without practical knowledge of other sciences the Holy Scriptures cannot be understood,' said St. Bonaventura in the thirteenth century re-echoing St. Augustine in the fourth. The school of the bishop's seat, whether in cathedral or monastery, perforce became a school of grammar, which was taught as preparatory and auxiliary to divinity, the primary object of the school's existence. To men not quite ignorant of Aristotle theological studies suggested problems which were philosophical; and this association of sacred and secular in due course gave rise to universities. The singers of a great church must add to a knowledge of musical notation the ability to read Latin words, even though, in default of grammar, the sense remained obscure. So the song school was created; it fluctuated throughout its history between the standing of a school of music and a grammar or a preparatory school. It was never an elementary school in the modern sense, a type of different origin.

In early days the bishop or abbot was the head of the cathedral or monastic school, and he was always its responsible chief; but as his duties became more onerous the care of the schools devolved upon a member of the chapter, usually the chancellor, but sometimes the precentor. Next, this officer (*scolasticus*, *archiscola*, or *scolarius*) tended to become in educational matters an administrator only; he might teach theology, but the grammar-teaching was customarily committed to a schoolmaster, a clerk in minor orders, in effect a layman. The scolasticus was virtually director of education under the local authority, the bishop, or 'ordinary'. No one might open a school or teach the liberal arts in the diocese without his licence, under penalty of trial in the spiritual court. The rudiments of such an administration may be traced back to the seventh century; at Reims *scolastici* of the ninth century are known by name; diocesan control was the rule throughout the Middle Ages. In time some of the universities emancipated themselves from this control, but its place was taken by the doctrine that only the Pope or the Emperor could found universities. Notwithstanding their clerical origin, the fact that the cathedral schools taught grammar, and sometimes at least one other ' liberal art ', gave to their instruction a value for others than clergymen. This lay character became more obvious as time passed; when the grammar school proved unable to meet a local demand a guild established one, or a school was added to an almshouse or attached to a chantry, either by express foundation or as a useful custom. But in all cases the bishop's licence was required; records show that attempts to evade this rule led to litigation which was sometimes carried to the highest court of appeal, Rome.

An echo of the bitter struggle between ' regulars ' and ' seculars ' of the Benedictine Age (ninth to twelfth centuries) is still heard in the dispute respecting the monks' share in teaching laymen. Some assert that the monks alone educated lay folk, others that monastic instruction was confined to teaching novices their *Rule*, the constitution of the monastic Order. It is agreed that during this period the great Benedictine houses were centres of learning which afforded a home for scholars, transcribed and interchanged books, maintained libraries. It is difficult to make a statement about their part in lay instruction which would be generally true at any time within the period, since circumstances differed with time and place. But their provision of separate schools for *interni* and *externi* at least points to teaching which was not limited to, if at all concerned with, the *Rule*; and there are recorded cases of men who were educated in convents yet did not become monks on completing their education. That not only abbots and priors but some simple monks were learned men inclines one to believe that where such scholars were found a fair measure of lay instruction was accessible to the *externi*. Certainly some English abbots maintained schools and schoolmasters and gave exhibitions to poor boys for the purpose of secular education. The growth of scholasticism and the study of law were powerful factors in the intellectual ferment of the twelfth century, and to these the monasteries contributed their share. Yet there is no reason to doubt that the cathedral and collegiate churches maintained their scholastic work wherever the monks failed to oust canons and clerks. The creation of that characteristic medieval institution, the university, was due to cathedral churches, not to monasteries, and the growth of universities ended the work of the latter as places of education, although the monks' successors, the friars, were conspicuous in university history. During the Benedictine age, there was marked educational activity in the cathedral schools of Reims, Laon, Chartres, Paris, Orléans, and Liège. Each of these centres owed its commanding position to the attraction of great teachers, who in the eager intellectual atmosphere of the twelfth century brought crowds, native and foreign, to the schools. The teaching at Chartres followed in the main the model of rhetorical instruction which Quintilian had described in the first century; had it prevailed generally, the revival of classical learning might have been advanced by two or three centuries. But Paris and its teachers of dialectic and theology overshadowed Chartres and made these the staple higher studies.

It is impossible to point to a particular year in the twelfth century as marking the beginning of the Bologna, Paris, or

Oxford *studia generalia*, or universities. When Abelard taught philosophy at Paris, when Irnerius lectured on law at Bologna, and Robert Pullus taught divinity at Oxford and Paris, they were sowing the seeds of great universities in soil already prepared by the scholastic labours of the cathedral and collegiate churches. Possibly similar local labours preceded the advent of Cambridge as a *studium* early in the thirteenth century.

The teachers and students of the first *studia*, settled in a not always friendly city, soon associated themselves in guilds, or *universitates*, for common convenience, safety, and freedom from extortion. The hierarchy of undergraduates, masters, and doctors, all duly ranked in a faculty of the Seven Liberal Arts and in at least one of the three faculties, theology, law, medicine, came later, but still early in university history. Yet the organization was very fluid at first ; and whenever Gown found cause of offence in Town, Gown migrated in a body, not being embarrassed by the possession of buildings or indeed of much property of any sort. The men and boys who came from all parts of western Europe to the *studia* made their own arrangements for board and lodging, sometimes with serious detriment to their morals and their pockets. A step in advance was taken when individual teachers opened boarding houses admitting students only ; and private charity maintained hostels for the benefit of the extremely poor. The Dominicans and Franciscans settled at the universities within the first quarter of the thirteenth century and they were joined by bodies of other ' religious ' before that century closed. The presence of these well-ordered houses of students living a common life and in time possessed of libraries, halls, chapels, and resident tutors, inevitably influenced their secular neighbours. The result was the creation of another characteristic medieval institution, the college, which was

firmly established at Paris, Oxford, and Cambridge, between
the years 1256 and 1284. Persistent tradition required that
fees should be low. The Lateran Council of 1179 decided
that in every cathedral church and in other churches where
it had been the practice, a master should be beneficed to
teach *gratis* the clerks of that church and ' other poor
persons ', ' poor clerks '. The repeated assertion of this
principle from the sixth or seventh centuries to the thirteenth shows that it was not invariably followed. Yet when
fees were exacted they were low. Grammar school boys at
Oxford between 1300 and 1347 paid a terminal fee varying
from 4*d*. to 5*d*., when the usual cost of a scholar's board for
one week was 8*d*., and a manuscript Donat, containing about
6,000 words, cost 3*d*. Writing, an ' extra ' taught inten-
sively, doubtless by a visiting expert, was charged 2*d*. per
week in 1347–8. Taking the term's fee as equivalent to half
a week's ' board ', it is very considerably lower than the
lowest fee charged to-day in any English secondary school.
Low fees, or no fees, implied the endowed teacher, whose
position was assured by the later creation of ' free grammar
schools '.

Maintenance was the poor student's difficulty. An
ancient obligation made ecclesiastical benefices chargeable
with a contribution to the support of students, one of the
recognized charitable acts ; at the university the college
organization soon developed not only the scholar on the
foundation, but also the servitor, or sizar, who received
commons or part commons for domestic service. Samson
(1135–1211), later the well-known abbot of Bury, was excused
school-fees on account of poverty ; he supported himself
at Paris by the alms which he received for carrying holy
water to parishioners' houses. There are several episcopal
orders of the thirteenth century directing that this office be
reserved to poor clerks, one bishop asserting that the benefice

was expressly created for them. In 1393 the Archbishop of Canterbury commends this 'laudable custom prevailing throughout England'—but he has to threaten penalties for its breach. Matthew Paris pictures a 'young clerk' of 1250 coming from a French village, 'bearing water in a little vessel with its sprinkler, and crusts of bread given to him for sprinkling holy water'. This clerk meets a papal agent who demands a tenth of the value of his benefice, to meet which and prolong a starved existence the mendicant sells his books and 'keeps school for many days'. The *aqua-bajulus*, or water-carrier, had a settled domicile; but the 'begging scholar' wandered from university to university gathering alms. His existence implied respect for even the humblest representatives of learning; but its toleration was open to abuse. In the fifteenth century young men, sometimes accompanied by yet younger boys, roamed over Germany begging and stealing, making their real or pretended zeal for knowledge an excuse for the life of a tramp. The Oxford Chancellor in 1461 licensed two begging students. University men came from all social ranks, the wealthiest and the poorest, but the great majority were probably drawn from classes which, while not indigent, were unable without assistance to maintain themselves throughout the prolonged university course, more especially if they proceeded to the higher degrees. It was to them that places were allotted by college foundation statutes. The phrase 'pauper et indigens', which so frequently defined the qualification for these emoluments, cannot reasonably be rendered 'indigent pauper', since it covered boys and youths in possession of an independent annual income equivalent to the customary charge for 'commons', i.e. board, for eighteen months or two years. A very burdensome charge fell upon the new-made bachelor, master and doctor, the burden increasing with the dignity. Rich men on graduation seem to have made it a point of honour to pay for the dinners and presents which their poorer fellow graduates were expected to provide.

The Latin, or grammar, schools were intended only for the boys, poor or rich, whose minds were of the scholarly type; they formed no part of a system of vernacular elementary schools. Not a few, perhaps very many, boys attending them dropped out of the course before ' grammar ' was completed; possibly the proportion of those who completed the study of the three ' arts ', grammar, rhetoric, logic, in the ' trivial schools ' was not great. But their failure was no substitute for elementary schooling as now understood. The duty of teaching *gratis* was laid upon the clergy, not excluding parish priests in villages, by a long series of councils, synods, and bishops' orders ranging over seven centuries from the sixth. But these were all framed *ad discendas litteras*, for the teaching of Latin ; the reiteration of the duty and the unsettled state of affairs, civil and ecclesiastical, during the earlier of these centuries, imply that this general provision was earnestly desired rather than commonly attained. The Decretals of Pope Gregory IX (1227-41) direct the parish priest to have his clerk to sing and read the epistle, to be able to keep school and to admonish parishioners to send their sons *ad fidem discendam*, to learn their religion, a phrase which later regulations make precise by specifying the Lord's Prayer, the Creed, the Hail! Mary, and other formularies. Such instructions regularized these parish, canonical or priests' schools, whose chief purpose was to give religious instruction to the boys *and girls* of the parish. Roger Bacon may have had such schools in view when he said (1267) that ' every one who desires it ' is ' instructed in those things which are of the faith'. Agnello, head of the first Franciscans in England (1224), is said to have ' received English lads into the Order

and, setting up schools for the poor, was zealous for study '.
Friars showed scant respect for the secular parson's jurisdiction and Agnello's schools may have been intended for
general parish use. It is far more probable that they were
meant to prepare boys for the novitiate, and that their ill-
educated pupils justified Bacon's complaint that boys of
ten and upwards ' who could read neither the Psalter nor
Donatus yet straightway after their profession were set to
study theology '. Leopold Delisle believed that, from the
thirteenth century, schools increased in number in rural
Normandy. There was a ' crowd of non-Latin schools,
song, writing, and reading ' in Troyes in the same century,
says another authority. Siméon Luce thought that during
the most disturbed years of the fourteenth century most
French villages had their schools. In 1400 Gerson, the
Paris *scolasticus*, inquired whether each parish had its school
and directed the establishment of one where one did not
exist.

These parish schools contained possibilities of development. Here and there the parson himself or a clerk in
minor orders might teach reading, either from goodwill or
for pay, like the priest to whom John of Salisbury and
another little boy were sent (*c.* 1130) ' to learn the Psalms ',
that is, to learn reading and begin the study of Latin. In
France at least such cases were not uncommon ; as economic
change made the advantage of vernacular instruction more
evident, the demand came from even humble quarters.
French priests alleged their canonical obligation as a reason
for keeping charity schools, independent of the *scolasticus*,
in which religion, reading Latin words, writing and summing
were taught. These seventeenth-century schools probably
had less systematic medieval forerunners. To these
possible opportunities of elementary instruction may be
added the song schools and the services of private teachers,

as well as the express provision of elementary schools during the closing century or two of the period. Song schools were originally liturgical only in purpose, but they followed the general tendency of schools to overstep their original bounds and the instruction which they gave was utilized by others than choristers. A record (York, 1367) complains that to the Precentor's prejudice ' chaplains, holy-water carriers, and many others keep schools of song and for instructing boys in singing, in parish churches, *houses, and other places* '. Perhaps these really were rivals of the cathedral song school; more probably they met a demand for teaching reading greater than that school contemplated. Anchoresses, female hermits, often dwelling on the outskirts of towns, also taught children, although authority frowned upon the practice. Teaching to read the mother tongue was no part of the grammar school's business. Yet there are indications that many could read, even amongst the sex which was excluded almost, if not quite, entirely from grammar schools. Before the close of the twelfth century a French devotional book appeared which was translated into English about a century later as *The Lay Folk's Mass Book*. In the greater German cities children learned to read and write under private teachers, men and women. English parents or god-parents were enjoined to teach their children the Lord's Prayer, the Creed, and other formularies in English long before the invention of printing; *Primers* partly at least in English appeared, containing these and similar matter. A mass of correspondence dating from times before and on the eve of the invention of printing (1440–50) has been preserved in this country, much of which is now in print. Men and women in quite humble walks of life, whose circumstances make it unlikely that they had had schooling in ' grammar ', are amongst the correspondents. The earliest English printed books (1476, &c.)

were in the mother tongue and were such as would especially appeal to women and to persons ignorant of any language but their own. The large number of controversial English books imported from the Continent between 1500 and 1550 points to readers of the same type. Dr. A. W. Reed found in the Record Office a document which revealed a party of village girls of humble rank reading English books in an Essex village church on Ascension Day in 1534. Who taught them to read?

By this date the ecclesiastical provision of schools had proved inadequate to the needs of a community outgrowing feudal conditions. Commerce and industry required that schools should supply in quantity and kind what it was not the Church's function to furnish. Guilds and municipalities set up schools, at first to teach the customary studies; but it proved necessary to supplement these Latin schools by purely elementary schools. In 1338, Florence, then a great commercial and industrial centre, taught reading to boys and girls in large numbers; it had also six schools where boys learned summing by the abacus, or counting-board, and by algorism, that is, summing by the decimal notation of integers. Commerce and industry need large numbers of clerks and work-people able to read and write and cast an account. Provision for this was made in German cities by the starting of 'German Schools' during the fourteenth century, at which time the earliest German universities, Prague, Vienna, Heidelberg, Cologne, and Erfurt had their beginning. England passed from the agricultural to the industrial and commercial stage in the following century, when 'Writing Schools' began to be established to teach boys 'the three R's', that, as a foundation deed of 1483 says, 'they may be more apt for the mechanical arts and other worldly affairs'. Schools of this kind, and more particularly the irregular practitioners who preceded them

in the days of manuscript books, made possible the rapid
advance of the art of printing, the latest of medieval inventions. For the vast majority of girls the standard of school
instruction (where any was given) varied but little throughout the centuries ; to become proficient in home-making
and scrupulously to discharge their religious duties sufficed.
For the last purpose reading was an advantage and to that
their schooling was mainly directed. But in Paris girls had
the opportunity of learning the rudiments of Latin accidence
equally with little boys, though separate schools were kept
for the sexes. These ' Little Schools ' were not elementary
but preparatory to the grammar schools ; they therefore
taught reading and rudimentary Latin grammar. The
name of a Parisian schoolmistress who kept such a school in
1292 is on record. In the following century the Paris
scolasticus, when summoning assemblies of the teachers of
the Little Schools, included ' honourable women keeping
and teaching schools in the art of grammar '. Mr. Leach
found a reference (1404) to a ' magistra scolarum ' at
Boston. Since ' magister scolarum ' is the technical term
for the master, i. e. head master, of a grammar school, it would
appear that Boston taught some girls Latin at that date.

To what extent did nunneries assist lay education ? No
brief answer can be satisfactory ; practice differed in
different times, countries, and nunneries. The convents of
the early centuries were the homes of some secular women
of high rank whose upbringing was that of the castle, not
of the school. Bishops frequently forbade nuns to receive
seculars for education, a prohibition perhaps as frequently
disregarded ; the more strictly a convent interpreted its
Rule, the less would it offer education to secular girls.
The studies of two girls, both seculars, in a ninth-century
Flemish nunnery, as described by Miss Eckenstein, comprised reading, writing, drawing, illuminating, spinning,

weaving, needlecraft; but these were exemplary pupils.
If writing, drawing, and illuminating be subtracted and
religious instruction added, this list is fairly representative
of what the generality of those girls learned who had any
schooling at all at any time during the Middle Ages; the
teachers required but little book-learning. Some French
and English nuns of the seventh and eighth centuries were
sufficiently instructed in grammar to make Latin verses
and to write Latin letters; a tenth-century German nun,
Hroswitha, wrote half a dozen plays whose mixture of
dramatic narrative and irrelevant pedantry does not conceal
their model, Terence. But the standard of the nuns' own
education declined in time. During the fourteenth century
while Latin remained the official language of English
authorities addressing monks, French at first and English
later were employed for nuns in like case. From that time
to the Dissolution in 1537 English replaced French, as it
did in the grammar schools of England after the Black
Death of 1348-9. Formally, nuns were literate; but this
need not mean more than ability to read the Latin Psalter
without an accurate knowledge of the meaning; in 1308
the Bishop of Exeter enjoined the Polsloe nuns to prefer
Latin in conversation, but permitted a relaxation of the
strict demands of grammar.

If Froissart's poem, *Espinette Amoureuse*, is autobio-
graphical, he went to a school (about 1350, or earlier) where
both young boys and young girls were taught together.
If the practice in the Low Countries was the same as in
England, Froissart's school was probably in a nunnery.
Miss Eileen Power has examined visitation injunctions,
account rolls, and other matter relating to forty-nine
nunneries, the dates ranging from the late thirteenth
century to the Dissolution. These convents were authorized
to receive young girls, or young girls and still younger boys

for education, the maximum ages being 12–14 and 9–10 respectively ; and the practice was more generally followed in the early sixteenth century than in preceding times. It seems to follow that medieval nunneries taught only a small fraction of the children of school age. In any case, for most girls facilities for schooling were meagre, yet current opinion was satisfied. Of girls who belonged to the landed class more is said below.

The arbitrary divisions ' ancient ', ' medieval ', ' modern ', obscure the thread of continuity running through Western education from the days of the Roman Empire to the present. When the Christian Church of the fourth century acquired political standing, it was by force of circumstances compelled, however unwillingly, to employ the rhetorical instruction which Rome had adopted from Greece and which Quintilian had fully described. There was no alternative. The study of Scripture was of all studies most congenial to Christian sentiment, and Scriptural study could only be pursued through ' grammar ', that is, language and literature. But some Latin and Greek literature, especially the poetic literature, was offensive to Christian theology and morals ; Christians of the second century had scrupled to send their children to school for that reason and because attendance involved sharing in pagan rites and countenancing pagan beliefs. Yet it was these schools or none ; the Christian catechetical schools did not profess secular knowledge, but limited their teaching to divinity and apologetic.

Christian thinkers from Tertullian in the second century onwards agreed that this pre-Christian learning was necessary to an understanding of the Scriptures. The situation was further embarrassed by the admiration which many felt for the purely human, aesthetic, and spiritual qualities of the Latin and Greek classics; and after Christianity had become the State religion there must have been many professing Christians whose sympathies could not be divorced from the literature which had been the core of their own schooling. So the rhetorical education, which had formed St. Jerome, and of which St. Augustine, before his baptism, had been a professor, became in due course the accepted mode of Christian schooling, notwithstanding the occasional frowns or active discouragement from the authorities. Thus the schools of the medieval Church preserved the memory, howbeit blurred and imperfect, of the old civilization, and carried onwards a limited knowledge of its literature, which remained the staple of European higher education down to the other day. In the West, such Greek authors as were known—Aristotle, a little of Plato, Homer—were best known through Latin versions. A reputation for Greek scholarship was not infrequently accorded to men whose Greek was limited to a knowledge of its notation and odds and ends of words with which they interlarded their writings. Nevertheless a thin stream of Greek scholarship never entirely ceased to flow until it became a broad river at the Renaissance. Latin was the real vehicle of medieval learning, and Latin classics, particularly the poets, did not lose their hold even in times when the Fathers and Christian Latin poets formed the favourite reading. Just as the Psalter was the boy's first book, so Ovid was his first 'classic'; Virgil was looked upon as half a Christian, Cicero was the model orator and an authority on philosophy and religion, Seneca was read as moralist and as man of science. Quintilian was still the authority on rhetorical education, although familiarity with the *Institutio Oratoria* waxed and waned in a strange fashion through the centuries, until Poggio in 1416 found a dust-begrimed yet complete text in the St. Gall monastery.

Greek astronomy, mathematics, medicine, and science passed to the West through the Semitic peoples, the Arabs and Jews of Spain being the most active agents. The Jews as speakers of Hellenistic Greek from the days of their dispersion formed a broad channel of Greek learning to the East; and the Arabs, whose conquests in the tenth century extended throughout the southern coasts of the Mediterranean and to the greater part of modern Spain, became its eager students, the school of Cordova being especially famous in the twelfth century. This orientalized Greek science, or at least its astronomy and astrology, were in contact with the West as early as the tenth century. Venice was actively trading with the East in the eighth century; it was through the same city that in the late fourteenth century the revival of Greek study in the West had its beginning. Of all the Greek thinkers Aristotle exercised by far the greatest influence upon the ' Latins ' of the West. Abelard, who died in 1142, only knew the elementary parts of Aristotle's logical doctrine, ' the old logic '. By 1150 the whole of that doctrine—the ' new ' and the ' old logic '— had become known to the West; and by 1200 most of his physical, metaphysical, and moral writings, ' the Three Philosophies ', were accessible in Latin translations. These, not being direct from the Greek but having filtered through two or more Semitic languages, were so very faulty that Roger Bacon, who pleaded for a more general study of the originals, declared ' if I had the control of Aristotle's books, I would cause them all to be reduced to ashes, as their study is nothing but a waste of time, a cause of error, and the multiplication of ignorance beyond what their explanation is worth. And as Aristotle's labours are the foundation of all philosophy no one can gauge the loss to the West since its philosophers have entertained these faulty translations.' Their anti-Christian trend was a further incentive to recover the genuine Aristotle. The Latin occupation of Constantinople (1204–61) gave an opportunity which wandering Western scholars did not miss. Nor did Roger Bacon think that competent teachers were not to be found. 'Teachers are not wanting; for everywhere there are Hebrews, and their tongue is substantially one with Arabic and Chaldee, though different in manner. There are men in Paris and in France and in all the regions beyond who know what is needed for the purpose. But Greek is especially in accord with Latin; and there are many in England and France who are sufficiently instructed in it.' He goes on to say that it would be no great matter for the bishops and rich men to send for books and teachers to Italy, where in many parts clergy and people are pure Greek. 'This the saintly Bishop of Lincoln [Grosseteste] was wont to do.' At this time Paris possessed a College of Orientals versed in Arabic and other Eastern languages. The University in 1300 petitioned the Pope for a college to teach Arabic, Greek, and Tartar.

The Seven Liberal Arts formed the curriculum of school and university; upon them were erected the professional studies of divinity, law, and medicine. The Arts were in two groups, the *Trivium* of grammar, rhetoric, dialectic, and the *Quadrivium* of arithmetic, geometry, music, and astronomy. Pestalozzi's fundamentals of instruction, language, number, and (geometrical) form, probably owed nothing to the Arts for their conception; but they very well summarize the Seven. Of the Arts, the first was vital to them all. 'Grammar', said Rabanus Maurus (d. 856), 'is the knowledge which interprets poets and historians; it is also the method of correct writing and speech. It is both source and basis of the liberal arts.' Rhetoric, the art ruling literary expression in general, also included the composition of formal epistles; with grammar it constituted the course for even the best schools, though some, the 'trivial schools', added logic. Dialectic was differently interpreted at different times. In its most liberal sense it was that association of Greek philosophy and Christian divinity which gave rise to scholasticism; in its least liberal form it consisted of the barest bones of elementary, formal logic, a spare diet usually offered to university freshmen. The *Summulae* of Petrus Hispanus (d. 1277), which long continued to be the most widely read text-book of logic, makes claims which reflect the position of that study throughout the later medieval period. 'Dialectic is the art of arts, the science of sciences, furnishing the way to the principles of all methods. For dialectic alone discusses accurately the principles of all other sciences and therefore in the attainment of sciences dialectic should be the first.'

The boundary separating school from university was ill-defined. The 'grandes écoles', or grammar schools, of Paris were repeatedly forbidden to trespass upon university functions; French school-boys still take the bachelor's degree before entering the university. Rhetoric thus formed common ground; but in the university the art sometimes included an elementary study of law. Arithmetic also varied in implication. In Boethius's text-book it meant the doctrine of the properties of number, especially of ratio and proportion. In clergy-schools it was the *computus*, a body of rules determining the date of Easter and other points in the Church calendar; remains of it survive in the prefatory matter to the Book of Common Prayer. Here, of course, astronomy helped arithmetic. Again, arithmetic meant rules for working the abacus, or counting-board, by which calculations in money and similar concrete 'sums' were solved. In the eleventh century the abacus and its employment seem to have enjoyed something like a renais-

41. THE HOUSE OF LEARNING

from G. Reisch, Margarita Philosophica, 1503 (see pp. 271 ff.)

sance in the great schools of Reims, Laon, Fleury, and Liège. The introduction of the zero to the West from the Arabian mathematicians somewhere within or near the twelfth century made algorism possible, that is, calculation by the nine integers and zero as now practised. Of geometry and music it is unnecessary to say more than that the former was based upon Euclid, with some geography added, and that, as well as notation and singing, the latter included the numerical relations of musical sound. Astronomy, which never quite emancipated itself from astrology, included such observation as was possible with rudely fashioned instruments, the telescope not being one of them.

For nearly a millennium after the fifth century a farrago of prose and verse, called the *Nuptials of Philology and Mercury*, was used as a manual of the Arts. Philology represented the love of learning; Mercury, or Hermes, by reason of his functions, inventions, and patronage, was especially associated with education. As the author proposed to describe the various provinces of knowledge which constituted the curriculum, he employed the form of an allegorical marriage, the Greek god being united with a curriculum of Greek origin. The first two books are occupied by this ambitious but exceedingly dull and somewhat irrelevant allegory, the remaining seven, in the words of Sandys, ' talk undiluted and unmitigated text-book ', each art giving an account of herself.

The earliest university statutes (Paris, 1215) present only the most sketchy outline of a curriculum. They imply lectures in arts and theology. In arts, rhetoric, the Quadrivium and Donatus's *Barbarism* (a very brief tract on incorrect Latin, written and spoken) are subjects for lectures on festival days, when as a rule ' there shall be no lectures '. Ethics is an optional subject, while the other two Aristotelian

' philosophies ', with the writings of certain heretics, are prohibited studies. Heresy, theological and political, was rife and the most extreme measures were taken at that time to extirpate it. At Oxford in 1267 the candidate for the B.A. degree read grammar, Aristotle's logic, natural philosophy, and psychology. A drastic reform was effected at Paris in 1452 and the full arts course included grammar in more modern text-books, verse-making, algorism, logic, geometry, astronomy, and (subsequent to the bachelor's degree) mathematics (i. e. arithmetic, geometry, music), and Aristotle's three ' philosophies '. In 1458 Greek was taught in Paris by a Greek refugee and some seven years later an Italian taught it in New College, Oxford. Dr. P. S. Allen has identified three Greeks who were copying Greek manuscripts in England about this time. After the arts course came the professional studies, divinity, law, medicine. The contest between the Empire and the Papacy gave a great vogue to both civil and common law as profitable bread-studies.

A great change in the higher studies was wrought by the entry of the Mendicant Orders quite early in their history into the universities. The Dominicans of Paris and the Oxford Franciscans were conspicuous amongst the scholars of the time. St. Thomas Aquinas (d. 1274), the great Dominican doctor, sought a reconciliation between Christian divinity and Aristotelian philosophy. The Franciscans, and chief among them Duns Scotus (d. 1308 ?), greatly fortified scholastic logic. These two names represent a conflict in educational opinion. St. Thomas put intellect above will, just as modern education tends to value knowledge more highly than conduct. Duns agreed with St. Augustine in putting will first, a position to which our schools may be forced to return when it is realized that ' all knowledge ' is the province of few, if of any. The Friars were as regardless of academic practice as of parochial order, yet they desired to enjoy full academic privilege. So they presented for divinity degrees Friars who had not followed an arts course ; the secular university teachers, no doubt as anxious to maintain their own interests as to uphold an educational principle, insisted that the arts course was the indispensable preliminary to study in what were recognized as the superior faculties. In that sense the dispute was settled at Oxford in 1253 and at Paris about the same time. Thus a line was drawn between general and professional education ; yet the motive of the earliest university studies was primarily professional. The Dominicans, as disseminators of the Faith and its upholders against heretics, had special need of a knowledge of the biblical languages and of modern tongues ; as missionaries to the very poor, the Franciscans also needed to know vernaculars, and their settlements in town slums led them to practise medicine. In 1237 Friar Philip informed the Pope that Friars Preachers were being sent to Armenia to learn the language, that the houses of the Order had been enjoined to study Eastern tongues and that the Friars spoke and preached ' in new languages and especially in Arabic, which is more common amongst the people '. The Council of Vienne (1311) directed the Universities of Paris, Oxford, Bologna, and Salamanca to teach Hebrew, Greek, Arabic, and Chaldee, and to secure translations from those languages into Latin, a direction repeated at Basel in 1434.

The curriculum gives no place to experimental science ; the tradition inherited from the ancient education, the deference paid to the written word and the protracted length of the established courses explain the omission. Yet experiment, observation, and applied science were not absolutely neglected in medieval society, even amongst its scholars ; although they do not belong to ' education ', the

scientific studies of such men as Albertus Magnus and
Roger Bacon sowed seeds which had already come to
vigorous growth when Francis Bacon wrote of the inductive
method and slighted the work of men who were employing
it successfully. The first chapters of Genesis have been in
modern times the battle-ground between theology and
science; in the Middle Ages they constantly moved
thoughtful men to an interest in nature, as witness the
different books, each entitled ' The Six Days ', of which
St. Basil (d. 379) wrote the first.

When the child could read the letters, syllables, and
words of the Latin Psalter, Donatus's *On the eight parts of
speech* was his next school-book. This elementary Latin
accidence, the work of a fourth-century grammarian,
remained, virtually unaltered, for more than a thousand
years the foundation of grammar-learning and the master-
key to recorded knowledge. It made no pretence of assisting
the memory graphically. Ninth-century manuscripts and
sixteenth-century printed copies are alike in their long,
unbroken paragraphs, initial letters alone disturbing the
page's monotony. A few lines from a mid-fifteenth century
copy will show how little care was taken to help the pupil
in memorizing.

 ' Participiū quid est ꝑs orōis ꝑte capiēs noīs & verbi recipit enī
a noiē genᵍea & casᵍ a v̄bo autē tꝑa & sig̴ficacoēs ab utꝗ₃ num' &
figurā.'

More advanced than the Donat was the *Grammar* of
Priscian, who taught the subject in Constantinople at the
end of the fifth or beginning of the sixth century. The
work in eighteen books treated accidence and, in much less
fullness, syntax. This compilation remained the standard
book until it was formally superseded at Paris (1366) by the
Doctrinale of Alexander de Villa Dei. Yet a greatly reduced

Epitome of Priscian was printed at Venice in 1511. The
Doctrinale purported to be an intermediate book for junior
' clerks ' for whom Alexander must have felt some sympathy, since he presents accidence, syntax, prosody, and
figures of speech, under their repellent technical names, in
some three thousand hexameters of sorts. Certainly some
help was needed to get by rote the jungle of exceptional
forms which it contained. The book was freely used in
Continental universities and was in general school use in
Germany, but neither it nor its sixteenth-century successor,
also in verse, the grammar of the Fleming, Despautère,
attained corresponding favour in England. This country
had its own grammar reform in the late fifteenth and early
sixteenth centuries, which gave the English school-boy
a choice of text-books much better arranged for convenience
and compiled on more reasonable principles ; this was the
work of schoolmasters, of whom William Lily was chief.
While Ovid was the first genuine classic which the school-
boy read, the *Disticha de Moribus*, a series of sententious
couplets attributed to ' Cato ', was from early times the
favourite beginner's author, as being at once edifying
and ' easy Latin '. The book was one of the many translated into German by the St. Gall monk, Notker Labeo,
who died in 1022 ; school-boys were using it in the late
seventeenth century, when its moralizing function was
better fulfilled by Lily's *Qui mihi Discipulus*, a versified code
of school-room behaviour.

The continuity with the ancient civilization is illustrated
by the series of encyclopaedias which ranged from the
works of Varro, Pliny the Elder, and Martianus Capella to
the *Margarita Philosophica* of 1503. The Church's emphasis
on authority and on the written word made such works an
especially appropriate instrument of the education over
which the Church presided. They also gave opportunities

for ' editing' those opinions of antiquity which were repugnant to Christian belief or principle. In their general character they resemble the *Thirty Seven Books of Histories* of Pliny (A.D. 23–79), a miscellany of geography, man and his inventions, animals, plants, vegetable products, medicine, and medicinal plants, metals, pictures, colours, and gems. While its greater part is matter of fact, it yet finds room for credulous, even nonsensical hearsay. Into this world of things and no-things the medieval writers brought a world of ideas. *The Twenty Books of Etymologies or of Origins* of Isidore of Seville (570–636), to-day obtainable in one octavo volume of 900 pages, has chapters on law, the Scriptures, the offices of the Church, on God, angels, saints, on warfare, languages, cities, and the things of everyday life, household furniture included. Isidore differs from Pliny in the attention which he gives to the meaning of terms, thus producing a modern dictionary rather than a modern cyclopaedia, a feature which marks his successors' similar books. It exposes the narrow limits of the writers' knowledge.

Medieval education was based on the principle of authority; that fact and the material conditions under which instruction was delivered, determined its method. Lack of books in sufficient quantity and frequent errors of transcription in cheap manuscripts compelled the early medieval teachers to employ oral methods and in particular the crude expedient of dictating the text of the authority under consideration. As copies multiplied the need for dictation disappeared, but the oral tradition was then firmly established. With the correct text before his pupils, the teacher's proper business began; he expounded the text and made his commentary. If the teacher's reputation was great, the commentary was likely thereafter to be the invariable accompaniment of the text. The scarcity of reliable texts also threw much rote-learning upon the pupil; and to facilitate rote, there was much repetition, the compiling of *résumés* and the employment of mnemonics, in framing which medieval students were expert. The five apparently meaningless lines beginning ' Barbara Celarent Darii Ferioque prioris ', which still appear in text-books of logic, are the contrivance of an unknown genius, who brought into this compendious shape pretty well all, expressed or implied, that was needed to operate the syllogism successfully. The value of verse-forms in memorizing was well-understood. Roger Bacon mentions a ' versified Bible ' intended seemingly for children ; but he disapproves of it, because it abridged or mutilated everything. Teachers favoured the ' direct method ' and text-books were in Latin. As the facilities for multiplying manuscripts improved, epitomes were made for the pupil. After the tendency of all epitomes, such manuals tended in time to replace the original authors. The *Sentences* of Peter Lombard (second half of the twelfth century) and the *Summulae* of Petrus Hispanus became substitutes for the Bible and Aristotle's logic respectively.

But the method *par excellence* both of teaching and learning was the disputation. ' This exercise ', said Robert de Sorbon (d. 1274), ' is much more advantageous than reading, because it results in clearing up doubts. Nothing is known perfectly which has not been masticated by the teeth of disputation.' The university student maintained theses and disputed from end to end of his degree course ; but the exercise was not confined to universities. Lively pictures of London school-boys' public disputations are drawn by Fitz-Stephen (*c.* 1118) and by Stow, the antiquary, who took part in them as a boy (*c.* 1530–40). The method did not please the Renaissance scholars, yet English boys of the seventeenth century had manuals designed to help them to dispute in grammar. Disputation shared with rhetoric the obvious defect of encouraging readiness to argue for victory's sake with indifference to truth and the merits of the case ; but it gave a command over what was learned and made it real, it bred alert, inquiring, acute minds, and no doubt incited many to leave the beaten track and think for themselves. It may even have turned some to the too much neglected scrutiny of nature. In any case, the method of disputation provided a powerful demurrer to the excessive respect shown to authority and the readiness to accept palpable forgeries, when once stamped with an authoritative name, failings which sadly limited the usefulness of education. It was all very well for Tyndal at a later day to talk of ' the old barking curres, Dunce's disciples, and lyke draffe, called Scotists, the children of darkness ', but reasons are not wanting for calling Duns, ' doctor subtilis,' and the other skilful disputants, ' lucifers,' bearers of the light.

The distinct type of upbringing which aimed at educating men and women of the highest social class owed nothing to schools, yet its tradition may well be regarded as a legacy bequeathed to the days of universal, compulsory schooling. Boys of this class used the schools exceptionally, some certainly resorted to the universities ; most were brought up apart from schools. A great feudal establishment not only had its staff of ' clerks ' to transact business, it also included children and young people, the charges of the lord and lady to whose personal care they were committed for education. The object in view was preparation for the careers of action, of ruler and soldier, and in less degree the cultivation of the social amenities. In its later history, chivalric education evolved a regular series of stages from page to squire and thence to knight, with corresponding stages for the maiden ; it was as ' vocational ' as the clerk's, but it was addressed to the individual and tried to train a greater variety of aptitudes than did the school. In that respect it should be instructive to-day. Physical training, the use of arms, military studies, manners in hall and bower, games like chess and other social accomplishments were carefully practised. Women shared with men in out-door sports and in the ceremony and social intercourse, often on an international scale, which were associated with the tourney. The early upbringing of boys and girls was in women's hands ; the girls acquired an elementary, empirical knowledge of medicine and surgery as well as of needle-craft, domestic arts and management. Religious instruction invariably formed a prominent feature in girls' education.

The association between courts and letters was sometimes slight, sometimes close, as at the courts of Charlemagne and of our Henry II ; but the constant presence of ecclesi-astics and other clerkly persons makes absolute neglect of letters in great feudal households incredible. Charlemagne's so-called Palace School was exceptional in its attention to the liberal arts ; but that it was not due to the King's personality alone is shown in its maintenance by his grandson, Charles the Bald, at whose court (873-7) John the Scot taught Greek and neo-Platonism. Henry II not only encouraged learning in the clerks who were his able adminis-trators ; his care for letters fostered romance amongst his lay courtiers. In Henry III's time the Franciscan, Adam Marsh, regularly corresponded in Latin with Simon de Montfort and his wife. Of the eleven priests in the house-hold of the fifth Earl of Northumberland (1477-1527), one was a ' maister of gramer in my lordes house '. Children of rank are found from time to time living in convents for education's sake, a practice which seems to have increased during the pre-Reformation century. In such cases the pupils were not associated with the school (if any) attached to the community, but with the abbess or abbot personally. That is, they formed part of the household of a feudal magnate, exactly as did their equals brought up in a castle or manor house ; they were not at school.

The historical significance of this aristocratic education consists in this, that it was the channel through which the humanism of the classical revival became effective. The patrons and auxiliaries of Renaissance humanism were not schools and universities, but the princes and princely merchants of Italy ; its practitioners were wandering scholars or men like Emanuel Chrysoloras, who was invited in 1397 by Florentine magnates to teach Greek in their city. In the fifteenth century there was a steady flow of learners, lay and clerical, men of all ranks, from north of the Alps to the Italian cities where Greek could be learned from Greeks or from their Italian pupils. But the spread of humanism, aided as undoubtedly it was by this revived study of Greek, owed most to its Italian patrons and to the scholars who served them.

The influence of the classical revival upon the old chivalric education is exemplified in an essay, *On the freeborn way of life*, which Vergerius addressed about the year 1392 to a son of the lord of Padua ; it has been translated by Mr. W. H. Woodward. In this essay the chief liberal arts are arms and letters. ' So soon as he is able to use his limbs let him be trained to arms ; so soon as he can rightly speak let him be trained to letters.' The curriculum includes the Seven Liberal Arts, history, moral philosophy, poetry, and the poetic art, mechanics, perspective, the art and theory of war, military training. From these the pupil makes his selection, taking or leaving in harmony with his own capacity. ' The natural bent should be recognized and followed in education.'

This was liberal education as practised (1423-46) by Vittorino da Feltre in 'the House Joyous' of the Marquis of Mantua. Vergerius's counsel reappeared in Castiglione's *The Courtier* (1528) and again in Elyot's *The Boke of the Governour* (1531), works which became standard texts of this type of nurture, though they are but intermediate links in a long chain.

Brantôme says that Renée of France, daughter of Louis XII, 'knew history, mathematics, Latin, and Greek as well as any learned man of her time,' that Marguerite of Angoulême, sister of Francis I, 'learned, while quite a child, Latin, Spanish, and Italian,' and later 'a little Greek and Hebrew'. Marguerite of Valois, wife of Henry IV, spoke Italian and Spanish 'as eloquently as if she had been born, nurtured and brought up all her life in Italy and Spain. It was the same with Latin.' The Latin exercise book of Mary Stuart, written when as a child of ten she was being educated in the French royal family, is in the Bibliothèque Nationale. Everybody has heard of Lady Jane Grey's love of Greek and of Queen Elizabeth's Latin; indeed, the instruction given to these highly placed women has, time and again, been misrepresented as typical of women's education in the sixteenth century.

These names have led to the very verge and beyond the limits of the Middle Ages. Italian universities of the fourteenth and fifteenth centuries were active in the study of law rather than of letters; when the revival reached the universities outside Italy, those seats of learning retained the medieval form of their courses, but gradually modified its content in accord with the newer ideals. Yet the schools went very near to sterilizing the humanism of the Renaissance. Cicero's eminence as an orator was a medieval tradition which the classical revival in Italy turned into a cult; from Petrarch (1304-74) to Sturm (1507-89) scholars used the most absurdly exaggerated language in praise of ' Tully '. Papal secretaries and State bureaucrats strove to express official letters and documents not in the living Latin of their own day, but in the literary dialect of Ciceronian prose. To write such prose was a passport to public employment. Schoolmasters realized the bread-and-butter value of the accomplishment, and the main purpose of teaching and learning was the imitation of Cicero's periods. Sturm's school at Strasbourg (1538–81) made a show of teaching the Seven Liberal Arts, but its lengthy course of study was very obviously devoted to one aim, the mastery of Ciceronian prose, and the Strasbourg Gymnasium became the model of Protestant Germany and of Northern Europe.

Medieval education preserved the memory and many of the literary treasures of the preceding civilization ; it continued in its formal aspect the education current under the Roman Empire, it established a curriculum which suffered little disturbance until the eighteenth and nine-teenth centuries, and it framed an organization of schools and universities which is still in operation. To these it added the tradition of a local as well as a central adminis-tration. Its strength lay in unity of belief ; society as such held a common philosophy of life, most men were agreed in their idea of the universe and man's place in it. Con-sequently there was virtually universal recognition of one supreme educational end. But this agreement was always being threatened, until the individualism of the humanists and of the Reformation destroyed it. Unity of belief was both the strength and weakness of the instruction, since it exaggerated the claim of authority, particularly of the written word, and tended to keep to a routine, a tendency which was actual for centuries. Yet its favourite method of disputation served in great measure as a corrective; critics and objectors were never lacking, and so long as they did not contradict the Church's settled decisions, they were not molested.

Rashdall thought that medieval university education was too literary yet too practical, too dogmatic yet too disputatious, and that if these couples cancelled each other, imagination, taste, the sense of beauty were neglected. But this is to restrict education to the doings of schools and their like. The Middle Ages did not so restrict it. In the upbringing of the knight and dame, to whose tastes in great measure we owe the beginnings of modern literatures, there was a salutary correction to the hard intellectualism of academic training. Perhaps that is the great medieval contribution to educational theory and practice. As men said then, ' The greatest clerks are not the wisest men.'

J. W. Adamson.

6

LAW

i. CUSTOMARY LAW

I

MEN'S conduct is regulated by two forces—by their habits of mind and by compulsion from outside authority. The latter may appear in the form of commands sanctioned by penalties, but even such 'laws' require generally a measure of support from the opinion and habits of the people subjected to them in order to function successfully. Laws repugnant to the notions of right of a community or to its practical requirements are likely to be defeated by passive resistance and by the difficulty of constant supervision and repression. On the contrary, when public opinion and moral training dispose men to consider certain relations to be normal or certain acts to be reprehensible these convictions and habits form, as it were, a convenient soil on which the various legal rules can be firmly established. In advanced civilizations the complicated fabric of social relations requires an extensive framework of laws, formulated and applied by professional experts, while in earlier stages the balance has to be drawn the other way : the rules of human conduct stand in immediate contact with public opinion and social custom.

This was undoubtedly the case in the Middle Ages. The attempts of Charlemagne and other rulers to introduce decrees and to enforce laws were powerless so far as systematic legislation was concerned, although they left many traces in the shape of particular institutions. Even when political authority began to be consolidated again—in the twelfth and thirteenth centuries—writers on law explained that they had to deal mainly with customs and not with rules established by express legislation and embodied in an official code. Bracton and Beaumanoir drew to a large extent on the decisions of judges, but these decisions were given in conformity to the average customs of the ruling military class. Eike von Repgow and the provincial laws of Norway, Sweden, and Denmark summarize the customs in the Courts in comprehensive recognized statements without express reference to judicial decisions. Needless to say that earlier ' laws of the folk ' or barbaric laws (*Leges barbarorum*) are even more clearly products of popular legal lore interpreted with occasional chapters (*capitularia*) of royal legislation. All these documents and literary efforts serve the purpose of retaining the memory and fixing the traditional wording of customary rules, but they were not general ' sources of law ' in the sense of embracing the whole body of customary rules used by a particular nation or in a particular region. Law had to be sought and discovered primarily in the vast background of social intercourse. Judges, when they had to try disputed points, had not simply to apply officially established texts, but to discover the rules that had to be applied in the case. English and American judges have even now to deal with similar problems when they judge at common law, and in order to solve these problems they usually rely on a vast collection of precedents—a body of professional decisions. Medieval judges had to a great extent to discover the customary views and arrangements prevailing among the people in their society.

This feature of medieval jurisdiction had characteristic consequences : it became necessary to ascertain the nature and details of custom by applying for information to representatives or experts belonging to the community where the custom was in use. *Judgement* (*Richten*) had to be supplemented by *Verdict* (*Urteil*). This could be done in various ways. In the earlier period the presiding judge of the court—of a shire, or of a hundred, of a county (*tunginus*), the ealdorman or hundredealder—left the question as to the custom to be applied as well as the question as to facts to the doomsmen, who were either the whole body of suitors of the court or the representatives of that body selected for a long period for their experience and wisdom (the *scabini, échevins, Schöffen*). His own business was to conduct the proceedings, to announce the ultimate decision, and to give it effect as far as was possible in those days. The same course was adopted when the verdict (*Urteil*) was meant to be a general pronouncement as to existing custom, distinct from the sentence of the presiding magistrate or chief.

Two Bavarian records of the ninth century allow us a glimpse of the way in which the judicial functions were differentiated between the representative of public power— a Royal Commissioner or Count or other magnate holding pleas—legal experts (*iudices*), and the assembly of doomsmen. In 822 an Imperial Commissioner (*missus*) orders that the law shall be decreed between the parties : Kieselhard, a public judge, was first in making a pronouncement in accordance with the law of the Bavarians. In the same year there is a record of the names of those who took part in making the ' decree ' in accordance with the law of the Bavarians : Kieselhard, Count Luitpold, and several vassals of the Emperor are mentioned by name ; at the close ' the whole people proclaimed with one voice that this was the law of the Bavarians '.[1]

In Scandinavian countries such pronouncements were

---

[1] Bitterauf, *Traditiones Frisingenses*, NN. 472 (referred to by Brunner, *Deutsche Rechtsgeschichte*, i, 204, n. 40).

sometimes made systematically in the form of addresses to the popular assembly (the Thing) by elected lawmen (*lagman*). The expert in customary law speaking before the All-thing in Iceland delivered an actual course on the various topics extending over the sessions of three years. The Carolingian practice of sending commissioners of the central government into the provinces for the control of administration and the holding of certain pleas led to the development of another method of inquiry into custom. The *Missi* or itinerant justices summoned trustworthy men from the country to give verdicts as to facts known in the locality concerned, and questions as to local or special customs were treated as such facts. The juries of Norman and Angevin England, the 'enquête par jurés' in France, were used in this way to ascertain customs diverging from the ordinary practice of the Royal Courts, while 'notorious' customs (*coutumes notoires*) were referred to by justices from their own knowledge without further inquiry.

A few examples will illustrate these points. In a trial of 1065 concerning the abbey of St. Trond in Lorraine the oldest inhabitants of the country were asked to declare faithfully what they had learned from their predecessors or held themselves up to the present time.[1] In a case before the Common Bench at Westminster (1224) it was asserted by the defendant that by the custom of the Manor of Bray in Berkshire if a daughter remained unmarried with her parents 'at the hearth' she succeeded to the whole inheritance on the decease of the latter. The Court directed an inquest by jury to be held in order to ascertain whether a daughter who had been married, so that she lived outside the tenement, could claim her portion in the tenement on the demise of her parents.[2]

The finding of such a jury was conclusive if unanimous.

[1] Grimm, *Rechtsalterthümer*, 4, ii, 386.   [2] *Note Book* of Bracton, 951.

As this was not always the case, jurymen were sometimes subjected to searching inquiries by the judges and might be dismissed and replaced by others.

The formulation of custom was not the privilege of any particular class—every social circle had its peculiar notions and habits and might be asked to state them. The Crusaders in Palestine followed different rules of law in the Courts of the knights and in those of the *bourgeois*. In Germany the law of the fiefs (*Lehenrecht*) was obligatory for the military class, while townsmen lived by *Stadtrecht*, peasants by *Hofrecht*, and manorial officers by *Dienstrecht*. In England the villains were refused access to the King's Court, but were protected in civil cases by the ' custom of the manor '.

The ideas of justice current in this age were not connected with assumptions as to the natural equality or freedom of men, but with a notion of stability of rights and duties. It was generally recognized that there were bound to be great differences in men's station in life, in the burdens and advantages appropriate to these stations, but every group of men, however lowly, claimed in justice to be ruled by settled customs and not by arbitrary power. This was an illusion as far as the opposition to change was concerned : social life in those days as at any other time was in process of flux, but the tendency towards customary arrangements gave a characteristic aspect to the juridical thought of this time. It helped to preserve for centuries any ancient conceptions and it provided a practical counterpoise against violence and oppression. The admission and preservation of customary rights by classes that seemed to be at the mercy of barbaric masters is perhaps more remarkable than the insurrectionary movements which helped some groups —e.g. the boroughs—to attain a formal improvement of their condition.

It would be impossible in this short chapter to trace the

consecutive stages in the formation of European customary
law. It may be mentioned, however, that the origin of
some of these rules may sometimes be derived from pre-
historic antiquity. A curious instance of the tenacity of
ancient custom is presented by the history of the law of
intestate succession. According to Glanvill the personal
property of a deceased person was to be disposed of under
the supervision of the ecclesiastical Courts. The goods
should be distributed in three parts—one going to the wife,
another to the children or next of kin, and a third being
disposed for the benefit of the soul of the deceased.[1] This
custom left a deep trace in English law inasmuch as the
probate of wills and the administration of a deceased person's
estate remained up to 1887 in the hands of ecclesiastical
courts. On the other hand, the attribution of one third
of a man's fortune to benefactions for the benefit of his soul
is connected with a primeval belief that the deceased man
ought to keep part of his belongings for his own use in after
life. At the funeral of a Russian chief, probably of Scandinavian origin, described in the tenth century by an Arab
traveller, Ibn Fadhlan, one third of the warrior's arms and
apparel together with his favourite wife and his dog was
burnt with him on the pyre, and the funeral of Scyld was
conducted in a similar way according to the description in
the Old English Song of Beowulf. Traces of Celtic and
pre-Celtic (Iberian) customs are also frequent. We may
note among them the practice of marriages concluded for
a year and a day, of which there is particularly graphic
evidence from Ireland. The ' coibche ' unions were celebrated amid great rejoicings at public festivals (Leinster
custom). They were consolidated as permanent marriages

---

[1] In Normandy the goods of a man who had left no will with some
bequest for the good of his soul in the course of his illness were forfeited
to the King. See *Ancienne Coutume*, A. Tardif, App. 12.

after the birth of children or in case of pregnancy. Such trial unions are not unknown even at the present time in certain outlying districts of Bavaria and Central Germany.[1]

In many of these cases it is not easy to distinguish between traditional folklore and results of adaptation to similar circumstances. Striking analogies may sometimes be observed in surroundings in which there does not seem to be any possibility of direct tradition or of loan. The famous story of Shylock claiming a pound of his debtor's flesh is hardly derived directly from the rule of the XII Tables ordering the cutting to pieces of an insolvent debtor, but both claims are rooted in the same soil—in the notion that one of the methods for securing the payment of a debt was to make the debtor bodily liable to the creditor, a view widely spread among the barbarians, and leading to various unpleasant consequences for the obligee in case of insolvency. In Frankish law a slayer who was unable to pay the composition fine of the heirs and kindred of his victim applied for assistance to his relations, and if the payment still remained incomplete, he was produced at three meetings of the local court (*mallus*) before being handed over, if unredeemed, to the mercy of his adversaries. In Muscovy any insolvent debtor was put up in the market-place and flogged (*pravej*) on the chance of some one redeeming him for the sake of relationship, friendship, or charity.

II

If we consider medieval legal customs in the bulk, it is easy to see that there are three departments of social life which have been particularly affected by them—namely, family law, land law, and commercial usages. The basic institution of all societies is the family group : it is least dependent on class distinctions in its fundamental arrange-

---

[1] Ehrlich, *Grundlage der Sociologischen Rechtswissenschaft.*

ments and, on the other hand, its organization exerts its influence on all social grades of the people. No wonder that it is very slow in its development and does not easily give way before cultural changes. Though our present family system is undoubtedly experiencing a crisis, it still bears marks of ancient custom in all its parts. The monogamic group held together mainly by the authority of the father of the household has been modified in many respects, but the principal alterations, such as the safeguarding of the property rights of married women, the emancipation of grown-up and self-supporting children, the lessening of parental authority, the increasing facilities for divorce, have been brought about in comparatively recent times and have not entirely obliterated the peculiar features of the strict monogamic household of old times. Some people are shocked by the requirement of the marriage service that the bride should promise obedience to her husband ; in France the fundamental legal rule governing the marriage union is still Art. 213 of the Civil Code, which declares that the husband owes protection to his wife, and the wife obedience to her husband. The details derived from this principle in subsequent clauses impose many substantial disabilities on the subordinate partner. In regard to parental authority the Code of Napoleon also kept close to the traditions of the pre-revolutionary customary law, and the reforms brought about by nineteenth- and twentieth-century legislation have been gradual and incomplete. It is not my object to prove that this tenacious adherence to traditional rules in family organization has been a proof of moral sanity and practical common sense outweighing apparent advances in the sense of individual equality and freedom. For the special purpose of this chapter it is important to notice that the resistance of family organization to change is directly connected with the force of social habits which have reached the form of customary law. They constitute a psychological foundation for conventional and legal rules that corresponds to average interests and habits of the mass of the people, and with such psychological facts express legislation and professional jurisprudence are bound to reckon.

Looking back on the customary history of the family group in European society we perceive that its foundation in the Middle Ages was laid by a contractual agreement between the bridegroom and the father who gave away the bride, with the support of kinsmen on both sides. The agreement took the form of a *purchase*, the power over the bride was bought (*mundi kjøbt* in Norway). The 'consideration' for the surrender of the bride consisted in various gifts—a payment to the father or guardian and his kindred, a 'morning gift' to the bride herself, a promise as to dower in case of widowhood (*witumo*). The bride's side gave corresponding presents to the kinsmen of the bridegroom and a marriage portion was assigned to the bride as her outfit in clothes, trinkets, house implements. The principal act of the marriage was the exchange of promises and gages between the two kindreds—the *wedding* (from wed = gage and pledge).

'If people want to wed a maid or a wife and this is agreeable to her and to her kinsmen, then it is right that the bridegroom should first swear according to God's right and secular law and should wage (pledge himself) to those who are her forspeakers, that he wishes to have her in such a way as he should hold her by God's right as his wife—and his kinsmen will stand pledge for him.

'Then it is to be settled to whom the price for upfostering her belongs, and for this the kinsmen should pledge themselves.

'Then let the bridegroom declare what present he will make her for granting his desire, and what he will give if she lives longer than he does.

'If it has been settled in this way, then it is right that she should enjoy half the property, and all if they have a child, unless she marries another man.

'All this the bridegroom must corroborate by giving a gage, and his kinsmen stand to pledge for him.

'If they are agreed in all this, then let the kinsmen of the bride accept and wed their kinswoman to wife and to right life to him who desires her, and let him take the pledge who rules over the wedding.

'If she is taken out of the land into another lord's land, then it is advisable that her kinsmen get a promise that no violence will be done to her, and that if she has to pay a fine, they ought to be her next to help her to pay, if she has not enough to pay herself.' [1]

The second act was the conducting of the bride to the bridegroom's home—the bridal run (*bryllup*, Scandin.), which still preserved reminiscences of the ancient marriage by capture in some of its folklore episodes, for instance in the simulated fight in Irish custom—the friends of the parties throwing shafts at each other. The influence of the Christian Church made itself chiefly felt by the requirement of an express consent of the bride which turned the agreement into an exchange of promises between the spouses. The specific benediction which formed the central point of the modern Church Office became essential as a result of a slow process of development. The principal feature of marriage from the point of view of the early Church was the exchange of binding promises. Records of the Churches of York and of Ripon testify to a number of marriages without Church ceremony, concluded by the exchange of promises *de presenti* (immediately binding), confirmed by 'handfasting'. At Easingwold in 1484 a man says, 'Here I take the, Margaret, to my handfast wif, to hold and to have, at bed and at burd, for farer for lather, for better for wars, in sekenes and in heil, to dethe us depart, if holy kirk it will ordand, and thereto plight I the my trowth.' [2]

---

[1] Liebermann, *Gesetze der Angelsachsen*, i, p. 442.

[2] *Acts of the Chapter of the Collegiate Church of SS. Peter and Wilfrid, Ripon, 1452-1506* (Surtees Society, lxiv, 1875), p. 159.

On becoming the wedded wife of a man the woman did not surrender to his arbitrary mercy. She could appeal to the protection of her kinsmen in case of need, and the Northern Sagas contain many stories of married women who lean on their kinsmen for support in their quarrels with their husbands. The guaranteed dower was a recognized legal institution. Its importance may be seen from the fact that in English law a life interest on one third of the husband's inheritance in land was regarded as the average dower; in France it amounted to one half. But the husband was according to most customs to act as the manager of the wife's property brought in at marriage or acquired after marriage. Even if he disposed of such property as if it were his own she could not prevent him or oppose him in his lifetime. But she could attack his acts after his death and claim what was hers by right. This position produced in English procedure a specific right of action—the writ of entry on *cui in vita*, that is on the ground that a woman had been unable to contradict her husband in his lifetime.

The aim of marriage from the point of view of customary law is not the gratification of personal affection, but the procreation of legitimate offspring : people marry *liberorum querendorum causa*, as they said in Rome. A barren marriage was not only a misfortune, from the popular point of view, but a ground of divorce. If a man died leaving his wife pregnant the birth of a live child was an event of decisive importance in regard to the inheritance. If the child was born alive ' with skin and hair, with nails and navel ', and it was heard to shriek within the four walls of the room, the rights to the property of the father and the mother were joined in its person and inheritance passed from it as if it had continued alive. If, on the other hand, the baby was stillborn or there was no offspring at all the paternal and the maternal contributions to the household were severed and each fell back to the original kindred from which it had come—*paterna paternis, materna maternis.*

In normal cases, when the father and mother lived long enough to rear and educate children, the father exercised discretionary power over his offspring. All children borne by the wife in a state of wedlock were presumed to be the legitimate offspring of her husband, and it was almost impossible to overthrow this presumption. The Roman maxim *pater est quem nuptiae demonstrant* held good in the medieval secular courts, and as for the ecclesiastical jurisdiction it favoured in every way the legitimation of children, even of those born out of wedlock, if the parents had subsequently gone through a form of marriage. English laymen opposed such subsequent legitimation as contrary to popular custom—' Nolumus leges Angliae mutare ' proclaimed the English magnates at the Council of Merton in 1234. But on the other hand they were exceedingly lenient in the treatment of illegitimate offspring. Bastards were commonly educated with children issued from regular marriages, and although they did not enjoy equal rights to property with their more fortunate brothers and sisters their position in the household was usually a tolerable one, and some, like William the Conqueror, achieved a brilliant career in spite of the initial blemish of their birth.

Emancipation from the father's authority was granted as a natural outcome of a separate settlement and of the creation of an independent household. If the outgoing son was given a considerable outfit to start with, this reduced his eventual claims to his father's succession unless he gave back into hotchpot the provision that had been made for him by his father in the latter's lifetime. The French thirteenth-century lawyer Beaumanoir states in his ' Custom of Beauvaisis ' that although parents may endow one or the other of their children in their lifetime, especially on the occasion of their marriage, such gifts must not be so considerable as to leave the other children disinherited (*orphelins et déshérités*). It happens commonly that the father or the mother is more fond of one of the children than of the others, and is therefore inclined to increase that one's portion by gifts, but if such donations are too outrageous, the judge should intervene and give redress.[1]

A very common and characteristic institution was the joint household (*compaignie, Gauerbschaft*) kept up by several relations, independent in their personal status. Married sons remained in this way in the household of their father, several brothers kept up a joint household after the death of their father (*parage*), &c. Such an association was a voluntary one, and its members were free to demand partition, but its frequent occurrence in the lower strata of society testifies to its value in the difficult economic and political conditions of the Middle Ages.

III

The land-law of the Middle Ages is characterized by a sharp contrast between the customs of the military class and those of the rest of the population. The notion of freedom was relative, admitting of many grades and shades, and a considerable number of small rent-paying freemen stood between the two principal orders, the knights (*milites*) and the serfs, as *socmen* and *franklins* in England, as *villains* and *roturiers* in France, as *Lassiten* or *Liten* in Germany. Their customs presented many peculiarities, but on the whole the main cleavage ran between the armed people and the unarmed labourers. We need not speak of the law of the fiefs (*Lehenrecht*) which is so prominent in the plead-

[1] Beaumanoir, ed. Salmon, p. 482.

ings and decisions of the higher courts. It should be noticed, however, that it was based on the fundamental conception of *tenure*, that is of a holding conditioned by service and always combining the claims and interest of two persons in each unit of property—the rights and duties of the lord with the rights and duties of the tenant. The lord's *estate* in the land was a direct or *eminent* domain, the tenant's estate a useful domain (*dominium utile*). Thus the old term *dominium* which had indicated in *Roman* law an absolute ownership excluding all other appropriation and involving the right to use, to abuse, and to destroy at will, had become split into two rights balancing each other.

A natural consequence of this modification of the concept of ownership in feudal land-law consisted in the fact that ownership of land was not sharply distinguished from possession of land. The two notions were distinct, but it was not easy to hold them separated in practice. We come to understand the situation better if we consider our own law as to movable goods. If I lose my umbrella and some one picks it up and uses it, after a certain time it may be difficult for me to establish my property right to it : the presumption will be in favour of the actual user. This is expressed in French legal language in the terse sentence : *en fait de meubles la possession vaut titre*. In medieval jurisprudence the actual ' seisin ' of a plot, the fact that a man dwelt on it, gathered the harvest, cut the timber, established a presumption of title which could be defeated by proving a better right, but which was *prima facie* protected and not easy to contest. As a matter of fact the tenure of land was to a great extent a relative notion, very different from the uncompromising ownership established in Rome by *dominium ex iure Quiritium*. In the law of Latin countries—Italy, France—the influence of Roman traditions in this respect was still noticeable, while in Germany, England, and

Scandinavian countries the relative character of appropriation was particularly marked. Yet, even in the South,
customary rules were affected by the indistinct nature of
seisin. The defence of possession, the development of
possessory remedies are characteristic of the Middle Ages.

These observations will help us to comprehend the law of
base or *servile tenures* that governed the life of the bulk of
the population in Feudal Europe. It might be said from
a strictly theoretical point of view that the rural population
was deprived of ownership : whatever an English villein
possessed belonged to his lord. Such arguments are often
produced in trials and summarized in treatises in the course
of the Middle Ages. But in actual life the rights of rustics
in respect of their holdings, their claims as to pasture and
wood, their succession and their transactions were formulated and applied in accordance with ' customs of the manor '
which might be occasionally infringed, but which provided
the general framework of their social life. The Court Rolls
of St. Albans or of Ramsey Abbey are records of an administration of justice and police similar in detail to the usages
of the royal courts. We find from the Court Rolls of
St. Albans that ' a remarkable custom is that of obliging an
incoming tenant, who takes up servile land, to make a contract with the lord that he will be obedient to him in all
things, in Scot and Lot, Tallage, and Services, both in body
and in goods as are all the other villeins. The tenant then
seals this document with his own seal. Traces of this custom
are clear in the Court Rolls at the end of the thirteenth
century and well on in the fourteenth century, but in the
Codicote Cartulary we have the actual *scriptum* of the
earlier date.' [1]

The tenant right established by them did not differ in

[1] Miss Levett, *Transactions of the R. Hist. Soc.*, 4th series, vol. vii
(1924), p. 69.

substance from the customs of privileged classes—the peasantry of ancient demesne in England or the colonists protected by a charter in France, although they differed in regard to access to the courts. Here is an instance of a stand made by the peasant in an ancient demesne manor against exactions of the steward.

'John William's son is attached on the security of John Dyke and Nicholas in the Nook for not coming to the lord's ploughing. And the said John comes into court and says that he has no beast of his own wherewith he can plough and has only borrowed beasts, and he says and alleges that so long as he borrows beasts for ploughing he is not bound to do any ploughing for the lord, and as to this he puts himself upon the Ramsey register. Therefore let the register be inspected before the next court.'[1]

The fact that medieval land-law was constructed to fit two strata of society, an upper and a lower one, produced a cleavage between bookright and folkright, between the law administered in the Royal Courts and the customs operative in the daily life of the rural population. One of the most striking expressions of this dualism is found in the customary institution of the *holding*; the standard tenement held by an average rustic of free or unfree origin. We are so familiar with the treatment of land as a marketable commodity, exchangeable in various quantities against various prices in money that we are puzzled when we find all over Europe in the first centuries of the Middle Ages plots cut out in accordance with some simple scale. There is the English *hide* of some 120 acres of arable, composed of four *virgates* or *yardlands* of about 30 acres and of eight *bovates* (*oxgangs*) of 15 acres each. There is the German Royal *Hufe* of 120 *morgen* (dayworks) and the common *Hufe* of 30 *morgen*; there is the *mansus* of Latin countries, containing in some cases 12 *bunnaria* (*Polyptique d'Irminion*); there

---

[1] *Select Pleas of Manorial Courts*, Selden Society, vol. ii, p. 111.

is the *bol* of Denmark and the *attung* of Sweden, of varying size, but equalized in each particular region. Bishop Arne Suneson in his thirteenth-century version of the law of Skaane (Southern Sweden) tells us that ' by the use of the surveyor's chain the whole villa is divided into equal parts, which in the mother tongue they commonly call *boel* (cor. *bol*) and we in Latin may call *mansos*, for the purpose of equalizing the estates and plots to the adjoining estates '.[1]

How is one to explain such regularity in the presence of legal rules which allowed transfer and partition of property, and admitted sons and even daughters to shares in the inheritance of their deceased parents? The natural effect of alienation and partition is inequality—the accumulation of property in the hands of some and the morcellation or absence of property in the case of others. Have we to suppose that some artificial measures were taken to ensure equality among the rustics? The key to the solution of the riddle is supplied by the nature and names of the units of rustic tenure and of the shares into which they are apt to fall. These units and these shares are not haphazard accumulations of a number of acres—they are organic units of cultivation which could not be interrupted at pleasure. In the main they are areas with appendant rights appropriate for the normal work of a plough-team. The large plough-team of eight oxen wants a hide as a basis for its working power—it is a full plough land. Under favourable circumstances it will embrace 160 or 180 acres of arable, although its taxable (geldable) estimate (*wara*) will be assessed at 120 acres. In connexion with it there will be various rights of usage in respect of pasture, wood, turf, fisheries. A big unit of this kind is only exceptionally held by a peasant—generally they are possessed only of fractions of it—appropriate for cultivation by a yoke of

[1] Grimm. *Rechtsalterthümer*, ii. 65.

four oxen (*iugum*) or a plough team of two oxen (yardlands) or even of a fraction corresponding to the toil of one ox (oxgang). In the case of such fractional plots co-operation was adjusted in accordance with simple and natural divisions of the team and not as a result of complicated and shifting reckoning. The proportional distribution of shares in the land follows in this way on lines indicated by agrarian organization. The consolidation of holdings in connexion with their agrarian use and value was by no means confined to servile tenements. In Norway the most privileged form of peasant holding, the *odal*, was constituted as a unit not to be cut up between co-heirs, but to pass to one of them, generally the elder, while the younger were provided with an outfit to start in business outside the *odal* farm or as dependants of its representative. The consolidation of smaller agrarian holdings was even more necessary as long as society lived mainly in a state of natural husbandry. When men had to content themselves with cottages and orchards of some 5 acres or less, they could not any longer take part in the normal cultivation of the field, they were therefore classed as mere cottagers in opposition to tenants ' with fields ' (*in campis*). The tendency of rustic land tenure under natural husbandry conditions to form regular holdings on a scale proportioned to the plough team and its constituent element is, of course, connected with the fact that householders reckoned not with values in exchange estimated in money, but with values for consumption, estimated in average requirements per worker and per family of workers. In Scandinavian countries and in the east of England permeated by Scandinavian influences land was sometimes estimated in *man-lots*.

In the course of economic evolution the standard holdings get disrupted, the number of irregular plots increases and estates are valued. In connexion with this process we observe another feature of medieval agrarian organization, namely the wide diffusion of the so-called *open field system*, i.e. of the cultivation of the fields not in separate plots but in contiguous *furlongs* and *shots*, subdivided into strips attributed to the various householders while the crops are growing and thrown together for common pasture after the harvest and before the new sowing season. It was not the only system used in the Middle Ages—in parts of France and in Italy the cultivation of small areas by isolated and independent householders was still prevalent in connexion with intensive ploughing and the culture of olives and vines. But the most common form of agrarian organization was the open field system with its inconvenient intermixture of strips and its obligatory rotation of crops. The single householder could not, without infringing customary rules, improve or vary the management of his own land : his strips were shares in a higher unit of cultivation—the township, the ' by ', the Dorf. In a case of 1370 the free tenants of the hamlet of Handborough near Oxford sued the Abbot of Eynsham because he had disturbed the customary order of rotation of crops in the township by substituting a four-field system for a three-field one : they complained of having lost in proportion pasture rights which they used to exercise every third year over the commons.

There were several forces which converged to maintain this peculiar system—the necessity of providing sufficient pasture for the cattle and especially the oxen and horses engaged in ploughing, harrowing, carting : while the villagers could not rely on the free waste of moors or alps they were bound to use the village commons and greens for their cattle. There were traditions of communal rights as to land which did not amount to a denial of individual tenant right and ownership in the strips, houses, orchards, and gardens, but constituted a kind of eminent domain or superior interest in the soil that enabled the township in cases of emergency to exercise a decisive influence on the settlement and land allotment.

On one occasion ' the peasants ' were removed from a certain area comprising ' eight hides of villein land. Of these eight hides one-fourth was taken, and it was reckoned that this fourth was an equivalent to the one-third of the park and of the demesne farm, which ought by right to have gone to the lord de la Lege. On the basis of this estimation an exchange was effected. In the time of the war (perhaps the rebellion of 1173) the eight hides and other hides in Segheho were encroached upon and appropriated unrighteously by many, and for this reason a general revision of the holdings was undertaken before Walter de Wahull and Hugh de la Lege in full court by six old men ; it was made out to which of the hides the several acres belonged. At that time, when all the tenants in Segheho (knights, freeholders, and others) did not know exactly about the land of the village and the tenements, and when each man was contending that his neighbours held unrighteously and more than they ought, all the people decided by common agreement and in the presence of the lords de Wahull and de la Lege, that everybody should surrender his land to be measured anew with the rood by the old men as if the ground had been occupied afresh : every one had to receive his due part on consideration of his rights. At that time R. F. admitted that he and his predecessors had held the area near the castle unrighteously. The men in charge of the distribution divided that area into sixteen strips (*buttos*), and these were divided as follows : there are eight hides of villein land in Segheho and to each two strips were apportioned.' [1] Such readjustments as this are described at length in Swedish and Danish laws.

---

[1] See *Villainage in England*, pp. 233-4.

The co-operation between neighbours (Norwegian *Grande*) was more than a matter of simple agreement : it assumed the character of a customary establishment which necessitated for its alteration the consent of all the members of a township. The village formed a community, and was recognized and exploited as such a community by the lord, and by public authority. The villata is frequently mentioned as acting as a unit in English records : it is normally represented by the priest, the reeve, and four villagers. This kind of community did not aim at regulating the needs and advantages of the individuals comprised in it : it reckoned with the holdings which were in *scot* and in *lot* in the township. The question of redistribution was raised only in exceptional cases. As a rule the pressure of population was met either by emigration of single adventurous individuals or by the colonization and reclaiming of new soil.

In sketching the customary arrangements of open-field peasant life I do not presume to describe a uniformly prevalent system : as I have already said, agrarian conditions were exceedingly varied in Western Europe. But the Court Rolls, the Weisthümer, the field-maps and extents are there to show that we are dealing in this case with widely prevalent customs, the last vestiges of which we may observe even now, after the great enclosure movement of modern centuries, in the *commons* scattered in the midst of our present-day enclosed estates.

IV

The customs of townspeople present two aspects : in one sense they have kept traces of many archaic views and institutions, on the other hand they are the outcome of economic and social progress. This contradiction is not difficult to explain : the close associations of burgesses made it possible for them to resist encroachments to which the less organized villagers had succumbed. At the same time the fact that industry and trade were mainly concentrated in the towns was bound to exercise its influence by introducing new ideas and facilitating intercourse in every way.

One of the most tenacious survivals of old times was the use of the wager of law in procedure before the courts of boroughs. The great advantages consequent on the introduction of the system of inquests in the Royal Courts were brought about by the exercise of the Royal prerogative with the help of a powerful administration. The boroughs were less fortunate in these respects and clung to more antiquated methods of conducting trials. We have, e.g., the following notice from London (A.D. 1319) : [1]

> 'There is an old custom of the city that when any London citizen is to purge himself at an eyre of the crime of high treason, he should purge himself with 36 men from each side of Walbrook, and of old it was held that if any of the said men thus chosen should die between the time of their election and the purging of the said citizen, then the rest of those living swore on the dead man's grave that if he were alive he would have sworn the same oath which they swear.'

The number of compurgators is exceptionally large in this case on account of the accusation of high treason. In ordinary cases 12, 6, or 3 men were called upon to corroborate the oath of the principal compurgator, for instance in the laws of the four burghs of Scotland. [2]

> 'If a burgess be charged by a countryman for stolen goods, found in his own house and in his seisin, and can deny the theft as a free burgess against a countryman, and can say that though he has no warrantors yet he bought the goods which are challenged lawfully in the borough market, the burgess shall purge himself by the oath of twelve neighbours and lose only the goods claimed. And he shall swear that he knows not where the door opens or shuts of the house of the man from whom he bought the goods.'

[1] *Borough Customs*, vol. i, Selden Soc. Publ., vol. xviii (1904), p. 49.
[2] *Ibid.*, p. 58.

Another peculiar feature of borough customs is the wide latitude allowed to self-help. As in primitive tribal societies, claimants of rights are commonly called upon to take the law into their own hand without even waiting for the help of executive officers. The topic of distress is one of the most developed in the collection of customary rules. Of course the person distraining had eventually to justify his conduct in a court of law and to be prepared to defend an action in replevin. The customs of Winchester (about 1280) provided the following means of putting pressure on a tenant who failed to pay his rent.[1]

'The custom of year and day aforesaid is this, that if there is any one who takes the rent of any tenement in the franchise of the city aforesaid, and finds his whole rent in arrears for a year and more, and can find nothing there to distrain, and there is a house there and people living in it, by leave of the bailiffs of the town he may take the doors and windows, and if by this he cannot get his due for his tenement and can find no other distress, by award of the court and the view of the alderman of the street and of his serjeant there shall be put a stake or a lock where there is a door, and the cause shall be enrolled in court and sued from week to week for a full year and a day from the first day of the suit, and if still no one comes to make satisfaction the tenant shall lose without recovery, whether he be of age or no, albeit so that before the judgment passes he may make satisfaction, the which judgment shall not be delayed to the damage of the demandant.'

In regard to substantive law the most curious tenacity is displayed in customs touching family rights and duties. The fifteenth-century Custumal of Dover, for instance, formulates clearly the restriction on alienation imposed by family ties and known in France under the name of ' retrait lignager '.[2]

'*Dover*, cap. 13.—Nota de vendicatione tenementi venditi. And if eny man or woman be in will to sell his herytage within

---

[1] *Ibid.*, p. 302.   [2] *Ibid.*, ii, p. 72.

the fraunchyse, the next of hys kyn shall have it afore all other :
and though the sale be made to any straunger, yf eny man that
be of kyn come in to the courte anone as he hath knowlege of the
sale and cleyme the bargayne, he shall have it by awarde of
the mayre and juratts and lesse pryce be every powdne xiid,'
of the which overplus the seller shall answer to the straunger.'

There are repeated declarations in the Custumals against
the attempts of lords to claim the wardship of burgesses
under age as if they were holding by military tenure.
Burgesses keep up strenuously the ancient folkright in
accordance with which the wardship of infants is to be
exercised by their next of kin.[1]

'*Bury* (about 1200). In the vill of St. Edmund, because it
was a borough, the custom was that the next of blood should
have the wardship of the child with his inheritance until he
came to years of discretion.'

This is one side of the legal life of the boroughs. As
against it we have to notice new rules in all matters connected with trade. Some of these rules are more characteristic of the conditions of town life than indicative of progressive tendencies. We hear, e.g., of the custom by which
any member of a borough or privileged market town could
claim a share in a bargain made by a fellow townsman. In
St. Omer, for instance (twelfth century),[2]

'the merchant gildsman had an option of first purchase, as
against the stranger to the gild. In the next clause it is ruled
that if any gildsman had agreed to a price for the purchase of
goods, other than victual, and of the value of five " gros sous "
and upwards, other gildsmen who " supervened " could claim
to go shares in the merchandise at that price. The saving clause
concerning victual goes to prove that membership of the merchant gild was not necessary in this case, and that all inhabitants
had their " lot " here, as was commonly the rule. The merchant

[1] *Borough Customs*, ii, p. 145.   [2] *Ibid.*, p. lxix.

gildsmen's rule was intended to secure equal opportunity for sharing in wholesale purchases of raw material and materials for trade, not for household consumption.'

The most important contribution of town life to the development of law was connected with the history of contract. While this important branch of law remains in the background in the common law of medieval England, the borough custumals and especially the records of fairs and markets contain abundant materials illustrating varied transactions of sale and purchase, of loan and hire, of suretyship and agency, &c. An important factor making for the widening of the outlook consisted in the pressure and participation of foreign merchants in the principal centres of export and import trade. The law merchant of the thirteenth and fourteenth centuries was a kind of *ius gentium*, of international private law, made to fit the notions and requirements of men from neighbouring places and even from other countries. A case tried in the fair court of the Abbot of Ramsey in St. Ives may serve to illustrate some of the questions which arose between the persons who transacted business at such a fair.[1]

'John Francis of Derby was attached to answer Richard of Fulham, citizen of London, in a plea that he (John) render to him ten marks which he owes him and unjustly detains etc. . . . .

'And thereupon William of Daventry and Adam of Burton, servants of the abbot of (Burton)-on-Trent, come and say that the process of the plea and execution of judgment for the said horse ought not (to be made) against (the said John) in this matter; for they say that, on the day on which the said Richard was attached to sue the said John Francis for the said debt, he (John) had no right or property, art or part in the (said horse). For they say that on the day of the said attachment the said horse belonged to the abbot, their lord, and was entrusted to them as his servants to be put on sale in this fair; and this they

[1] *Select Cases corncerning the Law Merchant*, Selden Soc., vol. xxiii (1908), vol. i, pp. 89, 90.

are ready to prove in any way that the court shall award according
to the law merchant. . . .

'And the said Richard says that the said William and Adam
should not be admitted to make such proof, for he says that
when anyone should make proof of the ownership of any merchandise or of any other thing, it is necessary that he whose
ownership is alleged should appear in his own person to make
(proof), and the said William and Adam are entirely extraneous
for the making of such proof. He craves judgment whether they
ought to be admitted to make such proof etc.

'And William and Adam say that it is entirely necessary that
they should be admitted (to make this proof), for they say that
when perchance any merchant, dwelling in remote parts, whosoever he may be, whether earl or baron, bishop or abbot, or any
such person of rank, should deliver his merchandise and goods
to any servant of his to have them put on sale in any fair, if any
one caused such goods and merchandise to be attached by reason
of a debt owed by another person, it would be hard and incon-
sonant with right if such servants, in whose possession such
goods and chattels were when they were attached, should not
be admitted to make such proof in the name of their lord. And
they still crave to be admitted etc.

'And thereupon all the merchants of the said fair, both
natives and foreigners, to whom judgments belong according to
the law merchant, having been called for this purpose and con-
sulted, say that they (William and Adam) may properly be
admitted in this and similar cases according to the law merchant.'

One of the principal consequences of this method of
treating commercial cases was the formation of usages and
customs of law merchant free from the extreme formalism
of procedure characteristic of the courts of common law.
Parole agreements were constantly made before witnesses
and binding consent between the parties was established
by the acceptance of a God's penny and of a drink. In
order to provide a material security for the payment of
the price a sum of money or some valuable object was given
as 'earnest'.

'William Fleming complains of Matthew Tanner, for that he
has unjustly broken a covenant with him for a cask of beer, which

he (William) bought from him for two marks of silver, in his (Matthew's) house in the vill of St. Ives on Tuesday after the close of Easter in the nineteenth year of the reign of King Edward; and to bind the purchase he (William) paid him a farthing as a God's penny and a pottle of beer worth a penny as beverage, with the understanding, to wit, that the said cask should remain in the house of the said Matthew until the beer of the said Matthew should be entirely sold, and then, at any hour at which the said William wished, he could broach his said cask. And to confirm this covenant the said William deposited his wife's surcoat worth 16s. as gage for a half-mark, payable to the said Matthew as earnest-money on the day of the contract.'

The lasting influence of commercial customs of this kind is particularly significant in a review of the Legacy of the Middle Ages: the Law Merchant continued to govern English trade until the second half of the eighteenth century, when Lord Mansfield received its rules as part of the Common Law instead of establishing them in particular cases as a fact by the evidence of experts.

A curious feature in the history of municipal customs is the spread of certain formulas by loan from one to the other. In all the countries of Western Europe there occurs the same phenomenon of a radiation of franchises and customs from certain countries to neighbouring and even to distant localities. The charters of Lorris in Gatinais and of Beaumont in Argonne have been copied again and again by hundreds of other communities; the same happened to Freiburg in Breisgau in Western Germany and to Magdeburg not only in Eastern Germany, but in Lithuania and Poland. A remarkable case is presented in England by the Custom of Breteuil. This medium-sized town situated in the present department of Eure on the confines of Normandy may be regarded as the parent municipality from whose charter of liberties a number of towns in England and Wales and Ireland—Hereford, Shrewsbury, Preston, Rhudlan, Cardiff, Drogheda, &c.—have copied their privileges and customs. We can trace to some extent the genealogical lines on which these transmissions were effected.

A Norman baron of Scandinavian descent, William Fitz-Osborn, came over with William the Conqueror and received the honour of Hereford as a reward of his services in addition to his fiefs of Breteuil, Cormeilles, and Verneuil in Normandy. On his death in 1071 his two lordships—the English and the Norman one—were divided for the time in the hands of his sons, but the municipal policy of his house remained the same on both sides of the house and we read in Domesday that Hereford, Cardiff, and Drusany were enjoying the liberties of Breteuil. The customs of Preston present the fullest record of the practices adopted on the pattern of Breteuil and, although it would be impossible to assert that every single clause of the custumal of Preston is derived from the uses of Breteuil, there can be no doubt that most of them belong to the group which went under that name in England and had actually grown by adoption and imitation from the original stock transferred from Normandy.

Now a good many of the clauses of this custumal and of similar charters elsewhere are concerned with exemptions and alleviations of exactions—e.g. the rule that no fine for transgressors may exceed 12*d.* except in three cases of grievous crimes from which fines are due to the King. There are also a number of instances in which customs appear which have no reference to the fixation or concession of seignorial rights. Cl. 3, for instance, deals with the protection of villeins who have dwelt for a year and a day in the town against pursuit by their former masters. In the same way the settlement of a new-comer within the precincts of the town, although it requires the unanimous consent of the original burgesses, is deemed legalized by an unchallenged residence of a year and a day, a rule that reminds us forcibly of the famous cl. 45 of the Lex Salica. The same customary period of limitation occurs in cl. 7 in regard to dispute as to the possession of tenements by burgesses.

Cl. 33, again, directs that in case a claim of debt is not satisfied by a burgess the creditor was to be paid from the fund of the community and the provost was enjoined to levy the sum from the property of the debtor. This regulation can hardly mean anything else but a guarantee of the faithful execution of obligations incurred by burgesses in respect of outsiders, especially foreign merchants—a provision designed to sustain the credit of the town and possibly to safeguard it against reprisals. The guild of the town is sometimes mentioned in custumals derived from the charter of Breteuil, and these mentions may serve as an indication of the fact that the whole domain of municipal government and social relations had come to be ordered on lines similar in substance and form. This seems to be the natural explanation of the fact that the inhabitants of towns and regions politically independent of one another framed their laws on the same pattern. Imitation in these cases was a device contrived for the sake of obtaining ready-made formulas for things which were much alike in reality and needed no separate elaboration.

Something similar took place in yet another department of law, namely as regards maritime customs. We observe here most striking instances not only of transmission from one people and country to another, but also of tenacious customs bridging from epoch to epoch over hundreds of years. The other day an American lawyer examined a case tried by the courts of Illinois (*Richheimer* v. *the People*) in the light of the juridical treatment of the rights and remedies of an Athenian banker in respect of a cargo bought with money lent by him and claimed by a creditor of the ship's captain as a pledge for another loan.[1] And indeed, if we wish to trace the development of doctrines as to risks, interests in maritime adventure, jettison, shipwreck, hypothecation on ship and cargo, bills of lading, rights and duties of mariners, of skippers, of supercargoes, we may well start from the laws obtaining nowadays, but we should have to look back for the reason of their formation and the conditions of their application not only to the customs of the Dutch, the Spaniards, the Portuguese, but to the compilations of Mediterranean usages called the Consulate of the sea, the laws of Gotland, the usages of Oléron in Gascony, the Statutes of Ragusa, the practice of Venice, of the Genoese, of Pisa, of Amalfi, the Byzantine legislation of the Basilica (liii), and of Justinian's *Corpus iuris* (Dig. xiv. 2), the Rhodian law, the speeches of Demosthenes (v. Lakritos, v. Phormion, v. Zenothemis).[2]

The continuity of development has sometimes been recognized expressly in modern judgement. Brett, J., referred to the Rhodian law on jettison as preserved in Dig. xiv in *Burton* v. *English* (1883).[3] But of course during the centuries of its history maritime law underwent many modifications of details in connexion with changes in economic and social conditions or with naval technique. An important characteristic of maritime trade in the ancient world was its treatment as a series of adventures. The ship or the cargo carried by it were not owned directly by some capitalist and if, as was mostly the case, the ship

---

[1] Zane on *Zenothemis* v. *Demon, Mich. Law Rev.*, 1925.

[2] See Ashburner, *The Rhodian Law, passim.*

[3] Brett, J. (221): 'This does not arise from any contract at all, but from the old Rhodian law, and has become incorporated in the law of England, as the law of the ocean. It is not a matter of contract but a consequence of the common danger, where natural justice required that all should contribute to indemnify for the loss of property which is sacrificed by one in order that the whole adventure may be saved.'

had been built and fitted out on borrowed money, if the cargo had been bought as a result of a loan, the lender had to face not only the usual risks of failure or dishonesty on the part of the borrower, but also the risks of the voyage in stormy seas, with insufficient technical means, in constant danger from pirates.

Insurance provides against such or similar risks nowadays, but insurance had not been worked out in antiquity or in the Middle Ages. Consequently risks had to fall on the parties to the adventure and for practical reasons they fell on the lenders, who were usually merchants or bankers conducting business from a safe place—from Athens, or Rhodes, or Amalfi, or Venice, or London. The borrowers might be seafaring, skilled and audacious, but not provided with extensive possessions within the reach of creditors. On the other hand, if the lenders bore great risks, the borrowers had to submit to heavy burdens—interest on maritime loans was reckoned at a higher rate than on ordinary ones. The usual rate in Athens was 18 per cent., in the Middle Ages it might rise to 24 per cent. and higher in spite of the condemnation of usury by the Church. The only result of this condemnation was that the interest charged was concealed by means of some device in the apparent tenor of the contracts, e.g. by including the stipulated interests in the sum of the capital lent. A certain mitigation of these exorbitant conditions was conceded when the borrower of money to be invested in grain or some other cargo could offer in hypothecation as a pledge not only the cargo concerned in the adventure, but goods in other ships, or stock on land, or a landed estate.[1]

Another feature of the maritime adventure was the distinction between the economic factors concerned in it. Roman jurists distinguished between the owner of the ship,

[1] Ashburner, *Rhodian Sea-Law*, pp. ccx, ccxvii.

the *exercitor* who rented it, the *magister* who was responsible for the material arrangements on board, the captain, and the merchant who invested money for the enterprise. Of course these various activities could be combined in many ways—the merchant may have been the owner of the ship, or the *exercitor* may have acted as a *magister* and so on. But the factors could also appear personified in the shape of different sharers. Their interests fall in any case into three main groups—those connected with the ship, those connected with the cargo, and those connected with the freight. A natural modification was effected in the Middle Ages as regards the third group. It was not only the owner of the ship, the purser (*magister*), and the captain who were interested in the freight, but the crew at large (*nautae*), who had ceased to be recruited from slaves, as in ancient Greece or Rome, but were as a rule free or half-free. In any case the arrival of the ship at the end of the agreed voyage was the occasion for settling accounts and winding up transactions.[1]

The customary conception of maritime adventure produced drastic effects in cases when a ship, in difficulty through storm, collision, grounding on rocks or sandbanks and the like, had to be saved by sacrificing part of its cargo or apparel. Such a ' jettison ' (*iactus*) raised intricate questions as to the attribution of damage and responsibility.

This gives rise to the law of ' average ' which goes back in its growth to the maritime customs of the Greeks and produces many subtle distinctions in medieval maritime custom. It amounts in substance to the recognition of the fact that sacrifices or expenses incurred by the ship in order to save the cargo as well as itself and the crew ought not to be borne exclusively by the ship's owners but should be shared by the other associates of the enterprise—the owners

---

[1] *Table of Amalfi*, c. 23 ; *Black Book of the Admiralty*, iv. 17 f.

of the cargo ought to be charged with a contribution and corresponding deductions should be made from the freight. Vice versa, the jettison of part of the cargo in order to save the ship by easing it should be apportioned according to certain averages between all the three groups of partners interested in the ship, the cargo, and the freight. The customs of Oléron, chs. 3–7 (Black Book, ii, 212–18), and the Table of Amalfi (cl. 27) may be cited in illustration of the way in which particular points arising from the general doctrine were treated.

In conclusion I should like to emphasize the view that has been expressed again and again in different parts of this survey. The formulation of legal rules and the determination of vested rights in the Middle Ages was connected in the last resort with habits and considerations of business life and social intercourse : judges settled disputes and rulers issued statutes in accordance with their professional training, their political insight and their sense of justice, but all these operations of the minds of the leaders had to conform in one way or another to the customs of the folk—the broad indications of everyday experiences and practice.

Paul Vinogradoff.

ii. CANON LAW

In the spiritual heritage of the Middle Ages to which we have succeeded, there is nothing that has remained so unaffected by the changes of time as the legal system of the Roman Church. Decretals and canons of a date earlier than the fifteenth century still govern the administration of the best disciplined and, from the point of view of numbers, the greatest of all monarchies—that of the Sovereign Pontiff—and regulate the religious and social life of the three hundred millions of the faithful of whom it is composed. The code published in 1234 by order of Gregory IX, the latest addition to which dates from 1317, was itself in force until 1918, while the substance of it may be found incorporated in that by which it was then replaced. Churches, moreover, which have separated from Rome, retain in their present constitutions many elements whose origin may be traced to the time when Christendom was one. Nor indeed has secular society, though many of its former links with religion have been broken, entirely rid itself of canonical conceptions. The principles developed by the Church and applied by her during the period when no one disputed her control over all civil matters in which the salvation of souls was concerned, still underlie a considerable portion of the common law of the west, and are predominant in large provinces such as those of marriage or of obligations. And of the ideas by which modern politics are inspired, some, as for instance those of submission to the authority of the State or the protection of the oppressed, were sedulously fostered by the canonists, while others, such as liberty of opinion and the abolition of privileges, owe their origin or their prominence to the reaction which set in with the Renaissance against the public law of the Church.

In order to understand the condition and tendencies of the modern world, it is necessary to determine doctrines to which it is found to be in opposition, and—more important still—to inquire how much in our religious organization, our legal customs and our conception of law is a survival from the Christian Middle Ages. Three fundamental problems may be said to call for solution. First, in what ways was the systematization of the canon law effected in the years between the coming of Gregory VII (1073) and the Great Schism (1378); in other words, of what elements and by what methods was the *Corpus Iuris* of the Church compiled, and what was the scope of its rules? Primarily this *corpus* defined the constitution of the Church. In our second section, therefore, we shall describe the classic theory of the clerical order, of the hierarchy and of the relations between the 'two powers'. Finally, since the classic law regulated the life of the faithful in all its aspects, political, social, economic and penal, we must examine under these heads the way in which the Church formulated for the use of all Christians a complete code of precepts and sanctions.

I

From the earliest times the Church had found it necessary to draw up rules of government and to define the obligations of her members in order to preserve her unity, to maintain her worship, to ensure the exercise of charity and the practical application of the evangelical virtues. Holy Scripture and Apostolic tradition formed the basis of her law; custom and papal and conciliar decrees added, as need arose, other provisions relating more particularly to matters concerning the hierarchy. The constitutions of the Christian Emperors determined the temporal position of the Church, the privileges of clerks and ecclesiastical property; the Fathers, notably St. Augustine, gave precision to her social theory. Conciliar canons and papal decrees, to which were often added excerpts from the Scriptures, from the Fathers or from secular law, were early formed into collections. In the sixth century the Roman Church adopted a collection made by Dionysius Exiguus, which contained, in addition to the canons of the great councils of the east, a series of decretals. This collection gained considerable authority in the west. It was formally bestowed (774) by Pope Hadrian, with certain additions (*Dionysio-Hadriana*), upon Charlemagne, whose approval (802) gave it official sanction within the Empire. But the appearance of the *Dionysiana* did not prevent the appearance of an abundant crop of private collections. To the period of purely local collections, arbitrarily drawn up in the sixth century for churches which the barbaric invasions had isolated, succeeded that of national or regional collections— *Hispana, Hibernensis*, the collection of Angers (of the seventh and early eighth centuries), not one of which was either universally accepted or logically arranged. And since these collections did not meet all the needs of the Church, private enterprise filled in the gaps in the law. The Celts introduced upon the Continent the use of Penitential Canons, usually anonymous and always of a non-official nature, thus providing a large variety of penances applicable to the different categories of sins. During the ninth century a group of Frankish clerks, in order to defend the bishops and ecclesiastical property, forged apocryphal collections, of which the False Decretals are the best known. In the eleventh century the collection most widely current was the *Decretum* of Burchard, Bishop of Worms, drawn up about 1012. As Paul Fournier, who has studied them all, has convincingly shown, neither this collection nor any of those current at the time were regarded as adequate by the reforming party in the Church. Not one of them included sufficient decisive texts, coherently arranged, upon the subjects of principal interest to the reformers, the primacy of the Apostolic See, the validity of the sacraments, the coercive power of the Church, investiture, nicolaism, simony. And further, the hall-mark of universality, bestowed only upon the rules promulgated or approved by Rome, was absent from these strings of local councils, penitential canons, apocryphal decisions, which composed the majority of these collections, and especially the *Decretum* of Burchard of Worms. The first task of the reformers, therefore, was to revise the contents of the collections. As it was their declared intention to avoid all innovations and merely to restore the former discipline, it was to ancient sources that they turned in their search for all decisions possessed of a universal character, such as would further their purpose and could replace the fragmentary texts of whose origin and doctrine they had become suspicious. As a result of detailed investigations in the libraries of Italy, there were brought to light many texts hitherto either unknown or ignored in the west, canons of general councils held after the fall of the Roman Empire, papal letters, fragments of patristic writings, extracts from the *Liber Pontificalis*. Knowledge of these was diffused by means of several collections, and particularly by the one in Seventy-four Titles (*c.* 1050) and the collection of Anselm of Lucca, which contained the elements of a complete theory of the ecclesiastical hierarchy.

Many problems which arose in the eleventh century concerning the status of persons and property (marriage, contracts, crime), and of which the canons offered no comprehensive solution, had been solved by the Roman Law. The discovery of the famous Florentine manuscript of the

Digest, perhaps by one of the clerks working in the Italian libraries on behalf of the reformers, came as a welcome aid to the post-Gregorians. Since 1090, the collection *Britannica* had included about a hundred excerpts from classical jurisconsults, and the canonization of the Roman Law was necessarily continued by the Church, as she worked towards the completion of her legal system, and thus encroached upon the province of private law. Both pre-Gregorians and Gregorians therefore revised the contents of the collections, but they could not prevent the survival of texts of German or Celtic origin, the suppression of which they had so ardently desired. Almost the whole of the *Decretum* of Burchard of Worms was included (*c.* 1095) in the *Decretum* of Yvo of Chartres, itself the source of the same author's *Panormia* which enjoyed a great reputation in the twelfth century. The confusion, in fact, which the reformers had sought to remedy remained. Several families of texts, several types of collections were competing with one another, and numerous contradictions became apparent between the texts appealed to on the one hand by the champions, on the other by the opponents of reform, contradictions of which men were more readily aware in a period of unification and of renewed study of law and of philosophy. The Pope could hardly think of enforcing on all alike, by the mere exercise of his authority, those collections with whose views he was in full agreement, not only on account of the reputation enjoyed for so long by the texts which these rejected, but also because the enforcement in their entirety of the ideas of the reformers seemed at the end of the eleventh century to be in practice impossible. On political grounds, a compromising, harmonizing process seemed advisable; and the trend of legal science was drawing men's minds to the same conclusion. A new method of interpretation grew up, of which Yvo of Chartres

and Bernold of Constance were, at the end of the eleventh
century, the first exponents. Their chief merit is to have
separated precept from counsel, and to have marked off
from principles of eternal validity the variable elements
of the law, which had been suggested by particular circumstances, whether of time, place, or persons, and the enforcement of which other conditions might render unseasonable.
This amounted to the recognition of the relativity of rules
and provided a technical method of harmonizing contradictions. Partial use was made of it by Algerus, a canonist
of Liège, while the range of its possibilities was extended
by Abelard in his *Sic et Non*. Shortly after the year 1140,
Gratian, a Bolognese monk, applied this new dialectic to
the whole mass of texts handed down by the collections—
conciliar canons, decretals, fragments from patristic writings,
and excerpts from the Justinian compilations. On each
question he proposed the texts *pro et contra*, as in two
pleadings, and sought for an explanation of the divergence
by careful definitions of the meaning of the words and of
the precise applicability of the rules. His *Decretum* was
a private work, but was so generally used in the universities
and courts of the Church that it became the foundation of
the classic law.

Gratian had almost succeeded in separating theology and
ecclesiastical law and had collected and classified all the
important texts. His work nevertheless was not final.
On many points the solutions he offered were hesitating or
fragmentary. And new problems were arising in the
Church, the result of new and unforeseen events of which
the Crusades are an example. The development of trade,
the substitution for the chivalrous ideal of that spirit of
cunning, to which satirical literature from Renard the Fox
to Piers Plowman bears witness, determined the Church,
now reaching the zenith of her power, to transform into

law many a rule that had hitherto been of merely moral obligation.

In order to complete the system of public and private law of the Church, the Popes summoned general councils, the Third (1179) and Fourth (1215) Lateran, the First (1245) and Second (1274) Lyons, Vienne (1311), and added to the number of decretals, the additions of Innocent III (1198–1216) being particularly important. Of these canons and decretals private compilations were made, and then in 1234 appeared the first official collection, by order of Gregory IX. Decretals and canons of oecumenical councils of a date subsequent to this were codified by order of Boniface VIII (*Liber Sextus*, 1298) and of Clement V (*Clementinae*, 1317). The texts to be found in these three collections had legal force. They represented the whole of the papal codification and therefore of the official and universal law of the Church in the Middle Ages.[1] Many canonists, and especially University professors, set about explaining the meaning of each text of the *Decretum* or of the Decretals (and so were called respectively Decretists and Decretalists), or systematically expounding the rules (*Summae*). The most famous of these commentators, who exercised a great influence upon the ideas and jurisprudence of their time, were Rufinus († 1203), Huguccio († 1210), Innocent IV († 1254), Hostiensis († 1271), Joannes Andreae († 1348). The majority of the remaining doctors confined themselves to faithfully copying these masters, and the *Speculum iudiciale* of Wilhelmus

---

[1] In the year 1500 two other series (*Extravagantes* of John XXII, *Extravagantes Communes*) were added to these three collections by Chappuis. The whole, formed by the *Decretum* and these five compilations, of which two were merely of a private nature, like the *Decretum*, received the title of the *Corpus Iuris Canonici*. Gregory XIII authorized and ordered to be published a corrected edition at the end of the sixteenth century, this being the only one used by the Church until 1918.

Durandus († 1296). A clear picture of the state of the law and of canonistic science at the very close of the Middle Ages is given by Panormitanus († 1445). Neither law nor science, however, was characterized by the dogmatism that one might expect, for the rules of the canon law were both formulated and applied with a remarkable absence of rigidity. The feature of the law which had the most disquieting consequences in the eyes of the canonists was its general character. For this a remedy was to be found both in particular laws (privileges) formulated for particular persons or groups, in derogations from the law as usually enforced (dispensations) granted by the legislative authority—usually the Pope—when circumstances rendered such a course advisable. A second danger was that the purpose of the law might be defeated, either by malicious use of the powers it conferred or by artful evasion of the restrictions set by it on individual rights. Canonists and civilians were at one in forbidding acts of unfair competition, exercise of rights with the object of injuring another (the historic precedent of the doctrine of *abus de droit*), and acts in deceit of the law. Finally, since the law could not make provision for every hypothetical case, the door was always open to custom. The danger of unauthorized rules was met by the canonists in this way : they declared custom to be binding only when it is reasonable, i.e. when it is in accordance with the principles of the Church, and with the assumed intention of the legislator, and when it has been in use for a sufficient length of time (*legitime praescripta*). The decision as to the presence of these qualifications lay with the judge. If proved to satisfy these requirements, a customary rule might, at least from the time of Gregory IX, supersede statutory law. Thus to the old rigidity of the civil law was opposed the equity of the canon law, exemplified in the intelligent, loyal, and benevolent interpretation and application of its rules.

A system which allowed so much freedom to the legislator and which was tempered by so judicious a method of interpretation could and ought to possess great logical consistency, and it is this which gives its most striking feature to the law of the Church.

II

In the thirteenth century the canons provided all the elements of a perfect system of organization for the Church. They reduced the laity to a condition of passive obedience and regulated in every detail the life and position in the hierarchy of the clerks, who from the earliest centuries of the Christian era had been regarded as the inheritance of the Lord (*sors Domini*), and whom the word Church was normally used to describe.

The definition of clerk embraced every one who had received the tonsure. From the sixth century onwards the tonsure might be given without ordination. In spite of Celtic opposition, Rome insisted everywhere on the form of the *corona*. The clerk, if he was to exercise spiritual functions, must have received orders, whether minor or major. From the thirteenth century the sub-diaconate was considered as the first of the major orders, the second being the diaconate. The two higher grades, priesthood and episcopate, formed the *sacerdotium*. The clerk received his orders in succession, one after the other and not *per saltum*, after the lapse of certain intervals of time (*interstitia*), and on condition that there was no impediment through incapacity or irregularity. For candidates for ordination the Church laid down very precise regulations on age (a priest or bishop must have reached thirty years), and also on their necessary physical and intellectual fitness and moral and social standing. These conditions being satisfied, ordination was conferred by a competent bishop, competence depending usually upon the domicile of the ordinand or of his parents. In the thirteenth century, after much controversy, the validity of ordination conferred by a heretical, schismatic, or simoniacal bishop was allowed, provided that such a bishop, having been himself regularly consecrated, had received his authority in unbroken succession from the Apostles, and that neither the matter, form, nor intention required by the Church had been wanting. Ordination conferred an indelible character, which could not be effaced by the most severe penalties inflicted by the Church on the clerk, though by deposition he was reduced to lay communion, and by degradation his clerical privileges were withdrawn. Hence a valid ordination could never be repeated. The clerks formed an order apart in the Church and were bound by a strict code of obligations. To engage in any secular occupation was forbidden them, especially in those of commerce, of arms, in the practice of medicine or of law. Worldly distractions were prohibited and the association with women. They might lodge only with persons free from all taint of suspicion. In order to bear witness to their renunciation of the world, they were compelled to dress in plain clothes of sober hue. Upon clerks in major orders, the popes in the eleventh century imposed the rule, already formulated in the fourth century but for long afterwards neglected, of continence, under pain of the most severe penalties. The Second Lateran Council in 1139 declared the marriage of a clerk to be void. His ordination determined the spiritual power and place in the hierarchical order of every clerk, his office defined the sphere within which these powers were to be exercised and his position in the hierarchy of jurisdiction. No ordination without a title was a principle almost universally observed from the earliest centuries of the Middle Ages. Orders were conferred with a view to the exercise of a definite function within a definite church. It was the duty of the bishop to provide for the maintenance of the clerks whom he ordained. The method of dividing the revenues of the diocese was fixed by canons in different ways in different countries. From the early Middle Ages onwards the revenues of the church to which the clerk was attached, or part of them, constituted his benefice, the permanent endowment of his office. The idea that the maintenance of the clerk must be guaranteed was looked upon as the justification for this benefice. From the thirteenth century the conclusion was drawn that every clerk who enjoyed adequate revenues from whatever source could be ordained. The man ordained without a title was received into a diocese, and the bishop, by *missio canonica,* assigned him his official position within it. This regulation of the beneficiary system belonged in the classic period of the canon law to *ius commune.* Only an outline can here be given of its many complications. When a benefice fell vacant the designation of the titulary, which conferred simply *ius ad rem,* i.e. a personal right to get the benefice, might depend in varied ways upon either an ecclesiastical or a lay person, and numerous conditions were imposed upon the candidates. The collation properly so called, which conferred the *ius in re, plenum ius,* a full right of administration and jurisdiction, belonged in general to the ordinary of the place. Finally the new titulary took formal possession. Henceforward to his obligations as a clerk were added the obligations of his charge : he was bound to perform his duties and to reside, and he could not become a candidate for other benefices.

The constitution of the administrative and official framework was practically uniform in all Christian countries. For the spiritual needs of the people the country districts and towns (in the latter the system did not become general until the twelfth century) were divided into parishes, at the head of which was placed the *parochus* with cure of souls. In the ninth century neighbouring parishes began to be grouped into deaneries, presided over by an arch-priest, who summoned together from time to time all the clerks of his district (*calendae*). These rural chapters acquired in the thirteenth century a legal personality and were provided with a constitution. All these inferior organisms were subdivisions of the diocese and were dependent upon the bishop. To him was committed, throughout the whole of his jurisdiction, the care of doctrine, the distribution of spiritual benefits, legislative authority (in so far as was allowed by *ius commune*), the super-vision of the clerks and the administration of ecclesiastical property. His contentious jurisdiction had reached its culmination in the thirteenth century. *Ratione personae*, he was the judge in all cases which concerned clerks and the numerous classes of persons assimilated to them, and those who had need of his protection. *Ratione materiae*, he was the judge in all spiritual and mixed causes, such as concerned heresy, sacrilege, oaths, marriage, ecclesiastical property, wills, and burials. At the beginning of the classic period these great powers were limited by those of the archdeacon, who had his own jurisdiction which tended to absorb that of the bishop. In the thirteenth century, however, the importance of the archdeacon's position declined and from that time onwards the bishop had regular assistants whose authority was revocable as having been received from him. These were the official, with control of all affairs of litiga-tions, and the vicar-general, at first, it seems, appointed temporarily during the absence of the bishop as his proctor, and later permanently with authority to act in the bishop's stead in all administrative affairs.

The power of the bishop was now shared only by the

canons. The practice of the common life, commended to clerks from the earliest times, had been regularized in the eighth and further developed in the eleventh century, and had resulted in the formation of cathedral chapters. In these each member had his own duties and prebend, and together they acted as a council for the bishop and administered the diocese during the vacancy of the see. In the thirteenth century the chapter reserved to itself the right granted by the canons to the assembly of the faithful, of appointing the new titulary. The arrangement of dioceses into provinces, an arrangement borrowed from the administrative system of Rome, had gone to pieces during the period of barbarian rule, but was restored by St. Boniface and Charlemagne. The position of the metropolitan was still of some importance in the period of the classic law. He confirmed and consecrated his suffragans, conducted visitations in their dioceses, summoned them to provincial synods over which he presided, and heard cases on appeal from their courts. Nevertheless the Pope, who by the granting of the pallium stressed the strict dependence of the metropolitan upon the Apostolic See, did not augment this intermediate power. To the patriarchs and primates little was left but the honour of the title. It is a natural tendency with all centralized monarchies to restrict the number of powerful intermediaries and to control their subjects either directly or through the medium of trusted agents.

The Pope ruled over the whole Church. He was the universal legislator, his power being limited only by natural and positive divine law. He summoned general councils, presided over them, and his confirmation was necessary for the putting into force of their decisions. He put an end to controversy on many points by means of decretals, he was the interpreter of the law and granted privileges and

dispensations. He was also the supreme judge and administrator. Cases of importance—*maiores causae*—of which
there never was a final enumeration, were reserved for his
judgement. Whilst episcopal impositions were closely
defined and regulated the Roman fiscal system (tithes,
annates) grew and increased from the time of Innocent III.
The general superintendence of ecclesiastical property
belonged to the Pope, who was considered by some to
be the owner or *dispensator principalis* of the *patrimonium
Christi*. Even spiritual powers became concentrated in his
hands. He alone could absolve from certain grave sins, of
which the first to be specified (1131) was assault upon
a clerk. He, as trustee of the Treasury of the Church,
monopolized, or nearly so, the distribution of indulgences,
which, in the eleventh century, had been organized by the
bishops. Further, he claimed for himself the canonizing of
saints. The bishops, whose jurisdiction was thus severely
limited, were strictly dependent upon the Holy See. From
1059 they were required to take an oath of obedience, and
the administration of their dioceses was effectually supervised by legates, of whom a certain number, *legati a latere*,
were cardinals and possessed of very extensive powers.
The Pope could create, divide, and suppress bishoprics,
confirm, translate, and depose bishops, and gradually reserved
to himself the right of nomination in more and more
instances. At the same time he often deprived them of
their right of disposing of minor benefices, to which he
himself appointed by means of provisory mandates (the
earliest is of the year 1137), expectative graces, and commends ; the last method, which was also practised in the
case of bishoprics and abbeys, was extensively adopted as
early as the thirteenth century with a view to concealing
pluralism. Finally also the monks, who were to be found
in every diocese, were brought into strict dependence upon

the Pope, and by their triple vow of poverty, chastity, and obedience were completely under the control of the Church. The authorization of the Pope was necessary for the institution of an order and also for any change in its rule. The decretals had carefully regulated the manner of governing the monasteries and defined the conditions required either for profession or for dispensation from vows, the intervention of the Holy See being frequently necessary in the latter case. The majority of monasteries—from the time of Urban II all those who obtained the *libertas Romana* by commending themselves to Peter—were exempt from episcopal jurisdiction and directly dependent upon Rome.

This extreme centralization had as its necessary result the development of the curia. The cardinals, who had been originally the titular heads of the principal churches in Rome and who had already been called upon by the Pope to help him, now took from the time of the Gregorian reforms a more and more active part in the government of the Church. From 1059 they enjoyed a preponderating influence in the elections to the papal chair, and in 1179 under Alexander III this became their exclusive privilege. He who obtained two-thirds of the votes of the Sacred College, whose procedure under the title of Conclave was defined in the thirteenth century, was held to be elected. In 1245 they acquired precedence over archbishops. They were the councillors of the Pope and occupied the most important places in the offices and tribunals of the curia, the apostolic *camera*, chancery, and *penitentiaria*.

The study of this hierarchical system leaves the impression of a powerful unitary organization. Beneath the surface, however, it was divided by conflicting interests and tendencies, and the dominating position of the papacy was threatened by forces which it had for the time being overcome. The conflict of interests in the diocese of regular and secular, of bishop, chapter, and archdeacon, may have been favourable to the development of the Roman system of centralization. In all the groups of secular clergy there were, however, to be found causes of complaint against the papal power. From the thirteenth century onwards many of the bishops and chapters were restive under the papal impositions of tithes and the restrictions placed upon their judicial powers and rights of collation to benefices. The fourteenth century gave birth to the conciliar movement, and the Sacred College itself now became restless and at times claimed the right to dictate the policy of the Pope it was going to elect. But in the classic period the most effective opposition encountered by the Holy See originated in the secular states. The definition of the relations between the ' two powers ' was the classical subject of debate among the Popes and canonists in the Middle Ages. Those who were haunted by the dream of unity attempted to justify theocracy, that is to say the sole supremacy of the Vicar of Christ, with a wealth of imagery and symbols. The two swords spoken of in the Scriptures, and representing the spiritual and temporal powers, belonged to the Pope, the first being used by the Church, the second on her behalf, *ad nutum et patientiam sacerdotis.* This theory found expression in various polemical writings of the period and inspired certain solemn pronouncements of the time, the *dictatus papae,* drafted during the pontificate of Gregory VII, the bull *Unam Sanctam* of Boniface VIII (1302). As a consequence of it Popes claimed the right of appointing and deposing kings, of passing judgement upon secular laws, and disposing of whole provinces. This conception of the direct power of the Pope over princes was more explicitly affirmed in periods of conflict. Thus in the Gregorian collections were to be found all such texts as would support the papal supremacy, even in temporal affairs, and especially those which seemed to establish his right to dispose of the empire. In general, however, the Popes contented themselves with the claim to intervention in secular matters *ratione peccati*. Princes were regarded as dependent upon them not as vassals—unless they had voluntarily done homage as such—but as Christians. To this theory of theocracy was opposed that of imperial absolutism. At the same time amongst both parties were to be found more balanced minds who hoped to establish the peace of the world, not by the subordination of one power to another, but by the co-ordination of one with another. This theory of the independence of the temporal and spiritual powers had been defined in a famous decretal of Gelasius and was accepted by the Bolognese school from the eleventh century onwards. And the great canonist Huguccio had expressly declared : *Utraque potestas scilicet apostolica et imperialis, est a Deo, et neutra pendet ex altera.* Dante summarizes this theory in certain lines of the *Purgatorio*, and elaborates it more precisely in the *De Monarchia*. It was adopted by almost all the decretalists of the fifteenth century, and its practical result may be seen in the Concordats.

Direct power, indirect power, co-ordination, phrases of such vague connotation can only express tendencies and aspirations. And to use them precisely, it would be necessary to take account of the circumstances in which they were coined, and of the various authorities on which they came to bear. For indeed there was no uniform principle which would embrace empire and communes, independent kingdoms and territories in feudal dependence on the Apostolic See. In their actuality such problems were of too complex and too individual a nature to be solved by general theories. They brought face to face with each other not two ideal persons, Church and State, clerk and knight, but, upon ground that bristled with practical difficulties, the contradictory and conflicting interests of all those who constituted on the one hand spiritual and on the other secular society. This entanglement of interests may in the first place be explained by the growth of ecclesiastical property. In the payment of tithes and in the making of pious bequests—customs which were now obligatory —the Church possessed fertile and constant sources of temporal wealth. In point of form, the Church's ideal of property was that it should be allodial or independent. But many churches had been built and endowed by individuals, who included them in their bequests; much ecclesiastical property, including even tithes, had been feudalized, and over all the State maintained or reasserted its sovereignty. In the Dark Ages the disposal both of ecclesiastical property and offices was as far as possible retained by the owners, overlords, and sovereigns. The Gregorian reforms definitely forbade the lay investiture of spiritual offices. As regards the minor benefices, the Church substituted for the ownership of the lord, the right of patronage, which included as its principal attribute the right of presentation. This was declared by Alexander III to be *ius spirituali annexum*, thus reserving to the ecclesiastical jurisdiction of the diocese cognizance of all disputed cases. Thus the independence of the spiritual authority, of the hierarchy, which the intimate connexion between the benefice and the priestly function had seriously compromised, appeared to be safeguarded. But from the twelfth century, although the Church admitted neither the private right of the lord nor arbitrary dispossession, the fiscal and judicial claims of the secular power were a perpetual menace to her privileges. The apparent indefinite increase of her possessions was a source of concern to sovereigns and overlords alike. For since the fifth century the rule had remained unchanged whereby the immovables of the Church were inalienable, that is they could not be sold nor be encumbered by real rights, except in case of urgent necessity, manifest utility, or for reasons of charity. Lay owners therefore ran the risk of being progressively expropriated, while the law of mortmain still more seriously endangered the freedom of alienation, so that the lords were deprived of their dues upon the transfer of property. The principle of the Church's right to acquire freehold property had been strenuously maintained by the canon law, but in practice compromises were arrived at, in the last instance a payment by way of compensation being made to the lord who suffered by some new acquisition of the Church. Such a payment was held to have exhausted the fiscal claims of the secular authorities. By Roman law these authorities could impose on ecclesiastical property only ordinary, not extraordinary taxes—the privilege of ' real immunity '—but this classification of taxes had disappeared for many centuries. The first denial of the Church's right to this immunity came from the communes, and was dictated, not by an anti-clerical spirit properly so called, but by their equalitarian principles, their emancipation from Roman law, and their exceptional needs. The struggles which had occurred in France and Italy, especially in Lombardy, between bishops and consuls, resulted in the third and fourth Lateran Councils. By these the conditions on which the so-called charitable subsidy was to be paid were defined. Churches were only to contribute to the expenses of the state for matters of general interest if the contributions of the laity were inadequate and after the consent of the bishop and clergy had been given and with the authorization of the Pope. This was in effect to leave to the Pope, who was omnipotent, the exclusive right to tax the Church. Of this right he made free use and especially to the advantage of the King of France. In the thirteenth and fourteenth centuries conflicts concerning ecclesiastical immunities arose less often between Pope and prince ; the stir caused by these quarrels in high places must not be allowed to create an illusion as to their number ; the conflict was between Pope and prince on the one hand and the national clergy on the other, whom their two ' protectors ' combined to tax unsparingly, either to meet the needs of a joint enterprise or as the result of the desire of each to please the other. What the clergy however obtained was the concession that the collection of taxes freely granted by them should not be in the hands of royal officials ; for to them entry into the domains of the Church was generally denied, even for the arrest of criminals who had taken shelter in consecrated places (right of asylum). This last point, however, was not strictly enforced, for the Pope, playing a conciliatory part, promulgated exceptions to the general rule.

The Church showed no less resolution in defending her clerks against the secular authorities than in defending her own property. By reason of their sacred character and their public duties, she had required and obtained as early as the fourth century their exemption from the performance of all personal obligations, military service (in feudal times men from ecclesiastical fiefs were led to the host of the overlord by an *advocatus*), the duty of watch and ward, labour services, the payment of extraordinary dues. This was the privilege of personal immunity. Above all they were exempt from the control of secular jurisdiction (*privilegium fori*). After many vicissitudes, this right was defined during the classic period. The criminous clerk, or one against whom a civil action (unless this concerned real property) was brought, could not be arrested by a layman nor be tried in a secular court, except in cases where the *traditio Curiae saeculari* was allowed. The officialities arrogated to themselves cognizance of actions which concerned every kind of clerk. In the thirteenth century the Pope defined with some strictness the classes of clerks who could not claim the privilege, in order that it might be confined to such as were faithful to their calling, wore the tonsure and clerical dress, and not be extended to married or apostate clerks, who were in effect living as laymen.[1] In France the secular courts in the thirteenth and fourteenth centuries did not question the principle of immunity, but they cited the decretals in opposition to the claims of the ecclesiastical courts, and little by little they formulated the view that disputes involving the public interest belonged to the royal jurisdiction.

The history of the legal privileges of the Church in the Middle Ages may be summarized thus. Their positive origin is to be found in Roman and early medieval law ; the Church, taking into consideration the reasons for their existence (the sacred character of ecclesiastical property and persons) and their justification in Holy Scripture, canonized the rules consecrated by law and custom. The papacy declared itself to be the guardian and moderator of these privileges, limited the powers of the ecclesiastical courts and conceded subsidies to the secular authority. The interests of the prince were served alike by violent publicists and by patient administrators little inclined for disputes and fearing censure. Conflicts of interest within the Church, various practical expedients of the state officials, temporary alliances between the Pope and the prince for overcoming the resistance of the national clergy, between prince and clergy to limit the power of Rome, between the Pope and clergy to resist secular exactions—such are the outlines of the picture presented by the history of the relations between the ' two powers ' in the Middle Ages, to be reproduced

[1] See the works of Génestal on the *privilegium fori*.

with a surprising variety of shade and detail. If on some occasions there were difficulties, on others Church and State combined to find a solution. Nowhere is this collaboration more noteworthy than in their efforts to maintain the unity of the faith. Since the time of St. Augustine the theory of intolerance was hardly questioned in the Christian world. Hence the legislation of the Roman Emperors against schismatics and heretics, hence crusades against dissenting sects and the organization in the thirteenth century of the courts of the Inquisition, with their secret procedure and the denial of the right of appeal. It was also this zeal for orthodoxy which compelled the canon law to forbid all relations with the excommunicated and to exclude Jews from public offices.

III

Thus the Church by a variety of means succeeded in maintaining the common faith. For Christian society she prescribed a discipline; prince and subject she instructed in their duties and their rights. The duty of the prince was to guarantee the reign of justice, the chief means to be used to this end being law, which should respect the rights of God and of the Church, and war. War was an act of vindictive justice which only the prince could perform. It must not be entered into with a view to conquest but only for the restoration of peace, the punishment of evildoers, and the recovery of stolen property. An attack made on another without justification, in a mere spirit of revenge or gain, was held to be unjust. In this way the Church limited the *casus belli*. In the feudal age the councils, in addition, attempted to alleviate the effects of a state of war by prohibiting it on certain days (truce of God), in certain places, and in respect of certain persons (peace of God). As for the subject, his first duty was to have a respect for authority; all power was of God, and the prince, by his consecration, had himself acquired an additionally sacred character. Indeed, obedience to positive law was canonically sanctioned by all the penalties known to criminal law, more especially those proper to homicide and carnal faults. Before God all men were equal, but human law had to blend in harmony inequalities of rank and status. From this inequality peace ensued, *pax, tranquillitas ordinis.* The canonists maintained the Roman tradition of a world immutably organized upon a hierarchic basis, a tradition dear to the Middle Ages. To them social inequalities appeared as a special dispensation of Providence, modelled on the Court of the King of Heaven and instituted for the salvation of souls. By Isidore of Seville and Rufinus for example, slavery, though never regarded with favour by the Church, was thought to help strayers from the right path to amend their lives. To remain in that state in which he was born and faithfully to fulfil the obligations which it entailed, such was the counsel which the Church gave to every Christian. In order to ensure the strict observance of the rules of their craft, the Church sanctioned the practice, common to many guilds, of requiring an oath on the admission of their members. On the other hand, in order to counteract whatever excessive harshness might be in her doctrine of absolute submission to the chances of birth, the Church had a twofold principle: the protection of the oppressed, the solidarity of the faithful. The Church's care for the oppressed was shown in the maintenance of charitable institutions and in the protection afforded to *miserabiles personae,* widows and orphans. Thus the Church courts had cognizance of cases in which widows were concerned, whenever justice had been denied, spoliation suffered, or dower-rights disputed. The conception of the solidarity of the faithful found its practical expression in public worship. All the faithful were received and incorporated within the Church at baptism, all shared without distinction in the same sacraments, particularly in those of Penance and the Eucharist. Since the Fourth Lateran Council all the faithful were bound to communicate once a year. All were alike bound by the rules of the liturgical year as to the order of public worship, days of fasting and of rest. The idea of the communion of saints found its highest juristic expression in the well-known theory of the Treasury of the Church, which seems to have been first fully developed towards the middle of the thirteenth century by Hugh of St. Cher. The merits of Jesus Christ, the saints, and the faithful still on earth were regarded as the common inheritance of all the members of the Church upon which they were permitted to draw, by means of indulgences, that were held to remit, wholly or partly, the punishments incurred by their sins.

The sacrament by which the Church exercised the widest influence upon general social life was that of marriage. In the tenth century she acquired the exclusive right of legislating on matrimonial matters and of jurisdiction not only over cases concerning the matrimonial bond, but also over all cognate questions, such as adultery, the legitimacy of children, separation *a mensa et toro*, and, to a certain degree, the financial relations of husband and wife. For a marriage to be validly contracted, neither rite nor formality was required. The two parties were themselves the authors of the contract and the ministers of the sacrament. The difficult point was to define exactly the nature of this contractual sacrament. Was it purely consensual, and therefore concluded from the moment of the exchange of promises, or was it in some sort a real contract that is completed only after consummation? In the early period of the canon law both these conceptions found support. Gratian still holds that the analogy of the symbol of the union of Christ with His Church required the *copula carnalis*. But from the time of Peter Lombard (*c.* 1153) the idea that marriage was completed by consent was victorious, an idea in conformity with the tradition of the Roman law and the general spirit of the canon law. It was not difficult to distinguish between the actual promise by which marriage was contracted and that made with a view to the future, the contract of betrothal, which could be broken in certain cases by either party and always by mutual consent. But the difficulty, which was sometimes perplexing, was to prove the existence of these purely consensual contracts. Such proof could hardly be supplied except by the agreement of two witnesses who had been present at the exchange of promises, or again by the possession of a certain legal status (*nomen, tractatus, fama*). Before the Council of Trent the presence of a priest was not required for the validity of a marriage and the practice of keeping parochial registers only began in the fifteenth century. Marriage before a notary was rare in the Middle Ages and the official documents settling the *dos* or the *donatio propter nuptias* were often drawn up before the celebration of the marriage. The consent must have been given with a clear mind and a free will; any error concerning the identity of one of the two parties, or some essential and distinctive quality of a party in view of which the marriage was entered into, or again the liberty of a party, rendered it null and void. Marriage could not be validly contracted under the influence of fear (*metus gravis*) or deceit. Besides defining particular conditions requisite for marriage, the canon law laid down certain general conditions necessary for the validity of the act of consent. The theory of impediments, diriment or prohibitive, was characterized in the thirteenth century by leniency and common sense. In general, the regulations as to age imposed by Roman law were maintained. But in view of its end marriage below the age of puberty was held to be valid where it was sanctioned by customs and the parties were *doli et copulae capaces*, able to beget children and capable of understanding the act they were performing. This consideration of the end of marriage caused the canonists to reckon impotence at the time of the mutual promise among the causes of nullity, in spite of the general principle of consent. The Church recognized the validity of marriage between slaves, between a freeman and a person of servile status, between catholics and heretics or those who had been excommunicated. In these last cases the impediment which had formerly been diriment became simply prohibitive. A difference of faith alone remained an obstacle as between a Christian and a heathen, since one of the parties would not have been baptized, a necessary condition for participation in any of the sacraments. Circumstances likewise compelled the Church to abandon the exogamic system she had formerly adopted, by which at the outset of the classic period, marriage between relations of the seventh degree was prohibited. Now in rural communities there was certain to be some connexion whether by blood or by marriage between all the inhabitants. By the Fourth Lateran Council the impediment of consanguinity was confined to relationship within the fourth degree. The rules concerning impediments through affinity were simplified and it likewise was restricted to connexion within the fourth degree. Finally, in classic law limitations were imposed upon spiritual relationship arising from sponsorship. Similarly rules concerning impediments penal in themselves were relaxed. Marriage was no longer forbidden, except occasionally, between the adulterous party who might become free and the fellow-sinner. Abduction ceased to be regarded as an impediment to marriage provided the *rapta* had been

set at liberty. In one point only did the canon law make
the doctrine of impediments more strict, namely in declaring
the marriage of professed religious and clerks in major
orders to be null. In spite of these relaxations, the obstacles
in the way of contracting a valid marriage were sufficiently
numerous to make it possible for parties to discover too
late that they had involuntarily disregarded some impediment. In such cases, in consideration of their good faith,
the children of the marriage were held to be legitimate
and all the consequences which would have resulted from
a valid marriage were admitted up to the day of the declaration of nullity. This was known as a putative marriage.
This important theory was developed by the decretists and
officially sanctioned from the time of Alexander III. In
order to obtain a declaration of nullity, or to prevent a marriage taking place on the ground of these various impediments, it was necessary to have recourse to legal action,
a course only allowed, however, with discretion. Prosecution by the ecclesiastical authority was rare and there was
a tendency to restrict the number of persons who might
make the accusation or denunciation. It was not lawful
for those unrelated to the parties, except in the absence of
near relatives, and amongst strangers preference was given
to those of known prudence. In this way the danger that
the validity of a marriage should be questioned by the ill-
informed and maliciously intentioned was avoided. Yet
though the canonists were alive to the necessity of placing
restrictions upon hasty accusation, they showed an equal
solicitude in allowing time to be no bar to the hearing of
matrimonial causes, in maintaining the imprescriptibility
of all proceedings and in permitting every decision to
be indefinitely open to revision. The sole object of
the legal action was to disprove the existence of the
sacramental bond. In the classic age, if this existed it was

indissoluble in every case, even if one party should have committed adultery.[1] The Church nevertheless instituted a legal means by which an end might be put to the common life without a divorce. This was the judicial separation, which continued to be called *divortium*, and of which the causes were fornication, apostasy, and grave cruelty. Thus in principle the matrimonial contract could only be dissolved by death. The surviving party might remarry, but while sanctioned in express terms by the Church, second marriages were not encouraged by her.

Before God the two parties to a marriage were equal and this doctrine of equality was first taught by Christianity. In practice it meant, above all, that the obligations, especially that of fidelity, were mutual. Nevertheless, the husband was head of the household, and in virtue of his position as such, he might choose the place of abode, reasonably correct his wife and demand from her such domestic duties as were consonant with her social position. Although the Church was less directly concerned with the pecuniary aspect of marriage, it was nevertheless a principle of the canon law, inspired by the idea of protection of the widow, that no marriage could be contracted without a dower. Even in the rules concerning the system of dowry (*dos*) the theories of the canonists have not been without influence upon secular jurisprudence, especially in the South of France. Influenced by practical considerations and by a particular

---

[1] If, however, a heathen, whose marriage by natural law was valid, were converted and the other party remained heathen and deserted him or encouraged him to forsake his religion, the new convert might remarry one who shared his faith (*privilegium Paulinum*). It should also be added that a non-consummated marriage was dissolved by the entry into a religious order of one of the parties and might in any case be dissolved by the pope. These last rules were a survival from the doctrine of Gratian, who regarded marriage as complete only after the *copula carnalis*.

interpretation of the system of Justinian they inclined towards the doctrine of the inalienability in value as distinct from an absolute inalienability *in specie*, a position which ensures both the protection of the dowry and the credit of husband and wife. Amongst the chief ends of marriage was the procreation of children. Classic law was severe in its treatment of bastards : it refused them Holy Orders and restricted their capacity. This attitude is explained by the leaning of the Church in favour of marriage, and more particularly by the campaign she undertook in the eleventh century against the concubinage of clerks. On the other hand the Church was anxious to allow legitimacy where possible, as the theory of putative marriage shows. Thus the scope of the Roman theory of legitimation was widened. Children born before marriage were legitimized of right without the necessity of complying with any of the conditions formerly required.

The study of the origins of the temporal property of the Church has shown the profound influence of the canon law upon secular life. Throughout the Christian world, laws concerning the transmission of property upon death had been materially affected by the action of the Church. It was under the influence of the Church that the practice of making a will became general, while the procedure required for its drawing up was simplified by the abolition of the Roman *heredis institutio*, and by the reduction of the number of required witnesses to two. The Church also exercised an influence on the rules of intestate successions. The late Sir Paul Vinogradoff observed that she was the most powerful opponent of the system which excluded women from the right of succession to land, and that she always looked favourably upon the view that land might be transmitted in the same way and with as little formality as money and movable property.

The sphere in which the direct influence of the canon law upon the secular law, as far as it concerned real property, was most strongly felt was that of possession. The two important chapters on law concerning first the protection of possession, and secondly acquisition by prolonged possession, were in fact re-written in the canonists. In order to protect the property of the Church against powerful lords who brought accusations against bishops, in order to seize their goods, the canonists of the ninth century had laid down the principle : *Spoliatus ante omnia restituendus.* The bishop who had been thus treated was restored to possession of his goods before any process for their recovery was started. This was nothing more than an exception in procedure, made for the advantage of determinate individuals who had suffered complete spoliation. In the eleventh century the principle of the *restitutio spolii* was extended by Gregory VII to civil processes, and in actual practice to persons other than bishops, sometimes even when only partial spoliation had occurred. Thus steps were taken towards the general notion of possessory remedy. But at present it was simply a question of an intermediate remedy involved in the course of an action, the application of which was entrusted to the judge's office. The decretists preserved in the *exceptio spolii* the principal features of this traditional remedy. But they added thereto an action in its own right ; in order to be reinstated, the aggrieved party must himself bring an injunction or a suit against the deforciant. This is a great novelty, the consequences of which can still be perceived in French law ; to the principle of the exception in procedure is now added the principle that spoliation and violence give rise to an action in reprisal. Roman law provided the bases for this theory ; but canon law substituted for the *deiectio*, on which the other system based the action, a far wider foundation. Every case of unjust deforcement of possession or quasi-possession, one might even go so far as to say every arbitrary obstacle offered to the exercise of a right, opens the way for this new canonical form of action which appears for the first time in the *Summa* of Sicardus of Cremona (*c.* 1180) under the name of *Condictio ex Canone Redintegranda.* By this *Condictio* the protection of possession went beyond the province assigned to it in Roman law. Not only were the causes of action extended, but the action lay in favour of any *de facto* holder (*detentor*) against the present possessor, even when the matter in question was a chattel or a mere right (for example an office, a benefice, or a family right). It was sufficient for a plaintiff to show that he had been in possession before the present possessor.

The above extension was accompanied by an extension of the doctrine of acquisition of title by prescription. Thus privileges and ecclesiastical local divisions were considered proper subjects for prescription, that is title was acquired by prolonged enjoyment. But here too canon law profoundly modified by extension the theory which it borrowed from Roman law. The Roman theory was that prescription only ran if the possessor had acquired under a *iustus titulus* (by sale, gift, exchange, and so forth) and was in good faith at the beginning of his possession : subsequent bad faith did not prevent time continuing to run. But in the eyes of the canonists, bad faith, whenever occurring, was a sin. The civil law punished the negligence of the owner who did not possess, the canon law reproved the sin of one who sought to prescribe without good faith. And this is why, shortly after Gratian's *Decretum,* which had only dealt with prescription as extinguishing rights of action, an anonymous author classifies as *furtum* the retention of an object, the true owner of which has come to one's knowledge. Nevertheless this doctrine was at first only applied to ecclesiastical property out of regard, according to Rufinus, to its immunity.

Stephen of Tournai considerably widened its scope by declaring that the retention of the property of another was forbidden by natural law and by the principles of equity. This was in effect to condemn the whole theory of prescription. Huguccio, with more caution, differentiated between the spiritual and temporal forum : prescription might justify possession before the law but not before conscience. Innocent III, in a famous decretal (*Vigilanti*), decided that he who claimed by prescription must not at any time have been aware that the object belonged to another. The commentators were long doubtful as to the exact import of this decretal and it provided an opportunity for the discussion of the great problem of the conflict of principles between the canons and secular law. From the fifteenth century, however, the requirement of continuous good faith became a principle of the secular law. It was adopted in Germany at the time of the Reception, it appeared in France in the Great Customal, and more recently in several Italian codes.

But the greatest influence of the doctrine of *bona fides* was destined to lie in the sphere of obligations, where it led to the completion of the Roman theory of contracts and pacts.

Roman law had gradually rid itself of formalism. Some centuries before the Christian era an agreement enforceable at law could only be created by means of ritual words and symbolic acts. From the period of the end of the Republic may be dated the beginning of real and consensual contracts, while certain pacts also became enforceable by action. But apart from these exceptions the rule remained that simple agreements by mutual consent were not legally binding, *ex nudo pacto actio non oritur*. In the Middle Ages, in order to make the promise more binding or simply to ensure its legal efficacy, the practice arose of taking an oath.

This was not readily accepted by the Church, and after recognition was accorded to the practice, she claimed the right of control over it. It was by this means that the competence of the ecclesiastical tribunals penetrated into the province of obligations. While the oath implied an obligation towards God, it was recognized that it also gave rise to an accessory obligation between the parties. It was a true formal contract, unilateral, having its cause in itself, and giving rise to an imprescriptible and perpetual obligation, whose scope was almost unlimited. It was used not only to give added force to agreements made within the terms of the civil law, but even to give validity to agreements entered into in direct opposition to the civil and even to the canon law. Examples would be the oath of a woman to respect an alienation of her *dos*, and an agreement under oath to pay interest. And it was a much debated question whether the oath only was valid, the agreement itself remaining of no effect, or whether the agreement was made valid by the oath. But between the promise made on oath and a simple promise there was no difference before God. All agreements, by whatever form they were entered upon, were binding upon the conscience. Not to fulfil the obligations of a pact was equivalent to a lie and the canonists of the twelfth century strove after a legal remedy for its non-fulfilment. According to Huguccio the duty of ensuring the carrying out of an obligation arising from a pact lay with the judge. According to Innocent IV, the only course open to the plaintiff was *denunciatio evangelica*. The general opinion, however, expressed in the *Glossa ordinaria* in the *Decretum* allowed to whoever wished to exact the fulfilment of a simple promise, a *condictio ex canone*. Thus was affirmed the principle, common to all modern law, of the essential part played by the will in originating obligations. That this theory of the pact (*pactum mutuum*) was directly contrary to a maxim of the Roman law and of secular legislation was somewhat embarrassing for the canonists. The attempts which they made to find a practical reconciliation between their theory and Roman law gave rise to the formulation of a new essential requirement of a valid contract, an element which the Romans had not clearly apprehended, namely the *causa*. An informal promise would, in most cases, be confirmed by a written act, *cautio*. Now the Roman texts, moreover, relative to the *querela non numeratae pecuniae* laid down that if the written act which established *mutuum* should contain a mention of the *causa*, this should constitute an acknowledgement of his obligation on the part of the promissor, and should be accepted as such by the judge, the burden of proving it invalid, so as to release himself, being laid on the promissor. If on the other hand the *causa* were not mentioned, the burthen of proof lay with the party insisting upon the fulfilment of the promise. These rules were recalled in a celebrated letter of Gregory IX to the prior of St. Bartholomew's, and the decretalists boldly drew from them the conclusion that all promises supported by *causa* were enforceable by Roman law. In the fifteenth century they forgot even the written act and thought only of the promise : *cautio seu debitum*, said Panormitanus. In other words, every pact for which there was a sufficient legal *causa* was valid. It mattered not that it was a pact *nudum a solemnitate* provided that it was not *nudum a causa*. On the definition of *causa*, the canonists were not, it is true, fully agreed, and in their very differences too they showed themselves the precursors of modern controversies. The general meaning on which all were agreed was the necessity of a purpose to be attained. There was *causa* if the promissor had in view a definite result, either some definite legal act or something more comprehensive such as peace.

And in order that morality might be safeguarded, it was not only necessary that the promissor should have an object, but that this object should be reasonable and equitable. Reason and equity were interpreted by the canonists in synallagmatic contracts as the exchange of strictly equal obligations, that is, the value of the service to be rendered by one party must be equal to that of the service to be rendered by the other. To find this balance was not always an easy task. The only simple case was that in which the object delivered was a sum of money, as would occur in a contract for a loan. Exactly the same sum must be repaid. Here we have the canonist theory of usury, with its prohibition of all lending at interest. But in the majority of cases the contract is concerned with the rendering of certain services, when it becomes a question of fixing a just wage, or with the conveyance of an immovable or of a movable other than money, when it becomes a question of fixing a just price, of determining the effect of a breach or non-execution of the contract by one of the parties. In all commutative contracts, the canonists, in order to fix the price, took account of the material object and the services to be supplied by the contracting party. Far from accepting the law of supply and demand as its base, they had an objective standard of value, which led them to postulate a fixed tariff. All productive work was worthy of a wage. The canonists justified the profits of the worker on the land, whose efforts are as tangible as their results and who wages an honest warfare with the soil. But they condemned mercantile profits, obtained without any transformation of matter, the result of speculation and bad faith.

These economic theories were founded upon the reasoning of Aristotle, upon the hatred of the canonists for all gain resulting from mere chance, and were perhaps due also to a feeling of distrust on the part of the Church as the owner of much landed property, for the merchant class, who in the communes were dealing the first blows at her power. In practice the theory of the just price led the canonists to adopt the strictest rules laid down by the civilians in the matter of *laesio* for cases of injury. And it was indeed this same idea of equilibrium and of commutative justice which gave rise to the theory of the termination of contracts. If one party did not keep his agreement, the other party was released from theirs, *non servanti fidem, fides non est servanda.* This maxim, which seems to have originated with Huguccio, had in the first instance the same meaning as the Roman maxim: *dolus dolo compensatur.* But already under Innocent III, a sometime pupil of Huguccio, the question was debated as one belonging to the sphere of contracts. In the saying of Huguccio, which he confirmed in three decretals, the Pope saw a mere interpretation of the intentions of the contracting parties, the operation of an implied condition; neither party was bound except on condition of performance by the other party. Both these conceptions, the penal and the contractual, were to be found in the writings of the canonists in the thirteenth century. What was common to both and also in the nature of an innovation was the attempt to base upon a general principle the different hypotheses upon which termination was admitted in Roman law.

The starting-point of the canonist theory of contract was thus the repression of sin, as that of the praetorian law was the repression of wrong. Wrong and sin indeed were not always clearly differentiated. *Crimen* and *peccatum* were frequently used synonymously in the earlier texts, for it was a confusion of which the canonists and civilians alike were guilty, and which was not without its results. In his *Mirror of Justices* Andrew Horn still classifies wrongs in accordance with the theological order of mortal and venial sins, and this was not without effect, since as the infinite variety of possible wrongdoing made any strict classification impossible, the number of wrongs might be freely extended, while the minute and detailed analysis of the circumstances of the sin, a practice popularized by the Celtic and Frankish penitentials and carried to an extreme by the casuists, provided an excellent model for modern criminal lawyers. This analysis of the circumstances is perhaps the greatest debt which penal secular law, and especially through the work of the old Italian criminalists, owes to the canon law. The conception of many wrongful acts—Bartolus instances particularly *furtum* and *iniuria*—was widened and modified. Above all, a method was provided for the precise investigation in any given case of the intention (which in itself is not a justification of the result, but which furnishes the means of assessing the responsibility of the criminal), and of the external circumstances of the act, especially of cases of necessity. It must be added, however, that while in general the canon law maintained the principle of personal responsibility for faults, it did not altogether escape the tendency common to all medieval legal systems, which is, in determining the penalty, to take account of the group as much as of the individual, and to obtain reparation, which should be complete, exemplary, and deterrent, by demanding it from the innocent if it could not be paid by the guilty. Canon law thus adopted the idea of group responsibility, the penal responsibility of the heir, of corporations and associations, of the family of the offenders who had injured the rights of the Church. It borrowed from the secular law the majority of its vindictive penalties, sometimes with modifications. Thus imprisonment, which had originally been purely preventive, became a true punishment, which involved solitary confinement in a dungeon for the moral safeguarding of the prisoners as well as enforced inaction for the purifying of their souls. The canonist idea of reformative penalties, excommunication, interdict, suspension, was not without originality. It had as one of its objects the amendment of the guilty person, although the Church was as solicitous for their repentance as for their amendment. The most important of these penalties was excommunication, which might be either a total exclusion from the Church (major excommunication), or merely an exclusion from participation in the sacraments and the liturgy (minor excommunication). In the preclassic period of the law all relations with the excommunicated were forbidden. But in the eleventh century this too severe rule was modified by numerous exceptions, and at the end of the Middle Ages, by the bull *Ad vitanda* of Martin V (1418), it operated only in the case of those who had been excommunicated *specialiter et expresse*.

Finally, while the ecclesiastical courts adopted little by little almost all the rules of the Roman procedure, they applied both discrimination and additions. From the Germanic law they borrowed certain features, for example the *purgatio*. In order to ensure the effectual prosecution of crime the Church introduced the system of denunciation, and to punish misconduct and scandals amongst clerks the inquisitorial procedure. The *ordines iudiciarii* of the canonists drew up detailed rules as to proof, especially proof by witnesses. In order to establish a fact two ocular or auricular witnesses were required, worthy of credence and agreeing in all points. The judge retained a great discretion in weighing the evidence, his sentence being dependent only on the testimony of the witnesses ' if he were thereto inclined '. No form of procedure has ever given a greater importance to the *officium iudicis*, and in no other has the search for truth been more effectively kept free from the shackles of formalism. We have already called attention to this feature in the case of marriage, and there is no better illustration of it than the theory of notoriety, according to which all notorious facts were adjudged summarily without formal accusation or right of appeal.

At the very time at which the system of the canon law was reaching completion the end of the Church's period of omnipotence was approaching. Internal revolutions—the transference of the Papacy to Avignon, the Great Schism, the Conciliar movement, the Reformation—brought temporarily to the ground the various organisms of which she was composed and deprived her of the allegiance of a great many subjects. The power of national states increased, and little by little the authority of the ecclesiastical hierarchy was restricted to spiritual concerns. Acting upon the theories of absolutism and of enlightened despotism, kings regained control of all temporal and even of ecclesiastical affairs (*iura circa sacra*). The State controlled the activities and censures of the Church, supervised its accessions of property, taxed its temporal possessions, bridled the religious orders, collated to benefices, sapped ecclesiastical jurisdiction. Its own powers increased at the expense of those of the Church, which were regarded as dependent upon concessions made by princes and therefore revocable, and sometimes as bold usurpations of public rights. The last period in this evolution was reached with the era of toleration (all forms of faith being on terms of equality) and the separation of Church and State.

The Church has not accepted this dispersion of her powers. On certain points she has enunciated her rights as dogmas. In proportion as her sphere of influence was diminished, the schools interpreted her principles more strictly in these, and these lost nothing of their severity in actual practice. Theological justifications replaced arguments drawn from positive law. Where formerly canonists had justified the immunity of clerks and ecclesiastical property by citations from the Theodosian code and from the decretals, for Juan Lopez (fifteenth century) or Girolamo Albani (sixteenth century) it sufficed to plead their sacred character and the support of Scripture, in which the priest, he said, appeared ' as a sort of angel or god '. On other points, for example in the sphere of economic relations, there was progressive adaptation of the law to changing conditions. As commercial ventures increased the importance of coin and as the Church had need of money and also of the means of investing her capital, the theories of usury and of a just price were modified, and nothing is more curious than to watch the ingenuity and casuistry of the theologians and canonists in their attempts to reconcile their principles with necessity.

One section of the classic law therefore has become obsolete, another has been modified. Yet another has remained intact and alive. We have noted at the beginning of this essay the careful way in which the Church has preserved her former discipline—what she has borrowed from the past is clearly seen in the rich apparatus of notes in the recent *Codex* (1918)—and also some important contributions of canon to modern law. The catalogue of these debts is not yet complete, for every year the most learned and most acute of our civilians and those least inclined to overrate the practical value of historical research make fresh additions to it. The point to be emphasized is that neither the canonists nor the civilians intended to draw up a list of mere ' relics '. The classic law is not dead ; its principles and the development of their consequences continues. Two examples will illustrate this point. First, the characteristic which appeared fundamental in the history of the hierarchy, that is centralization, was brought into prominence in the sixteenth century by the Council of Trent and by the popes, especially Pope Sixtus V, the founder of the Roman Congregations. The Vatican council (1870) defined papal infallibility and Rome continues along its monarchical way. And again, the ideas of good faith and equity which underlay the canonist theory of contracts still influence the legislators of to-day, and those shrewd conceptions of the just price and a just wage are more vital than any system that has been practically applied because they express our permanent ideal. Thus the present is linked to the distant centuries of Innocent III and Gregory VII ; and indeed even to those more distant, for many of the ideas which bore fruit in the classic age were the heritage of past civilizations. The care of the poor and the oppressed which was characteristic of Judaism, the Roman love of order and authority, the Greek conceptions of political economy and formal logic, the enthusiasm and scrupulousness of the Celts, which were shown more particularly in their penitential system—all these conquests of the human mind, which seemed to her in accordance with her fundamental principles, went to the enrichment of the Church's law, and were assimilated to her own doctrine after such modification and correction as was required to bring them into harmony with her own point of view. It is indeed the highest moral tradition of the West and of the Mediterranean peoples which has been gathered up and handed down to us in the classic law of the Church.

GABRIEL LE BRAS.

iii. ROMAN LAW

AMONG the most important of those treasures of the mind
handed down by the Middle Ages to modern times must be
reckoned the law of Rome. The complete rule and canon
of a highly organized and civilized society, it establishes
a satisfactory balance between each man's rights and his
duties, visiting their violation with fixed sanctions, and
laying down forms of procedure which permit of those
sanctions being applied with discernment or their rigour
relaxed. Over all stood an authority, powerful to protect
the life and labour of the individual, prudent to secure for
the whole people the full benefit of individual effort. The
formulation of Roman Law was the greatest triumph of the
ancient world. In it the Middle Ages had, of course, no
part; but they have transmitted it to us. The great
cataclysm of the invasions might easily have destroyed
Roman Law when it destroyed the political sovereignty of
Rome. To reawaken, to restore to life, to spread it far and
wide in everyday use, this was the work of the Middle Ages;
a work so well performed and so lasting that the Roman
system remained the common law of Germany down to the
promulgation of the German Civil Code of 1900; that it
governed the south of France till the Civil Code of 1804;
and inspired elsewhere almost every legal system of the
West. In short, the Middle Ages themselves were inspired
by certain general conceptions of Roman Law which were
only to find their full fruition in the world of to-day.

For this wonderful survival we must at once acknowledge
a great debt of gratitude to the Middle Ages. Nevertheless,
the medieval endeavour was simply to take practical advantage of this legal gospel of Rome; in so doing they occasionally altered and even falsified it, sometimes from

prejudice, sometimes in the process of adapting the law of Rome to the new conditions which it was called upon to govern. The varying perspicacity of interpreters, the requirements of practice, the new and sometimes contradictory aspirations of peoples, all these factors made for a partial deviation of medieval Roman Law from the historical law of ancient Rome. It follows that what they have handed down to us is a Roman Law very far from its early purity, complicated and tortured by the efforts of medieval thought. To sort out the legal stock-in-trade, and to ascertain what it is that modern society owes to ancient and what to medieval Roman Law would require an analysis somewhat too detailed for such an essay as this. It will, I believe, be easier and at the same time sufficiently accurate to give a general view of the great movement of ideas of which Roman Law was at once the axis and the instrument from the downfall of Roman sovereignty to our own day. To do so we will investigate three great questions : I. How and when was the renaissance of Roman Law in Western Europe brought about, and what has been in regard to it the attitude from time to time of scholars and practising lawyers ? II. Which are the great leading conceptions of Rome which struggled to life again in the Middle Ages and are being more fully realized to-day ? III. What procedure did the Middle Ages adopt in altering Roman Law to meet their needs, and how far can we follow their example?

I

1. It is universally recognized that the barbarian invasions of the fifth century did not, in Gaul, in Italy, or in Spain, destroy the practice of Roman Law. That practice survived among the romanized peoples and does not appear even to have been attacked by the invaders. In the midst of these populations the Barbarians insinuated themselves in ever-

increasing numbers, maintaining their own customs but respecting those of their neighbours, which it was the duty of the judges to uphold exactly as it had been while the lordship of Rome was still effective. This general survival is a phenomenon of which numerous explanations can be given. First of all, there is the great numerical preponderance of the romanized population in comparison with the original barbarian influx, a preponderance which made impossible the absorption of the Roman by the barbarian element; then there is the usual method of the invasion. As a rule the barbarians who established themselves on the soil of the Empire came there as auxiliaries forming part of the Roman army and subjected, at least as a matter of law, to the Imperial authority : they were mere garrisons without reason for meddling in the civil life of the populations in whose midst they were stationed. Later still, when at different dates in different localities the usurpations had caused the rejection by the barbarian chiefs of even their nominal subjection to the Empire, the persistence of Roman Law is explicable, not only by the previously formed customs of the diverse races, but also by the inadequacy of the barbarian laws, which were too rudimentary to regulate the much more complex and more active juristic intercourse of the romanized populace. Thus it comes about that even the barbarian texts themselves admit the existence throughout the West of two parallel streams of legal activity, a Roman and a barbarian stream. This state of affairs lasted several centuries, its duration varying in different regions according to the extent of their germanization, the importance of successive barbarian inroads, and even according to the changes and chances of political history. In France the South long continued to practise Roman Law in accordance with the *Lex Romana Visigothorum*, while the North more rapidly forgot it. In Italy Roman formularies continued in use in spite of the Lombard invasion. Nevertheless, a difference long obtained between the more germanized valley of the Po and the Romagna or the Marches which were less sensitive to barbarian influences. But everywhere the populace, Roman by race or culture, was the common prey of all the disorders begotten of conquest, blood feuds awakened by the helplessness of the judiciary, high-handed freebooting of banditti chieftains rebellious against every control ; and it was impossible that it should pass through such an ordeal unscathed. Ultimately in spite of the efforts of the Carolingian dynasty to restore civilization, the whole Western world, Gallo-Roman and barbarian alike, fell back to a stage of social development far behind that of pre-barbarian Rome. Roman Law, in those localities where it still subsisted, was forced to accommodate itself to the level of the general ignorance, was reduced to precepts more and more elementary, and, for the majority, ceased even to be intelligible. Of specific law there remained only a detritus of practice preserved in traditional usage. Continual retrogression had reduced popular mentality to the primitive, and forms of social life to the rudimentary : the Roman system was no longer the law adapted to their needs or their aspirations : inevitably the crude barbarian concepts held the field. From the tenth century the night grew darker and the West seemed incapable of drawing benefit from its old ties with Rome.

2. Very soon, however, a reaction set in almost everywhere. The cities, organizing themselves more compactly, began to feel a new security behind their walls. The national migrations were finished and the peoples of the West settled down at last to a sedentary state. Men of peace and social order gathered together of their own accord and placed themselves under the guidance of the lord of some neighbouring castle in order to put a stop

even by force to family war and to the brigandage of town against town. They were vigilant in maintaining the security of the roads, they protected the work of labourers and artisans, they fostered production and exchange. The West set itself to climb slowly back up the hill down which it had so quickly fallen. The return to an organized and peaceful state of society made possible a renewed understanding of the value of ancient discipline ; and when scholars discovered in ancient manuscripts the laws of Rome, of which the very existence had almost been forgotten, the admiration of contemporaries was unreserved and their hopes unlimited. Studious youth flocked in crowds to the Universities to hear the new gospel read and expounded, and returned filled with an overflowing enthusiasm. The *Corpus Iuris* of Justinian, like a great wave on an undefended coast, seemed likely to submerge Italy, France, even England, and to wipe out all trace of the customs which the narrow simplicity of the folk-lawyers had laboriously and often clumsily raised.

This renaissance of Roman Law came about first in Italy at the beginning of the twelfth century at the University of Bologna under a jurisconsult named Irnerius, of whom we know very little. He was the head of a school which quickly became famous throughout the West. He left equally famous disciples, known as ' the Four Doctors ' Bulgarus, Martinus, Ugo, and Jacobus, who were summoned, as imperial counsel, to sit in the Diet of Roncaglia (1158) by the Emperor Frederick Barbarossa. The four doctors in their turn trained up numerous successors ; and, driven onward by apostolic fervour or sometimes by the ups and downs of the intestinal squabbles of the little Italian towns to which they belonged, these successors went out to carry the good tidings, some to France as Rogerius, Azo, and Placentinus, others like Vacarius into England.

There has been much discussion about the causes and character of this renaissance. But it is now settled that it was neither so sudden nor so unforeseen as was at one time supposed. It was but the harvest of a seed-time dating back for nearly a century before. In Italy the memories of Rome were more tenaciously held than elsewhere. There the compilations of Justinian had been reproduced in more numerous manuscripts, having been brought direct into the exarchate of Ravenna by the Imperial armies. The cities of Lombardy had returned to great commercial prosperity and their inhabitants had felt the need of a deeper and more searching study of juristic relations. Already, in answer to this demand, law was being taught in the flourishing Universities of Pavia, of Ravenna, and perhaps even earlier of Rome. At Pavia the interpreters of Lombard law had even essayed to adapt their system to the varied juristic needs of an active commercial intercourse.[1] The restoration of Roman Law was only the last and the happiest of these efforts.

From the moment that lawyers applied themselves to study the *Corpus Iuris* of Justinian, they were captivated by its twofold superiority of theory and practice. Many were the specific solutions which they found there ready made, anticipating (even in details) the practical complications which their own minds were not yet trained to unravel. Their admiration was also commanded by the methodical way in which each concrete case was reduced to its juristic

[1] The famous Lanfranc was born at Pavia about A.D. 1005. He taught there for some time and afterwards went to France, where he founded the abbey of Bec, in Normandy, which rapidly became a great centre of learning, counting among its scholars Saint Anselm, Yvo of Chartres, and the future Pope Alexander II. After William's Conquest of England Lanfranc was chosen Archbishop of Canterbury in 1070, and it was he who brought to England the first fruitful seeds of Italian juristic thought.

essentials, and was ranged in the category or under the aegis of some commanding principle, whilst this principle itself was seen to be but the application of a more exalted and more general truth. What a gulf separated this harmonious, logical procession of ideas from the isolated, disconnected, and apparently arbitrary solutions which were all that even the most advanced of the barbarian codes could show! To crown all, these great principles themselves were found to be closely allied with the moral conceptions, the acceptance of which the Church had during twelve centuries been striving to secure against a welter of physical force. Such, for instance, was the notion of equity on which the earliest glossators argued at such length: such was that of the natural equality of all men which Justinian taught in spite of the harsh fact of slavery: such again was that of the sovereignty of the people to which imperial omnipotence had at least paid lip-service. To conclude, each man found in the law of Justinian his varying needs and aspirations satisfied without altering the solidity of its organization or the fair hierarchy of social orders which it establishes.

The first attitude of scholars brought face to face with these written monuments was one of devotion. They must search them and know them; and to this search they brought an unbounded faith which refused to admit in the imperial handiwork the possibility of either failing or contradiction. Hence the abundant wealth of purely explanatory literature; of glosses first grammatical and then juristic; of 'continuations' or *résumés* of whole titles which, when joined together, became the *Summae*; of *quaestiones* attempting to reconcile the contradictions of various Roman texts or later to solve a difficult case not expressly foreseen. Of all this mighty effort of interpretation and reconciliation achieved by the 'school of the glossators' the results were condensed during the first half of the thirteenth century into the ' Great Gloss of Accursius '. Such was its success that in certain towns, and even at times in University teaching, it usurped the place and the authority of Justinian.

During this century and a half the authority of Roman Law was so universally accepted that ancient usages and municipal statutes were lost in the flood, and lawyers could hardly think of reserving for them even the smallest corner in their daily practice. Nevertheless, the day came when a halt was called: towards the middle of the thirteenth century enthusiasm calmed down. The glossators, for all their good intentions, had singularly complicated the legal system even of Justinian, and had too often made of it a stumbling-block for the common people who were ignorant and without advice and had no instinctive tradition to teach them how to meet the many requirements of the Roman Law. Moreover, in daily use the classical doctrines sometimes did violence to the popular conscience ; for traditional conceptions (notably concerning the government of the family, succession, the property relations of husband and wife) and traditional procedure were very different from the conceptions and practices of Rome. Insensibly therefore, first in France, afterwards in Italy following the example of France, the popular will revolted and insisted on a respect for local usage. A complete theory was accordingly elaborated of the part which should be played and the legal force which should be wielded by custom ; [1] and

[1] The theory of the authority allowed to custom by the civilians, and still more the evolution of that theory, are too complicated to be dealt with in such a paper as this. The glossators did not deny the legal authority of custom ; but to reconcile the texts of the Digest which support it with the legislative omnipotence delegated to the Emperor by the people which finds expression in Justinian, they postulated for the validity of custom an Imperial grant (express, at first ; afterwards implied) of legislative authority. It is only the post-glossators who

even Roman rules were interpreted in a more attractive spirit and with more concession to popular ignorance. In England the movement amounted almost to an expulsion of the Civil Law. At the same time, its doctors were carried along by the great scholastic tide which was setting in favour of constructive logic, and tended to disregard the strict letter and to rally more to the principle which could be extracted from it. This principle they would enlarge and even modify so as to absorb into it customary conceptions, and to provide sanction for practices sprung of new-found needs. Moreover, from the middle of the twelfth century alongside the Civil Law and teaching in the same schools, the Church had worked out a new jurisprudence whose purpose was to comment on and to expand the new compilations of its confessors and pontiffs and to provide for the action of its special courts. This was the Canon Law, sprung like the Civil Law from Roman sources, but from biblical and sacred origins as well. Its legislation extended in part over the same ground as the system of Justinian, was inspired by the purest Christianity, and made the same unvarying and universal claim to the allegiance of all Christendom. The civilians could not possibly ignore this great movement of jurisprudence ; indeed they frequently took part in it, just as the canonists also worked in concert with them at the modification of Roman secular laws. Obviously, the reciprocal influence of the two systems on one another was inevitable.

All these new elements gave to the expounding of the law a new direction and called to birth a new school, that of the dialecticians, which closed and supplanted that of the

denied the necessity for such a grant and derived custom from juris-diction allowing that custom, like jurisdiction, could acquire validity by prescription. Besta, *Storia del diritto italiano*, i, pp. 433 and foll., 497 and foll. (1925).

glossators. Beginning in France during the second half of the thirteenth century, its earliest representative was James of Révigny, bishop of Verdun, followed by Peter of Belleperche, dean of the chapter of Notre-Dame of Paris, afterwards bishop of Auxerre and chancellor of the King of France. The principal representatives of this school among us are all Churchmen. By Cynus of Pistoia the school was carried into Italy, which it conquered; it attained its highest eminence with an Italian jurisconsult of the first half of the fourteenth century, Bartolus of Sassoferrato. Throughout the West, Bartolus achieved a fame comparable to that which a century earlier had belonged to Accursius, and left many disciples, of whom the most celebrated, Baldus, died early in the fifteenth century. This school was characterized both by its spirit of compromise with local and canon law and by its constructive dogmatism. It would use a logical formula at one moment to press to extremes principles which the sagacity of the ancient jurisconsults moderated by others acting in an opposite direction; at another to build up modern and customary ideas on a Roman foundation.

The doctrinal results of this new orientation of Roman Law were in unison with certain well-known historical events. In France, for example, the monarchy was growing stronger and at the close of the twelfth and beginning of the thirteenth century (Bouvines, 1214) had cast off the sway of the German Emperor. Nevertheless, in the eyes of the Romanists it was simply a local sovereignty legally subordinate to and contrasted with the Emperor, the principal characteristic of whose overlordship was (in abstract theory) that it knew no bounds. Long ages were needed to reduce this abstract supremacy over all Christendom to a harmless historical survival. Small wonder that the kings of France looked with some favour on the assertion before their tribunals of local custom to the prejudice of that Roman Law which savoured of the Emperor. Indeed, in alliance with the papacy they showed their hand still more clearly by measures discouraging the spread of Roman Law teaching. Although, therefore, during the thirteenth century there was reason to fear that in Northern as in Southern France the legislation of Justinian might stifle the existing growth of custom, in the fourteenth, on the contrary, the South alone remained subject, and in the North Justinian was reduced to the role of auxiliary or supplemental law, of written reason suggesting a solution when custom does not dictate one. Hence the great division of France into the territories of written and those of customary law.

This was the outward and visible result, hostile to Roman Law and in harmony with the liberation of the monarchy from Roman imperial suzerainty. But there was another and contrary result which illustrates the high degree of legal acumen already developed in France. The juris-consults of the North had all been brought up in the school of Roman Law. Custom was fluid, uncertain, contra-dictory ; it had never passed through the crucible of a pro-mulgation in writing or been refined by abstract juris-prudence. Inevitable comparisons must daily have shown the technical superiority of the Civil Law with its tabulated rules and fine distinctions : as witness Bouteiller, who in the fourteenth century and in Northern France stigmatizes the customary law as ' hateful ', and, though he admits its sway, packs his study of it with undisguised borrowings of Roman rules. Our custumals tell the same tale : the customary law, though officially victorious, romanizes more than ever before. At the same time and on the other hand by its resistance to the civilians in matters of deep-seated popular sentiment, custom becomes conscious of itself and is stripped of all but its irreducible essence. In the fourteenth and fifteenth centuries their Roman legal education has taught our customary jurists habits of mind to which their predecessors were strangers ; habits of exactitude, of steadfastness, and of rigorous logic in the handling of custom. They strive, sometimes even with the open assistance of the civilians, to grasp the Proteus of custom and pave the way for its codification. Such a work could not be accomplished without large borrowings from Roman Law, and many were the embryo principles of custom which had to be abandoned in favour of their Roman rivals. Roman influence, then, becomes more difficult to disentangle from the mass ; since it is exerted not only on the solutions adopted but on the whole spirit of their application.

In England no part of the realm was in direct contact with Italy ; the juristic unity of the whole country was maintained ; and the romanist influence was only felt, as it was in the North of France, by the channel of customary jurists of whom Bracton was the most authoritative. England, also, escaped much more quickly, the cycle of Roman influence ending in the course of the fourteenth century. The systematic abstractions of Roman Law had from the very outset bewildered English practitioners. For this very reason they had begun by rejecting the absolute ' dominium ' of the Romans (imported by Vacarius the glossator of Bologna) and had established their real property on the foundation of the purely relative protection afforded by the Assizes of Henry II.[1] As the years went by consecrating

---

[1] Henry II's advisers, notably Glanvill and the chancellor Becket, were thoroughly imbued with Roman jurisprudence ; and the assizes framed at their instance are no strangers to Roman technique. The affiliation of the Assize of Novel Disseisin to the *Interdictum Unde Vi* through the canonist *Actio Spolii*, and perhaps also that of Mort Dancester to *Quorum Bonorum* are very probable. Nevertheless, it is incontestable that the Assizes, descendants though they be of the

and developing this Royal Law of Assizes, the influence of Roman Law was stifled. But it reappeared even in the course of the thirteenth century when the triumph of the Law of Assizes was complete. Freehold having henceforth its protective sanctions, it was found necessary also to protect certain existing tenancies at will, certain tenures of less dignity than real property, and certain chattel interests in possession less than those of the proprietors who enjoyed the protection of the Assize. For this the civilian theory of possession furnished the materials : the ' action of trespass ' takes our thoughts back to the Roman interdicts. But though its Roman affiliation is probable, it is nevertheless uncertain ; and though the evolution in England of real and personal property follows a curve similar to that outlined at Rome by ' dominium ', ' possessio in bonis ', and ' possessio ', English Law preserves in this also a character all its own. Finally, the school of the dialecticians, as a school of law, had, properly speaking, no appreciable influence in England. It is from Azo and the school of Bologna that Bracton and his successors draw their inspiration. The fourteenth century was an unpropitious time for juristic speculation ; and the England of the fifteenth century turns its thoughts inward and becomes more and more estranged from the Continent and from Roman Law.

It is extremely probable that the great wave of Roman Law which overflowed England in the twelfth and thirteenth centuries reached Scotland almost immediately. True, it was not till the fifteenth and sixteenth centuries that Roman Law took root there so vigorously as to remain even to this day one of the most fertile sources of Scots law. But in the fourteenth century appeared Scotland's earliest juristic manual, the *Regiam Maiestatem,* which is little more

Roman theory of possession, resulted in the total overthrow and disuse of the Roman structure of absolute *dominium* as distinct from possession.

than an adaptation of the famous *Tractatus de legibus et consuetudinibus regni Angliae* of Glanvill ; and Glanvill's intimacy with Roman ideas is undeniable. In the twelfth century Robert, Bishop of St. Andrews, with the assent of King David I, promulgated to his clergy the *Exceptiones Ecclesiasticarum Regularum*, the parentage of which has been traced by recent scholarship to the Decretum of Yvo of Chartres.

From the first, Italy in general readily accepted the doctrine of the earliest glossators. To an even greater extent than in the South of France, popular usages were already strongly impregnated with Roman Law and even the Lombard element in them had already been transformed. Nevertheless, this must have cost the Italians an effort, since the Roman Law consecrated among them the supremacy of the germanic Emperor. The fall of Frederick II terminating this supremacy could not fail to be favourable to civilian influence, the more so that henceforth the enemy whom the Italian republics had to fear was no longer the Emperor but the Pope, against whom the Civil Law provided a bulwark. On the other hand, the growing commercial prosperity of the cities, and the rivalries between them accentuated the longing of single cities for juristic autonomy, for an individualism which the unitary principle of Roman Law could not satisfy. Hence originate numerous local statutes corresponding to the French custumals, which without rejecting the Roman Law as a common legal background step in between it and the people and render its application somewhat more distant. We have already mentioned the complaisance of the new school of the dialecticians with regard to these statutes ; and it is well known that Bartolus even took a leading part in elaborating the famous ' Statute Theory ' which resulted in the acceptance of rules permitting in certain cases the authority of

Statutes to transcend the limits of civic territorial sovereignty and thereby to place a check on the common law of
Rome. But, just as in France though even more noticeably,
the Roman influence was carried on by the romanization
of the Statutes (Balduinus at Genoa, 1229; Paul de Castro
at Florence, 1415).

The influence of the dialecticians or Bartolists pre-
dominated in France and in Italy until the sixteenth century,
when it fell under the attack of the historical school of which
we shall shortly speak. But first it will be well to mention
one of the latest conquests of this school, namely Germany,
where it held sway till the nineteenth, we may even say till
the dawn of the twentieth century.

We might perhaps have expected to find Germany among
the earliest and speediest conquests of the Roman *renaissance.*
The doctrine of the civilians reconstructed the imperial
omnipotence to the profit of the German nation, which
appeared as the successor of Rome and claimed title to
bring under her sceptre all Rome's ancient territories.
This was definitely the pretension of Frederick Barbarossa
at the Diet of Roncaglia, where, seated in his *consistorium*
and surrounded by the four doctors of Bologna, he added
two ' authentics ' to the ancient laws of Justinian. Nevertheless, Germany's first attitude was one of resistance.
Perhaps because the German folk was still too far removed
by the savagery of its manners from the full refinements of
Roman Law; perhaps because in the unending strife of the
twelfth and thirteenth centuries Roman Law appeared
as the banner of that domineering foreign civilization which
was made such a grievance against the Hohenstaufen;
in any case there is no trace of Roman influence in the
Mirror of Saxony (1215) and very little in the *Mirror of
Swabia* (1275). Moreover, both in political life and in
private affairs the conception of personal law was very

firmly and very widely held in Germany; the right, that is, of every man to live the law of his homeland, and even the law of his own social class, and to refuse obedience to any common discipline. This piecemeal tendency to individual autonomy brought about the eclipse of the Empire during the interregnum and the growth of a large crop of local independent legal systems in direct conflict with Roman unity. Civil Law was not entirely unknown, for the fourteenth and fifteenth centuries are marked in Germany by numerous little treatises which institute a frequent comparison between Roman imperial law and municipal usages. Rejected though it might be, its influence was none the less present. Add to this diversity of laws the multiplicity of jurisdictions each upholding the independence of its own jurisprudence, and we shall understand the chaos which was Germany in the fifteenth century. The remedy came from the very virulence of the disease. Commerce developed in Germany between city and city and held out its hands beyond the borders of Germany to the cities of Italy, France, Flanders, and elsewhere: men were forced of necessity to erect by common consent superior courts of intercommunal justice capable of rising above local divergences of legislation and of judging by the light of a common law of their own making. The groundwork was provided by the manuals of Roman Law in vogue at the universities which Italian jurists founded in Germany at this time; and some of these manuals enjoyed for this very reason an astonishingly wide popularity. At the same time in the most widely discussed cases, the practice grew up of an official submission of the issue to the masters of the universities for the opinion which they alone were competent to base upon broad reasons of equity. Bartolus provided an inexhaustible mine of solutions couched in peremptory form. Thus by its own excellence, by the fame of its interpreters, and without any definite legislative acceptance, Roman Law met the universally admitted need for a common rule and slowly but surely conquered a country which at the outset had been indifferent and even hostile. The crown and summit of this conquest was the foundation in the sixteenth century of the Imperial Court of Justice. This made the Roman Law the common law of all Germany— a position which it held down to the promulgation of the Imperial Civil Code in 1900. True that little by little during these four centuries its domain was circumscribed by various royal codes issued in the different kingdoms; but until 1900 the Roman Law was admittedly superior to these. Besides, what Germany followed was not the Roman Law of Justinian but the law interpreted and transmogrified by the Bartolists. In Germany, its latest conquest, that celebrated school continued to flourish long after the rest of Europe had deserted it for the historical school: of this we must now speak.

In the sixteenth century, as is well known, western Europe as a whole turned with enthusiasm to pagan antiquity. The happy outcome of a number of accidents had been to render possible the direct study of ancient texts; and men were alive to the mental squalor of preceding centuries and to the way in which the real facts of antiquity had been misunderstood by scholastic philosophy and religious prejudice. Youth and confidence were the order of the day; and in the glamour of Greece and Rome reason and liberty of thought were born anew. Learning was light-hearted, brave, and youthful, totally without reverence for the recent past: the leading strings of tradition were thrown away: nothing was left unquestioned. How could the Dialecticians survive such a mutiny with their abstruse involutions, their great piles of rubbish and puerilities? For there is no denying that the jurists of this school gave openings for criticism. Their desire to reconcile every contradiction, and to find Roman authority for practical solutions the reverse of Roman led to childish hair-splitting and great doctrinal uncertainty. They had covered the Roman texts with a parasitic vegetation so luxuriant as to alter their whole aspect. It is easy to understand the holy zeal with which the humanists set about the destruction of this sacrilege, and the renown achieved by those (of whom, in France, Cujas is the chief) who made it their life's work to restore the Roman compilations to their original purity. But from our present point of view the important fact is that the humanists in their single-minded restoration of the old Roman Law in its classical framework have finally banished it from the present to the everlasting calm of the past. They saved it from the distortions of everyday life and practice ; but they made of it for the future no more than a frigid work of art with no effective influence beyond that which a cultured mind may feel by the contemplation of an artistic harmony. The humanists, one might almost say, ended the popular destiny of Roman Law in the West.

Nevertheless, at first the success of the humanists was more apparent and resounding than deep or real. The hold of the Bartolists and of the glossators generally over the jurisprudence of the West was so close that the humanists themselves did not even think of pushing their doctrine to extremes. For nearly three centuries they claimed for the Civil Law, exactly as the Bartolists had done, a domain of general daily use. Not till the nineteenth century, hardly till the latter part of that century, did the humanist reform lead to its full results. Thus in the 'written law' territories of France it was not the Roman Law of Cujas which was held to be binding. Legal practice maintained its old habits of compromise and continued to approximate, with or without the aid of the revised Roman texts, to the solutions adopted in the neighbouring customary territories. The only effect of the renaissance was to establish a distinction between written law and Roman Law. In the customary territories the influence of Roman Law was felt in two different ways. The great jurists, Dumoulin, d'Argentré, Chopin, Lebrun, Pothier, were worthy successors of the ancient *prudentes* : in successive editions of the customs and in their own interpretation their art was shown in guiding custom on the road marked out by the great Roman signposts. They freed it from local peculiarities, and accentuated its common tendencies, paving the way for the fusion of all the customs in a united national law. Secondly, for lack of commentary on the varying local customs, lawyers were compelled to fall back on Roman Law in its great function of supplementary law or ' written reason ' : natural diffidence made them loath to give up the help of the great past. It was only very gradually that the elaboration of common principles from a converging interpretation made it possible for the boldest among them to appeal to a ' customary common law ' rather than to the ' supplementary ' Civil Law. This was due to the impact of the French Revolution.

Moreover, this ' written reason ' of Roman Law was a conception very close to the natural law which was the pride of the eighteenth-century philosophers throughout Europe. Now that the strict letter of the law was no longer held binding, it was easier to look upon it as a social ideal. To imitate the classical democracies, as the revolutionary thinkers conceived them, and to establish the sway of universal reason : with these aims in view the French Revolution proclaimed the great principles on which modern societies rest—some at least of which are (as we shall show) a legacy from Roman Law.

II

Let us endeavour to disentangle the main conceptions of
public and private law which the Middle Ages borrowed
from Rome and have handed down to us; and first of
public law. A bird's-eye view of modern public law in the
West will throw into prominence, among others, three great
governing principles. These are : (i) the idea of the State,
(ii) the idea of national sovereignty, (iii) the aspiration
towards an international polity. Let us examine the debt
of these conceptions to Rome, taking the two first together
since they are joined together in the same classical texts,
while the third is more widely scattered.

A. First, in the Roman world there was never any doubt
that the source of all public authority was the people.
The people alone had the right to make laws and to issue
commands ; it alone could defend the interests of the city.
The people is fully conscious of this supremacy and mani-
fests it by taking an active part in the civic life in its assemblies, in its public festivals, and in the army. The whole
public law is based on this notion of popular sovereignty.

Secondly, the organ of the people is the Roman State, the
respublica. Composed of all the citizens, the *respublica* is
nevertheless above them all, superior to each individual in
just that measure that the safety of all is more important
than the safety of one. It is invested with an unlimited
authority over the individual and the power to exact from
him the sacrifice of his personal interests, and even of his
life. The social discipline thus imposed on all citizens is
one of the most valuable achievements of the ancient world.
The Roman State was at bottom only the City grown larger,
the organ of collective defence against the world outside.
Born of the difficulties of life in a petty town standing
alone in the midst of a frequently hostile countryside, it

retained the same stamp even after it had grown to the furthest extension of the Empire. This absolute authority of the State is as noticeable in the late Empire as under the kings. It is this alone which can saddle a man for life with the duties of a *curialis* even against his own wishes, and makes possible the kind of state socialism which we meet with after Diocletian.

Thirdly, the last in this train of ideas which rule the public life of Rome is the delegation of the power of the State to civil servants entrusted with its exercise. The civil servant wields the powers assigned him not in his own name but in that of the State of which he is only the provisional incarnation. Two consequences follow. First, the civil servant partakes of the majesty of the *respublica* : thus the Emperor becomes an absolute master from the moment that the Imperial power is confided to him, and the *Lex Iulia Maiestatis* is extended to contempts of the Emperor or his images. On the other hand, the civil servant's authority belongs not to his person but to his office. He has no right to transmit it to his heirs, nor is he allowed to extract from it profit for himself as from his private property. He can only wield it for the interest of all and in the name of all.

The doctrine of the delegation of power by the people to the Emperor subsists even in the later Empire. Nevertheless, we must admit that in the practice of Imperial authority, eastern influences had mingled at this epoch a personal element with the old Roman traditions. Thus is established the hereditary transmission of the throne; and the privy purse of the Emperor, the ' fiscus ', absorbs the public treasury of the Roman State, the ' aerarium '. But these deviations were without serious doctrinal consequences.

The whole public system of Rome broke down in the course of the invasions. The invaders, grouped in families, in tribes, or in semi-nomad bands, knew nothing of the abstract territorial city of the Roman world. The tie which bound them together was essentially personal and private. The company follows its chieftain, trusting him so long as he is successful in his campaigns, scattering on his death or defeat ; but attached to him only by the bond of a personal oath. The chieftains themselves join the following of a more powerful chief to whom they swear fidelity for themselves and their men. The king is only the chief of a greater host, a character which he retains in France for long centuries and in Germany longer still. On this foundation of personal fealty rests the feudal regime which governed all Europe till the nineteenth century. Of this barbarian conception, we may say, are sprung those royal houses which still exist in western Europe ; allegiance and fealty to a dynasty embody a mystic sentiment of love for the person of the Sovereign regarded partly as the representative of the state of which he is the head but still more as the incarnation of a powerful ancestral protector and lord.

But the abstract conception of the Roman State reappears from the first moment of the renaissance of Roman Law. The minds of men had been made ready for it by the ceaseless efforts of the Church, which, although it had never appealed to the lay idea of public interest, had nevertheless endeavoured to wean the king or chief little by little from selfish desires by insisting on the duties and responsibilities of his office before God. It inculcated the duty to uphold the reign of peace among men, to make wide the bounds of justice and equity, to protect the weak, and to ensure the practice of charity and love between neighbours. The form was different but the substance was the same, namely, to make of the king the servant of the public interest, the *respublica*. For this tendency Justinian's texts provided a stronger and more exact foundation : a fragment from the institutes of Ulpian, which is reproduced twice over by Justinian (*Inst.* i. 2. 6, and *D.* i. 4. 1. 1, pr.), was the starting-point of all Romanist doctrine from the twelfth century. It runs thus, ' The prince's decision has the force of law; inasmuch as by the royal law passed concerning his authority the people has invested him with the whole of its own authority and power '. Two phases of constitutional doctrine are here reconciled together by the jurists of the classical period without distinguishing their historical succession. The first proclaims the principle of popular sovereignty : the right to command and therefore the right to make law belong to the people alone. This principle can be traced back to the earliest period in Roman history when the government of the city was made up of two distinct but allied parts, people and *patres.* From this distinction and this common sovereignty derives the celebrated formula S.P.Q.R. (*Senatus populusque Romanus*) which was placed at the head of all official acts. In the later Empire popular sovereignty has disappeared : its place has been taken by the imperial will. Hence the second principle which Ulpian gives us : that which the prince has declared to be his pleasure has the force of law. However, the new principle of imperial sovereignty was not in the eyes of the jurists incompatible with its forerunner, the sovereignty of the people : they explained the omnipotence of the Emperor by saying that the Emperor had received from the people the delegation of that sovereignty which properly belonged to it alone. This delegation had been made by a *lex regia* passed at the entry into office of each succeeding Emperor. Actually, the formality of the *lex regia* had disappeared in the later Empire. The Emperor was absolute : true, but that was the natural consequence of the popular sovereignty of which he was the incarnation. Popular sovereignty ; delegation thereof to the Emperor ; imperial or royal absolutism : such are the problems which Ulpian's text raises, and the solution which he gives them reconciles the ancient constitutional principles of Rome with the state of affairs introduced by the Empire. From the twelfth century onwards this text gave rise to ceaseless discussion among civilians and canonists alike. Oddly enough, it was the idea, first and foremost, of popular superiority over king or emperor which fascinated the minds of the majority of medieval thinkers from William of Auvergne, St. Thomas Aquinas, Bartolus or Dante down to Hotman, Althusius, or Hubert Languet. The religious wars of the sixteenth century made plain the dangers of extreme democratic doctrines and inclined men's minds towards the other aspect of the problem, namely, the absolute power of the Emperor. Then the old theory of a delegation by the people to the Emperor or king, a delegation henceforth deemed irrevocable, was used to justify the exaltation of despotism as, for instance, by Hobbes. At last, when in the eighteenth century the defences of royal absolutism are breached, Rousseau has but to proclaim the popular sovereignty inalienable and to give a new turn to the idea of delegation rendering the royal power limited, permissive, and revocable. All these various and (some might say) conflicting conclusions are drawn from the text of Ulpian inflected to meet the varying political circumstances out of which they arose : they are all, that is to say, of Roman origin.

B. Rome gave the world the ideal of universality and brought the same to fruition in her legal system. This was brilliantly shown by the great German civilian, Von Ihering, more than fifty years ago. Other cities of classical times were devoted to the narrowest parochialism. From the time of her great conquests onwards, the genius of Rome was exhibited in resistance to this tendency : she brought together under her aegis thousands of cities united in a single bond of peaceful progress and mutual respect : by regular slow steps she led up to the same degree of civilization men of widely different race : she satisfied local peculiarities at the same time that she exalted the traits common to all humanity. With the whole known world subjected to her laws she went far towards realizing the dream of a universal rule of equality over all the races of mankind. Christianity has only spiritualized the ideal which Rome inaugurated.

The Germanic invasions broke up this unity, and on the Roman soil sprang up a whole forest of petty local sovereignties jealous of their autonomy and in a perpetual state of war and brigandage one against another. But their peoples cherished the memory of the golden age of the great *pax Romana* ; and endeavoured with the aid of the Church to restore it first as the Roman Empire of the West under Charlemagne, and afterwards as the Holy Roman Empire. Stubborn facts, however, would not submit to such a construction, and the Germanic Empire was universal only in dreams. The national kingdoms rose against its pretensions and threw off all subordination ; and, the better to unite their jarring but reconcilable elements within, laid stress upon everything that divided them from the world without. Among men inspired with the lust of conquest and plunder a dominion built upon force without the cement of common sympathies is indeed a house of cards.

With less noise but more effect than the Holy Roman Empire, Roman Law in the Middle Ages filled the part of an international unifying agent. By the world-wide compass alike of its moral authority and of its practical application it achieved an influence comparable to that of Christianity itself, appealing to and ensuring their willing acceptance of the same ideas of equity and social justice, of discipline and administrative order. It inclined them to see their temporal interests in the same light and brought them together in the bond of a common civilization. Overstepping state frontiers, it united scholars in a great commonwealth of thought governed by the memory and the law of Rome, a commonwealth whose horizon was world-wide. The universities were open to all who hungered for learning and were filled with all the peoples of the earth. In them affinities of language, of race, of feeling, unknown or long forgotten, were discovered or renewed ; and those who went forth from them carried the good seed back to their homes. The renaissance of Roman Law in the twelfth century is the first and foremost glory of the universities.

We have said how numerous they were throughout the countries which had formed the Roman Empire. In the fourteenth and fifteenth centuries they become more local and more national : from our present point of view, there is a set-back brought about by wars and devastations and the return of local jealousy. The second renaissance, that of the sixteenth century, restores to the rejuvenated Civil Law its universal appeal. More than ever, the scholars of all nations are bound in a single brotherhood. By them are built those dreams of unity, of the universal republic, which haunted the vision of the eighteenth century, which fired the generous enthusiasms of the French Revolution, and have at last taken bodily form, from the anguish of the last great war, in the League of Nations. Submerged in the German flood, the Roman seed has nevertheless taken root, and to-day is struggling to bloom : to give mankind the freedom of the *pax Romana* instead of tyrannical strife.

This longing for unity engendered among the nations by the idea of Rome, yet found its quickest and fullest development in the internal life of certain countries. This was specially marked in France, where during the thirteenth and fourteenth centuries the educated classes of the different provinces were being drawn ever closer together by the intercourse of common universities, and where the royal house called to its councils the intellectual pick of every province and sent them forth again as its representatives in the government of the whole country. The national wars of the fourteenth and fifteenth centuries brought the most distant provinces together in the face of a common danger : from the sixteenth century onwards the abstract unqualified conception of the *respublica* was held in high honour by our legislators ; and the late Roman Empire became the model for a central bureaucracy growing ever stronger and controlling more and more completely the social life of the provinces. Under Francis I the Chancellor Duprat brought to power the representatives of the Civil Law Faculty of the University of Toulouse : the absolute monarchy which they inaugurated was to go forward in the footsteps of the Roman State and to bring about that centralization which the Revolutionary leaders, intoxicated with the strong wine of classical democracy, were to make still more complete.

Passing from public to private law, we find Roman influence on the legal systems of Europe still more marked. But so wide is that influence that we should have to examine every institution in minute detail in order to balance our account. There is no legal field where it is not felt ; on the other hand, there is none in which it has operated unalloyed.

The law of Things (*ius quod ad res attinet*) is the branch of law in which it appears most clearly. Though it may be true that the distinction between movables and immovables and the establishment of a different system of rules for each of these two categories are not of distinctively Roman origin, yet it would be hard to deny that the very conception of ownership, of its attributes, its bounds, and its indivisibility (as that conception is held to-day in France, in Italy, and in Spain) is taken directly from Roman sources. We can hardly doubt that the analysis of the distinction between property and possession is of Roman origin. Perhaps we may even attribute to the civilians in England the leading part in creating the system of personalty? In fine, on the Continent at least, the whole system of real actions and sanctions for the right of property is, we may confidently assert, derived from the *rei vindicatio*. The struggle was a long one which achieved these results. Not till 1789 in France, and later still in the rest of Europe, did the single Roman conception of indivisible ownership triumph over the piecemeal tendencies of the feudal doctrine of estates.

The law of obligations fell more quickly under the civilian sway. Barbarian practice and theory alike were rudimentary and inadequate to the widespread juristic relations of trade and industry renewed. The fine analysis of the intention of parties, the reasoned elaboration of the elements of contract, the classification of obligations, of their methods and effects: in all these things Roman Law stood alone and without rival in the Middle Ages. It was studied with such zeal and applied with so little resistance that the customs when cast into written form and published commonly omit all mention of the law of obligations. The triumph of Civil Law in this sphere goes back to the thirteenth and fourteenth centuries.

As much may be said of procedure in general; not for any lack of a barbarian theory of procedure but because that theory with its wagers of law, its narrow formalism, and its disingenuous subtleties was a shapeless mass totally unfit to stand up against the simple, clear, and orderly Roman procedural mechanism. In this field the Church contributed much to the acceptance of Roman methods.

On the other hand, in the domain of family law the

principal factor in the legal systems of the West has not been the Civil Law but the Church and Teutonic conceptions. There need be no surprise at this when we reflect upon the narrow foundation of the Roman family based only on power, on authority imperative, absolute and unyielding, and upon the obviously insufficient place allotted in its scheme to marriage and the common affections and interests of the two parents one to another and towards their children. What power of attraction could so mechanical an idea have in competition with the Christian family based entirely on ties of blood and mutual affection, upholding the kinship of all whom those ties unite and reverencing even in its discipline the personality of the child ? No doubt the Roman system did a great deal to soften the harshness of its early conceptions ; but its foundations remained unchanged, and its latest reforms, those laid down in Justinian's 118th Novel, were not known in Gaul until after the sway of Christian and Teutonic ideas was fully established in the West. The Teutonic family had been very much more open to Christian influences ; it extended ' as far as a single drop of blood could be traced ' ; it obeyed the collective will rather than an absolute chief : the feeling of common interest was more important than the dry categorical imperative of discipline.

Hence the ordinance of marriage and the arrangements of property between husband and wife belong to the Church. Instead of sanctioning, as at Rome, the entire separation of interests between spouses and the unqualified protection of married woman's property, the Church made the wife partner for richer for poorer, for better for worse, in the management of the conjugal patrimony. Hence also there survived for ages a family supervision for the benefit of the family over the disposal and transmission of ancestral property by its manager for the time being.

Nevertheless, even here where the governing ideas are not Roman, it would be incorrect to say that Roman Law has played no part. Let it suffice to instance the Roman institution of guardianship and the *in integrum restitutio ob aetatem* in the law of incapacities ; or to remind ourselves of the progress throughout the Middle Ages of the right to dispose of one's property on death. In France it is only with the Code of 1804 that we see the definite triumph of the Roman principle that a man's property at his death devolves as a single whole, and the technical details of the acquisition and even of the partition of such property. Although in France the partition of an inheritance is declaratory and does not involve a transfer of title, yet other rules of partition are undeniably Roman, as are also the theories of the payment of debts of the deceased, and of the lien established by operation of law over the property of the deceased in favour of the legatees.[1]

Enough has been said to show how thoroughly and by what manifold paths the Civil Law permeated during the Middle Ages the legal systems of the West. One might wish, perhaps, for a single striking formula to describe its general effect on the development of private law ; but it is not always easy to focus the leading idea quite clearly. Let me indicate only what appears to me the most marked trait of this Roman influence.

We may say, I think, that Roman Law more than any other theoretical factor has facilitated the passage of west European societies from the economics of the agricultural family to the rule of commercial and industrial individualism. It has not been the sole factor in this transition ; for the whole legal system of movable property, with its rapidity of circulation and its dearth of specific remedies, has been largely built up if not on Teutonic foundations, at any rate

---

[1] Cf. Code Civil Art. 1017 with Codex 6. 43. 1. 2.

upon modern legislative experiments necessitated by the low esteem in which feudal society held movable wealth. Roman Law, nevertheless, took the lead in the long stern fight, never crowned with complete success till the French Revolution, for the emancipation of the individual and of property from the ties of family or seigneurial collectivism. Let us dwell upon this for a moment.

In every primitive society where the State still lacks authority, its duties are discharged by an elementary organism, the family or the tribe. These duties do not usually stop at the protection of the individual; for in the general insecurity the group as protector must of necessity be vested with great authority over every one of its members. Nay more, within the group everyday life and work are hardly thought of except in common. The land, and frequently also the flocks and herds, are common property. Later, as the fear of outside attack becomes less pressing, each man tends to work for himself and to enjoy the fruits of his labour apart; he withdraws from the common effort and the common home; he feels the need of his own personality and separates himself whether with or without his share of the common patrimony. The development of commercial exchange and intercourse with distant lands, the growth of movable wealth, the temporary emigration of the most adventurous spirits, all accelerate this movement. Legislation favours more and more the accumulation of individual riches and becomes more hostile to the authority of the group. But for a very long time traces of an earlier state of affairs remain.

The historical process is a very common one, and the Roman world itself went through it. But at the moment of the German invasions Rome had long passed this stage and had arrived at an organization, to all appearances, fully individualist. The ownership of the clan, the control of the group over the alienation of immovables, impediments on free gifts by individuals whether *inter vivos* or *mortis causa*—all these things have disappeared. Roman Law consecrates the absolute and unreserved power of the individual over his property of whatever nature. The law of obligations in particular, completely freed from the solidarity of the family, has applied with increasing care the principles of individual intention and individual responsibility. The great doctrinal achievement of the *prudentes* lies in this principle of intention, accurately and unflinchingly worked out and placed beyond the reach even of judicial modification. The whirl of business, the safety of juristic intercourse, necessitated complete individual autonomy ; and by one of those curious contradictions of which life is made up that autonomy became the more stubborn in Rome that it was founded not on the solitary individual but on the group ; that narrow unchanging group of Roman society, the family incarnate in its chief and serving only as his pedestal. Here is one of the most distinctive characteristics of Roman private law : the absorption by the *paterfamilias* of the whole juristic life of the *familia* and the erection of his individual discretion, omnipotent and unfettered, in the very centre of private law. The *paterfamilias*, girt with the sole authority over the patrimony, is the triumphant champion of individualism in the classical law.

Over against this robust individual autonomy a very different state of affairs prevails at the time of the invasions among the Teutonic folk : great formless groups of kindred, their boundaries often ill-defined and devoid of any central authority. Sovereignty is diluted in the folk-moot. At one time, it may be, discipline was strong enough to make of the kindred an organization for battle ; but it had quickly been relaxed and survived only as a control over landed property vested first in the family as a whole, later in the individual kin in the order of their succession. In this mitigated form, with variations of time and place and becoming ever less burdensome, the authority of the family survives through the centuries down to the nineteenth, deteriorating slowly, with spasmodic revivals whenever care for the family property fostered by noble or conservative sentiment was for a time stronger than the desire for commercial freedom. Some centuries after the invasions alongside the family association there arises in the West, to meet the need for military protection, the feudal association with its strict hierarchy of ranks. To ensure permanence, this also is founded on the land of which the ownership is divided among successive holders, each lord in turn possessing the right to intervene in any alienation of land by his liegeman. Hence an alienation to be valid must receive the assent of all who hold sway over the land; a requirement which, though worn somewhat threadbare, survives down to the nineteenth century. Landed property, therefore, the most vital form of wealth through long ages, is hedged about by barbarian tradition with a network of successive impediments, designed, contrary to Roman ideas of liberty, to keep it in bondage and to render alienation a slow and difficult business.

Against this organization Roman individualism maintained unceasing combat. The first shock of the barbarian invasions from the fifth to the eighth centuries did not immediately reveal how violent was the conflict between the two societies, and the speedy triumph of Roman conceptions might have been expected. But the decay and eventual collapse of the Carolingian dynasty revived Teutonic barbarism and made the conflict obvious. The Italian renaissance of the twelfth century brought back the individualist principles of the Civil Law; and their action from that time onwards has been silent, steady, and unceasing.

That it took seven centuries to achieve the victory is no doubt due to the fact that only a complex social and economic civilization can appreciate to the full the attractions of individualist law ; but it is due also to the way in which our legal authorities made use of the Civil Law. This brings us to our last point.

III

Throughout the Middle Ages the Civil Law was the daily and hourly *vade mecum* of our jurists. Their own doctrinal inexperience held them spellbound before this orderly sequence of juristic commands, this wealth of dialectical ingenuity. They were attracted at the same time by the stubbornness of ancient principles and by the mental subtlety which was capable sometimes of interpreting them in a contrary sense. The Civil Law became to them an inexhaustible arsenal full of all manner of mighty weapons ready to be snatched up and wielded in the tussles of everyday life. Of these weapons they availed themselves in all sorts of causes, as the moment's need dictated, without troubling their heads about their suitability to the end in view. The Civil Law was even pressed into the service to combat its own essential principles, and we find Roman technicalities used as a brake to retard the progress of Roman principles. Of this the most striking example is feudalism.

Sub-infeudation involved the parcelling out of ownership in land, and a hierarchy of ownerships flatly contradictory to the indivisible and absolute Roman concept. Nothing less than the downfall of the fief at the French Revolution was needed to bring about the return of the West to the theoretic indivisibility of proprietary right. But it is not so often noticed that the feudal theory has, nevertheless, been built up entirely of Roman materials and by the

Romanists of the thirteenth to sixteenth centuries. They elaborated that queer creation of *dominium directum* and *dominium utile* ; at the same time they made the possession of land inseparable from the contractual obligations of the tenant which are a direct burden on the land. To effect all this they did but amplify the Roman notion of *actiones directae* and *actiones utiles* and the distinction between *dominium iure civili, possessio in bonis,* and the holding of provincial soil. At the commencement of the thirteenth century, feudal relations had not yet been clarified into a system of law and were still liable to be tossed about by every wave of changing circumstances. Had they continued in this condition they would have developed and become extinct side by side with the military service which they provided. But erected into real rights, of which the obligations were but the outward sign, they acquired the power to outlive the duties which were their justification. Bound together by the cement of Roman logic and Roman technique, they continued to weigh heavily upon western Europe for two or three centuries after the causes which had given rise to them had vanished. In the end it took the French Revolution to destroy that which the lawyers had built up by the aid of Roman jurisprudence, a building erected in flat defiance of the natural tendencies of Roman Law to meet the anti-Roman aspirations of medieval society.

In a narrower field we may also mention the theory of substitutions which was in high favour throughout western Europe from the fourteenth to the eighteenth centuries. It is well known how in many parts of northern Europe customary law withstood the introduction of the Roman testament, maintaining the unavoidable authority of intestate succession and family co-ownership. The testament is a mighty instrument in the hands of the individual to withdraw his patrimony from the unending sway of the family. In refusing to allow the right of testament, the northern countries naturally rejected the *institutio heredis*, which is its keystone. Nevertheless, they borrowed from it the *substitutio* that became in French Law the 'substitution fidéi-commissaire', which is merely a form of sub-institution; and this substitution they made a means not to facilitate the transfer of the property of the deceased to strangers in accordance with the will of the deceased, but on the contrary to assure its permanence from generation to generation in the hands of a single family by making void and of no effect any disposition by the representative of any one of these generations. Thus the individualist Civil Law is brought in to support the ingrained sentiment of family and nobility.

Thus it was that the whole Western world down to the French Revolution felt the influence, more or less direct, more or less general, of the Civil Law. The French Revolution inaugurated throughout the West a great effort of codification, which, albeit broadly inspired by Roman principles, has gradually eaten away the official and legal authority of Justinian's text. In this it has but carried on the movement which from the sixteenth century onwards has impelled modern Europe to cut out her own juristic habiliments for herself.

The publication of the French Civil Code in 1804 was the first great blow to the Roman supremacy. On one hand it re-established a single legal system for all France and put an end to the binding force of Justinian's law in the south. On the other hand, throughout the country the Civil Law was no longer allowed even the function of supplementary law. The Code was intended to be self-sufficient. Where the letter of the law is insufficient, the solution of every difficulty brought before our judges must be sought in its spirit. With us the legislator has been obeyed. During the first half of the nineteenth century the old quotations from the Digest and the Codex are still received ; but after that, in France at least, the echoes of the past are stilled.

Italy followed very much the same evolution as France, but more slowly and irregularly. Not till 1866 was her Civil Code published after more than half a century of ups and downs. Germany was still more tardy ; for, as we have already mentioned, she did not attain her Imperial Civil Code till 1900, and the Civil Law remained her common law until that year. We may add that on many points the German Code of 1900 is even now more romanized than the French Code of 1804.

Only in our own day, therefore, has the *Corpus Iuris* of Justinian been divested of binding force. Fourteen hundred years old in its latest recension, eighteen hundred years in the majority of its fragments, it has continued to rule the world through the greatest political and social upheavals ever known and has outlived by all these long centuries the civilization which gave it birth.

Must we say that Roman Law, now that its binding force has gone, has no longer a part to play in western Europe ? He would be a bold man who should say so, for it continues to be taught in all the universities. Roman Law is still the foundation for the liberal education of a lawyer, the training and the sharpening of his logical equipment. The methods of reasoning of the Roman jurists, their way of approaching a legal problem we still follow to-day. To their classifications we have returned after having long neglected and sometimes misunderstood them. Above all, we are still ruled by their idea of justice and their strivings after equity.

Ed. Meynial.

7

THE POSITION OF WOMEN

THE position of women has been called the test point by which the civilization of a country or of an age may be judged, and although this is in many respects true, the test remains one which it is extraordinarily difficult to apply, because of the difficulty of determining what it is that constitutes the position of women. Their position in theory and in law is one thing, their practical position in everyday life another. These react upon one another, but they never entirely coincide, and the true position of women at any particular moment is an insidious blend of both. In the Middle Ages the proper sphere of women was the subject of innumerable didactic treatises addressed to them, or written about them, and their merits and defects were an evergreen literary theme, which sometimes gave rise to controversies in which the whole fashionable literary world of the day was engaged, such as the debate which raged round Jean de Meun's section of the *Roman de la Rose* and Alan Chartier's poem *La Belle Dame sans Merci* at the beginning of the fifteenth century.

The characteristic medieval theory about women, thus laid down and debated, was the creation of two forces, the Church and the Aristocracy, and it was extremely inconsistent. The Church and the Aristocracy were not only often at loggerheads with each other, but each was at loggerheads with itself, and both taught the most contradictory doctrines, so that women found themselves perpetually oscillating between a pit and a pedestal. Had the Church, indeed, been consistent in its attitude towards them

D d

in the early days of its predominance, their position might have been much better or much worse. But it was remarkably inattentive to the biblical injunction against halting between two opinions. Janus-faced it looked at woman out of every pulpit, every law book and every treatise, and she never knew which face was turned upon her. Was she Eve, the wife of Adam, or was she Mary, the mother of Christ? 'Between Adam and God in Paradise', says Jacques de Vitry (d. 1240), 'there was but one woman; yet she had no rest until she had succeeded in banishing her husband from the garden of delights and in condemning Christ to the torment of the cross.' On the other hand, 'Woman', says a manuscript in the University of Cambridge, 'is to be preferred to man, to wit: in material, because Adam was made from clay and Eve from the side of Adam; in place, because Adam was made outside paradise and Eve within; in conception, because a woman conceived God, which a man could not do; in apparition, because Christ appeared to a woman after the Resurrection, to wit, the Magdalen; in exaltation, because a woman is exalted above the choirs of angels, to wit, the Blessed Mary.' It is extremely curious to follow the working of these two ideas upon the medieval mind. The view of woman as an instrument of the Devil, a thing at once inferior and evil, found expression very early in the history of the Church, and it was the creation of the Church; for while Rome knew the tutelage of woman, and barbarism also placed her in man's *mund*, both were distinguished by an essential respect for her. As the ascetic ideal rose and flourished and monasticism became the refuge of many of the finest minds and most ardent spirits who drew breath in the turmoil of the dying Empire and the invasions, there came into being as an inevitable consequence a conception of woman as the supreme temptress, 'ianua diaboli', the most dangerous of all obstacles in the way of salvation. It is unnecessary to enter fully into the ramifications of this attitude. Its importance is that it established a point of view about woman which survived long after the secular conditions which created it had passed away. In practice it had little influence upon men's daily lives; they continued marrying and giving in marriage and invoked the blessing of the Church upon their unions. But opinion may change irrespective of practice and the monastic point of view slowly permeated society. Tertullian and St. Jerome took their place beside Ovid in that ' book of wikked wyves ', which the Wife of Bath's fifth husband was wont to read aloud nightly, with such startling results. The clergy, who preached the ascetic ideal, were for many centuries the only educated and hence the only articulate section of the community, and it is not surprising that the fundamental theory about women should have been a theory of their essential inferiority.

This theory was accepted by the ordinary layman, but only up to a point. Outside the ranks of monastic writers and the more extreme members of a celibate priesthood, no one, save professional misogynists like the notorious Matheolus, took the evil nature of women very seriously, and most men would probably have agreed with the Wife of Bath's diagnosis,

> For trusteth wel, it is an impossible
> That any clerk wol speke good of wyves,—
> But if it be of hooly Seintes lyves,—
> Ne of noon oother womman never the mo.

What they did accept was the subjection of women. The ideal of marriage which inspires the majority of the didactic works addressed to women in the course of the Middle Ages is founded upon this idea and demands the most implicit obedience. It is set forth in the stories of Patient

Griselda and the Nut-Brown Maid, and the possessive attitude towards women is nowhere more clearly marked than in the remarks made upon feminine honour by Philippe de Novaire (d. 1270) in his treatise *Des quatre tens d'aage d'ome*. 'Women', he says, 'have a great advantage in one thing; they can easily preserve their honour if they wish to be held virtuous, by one thing only. But for a man many are needful, if he wish to be esteemed virtuous, for it behoves him to be courteous and generous, brave and wise. And for a woman, if she be a worthy woman of her body, all her other faults are covered and she can go with a high head wheresoever she will; and therefore it is in no way needful to teach as many things to girls as to boys.'

The subjection of women was thus one side of medieval theory, accepted both by the Church and by the Aristocracy. On the other hand, it was they also who developed with no apparent sense of incongruity the counter-doctrine of the superiority of women, that adoration (*Frauendienst*) which gathered round the persons of the Virgin in heaven and the lady upon earth, and which handed down to the modern world the ideal of chivalry. The cult of the Virgin and the cult of chivalry grew together, and continually reacted upon one another; they were both, perhaps, the expression of the same deep-rooted instinct, that craving for romance which rises to the surface again and again in the history of mankind; and just as in the nineteenth century the romantic movement followed upon the age of common sense, so in the Middle Ages the turmoil and pessimism of the Dark Ages were followed by the age of chivalry and of the Virgin. The cult of the Virgin is the most characteristic flower of medieval religion and nothing is more striking than the rapidity with which it spread and the dimensions which it assumed. She was already supreme by the eleventh century, and supreme she remained until the end of the Middle Ages. Great pilgrimages grew up to her shrines and magnificent cathedrals were reared and decorated in her honour, while in almost every church not specifically her own she had a lady chapel. In the thirteenth century—about the same time that Philippe de Novaire was deciding that girls must not be taught to read—Albertus Magnus debated the scholastic question whether the Virgin Mary possessed perfectly the seven liberal arts and resolved it in her favour. Her miracles were on every lip, her name was sown in wild flowers over the fields, and the very fall of humanity became a matter for congratulation, since without it mankind would not have seen her enthroned in heaven.

> Ne hadde the appil take ben,
>   The appil taken ben,
> Ne hadde never our lady
>   A ben hevene quene.
> Blessed be the time
>   That appil take was.
> Therefore we moun singen
>   ' Deo gracias '.

The cult of the lady was the mundane counterpart of the cult of the Virgin and it was the invention of the medieval aristocracy. In chivalry the romantic worship of a woman was as necessary a quality of the perfect knight as was the worship of God. As Gibbon puts it, with more wit than amiability, ' The knight was the champion of God and the ladies—I blush to unite such discordant terms ', and the idea finds clear expression in the refrain of a French *ballade* of the fourteenth century, ' En ciel un dieu, en terre une déesse '. One of its most interesting manifestations was the development of a theory of ' courtly love ', strangely platonic in conception though in many ways as artificial as contemporary scholasticism, which inspired some of the finest poetry of the age, from the Troubadours and Minnesingers of France and Germany to the singers of the ' dolce stil nuovo' and Dante himself in Italy. It is obvious that a theory which regarded the worship of a lady as next to that of God and conceived her as the mainspring of brave deeds, a creature half romantic, half divine, must have done something to counterbalance the dogma of subjection. The process of placing women upon a pedestal had begun, and whatever we may think of the ultimate value of such an elevation (for few human beings are suited to the part of Stylites, whether ascetic or romantic) it was at least better than placing them, as the Fathers of the Church had inclined to do, in the bottomless pit. Nevertheless, as a factor in raising the position of women too much importance must not be attributed to the ideal of chivalry. Just as asceticism was the limited ideal of a small clerical caste, so chivalry was the limited ideal of a small aristocratic caste, and those who were outside that caste had little part in any refining influence which it possessed. Even in the class in which it was promulgated and practised, it is impossible not to feel that it was little more than a veneer. Not only in the great *chansons de geste*, but in the book which the fourteenth-century knight of La Tour Landry wrote for the edification of his daughters, gentlemen in a rage not infrequently strike their wives to the ground, and the corporal chastisement of a wife was specifically permitted by canon law. The ideal of *l'amour courtois*, too, rapidly degenerated and its social was far less than its literary importance. It had a civilizing effect upon manners, but the fundamental sensuality and triviality beneath the superficial polish is to be seen clearly enough in the many thirteenth-century books of deportment for ladies, which were modelled upon Ovid's *Ars Amatoria*, so severely condemned by Christine de Pisan. It is probable that the idea of chivalry has had more influence upon later ages than it had upon contemporaries. As a legacy it has certainly affected the position of women in modern times, for whatever its effect upon medieval practice, it was one of the most powerful ideas evolved by the Middle Ages, and though it owed something to Arab influences, it was substantially an original idea.

Such, then, was the medieval theory as to the position of woman, an inconsistent and contradictory thing, as any generalization about a sex must be, teaching simultaneously her superiority and her inferiority. It was, as has been said, formulated by the two classes which were in power at the outset of the period, the Church and the Aristocracy. It is true that from the thirteenth century onwards a new force was added to these ; the Bourgeoisie began to make itself increasingly felt, and in some respects the Bourgeoisie showed a greater sense of the normal personality of women than did either the Aristocracy or the Church ; borough law had to take account of the woman trader, and in many towns there existed ' customs ' for the treatment of a married woman carrying on a trade of her own as a *femme sole*. These are in striking contrast with the laws regulating the position of the married woman under the common law, and although they were intended for the protection of the husband they were also an effective improvement in the status of the wife. But in the main the Bourgeoisie rose to importance in a world in which law and opinion had already hardened into certain moulds, and it accepted as a dispensation of nature those ideas about women and about marriage which it found in existence. Indeed the Bourgeois note in literature, which first makes itself felt in the *fabliaux*, is if anything rather more hostile to women than the clerical note and far more so than the courtly note, for except in the great mercantile families, whose wealth enabled them to move in the circle of the aristocracy, *Frauendienst* found little welcome   Nevertheless, the woman of the *fabliaux*, odious as she is, shows something of the practical equality which prevailed between men and women in the middle and lower classes; for if she is in subjection, the subjection is very imperfectly maintained, and the henpecked husband is a suspiciously favourite theme. There is a sort of poetic justice in the fact that men whose ideal wife was Patient Griselda not infrequently found themselves married to the Wife of Bath.

Two great bodies of opinion remained wholly unexpressed. The working classes, 'whose shoulders held the sky suspended' above Church and Aristocracy and Bourgeoisie alike, were to remain inarticulate for many centuries to come. That busy world of men and women, of which we catch a glimpse in court roll and borough record, rarely raised its voice above the whistle of the scythe or the hum of the loom. One other class, too, remained all but inarticulate, for we hardly ever hear what women thought about themselves. All the books, as the Wife of Bath complained, were written by men.

> Who peyntede the leoun, tel me who?
> By God, if wommen hadde writen stories
> As clerkes han with-inne hir oratories,
> They wolde han writen of men more wikkednesse
> Than all the mark of Adam may redresse!

Works written by women are rare (apart from the passionate love-letters of Héloïse and the outpourings of the great women mystics) and such poetesses as the troubadour Countess Beatrice de Die and the famous writer of *lais*, known as Marie de France, in no way detach themselves from the poetic convention of their day. The Legends of Good Women which sprang up to counteract the books of 'wikked wyves', the somewhat jejune *Biens des Fames* which replied to the much more vigorous *Blastenges des Fames*, were probably all the work of men. It is not until

the end of the fourteenth century that there appears
a woman writer to take up the cudgels for her sex and lead
a party of revolt against the prevalent abuse of women.
Christine de Pisan was skilled in all the courtly conventions,
for she made her living and supported three children by her
pen ; but there is both idealism and reality in her attack
on the *Roman de la Rose*, and in the educational treatise, *Le
Livre des Trois Vertus*, which she wrote for the use of women.

For the rest we must deduce the woman's point of view
from an occasional *cri du cœur* or half-humorous comment,
preserved not in literature but in real life. St. Bernardino
of Siena, in one of his vividly colloquial sermons, urges
husbands to help their wives and strengthens his plea by
one woman's words to him. ' Mark thy wife well,' he says,
' how she travaileth in childbirth, travaileth to suckle the
child, travaileth to rear it, travaileth in washing and cleaning
by day and night. All this travail, seest thou, is of the
woman only, and the man goeth singing on his way. There
was once a baron's lady, who said to me : "Methinks the
dear lord and master doth as he seeth good and I am content
to say that he doth well. But the woman alone beareth the
pain of the children in many things, bearing them in her
body, bringing them into the world, ruling them, and all
this oftentimes with grievous travail. If only God had
given some share to man ; if only God had given him the
child-bearing ! " Thus she reasoned and I answered :
" Methinks there is much reason in what you say." ' Something of the same spirit inspires an anonymous fifteenth-
century song, which strikes a note of naïve and genuine feeling :

> I am as lyghte as any roe
> To praise womene wher that I goo.
> To onpreyse womene yt were a shame,
> For a womane was thy dame ;
> Our blessed Lady beryth the name
> Of all womene wher that they goo.

A woman is a worthy thyng,
She dothe washe and dothe wrynge,
'Lullay! Lullay!' she dothe synge,
    And yet she has but care and woo.

A womane is a worthy wyght,
She serveth a man both daye and nyght;
Therto she puttyth all her myght,
    And yet she hathe but care and woo.

Only rarely was the prevalent theory, ascetic or romantic, broken by this domestic strain.

But the theory about women, inconsistent and the work of a small articulate minority as it was, was only one factor in determining their position and it was the least important factor. The fact that it received a voluminous and often striking literary expression has given it a somewhat disproportionate weight, and to arrive at the real position of women it is necessary constantly to equate it with daily life, as revealed in more homely records. The result is very much what common sense would indicate, for in daily life the position occupied by woman was one neither of inferiority nor of superiority, but of a certain rough-and-ready equality. This equality was as marked in the feudal as in the working classes; indeed it allowed the lady of the upper classes considerably more scope than she sometimes enjoyed at a much later period, for example, in the eighteenth and early nineteenth centuries. In order to estimate it, we may with advantage turn from theories to real life and endeavour, if possible, to disentangle some of the chief characteristics of the existence led by three typical women, the feudal lady, the bourgeoise, and the peasant. The typical woman must be taken to be the wife and more generally the housewife, but it must not be imagined that marriage was the lot of every woman and that the Middle Ages were not as familiar as our own day with the independent spinster. Then as now the total number of adult women was in excess of that of men. Reliable statistics are sadly to seek, but here and there poll-tax and hearth-tax lists afford interesting information. In the fourteenth and fifteenth centuries certain of the German towns took censuses, from which it appears that for every 1,000 men there were 1,100 women in Frankfort in 1385, 1,207 women in Nuremberg in 1449, and 1,246 women in Basel in 1454; the number of women was, it is true, swelled in these towns, because it was customary for widows from the country round to retire there, but a disproportion between the two sexes certainly existed.[1] It is, indeed, to be expected on account of the greater mortality of men in the constant crusades, wars and town and family factions, and the discrepancy was aggravated by the fact that the celibacy of the clergy removed a very large body of men from marriage.

Medieval records are, indeed, full of these independent women. A glance at any manorial 'extent' will show women villeins and cotters living upon their little holdings and rendering the same services for them as men; some of these are widows, but many of them are obviously unmarried. The unmarried daughters of villeins could always find work to do upon their father's acres, and could hire out their strong arms for a wage to weed and hoe and help with the harvest. Women performed almost every kind of agricultural labour, with the exception of the heavy business of ploughing. They often acted as thatcher's assistants, and on many manors they did the greater part of the sheep-shearing, while the care of the dairy and of the small poultry was always in their hands. Similarly, in the towns women carried on a great variety of trades. Of the five hundred crafts scheduled in Étienne Boileau's *Livre des Métiers* in medieval Paris, at least five were their monopoly, and in

[1] K. Bücher, *Die Frauenfrage im Mittelalter* (Tübingen, 1910), p. 6.

a large number of others women were employed as well as men. Two industries in particular were mainly in their hands, because they could with ease be carried on as by-industries in the home. The ale, drunk by every one who could not afford wine, in those days when only the most poverty-stricken fell back upon water, was almost invariably prepared by women, and every student of English manorial court rolls will remember the regular appearance at the leet of most of the village alewives, to be fined for breaking the Assize of Ale. Similarly, in all the great cloth-working districts, Florence, the Netherlands, England, women are to be found carrying out the preliminary processes of the manufacture. Spinning was, indeed, the regular occupation of all women and the ' spinster's ' habitual means of support ; God, as the Wife of Bath observes, has given three weapons to women, deceit, weeping, and spinning ! Other food-producing and textile industries were also largely practised by them, and domestic service provided a career for many. It must, of course, be remembered that married as well as single women practised all these occupations, but it is clear that they offered a solution to the problem of the ' superfluous ' women of the lower classes. Nevertheless, this equality of men and women in the labour market was a limited one. Many craft regulations exclude female labour, some because the work was considered too heavy, but most for the reason, with which we are familiar, that the competition of women undercut the men. Then, as now, women's wages were lower than those of men, even for the same work, and the author of a treatise on *Husbandry* was enunciating a general principle when, after describing the duties of the daye or dairywoman, he added : ' If this is a manor where there is no dairy, it is always good to have a woman there at a much less cost than a man.'

The problem of the unmarried girl of the upper class was more difficult, for in feudal society there was no place for women who did not marry and marry young. It was the Church which came to their rescue, by putting within their reach as brides of Christ a dignity greater than that which they would have attained as brides of men. The nunnery was essentially a class institution. It absorbed only women belonging to the nobility, the gentry, and (in the later Middle Ages) the bourgeoisie, and in practice (though not in strict canon law) it demanded a dowry, though a smaller dowry than an earthly husband might have required. But the spinsters of the working class were absorbed by industry and the land and did not need it. To unmarried gentlewomen monasticism gave scope for abilities which might otherwise have run to waste, assuring them both self-respect and the respect of society. It made use of their powers of organization in the government of a community, and in the management of household and estates ; it allowed nuns an education which was for long better than that enjoyed by men and women alike outside the cloister ; and it opened up for them, when they were capable of rising to such heights, the supreme experiences of the contemplative life. Of what it was capable at its best great monastic saints and notable monastic housewives have left ample record to testify. Even if it suffered decline and sheltered the idle with the industrious and the black sheep with the white, it was still an honourable profession and fulfilled a useful function for the gentlewomen of the Middle Ages. In the towns, and for a somewhat lower social class, various lay sisterhoods, grouped in their *Béguinages*, *Samenungen*, *Gotteshäuser*, offered the same opportunities.

But what of the well-born girl who was not destined for a nunnery ? Of her it may be said that she married, she married young and she married the man selected for her by her father. The careful father would expect to arrange for his daughter's marriage and often to marry her before she was fourteen, and if he found himself dying while she was still a child he would be at great pains to leave her a suitable dowry *ad maritagium suum* in his will. A girl insufficiently dowered might have to suffer that disparagement in marriage which was so much dreaded and so carefully guarded against, and even in the lowest ranks of society the bride was expected to bring something with her besides her person when she entered her husband's house. The dowering of poor girls was one of the recognized forms of medieval charity and, like the mending of bad roads, a very sound one. The system, of course, had its bad side. Modern civilization has steadily extended the duration of childhood, and to-day there seems something tragic in the spectacle of these children, taking so soon upon their young shoulders the responsibilities of marriage and motherhood. Similarly, since marriage is to-day most frequently a matter of free choice between its participants, the indifference sometimes shown to human personality in feudal marriages of the highest rank appears shocking. They were often dictated solely by the interests of the land. ' Let me not to the marriage of true fiefs admit impediments ' may be said to have been the dominating motive of a great lord with a son or daughter or ward to marry, and weddings were often arranged and sometimes solemnized when children were in their cradles.

Medieval thinkers showed some consciousness of these disadvantages themselves. The fact that all feudal marriages were *mariages de convenance* accounts for the fundamental dogma of *l'amour courtois*, so startling to modern ideas, that whatever the respect and affection binding married people, the sentiment of love could not exist between them, being in its essence freely sought and freely

given and must therefore be sought outside marriage.
' Causa coniugii ab amore non est excusatio.' Langland,
again, inveighs against the ' modern ' habit of marrying for
money and counsels other considerations ; ' and loke that
loue be more the cause than lond other [or] nobles.'

It is more rarely that the woman's view of a loveless
marriage finds expression, but once at least, in the later
Middle Ages, the voice of a woman passes judgement upon
it, and with it upon the loneliness, the *accidia* (as monastic
writers would have called it) of that life which medieval
literature decks in all the panoply of romance. The Saxon
reformer, Johann Busch, has preserved in his *Liber de reforma-
tione monasteriorum* (1470–5) a poignant dialogue between
himself and the dying Duchess of Brunswick.

> ' When her confession, with absolution and penance was
> ended,' he writes, ' I said to her, " Think you, lady, that you will
> pass to the kingdom of heaven when you die ? " She replied,
> " This believe I firmly." Said I, " That would be a marvel.
> You were born in a fortress and bred in castles and for many
> years now you have lived with your husband, the Lord Duke,
> ever in the midst of manifold delights, with wine and ale, with
> meat and venison both roast and boiled ; and yet you expect
> to fly away (*evolare*) to heaven directly you die." She answered :
> " Beloved father, why should I not now go to heaven ? I have
> lived here in this castle like an anchoress in a cell. What delights
> or pleasures have I enjoyed here, save that I have made shift to
> show a happy face to my servants and to my maidens ? I have
> a hard husband, as you know, who has scarce any care or inclina-
> tion towards women. Have I not been in this castle even as it
> were in a cell ? " I said to her, " You think, then, that as soon
> as you are dead God will send his angels to your bed to bear
> your soul away to Paradise and to the heavenly kingdom of
> God ? " and she replied, " This believe I firmly." Then said
> I, " May God confirm you in your faith and give you what you
> believe." '

But it is unnecessary to suppose that the majority of
feudal marriages turned out badly. The father is not

human who does not wish to do his best for his daughter,
and it was only in the most exalted rank that worldly could
entirely outweigh personal considerations.   Moreover, the
fact that most wedded couples began life together while
they were both very young was in their favour.   Human
nature is extremely adaptable, and they came to each other
with no strongly marked ideas or prejudices and grew up
together.   The medieval attitude towards child marriages
was that to which Christine de Pisan gave such touching
expression when she recalled her own happy life with the
husband whom she married before she was fifteen and who
left her at twenty-five an inconsolable widow with three
children.

> Il m'amoit et c'estoit droit,
> Car joenne lui fuz donnée ;
> Si avions toute ordonnée
> Nostre amour et nos deux cuers,
> Trop plus que freres ne suers
> En un seul entier vouloir,
> Fust de joye ou de douloir.

Certainly medieval records as a whole show a cameraderie
between husband and wife which contrasts remarkably both
with the picture of woman in subjection which the Church
delighted to draw and with that of the worshipped lady of
chivalry.   An obscure Flemish weaver of the sixteenth
century, writing to his wife from England, signs himself
with the charming phrase ' your married friend ', and of
medieval wives as a whole it may be said with truth, that
while literature is full of Griseldas and *belles dames sans
merci*, life is full of married friends.   The mothers, wives, and
daughters of the barons and knights of feudalism are sturdy
witnesses to the truth of Mrs. Poyser's immortal dictum,
' God Almighty made 'em to match the men.'   If feudal
marriages submitted them completely to their fiefs, they
could inherit and hold land, honours, and offices like men.

and are to be found fighting for their rights like men, while widows, in their own right or as guardians of infant sons, often enjoyed great power. Blanche of Champagne waged war for fourteen years (1213–27) on behalf of her minor son, and Blanche of Castile governed a kingdom as regent for the boy Louis IX. Indeed, the history of the early thirteenth century is strongly impressed with the character of those two masterful and energetic sisters, in beauty, talent, and iron strength of purpose the worthy granddaughters of ' the eagle ', Eleanor of Aquitaine, Blanche, the mother of Saint Louis of France, and Berengaria, the mother of Saint Ferdinand of Castile.

Throughout the Middle Ages, too, the social and physical conditions of life, the constant wars, and above all the slow communications, inevitably threw a great deal of responsibility upon wives as the representatives of their absent husbands. It has been asserted in all ages that the sphere of woman is the home, but it has not always been acknowledged that that sphere may vary greatly in circumference, and that in some periods and circumstances it has given a much wider scope to women than in others. In the Middle Ages it was, for a variety of reasons, a very wide sphere, partly because of this constantly recurring necessity for the wife to take the husband's place. While her lord was away on military expeditions, on pilgrimages, at court, or on business, it was she who became the natural guardian of the fief or manager of the manor, and Europe was full of competent ladies, not spending all their time in hawking and flirting, spinning and playing chess, but running estates, fighting lawsuits, and even standing sieges for their absent lords. When the nobility of Europe went forth upon a crusade it was their wives who managed their affairs at home, superintended the farming, interviewed the tenants, and saved up money for the next assault. When the lord was taken prisoner it was his wife who collected his ransom, squeezing every penny from the estate, bothering bishops for indulgences,[1] selling her jewels and the family plate. Once more it was these extremely practical persons and not the Griseldas, or the

> store of Ladies whose bright eies
> Rain influence and judge the prise,

who were the typical feudal women.

Christine de Pisan, in her *Livre des Trois Vertus* (*c.* 1406), sets down the things which a lady or baroness living on her estates ought to be able to do. She must be capable of replacing her husband in every way during his absence; ' because that knights, esquires and gentlemen go upon journeys and follow the wars, it beseemeth their wives to be wise and of great governance, and to see clearly in all that they do, for that most often they dwell at home without their husbands, who are at court or in divers lands.' The lady must therefore be skilled in all the niceties of tenure and feudal law, in case her lord's rights should be invaded; she must know all about the management of an estate, so as to supervise the work of the bailiff, and she must understand her own métier as housewife, and be able to plan her expenditure wisely. The budget of a great lady, Christine suggests, should be divided into five parts, of which one should be devoted to almsgiving, one to household expenses, one to the payment of officials and women, one to gifts, and one should be set apart to be drawn upon for jewels, dresses,

---

[1] These were common during the Hundred Years War. Archbishop Kempe's York Register, for instance, contains an indulgence of 28 days to raise £50 required for the ransom of Richard Botiler of Shropshire, taken captive in France, to be paid either to him or to his wife Elizabeth (1443), and another on behalf of Elizabeth wife of Sir John Holt, also a prisoner. *Test. Ebor.* (Surtees Society), ii, p. 31 (note).

and miscellaneous expenses as required. The good management of a housewife is sometimes worth more to a lord than the income from his tenants; and in every class of life it is the wife's function to dispose wisely of her husband's resources according to his rank, whether it be the baron's patrimony or the labourer's wage. Christine de Pisan was writing about how a lady ought to behave, but from many records we know that the ideal was carried out in practice. No more striking witness to the confidence reposed by husbands in the business capacity of their wives is to be found than the wills and letters of the later Middle Ages. It is impossible to read through any great collection of medieval wills, such as the *Testamenta Eboracensia*, published by the Surtees Society, without observing the number of cases in which a wife is made the executrix of her husband's will, sometimes alone and sometimes as principal in conjunction with other persons. More than once a touch of feeling enlivens the legal phraseology, as when John Sothill of Dewsbury bids his executors, 'I pray you, pray Thomas my son in my name and for ye lufe of God, yat he never strife with his moder, as he will have my blissyng, for he sall fynd hir curtos to del withall'. Letters tell the same tale. The Paston Letters, for example, give a remarkable picture of the hard-headed business woman in fifteenth-century England. No one could really like Margaret Paston, who bullied her daughter and kept the only soft corner in a peculiarly hard heart for her husband, but she was exceedingly competent and managed his property for him with the utmost success, collecting rents, keeping accounts, and outwitting enemies, and she seems to have taken it as part of the day's work to be besieged in her manor, and to have the walls of her chamber pulled down about her ears by armed men.

But it was not only on exceptional occasions and in the

absence of her husband that the lady found a weight of responsibility upon her shoulders. It is true that her duties as a mother were in some ways less arduous than might have been supposed. Large families were general, and the death-rate among children was high (as may be guessed from many a medieval tombstone, in which little shrouded corpses are ranged with living children behind their kneeling parents), but the new-born child, in the upper classes at least, was commonly handed over to a wet nurse and it is sometimes mentioned as a sign of special affection in a mother that she should have fed her own children at the breast. Again, the training of the young squire often took him at an early age from his mother's society, and it was customary to send both boys and girls away to the households of great persons to learn breeding, although no doubt they often remained at home. In any case the early marriages of the day meant short childhoods. Books of deportment are singularly silent, as a whole, on the subject of maternal duties; they were (as might be inferred from the shocking behaviour of Griselda) overshadowed by those of the wife. But if the nursery was not a great burden, housekeeping in the Middle Ages, and indeed in all ages prior to the Industrial Revolution, was a much more complicated business than it is to-day, except for the fact that domestic servants were cheap, plentiful, and unexacting. It was no small feat to clothe and feed a family when households were large, guests frequent, and when much of what is to-day made in factories and bought in shops had to be prepared at home. The butter and cheese were made in the dairy and the beer in the brewhouse, the candles were made up and the winter's meat salted down in the larder, and some at least of the cloth and linen used by the household was spun at home. The lady of the house had to supervise all these operations, as well as to make, at fair and market or in the nearest town, the necessary purchases of wine and foodstuffs and materials which could not be prepared on the manor.

The country housewife, too, was expected to look after the bodies of her household in sickness as well as in health, and it was necessary for her to have a certain skill in physic and surgery. Life was far less professionalized in the Middle Ages ; a doctor was not to be found round every corner, and though the great lady in her town house or the wealthy bourgeoise might find a physician from Oxford or Paris or Salerno within reach, some one had to be ready to deal with emergencies on the lonely manors. Old French and English metrical romances are full of ladies physicking and patching up their knights, and household remedies were handed down with recipes for puddings and perfumes from mother to daughter ; such knowledge was expected of them, as it was expected of the ' wise woman ', who mingled it with charms and spells. There exist also various treatises on the diseases of women which are obviously written or translated for their own use, and in an English version of the *De Mulierum Passionibus* (attributed to Trotula), the translator asserts himself to have undertaken the work in order that women shall be able to diagnose and treat their own diseases ; ' and because whomen of oure tonge donne bettyr rede and undyrstande thys langage than eny other and euery whoman lettyrde rede hit to other unlettyrd and help hem and conceyle hem in here maledyes wt.owtyn shewyng here dysese to man, i have thys drauyn and wryttyn in englysh.' [1] If, however, a woman set up practice as a physician outside the limits of her home and pretended to something more than the skill of an amateur

---

[1] MS. Bodl. Douce 37 (Western 21611), f. 1b. There is a similar fourteenth-century English treatise on gynaecology, written ' that oon woman may helpe another in her sykenesse ', in Brit. Mus. MS. Sloane 2463. I owe these references to the kindness of Dr. Singer.

or a witch, there forthwith arose an outcry which seems to foreshadow the opposition of the medical profession to the entrance of women in the nineteenth century. The case of the doctors was a respectable one; the women had no medical degrees and therefore no knowledge or training.[1] Nevertheless there were women here and there who acquired considerable fame as physicians. The most interesting of them is the well-born lady Jacoba Felicie, who in 1322, being then about thirty years of age, was prosecuted by the Medical Faculty at Paris on a charge of contravening the statute which forbade any one to practise medicine in the city and suburbs without the Faculty's degree and the Chancellor's licence. Various witnesses were called to testify that she made use of all the usual methods of diagnosis and treatment, and several of them said that they had been given up by various doctors before being cured by her and set forth the names of these legitimate but unsuccessful practitioners, which was perhaps a little hard on the profession. Her skill seems to have been undoubted, one witness stating that ' he had heard it said by several that she was wiser in the art of surgery and medicine than the greatest master doctor or surgeon in Paris'. Nevertheless she was inhibited, although she made an eloquent and sensible defence; but as she had already disregarded a previous inhibition and a heavy fine, she probably continued as before to practise her healing profession.

The lady was thus obliged not only to be housewife in her own capacity, but amateur soldier and man-of-the-house in her husband's absence, and amateur physician when no skilled doctor could be had. She was also obliged to be something rather more than an amateur farmer, for the comprehensive duties of a country housewife brought

---

[1] Trotula and the famous women doctors of Salerno are rapidly melting away under the cruel searchlight of modern research.

her into close connexion with all sides of the manorial
economy. It is plain from medieval treatises that a general
supervision of the manor farm was expected of her, over and
above that of the dairy, which was her special province.
Christine de Pisan's great lady must understand the choice
of labourers, the seasons for the different operations, the
crops suitable for different soils, the care of animals, the
best markets for farm produce. Stoutly clad, she must
tramp up and down the balks, ' par devers ses grans prairies
et frais herbages ', and through the young coppices, to
oversee her cornfields and pastures and woods. She must
have a watchful eye upon her labourers, too. ' Let her go
often into the fields to see how they are working, . . . and
let her be careful to make them get up in the morning.
Let her wait for no one, if she be a good housewife, but let
her rise up herself and throw on a houppelande, and go to
the window and shout until she see them come running out,
for they are given to laziness.' Deschamps' satire on the
manorial housewife was evidently drawn from life :

> J'ai le soing de tout gouverner ;
> Je ne sçay pas mon piet tourner
> Qu'en vint lieux ne faille respondre.
> L'un me dit : ' Les brebis faut tondre ' ;
> L'autre dit : ' Les aigneaulx sevrer ' ;
> L'autre : ' Il faut es vignes ouvrer ' ;
> L'autre s'en va a la charrue ;
> L'autre dit : ' Getter fault en rue
> Les vaches aprés le vachier ' ;
> L'autre dit : ' Il faut escorchier
> Un buef qui s'est laissé mourir ' ;
> L'autre dit : ' Il faut recouvrir
> Es estables et sur la grange.'

An equally good portrait of a town housewife, belonging
to the *haute* bourgeoisie, is to be found in the remarkable
book which an elderly citizen, the Ménagier de Paris, wrote

about 1392–4 for the instruction of his child wife. The tenderness of its tone and the extremely practical nature of the information contained in it, make this treatise unique among the innumerable didactic works addressed to women in the Middle Ages. The Ménagier explains to his young wife that he has undertaken the work in response to her request that he would teach her and because she would certainly marry again after his death, in which case it would be a great reflection *upon him* if she were not wise in all that concerned the care of house and husband ! And truly the second husband of the Ménagier's wife must have been a happy man ; if, indeed, he did not suffer the penalty described by another fourteenth-century bourgeois, Paolo di Certaldo of Florence, who says : ' If thou art able, beware of taking a widow woman for thy wife, because thou wilt never be able to satisfy her, and every time thou refusest her anything she may ask of thee, she will say, " My other husband did not treat me thus ! " Yet truly, if thou hast already had another wife thou mayst take her with greater safety, and if she saith, " My other husband did not treat me thus," or " Blessed be the soul of So-and-so," thou canst reply " Blessed be the soul of Madonna So-and-so, who did not cause me this tribulation every day ! " ' The Ménagier planned his book in three sections. The first deals with the lady's moral and religious duties, deportment, and duty towards her husband ; ' because these two things, to wit the salvation of your soul and the comfort of your husband, are the two things most chiefly necessary, therefore are they placed first.' The second and most interesting section deals with household management, the choice and treat-ment of servants, the best methods of airing, mending, and cleaning dresses and furs, the best recipes for catching fleas and other ' familiar beasts to man ' and for keeping bed-rooms free of mosquitoes and barns of rats, the art of gardening, and above all the choice and preparation of menus suitable for every sort of meal. 'The fourth article is that you, as sovereign mistress of your house, may know how to order dinners, suppers, meats and dishes and be wise concerning butchers' and poulterers' lore and have knowledge of spicery, and the fifth article teaches you how to command, order and devise and have made all manner of soups, stews, sauces, and other viands, and the same for invalids.' He is truly the Mrs. Beeton of the Middle Ages; and it may be remarked that his ideas as to quantity in ingredients are very similar. The book closes with a third section, planned but unfortunately unfinished, which deals with the lady's amusements.

The Ménagier's book tells us more about the domestic economy of a wealthy citizen's home than any other medieval record. One of its most valuable characteristics is the particularity of his instructions for dealing with domestic servants. In the management of her ménage his young wife is assisted by a steward, Master Jehan *le dispensier*, and by a sort of duenna-housekeeper, Dame Agnes *la béguine*, and the choice of servants is left entirely in her hands, with their assistance. There were in Paris at the time *recommanderesses*, or women keeping what would to-day be called registry offices, and the great ordinance of 1351, which fixed wages after the Black Death, allowed them 18*d.* for placing a chambermaid and 2*s.* for a nurse, ' a prendre tant d'une partie comme d'autre '. The Ménagier warns his wife to engage no chambermaids ' until you first know where their last place was and send some of your people to get their character, whether they talked or drank too much, how long they were in the place, what work they were wont to do and can do, whether they have homes or friends in the town, from what sort of people and what part of the country they come, how long they were in the place and why they left'. On engaging a girl she is to cause the steward to enter in his register her name and that of her father and mother and kinsfolk, the place where they live, the place of her birth and her references. The closest supervision is to be maintained over the manners and morals of maid-servants and their mistress should set them a good example in all things. They are to be well fed and allowed due time for recreation, young and foolish girls are to sleep in a room adjacent to her own and without low windows looking on to the road, and ' if one of your servants fall ill, do you yourself, laying aside all other cares, very lovingly and charitably care for him or her'. The daily work of the servants is set down with even greater care, the sweeping and cleaning of the house in the morning, the feeding of pet dogs and cage birds, the airing of sheets, coverlets, dresses and furs in the sunshine so as to preserve them from moths, together with sundry recipes for getting rid of spots, the weekly inspection of wines, vinegars, grains, oils, nuts, and other provisions by the steward, and the admonishment of Richard of the kitchen to cleanliness. Every man and maid must have his or her specific work to do, and the steward, the housekeeper and the young mistress must watch carefully that they do it.

But the work of the bourgeoise housewife is by no means confined to running her house and managing her servants, for she, no less than the lady of a manor, must be ready, if need be, to take her husband's place; and she commonly knows a great deal about his business. William Warner of Boston, trading in Zealand, habitually sends home to his wife Iceland stockfish and other goods, that ' she shulde putte the marchaundise to sale as she dydde other mar-chaundise'. Almost all guild regulations forbidding the employment of women make exception for the craftsman's wife and daughter, who are expected to help in the workshop and need no formal apprenticeship. The training thus acquired enabled a widow to carry on her husband's trade and to complete the training of his apprentices and thus we find widows not only engaged in small crafts but in mercantile operations on a large scale, like Margery Russell of Coventry, who obtained letters of marque against the merchants of Santander and seized two of their ships. Nor was it only as their husband's representatives or widows that married women came into the labour market, for they frequently carried on separate businesses as *femmes soles*, and it has already been pointed out that many town regulations took cognizance of this fact and allowed them to be sued for debts and punished for misdeeds as though they were single women. With single women they shared in the textile and food-producing industries, and there were other women besides the Wife of Bath who carried on the business of clothiers—

> Of cloth making she hadde swiche an haunte
> She passed hem of Ypres and of Gaunt,—

though possibly they did not all wear out five husbands in their spare time, like that redoubtable lady.

The lower we move in the social scale the more laborious, naturally, was the housewife's life, because she would commonly be obliged to help with her husband's craft or to carry on some by-industry of her own, as well as caring for house and children. Below the ranks of the gentry and the richer bourgeoisie few housewives were able to concern themselves solely with their homes, which were frequently supported by the earnings of wife as well as of husband. Most laborious of all was the lot of the peasant woman living upon the land. Of her indeed the proverbial adage was true:

> Some respit to husbands the weather may send,
> But huswiue's affaires haue neuer an end.

It is true that manorial customs usually exempted the villein's wife from the obligation to labour on the lord's land, but her toil could rarely be spared upon her husband's holding, the inevitable by-industry occupied what time she could spare from the fields, and in her one-roomed or two-roomed cottage, dark and smoky and often shared with the animals, as Chaucer has drawn it in his tale of Chauntecleer and Pertelote, she must labour unceasingly. There are few passages in medieval literature more poignant than that in which Langland has described ' the wo of these women that wonyeth in cotes '.

Nevertheless, the life had its compensations. In Western Europe at least the small cultivator of the village advanced steadily in freedom and prosperity during the Middle Ages, and *fabliaux* often show us the well-to-do villein—

> Jadis estoit uns vilains riches
> Qui mout estoit avers et chiches.

If manorial custom looked upon women mainly as replenishers of the estate with labour and forced the villein to pay merchet and leyrwite for his daughter, it also not infrequently showed special consideration for his wife while she was fulfilling her essential function. Sometimes the villein's wife in childbed is excused the annual tribute of the Shrovetide hen, sometimes she may claim a load of firewood, sometimes she may even fish for herself in the lord's strictly preserved brook. At Denckendorf in Württemberg each lying-in bondwoman received two measures of wine and eight white loaves at the christening of her child. Harsh and coarse and laborious as it was, the peasant woman's life had its rude gaieties, and there is some truth in Christine de Pisan's judgement, ' Comment qu'elles soient nourries communement de pain bis, de lait, de lart, de potaige et d'eaue abuvrées, et que assez de poine troyent, est leur vie

plus sceure et mesmes en plus grant suffisance que telles [qui]
sont bien haultes assises.'

This tale of busy and hard-working lives lived in lord's
manor, in burgess's house, and in peasant's cottage has taken
little account of the amusements of the medieval woman.
Yet there were many. The Ménagier de Paris, a wealthy
man with a house in the country as well as in Paris, could
plan for his wife the characteristic diversions of the upper
class, and the third section of his book shows us the lady at
play. He has already, in a previous section, said something
about his wife's employment in her hours of ease : ' Know
that it doth not displease, but rather pleases me, that you
should have roses to grow and violets to care for, and that
you should make chaplets and dance and sing ; and I would
well that you should so continue among our friends and
those of our estate, and it is but right and seemly thus to
pass the time of your feminine youth, provided that you
desire and offer not to go to the feasts and dances of lords
too great, for that is not seemly for you, nor suitable to
your estate and mine.' Romances and miniatures both
show how fond medieval ladies were of feasting and dancing,
and of making garlands in gardens with stiff raised beds,
fountains, arbours, and 'flowery medes', such as the pleasaunce
within a fortress so charmingly described in the *Roman de la
Rose*, or the ' garden fair ' in which King James of Scotland
saw the lady Johanna Beaufort walking. Apart from these
pleasures, the Ménagier wishes his wife to take her part in
the other outdoor and indoor amusements suitable to her
station. In fair weather she will go hawking and his third
section therefore contains a detailed treatise on that art.
In foul weather she will sit indoors with other ladies of her
age and rank, and they will play, not only at chess and
tables, but at games which we have long since relegated
to the nursery, blind man's buff, or *pince-merille*, and

innumerable question-and-answer games and riddles, like the favourite games known as *Le roi qui ne ment pas* and ' Ragman's roll '. Or else they will sing and tell stories to each other, for the setting of Boccaccio's *Decameron* was a common one in the Middle Ages and every well-educated lady must have a store of such tales at her finger-tips, and must be able to play her part wittily in the long ' debates ' and ' *tençons* ', in which love was ever the favourite theme. It was the Ménagier's intention to complete his book by a collection of games and riddles, but either death interrupted him or he wearied of his task, for his third section lacks the two ' articles ' which were to have contained them. But at all events his wife must have shone in the telling of tales, for all his admonitions to her are illustrated by stories, *exempla* as the preachers called them. He apologizes to his wife for including the tale of Griselda with the explanation, ' know that it never befel so, but thus the tale runs and I may not correct nor alter it, for a wiser than I made it ; and it is my desire that, since others have read it, you also may know and be able to talk about everything, even as other folk do.'

Oral narratives, indeed, played a great part in the amusements of the age and took the place which is filled by books to-day. Although such collections as the Paston and Stonor letters make it clear that the fifteenth-century gentry, both men and women, could read and write, books were rare before the invention of printing, and the wills of layfolk show very few besides service books of one sort or another, primers, psalters, and the like. But occasionally we hear of others. Sir Thomas Cumberworth (1451) leaves to his fortunate niece Annes ' my boke of the talys of cantyrbury ' ; Joan, widow of Sir Robert Hilton of Surrie (1432), leaves her sister Katherine Cumberworth ' unum librum de Romanse incipientem cum Decem Preceptis Alembes ' and

her niece ' unum librum de Romanse de Septem Sages '.
Sir John Morton of York (1431) leaves Joan Countess of
Westmoreland ' unum librum de Anglico vocatum Gower
pro remembrancia ', and John Raventhorp, a York chaplain
(1432), leaves ' librum Angliae de Fabulis et Narracionibus '
to Agnes of Celayne, his servant for many years. In general,
however, the imagination of a medieval lady was fed by the
telling of tales, whether by preacher, *jongleur*, or by her
companions, rather than by the reading of books.

For the town housewife there were a multitude of amusements, such as those in which the Wife of Bath delighted,

> visitaciouns
> To vigilies and to processiouns,
> To preching eek and to thise pilgrimages,
> To pleyes of miracles and mariages.

Women readily flocked to hear sermons, when a good
preacher was at hand. Indeed, if Bernardino of Siena or
Berthold of Regensburg were at all typical (which it is to
be feared they were not) sermons must have been as entertaining as they were instructive. They were always interlarded with *exempla*, and some moralists (among them
Dante himself) complained that these anecdotes were often
trivial, not to say improper, and crowded out the solid
teaching which should have informed the sermon, ' but one
halfpennyworth of bread to this intolerable deal of sack.'
Often, however, the listening women would find their
foibles scourged, particularly their too gay attire, their
crested shoes, long trains, bare bosoms, and horned headdresses. Sometimes excitable ladies took these admonitions
seriously. ' As in the days when the Breton Thomas Couette
preached,' says Mr. Owst, ' and French womenfolk, stung
to the heart, made public bonfires of their favourite orna-
ments and vanities, so two centuries later their sisters of
Italy were wont to do the same in the piazzas of Siena and

Florence at St. Bernardino's bidding. "Tables, cards, dice, false hair, rouge-pots, and other tribulations, even to chess boards " had been known to enter the flames. But with the enthusiasm of the sermon over and the preacher gone, they were liable to that same reaction which befel certain remorseful ladies once driven to make good the loss of their horned headdresses, of whom it was written that " like snails in a fright they had drawn in their horns, but shot them out again as soon as the danger was over ".'[1] But St. Bernardino deserved well of the women who flocked to hear him. He was always urging their husbands to show them consideration and praising their housewifely virtues, while he scolded their vanities. He even declared on one occasion that ' it is a great grace to be a woman, because more women are saved than men ', and on another he drew a heartrending picture of the discomfort of the bachelor's unkempt home, ending up, ' knowest thou how such a man liveth ? even as a brute beast. I say that it cannot be well for a man to live thus alone. Ladies, make your curtsey to me ! ' And it is to be hoped that they did.

Such, then, was the daily existence of some typical medieval women. If medieval civilization is to be judged by it, it must be admitted that it comes well out of the test. It is true that the prevalent dogma of the subjection of women, becoming embedded in the common law and in the marriage laws, left to future generations a legacy which was an unconscionable time in dying. It is true that woman was not legally ' a free and lawful person ', that she had no lot or share then, or indeed until the twentieth century, in what may be called public as distinct from private rights and duties, and that the higher grades of education were closed to her. On the other hand, she had a full share in the private rights and duties arising out of the possession of

[1] G. Owst, *Preaching in Medieval England* (1926), p. 190.

land and played a considerable part in industry, in spite of the handicap of low wages and sometimes of masculine exclusiveness. The education of the average laywoman compared very favourably with that of her husband, and some ladies of rank were leaders of culture, like the royal patronesses of the troubadours, and occasionally blue-stockings, like Christine de Pisan. Although there was small place in the society of the upper classes for the independent unmarried woman, she found an honourable occupation for her activities in monasticism. In every class of the community the life of the married woman gave her a great deal of scope, since, as has already been indicated, the home of this period was a very wide sphere ; social and economic conditions demanded that a wife should always be ready to perform her husband's duties as well as her own, and that a large range of activities should be carried on inside the home under her direction. Finally, while the Middle Ages inherited the doctrine of the subjection of women, in some degree at least, from the past, it evolved for itself and handed down to the modern world a conception of chivalry which has had its share in the inspiration of poets, the softening of manners, and the advance of civilization. Taking the rough with the smooth and balancing theory against practice, the medieval woman played an active and dignified part in the society of her age.

EILEEN POWER.

8

THE ECONOMIC ACTIVITY OF TOWNS

SCHOLARSHIP, like everyday life, has its fashions. The origin, the constitution, and the policy of towns have so engrossed the attention of students that relatively little has been written about the contributions that towns have made to later history. The destruction of village economy, with all that this meant for social development, is one of the most general of the town's early accomplishments. Villages, in the form of manors, were not destroyed but village economy ceased to exist, as town economy came into being. Of course, agriculture continued as a form of production, and rural life even developed elements of unwonted prosperity, but the new commercial community, the town, reduced the neighbouring villages, or manors, to a state of subordination. Here was a conflict in the making, silent but far-reaching. The manors were owned singly or possessed in groups. Here a monastery held twenty manors, there a bishopric possessed forty, sometimes as far apart as fifty or a hundred miles. Foodstuffs were sent to the monastery or the palace in the form of rent or products of demesne-farming : sheep were driven and bacon and grain were carted long distances to the lord's place of consumption. The town, however, challenged this clumsy and uneconomical distribution of products. It set itself up as a local market centre, cutting right across the old grouping of manors. So that henceforth there were two rival systems : the old feudal-manorial arrangement of scattered village communities attached to a private household often quite remote, and the new compact group of manors looking to a town as their focal centre. In the more remote parts of northern and eastern Europe, elements of the manorial system long survived, while in the west and the south (in those parts where it had existed) manorialism died out relatively rapidly. However this may be, there was now a new centre of gravity in the town. The relative self-sufficiency of the individual manor sooner or later gave way to exchange relationships with the town; and the sending of the manorial surplus to the lord's seat gave way to disposal of it at the nearest market town. The tenants also learned to market such surplus as they had, and ambitious ones preferred to give their lords money in lieu of labour. Old-time service was thereby rivalled and in places soon supplanted by money payments: custom was giving way to contract. The cash nexus of modern society was beginning; this was the entering wedge of commercial competition. Perhaps all this is not so much the contribution of the town as the town itself.

The town brought in not simply a new economy or organization but a capacity for accelerated change or progress. There had been changes, of course, in the pre-urban stages of society, whether in village economy or an earlier condition, but the changes had been slow. Henceforth the town, in the course of three or four centuries, displayed a remarkable capacity to progress. The infant struggling town was almost wholly commercial, with a market-place and, more characteristically, a group of stores or shops. Such were Lynn and Sandwich, Cambridge and Andover in England, many north German towns, and Russian towns even up to the present day. Some of these towns came to add manufacture to commerce, that is, became highly skilled in the making of various commodities: copper utensils in Dinant, wooden wares in Nürnberg, and woollen cloth in Ghent and many other centres. This may be called the second phase of town growth. A smaller number of towns attained political and even cultural importance, becoming indeed the seats of the new art and the new learning. The capacity for such progress lay not in the people alone but in the organization of town affairs. Above all else, there was opportunity for specialization in trade or manufacture, law or medicine, painting or sculpture. And of almost equal effect there was the stimulus that comes through fresh contacts, when Londoners met Lombards and when Venetians traded in the east. The brain and nerves of the townsmen worked with quickened pace. Life became a game in which all faculties, physical and mental, could play a part. The town, indeed, became the sink of human energy, while the country remained the reservoir. The town gave leadership, while the country supplied the leaders. It is fitting that civilization has been etymologically identified with the work of towns.

To the progress of industrial organization from primitive manufacture for home use up to the modern factory system, the town made its contribution. Before towns came into existence, all manufacture had been for use, not for sale. This system gave way, or tended to give way, to the retail handicraft system, as industry was developed in the towns. In the new system goods were still made by hand, but for sale, not for use. The consumer, however, was at first near at hand and purchased his manufactured wares directly from the handicraftsman. The great advance lay in the fact that some persons were at last engaged in the making of wares for sale, while formerly agriculture and manufacture had been joint occupations. Here is the beginning of industrial specialization which has gone on to our day as a giant force in production. At first retail handicraft was only to fill an order, but later goods were made up for chance sale. At this point industrial capitalism shows its head in investment in raw materials and finished products. In the fourteenth century, in southern and western Europe, a further step was taken when industrial and commercial capital and management were specialized. In short, retail handicraft became wholesale handicraft. In this latter system handicraftsmen engaged chiefly in the manufacture of goods, selling their products to merchants who in turn disposed of them either directly to consumers or indirectly to consumers through other traders. Goods were still of handicraft production, made by hand, but the handicraftsman did not retail his wares to the consumer : he had to operate through a specialized middleman. So long as the handicraftsman was free to sell to any merchant, and so long as he was the owner of his raw materials and tools and commanded a profit (rather than a wage) from his enterprise, little could be said against the new system. But when in the early modern period industrial entre- preneurs arose who reduced the handicraftsman to economic dependence (putting-out or commission system), the new system stood condemned first by the sufferers and later by the general public. For industry, the change from retail to wholesale handicraft meant specialization in function, the separation of industrial from commercial capital, a larger supply of goods, and greater skill. It also was the beginning of the subordination of the workers and their exploitation. Revolts and civic turmoil in the larger industrial towns of the Middle Ages were the signs of the slowly developing system of wholesale handicraft.

The example and the tradition of revolt may be set down as a legacy of the medieval town to modern society. To the uprisings of peasants were added the revolutions of towns- men. By such means has the commonweal been purged and the social health maintained. Of course, not all town revolts were industrial. It is true that those in Ghent

(1343–5) and Florence (1378) were largely struggles between small industrial masters on the one hand and large commercial masters on the other, but then there were also contests between rival factions of equals and between the whole community on the one hand and on the other a harsh illiberal lord who refused to extend the town's liberties. But the point remains the same : men and classes conscious of their value to society will and do rise to increase their share of the total income. The social philosophy, which is now accepted, was held in the Middle Ages, if we may judge motive from act, that to the producers belong the products. Unfortunately for society, there was not then, as there is not now, any easy means of deciding between the claims of the producers.

In the more technical or mechanical aspects of production, there was noteworthy progress in medieval towns. The urban community learned how to build light, yet convenient, houses. It paved some of its streets and market-places. It erected fulling and grist mills driven by water-power. It improved processes of manufacture, such as the dyeing of cloth, the preparation of leather, the making of copper and pewter utensils, and the decoration of pottery and wooden wares. The crafts of goldsmiths, glass-makers, and sculptors became arts of high order. The most notable mechanical invention was the printing-press with its movable type, a promise at once of the spread of culture and the extension of mechanics and production. This last improvement, we may feel sure, owed nothing to antiquity. It was to make the town the purveyor of secular learning in rivalry with the monastic copyist and illuminator.

In contemplating the benefits of the mechanical process of printing, we should not forget the commercial organization which made it possible. If men produced simply for their own use, or if they manufactured for sale directly to customers, there would have been no future for the printing-press with its capacity to cater for a wide market. In other words, it owed not a little of its success to the commercial organization of the times. The key to this commercial organization is specialization. Some town traders dealt wholly in local products such as corn, meat, and poultry. Others traded in distant wares such as salt, leather, and wine. A third class, such as mercers, drapers, ironmongers, and haberdashers, handled only or chiefly manufactured wares. Such merchants bought from original producer or importer and sold most commonly to retailer or to exporting merchant. There was once a controversy among German scholars as to whether there really was an out-and-out wholesaler in the medieval period. The fact that town regulations usually forced importers to sell to consumers for a period after their arrival in the town with goods, points to the cardinal fact that, although many merchants might prefer the wholesale trade, they were not allowed to be exclusively wholesaling merchants. The significance of such specialization as has been indicated points to greater mercantile skill, longer journeys, larger stocks, and the great strength which merchants possessed in their contest with other merchants for markets and with industrial masters for industrial control. All this is modern in the extent of its dominance, not in its origin.

Out of all this merchandising, developed commercial ideals, habits, and law of great significance for subsequent times. The belief in a fair customary price is a medieval inheritance, though there were plenty of breaches when opportunity served. Merchandising was then a dignified and leisurely enterprise, as many people to-day still think it should be. Wares should be of high and standard quality. Debts should be paid when due. Such ideals arose out of the very necessities of direct trade between merchant and retailer, retailer and consumer. But not everything was left to mere custom or passive sanction. The law merchant stood above the floating custom as a crystallized body of practices which could be, and were, enforced summarily in courts hastily improvised by merchants who were at one fair to-day and another to-morrow. In the towns themselves many of the customs were made the formal laws of the municipality. Such laws constitute an important part of our present-day system of commercial intercourse, the irreducible and little-questioned part of our economic order.

In our present economic activity we find and accept many instruments which were really of medieval invention or development. Although money in one form or another is pre-urban, coined money is a town improvement. Of course, there is a question as to how much the medieval town owed to the ancient city. But modern European coinage owes its start to the medieval system with its units of pound, shillings, and pence, and their variations. Paper money, in the form of certificates of municipal indebtedness, goes back at least to the thirteenth century, when in some Italian towns these certificates were declared acceptable in payment of debts to the state, and in Como in 1250 they were made the equivalent of metal coins. Of course, it is well known that bills of exchange were passed from hand to hand as money—up to the date when they became due. Weights and measures, as well as money, were provided by the town. In England and France the sovereign made more or less successful efforts to standardize these local units. The towns do not seem to have come together to make their systems uniform, but practical treatises were privately compiled to assist the trader in his reckoning of prices in terms of strange weights and coins.

At the top of the exchange mechanism stood the bank, which we are rather too prone to regard as a modern institution. Private banks developed most rapidly in Italian cities, their activities extending to distant lands. Jews and gentiles, Florentines and Lombards, engaged in activities which we now call the banking functions. They changed money, purchased specie, received deposits, cashed cheques, and extended credit to customers. The Bardi and Peruzzi were famous bankers in Florence, the Pisani and Tiepolo families in Venice. Apparently such banking houses arose out of the business of merchandising as well as of money changing. Of public banks, there are but a few examples, and these come from fifteenth-century Italy and Spain. The best known is the Bank of St. George in Genoa, which, though originally a society of state creditors, came to receive deposits and transfer credits, and in modern times, indeed, became a full-fledged bank of great economic and political import in Genoa and an example for other countries. Public banks arose in Venice only in the sixteenth century, though private banks had been set up in that city centuries before. The *montes pietatis*, charitable loan institutions provided by some Italian cities, did some of the work of banks but had little influence on the history of banking. In general, the banks provided a more effective instrument for the utilization of capital and facilitated the exchange of goods and services. The history of banking is the story of halting trial and grievous error; the learning process has been long and arduous. Not the least part of this process consisted of the early banking experiences of the medieval period.

Without book-keeping, bankers, and in fact business men in general, could make but little headway. Single entry arose wherever commerce was well developed. Double entry was apparently an Italian contribution. The style of Venice was most marked and praised, though, it would appear, we actually have earlier examples of the use of double-entry in Genoa (1340) than in Venice. The first known treatise on double-entry, compiled by the Venetian Luca Pacioli, was printed in 1494. Other Venetians wrote text-books on the subject, and European towns generally were, by the middle of the sixteenth century, in a position to learn the art. There can be no question that the fundamental principles of accounting, on which our big business units and our government departments are to-day operating, had their beginning in Italian practices of the fourteenth and fifteenth centuries.

For the earliest-recorded instances of the combination of business men to form new business units, we have also to go back to Italian cities. Family partnership of brothers or other relatives, those eating bread in common (*companis*), was a widespread spontaneous growth in local as in distant trade. It had no special place of origin and no clearly marked history. Ship partnership, however, arose in Genoa not later than the twelfth century, and presumably spread from that city. Some one possessing capital would entrust it, either in the form of goods or money, to a trader going abroad to traffic for profit. The capitalist (*commendator*) remaining at home would contract with the active partner to receive a share of the profits or a rate of interest. In the former case he would be somewhat in the position of a stock holder, in the latter of a bond holder. On the Continent such a scheme for carrying on business developed great popularity down to the nineteenth century. The silent partner investing the capital might be, and indeed often became, a group of persons holding joint stock, while the actual management was entrusted to the chief or active partner. But it was the joint-stock form that finally won. This joint-stock was not in itself a new but an old rival and competing form of business combination. In the early part of the fifteenth century the joint-stock principle was in operation in the Bank of St. George in Genoa (1409 ?) and in the iron industry of Leoben (1415). There is a difference of opinion as to the importance of these early joint-stock companies up to the time of the formation of the Dutch, English, and French East India companies. Of their existence, however, there can be no doubt, nor can there be any question as to the importance of a business combination which has so effectively mobilized capital for the pursuit of business on a large scale.

It is not in business combinations, however, but in business associations that we find the experience of the medieval town most rich. While combination leads to the formation of new units jointly sharing profit or loss, association leads simply to a convenient grouping of units which themselves remain independent as before, at least in all essentials. The association which came first and lasted longest in some towns was the merchant gild. This was made up of men of all trades, and sometimes included professional people, even rural landholders of the district. At times it was even open to alien merchants trading in the town. There is much difference of opinion about the date and place of origin of the merchant gild and about its relation to the town government, but hardly any concerning the importance of its work. Over the trade and manufacture of the town the merchant gild in the early Middle Ages, and especially in the smaller towns, had general supervision, though probably not final control. The merchant gild was analogous to the modern chamber of commerce, commercial club, and civic association, though it is doubtful whether the modern could be shown to have any lineal descent from the medieval institution. Although the modern associations have been born again in the period since the seventeenth and eighteenth centuries, nevertheless the task of public economic regulation and civic improvement begun by the merchant gilds has been continuous in the towns since at least the eleventh century. It is no small praise to have begun a work which has continued for nearly a thousand years.

As the merchant gilds proved inadequate craft gilds took their places. They were both associations of business men seeking the fullest measure of advantage for themselves and their town. As urban communities increased in population and in complexity of economic activity, the old general association was found to be quite incapable of looking after the needs of the town. Accordingly, craft gilds, or associations of the members of one single craft, arose to care for the individual trades. Butchers, poulterers, bakers, cornmongers, and salters had their gilds; also weavers, fullers, and dyers; carpenters, masons, and thatchers; shoemakers, cobblers, lorimers, and saddlers; mercers, drapers, ironmongers, and haberdashers; vinters, taverners, and brewers; barbers, doctors, judges, scribes, and parish clerks. Up to the twelfth and thirteenth centuries there had been no such array of formal specialization as is represented by the craft gilds. Although some crafts were unorganized because of their insignificance and others because of popular hostility, nevertheless, in the fourteenth century, which was the heyday of their power, there were scores of gilds ready and able to promote the interests of their particular crafts. Generally speaking, the gilds enrolled the apprentices and journeymen as well as the masters, though it was only the last-named who had any influence in the management of the association. This was not a matter of moment so long as all apprentices became journeymen and practically all journeymen moved up to the rank of masters. Although the jealousy that one craft felt of another was probably rooted in human frailty, nevertheless, the gilds strengthened and perpetuated this feeling when they secured the enactment of laws limiting the activity of their rivals. A well-known instance was the restriction of cobblers to repairing old shoes and shoemakers to making new ones. A much more significant accomplishment of the gilds was the regulation of their own crafts, whether commercial or industrial, economic or professional. It is at least a plausible attitude to take at this distance that such regulation, while it tended to become restrictive and hampering, was at first helpful in the inculcating of high ideals of manufacture and commerce, labour and service.

An attempt, beginning in England, has been made in recent years (1912, 1915 f.) to found a new brand of socialism half-way between state socialism and syndicalism. This is called gild (or guild) socialism. The socialist gilds are to be not urban but national; and they are to manage the means of production which are actually to be owned by the state. Otherwise these modern bodies are supposed to resemble the medieval gilds. The cardinal idea is that the new gilds are to contain a harmonious group of workers from the apprentices up to the managers. Apparently it is thought that the medieval gild was a body of this kind. Such harmony as did exist in the medieval gild, however, was probably due to the dominance of the masters and the expectation that each apprentice and each journeyman would some day rise to the master class, when he would have his turn at lording it over his fellows. When the journeymen at length endeavoured to set up a separate association of their own they met the fiercest kind of opposition. In one other respect there has been some misunderstanding. The new socialist movement is to be founded on the craft, as distinct from the trade, principle. That is, for example, masons, painters, plasterers, and carpenters are to give up their separate trade unions in order to form a craft union of house builders. But in the Middle Ages there was no gild of house builders, so far as I have discovered, and indeed these particular callings of masons and the like, as well as those of weavers, fullers, dyers, and shearers of the cloth industry, had been organized in the craft-gild system. In other words, it is somewhat erroneous to identify craft gilds with a lack of division of labour. But, of course, the main idea of significance here is that the medieval craft gild should have left behind it a legacy embodying ideals of service in our day, or indeed any legacy that would be of assistance in the solution of modern industrial problems.

Because of changes in market, and therefore also in industrial, organization, many craft gilds were transmuted into something quite different from what they had originally been. In London these new associations were called livery companies. Other large cities on the Continent experienced the same kind of change. The new livery company, frequently incorporated, was an oligarchy, control lying in the hands of those members rich enough to provide a costly livery and to meet other charges. Below the livery were the poorer masters with but little power or influence in the affairs of the gild. Below them were the journeymen who, in many crafts, no longer had any real chance of becoming masters at all, unless they took jobs into their own homes and became sweated workers. Sometimes they went into the country where restrictive rules did not run, where they did not have to pay a heavy entry fee to become a master, or provide an expensive masterpiece as proof of their skill, as was required on the Continent. Analysed differently, the livery company was a craft gild made up of poor masters, in many cases handicraftsmen, who constituted the rank and file of the craft on the one hand, and on the other hand rich masters or merchant entrepreneurs who were often the employers of the poor handicraftsmen working in their own houses. Such was the actual inheritance of medieval associations to the modern period. Indeed, these companies have lived on in London, even to the present moment, and, it may be noted, still have a dominant place in elections in the City of London. A few of them are actively connected with their trade, for example, fishmongers with the fish trade ; some, notably the brewers, are made up only of persons engaged in the business they nominally represent. There is a movement to rehabilitate those companies which, beginning with the sixteenth century in most cases, had tended to divorce themselves from their trade or craft and to become festive and charitable associations, or indeed to become moribund.

As capital gradually got control of some of the craft gilds, or livery companies, there was a movement on the part of journeymen to secede. Usually, under the guise of religious worship, brotherhoods of journeymen were formed to carry on an economic struggle against the rich who dominated the old-time associations of their craft, or the great entrepreneurs who were gradually overwhelming the small masters and making it difficult for the journeymen to become masters at all, at least in the sense of retail handicraftsmen selling to any customer that pleased them. In England these brotherhoods failed to make permanent gains ; that is, they failed to attain a status of independent trade unions, as we should say to-day. In parts of Germany, however, their independence was recognized, after a long struggle. In Colmar, at the close of the fifteenth century, the journeymen bakers struck for the recognition of their brotherhood. After having waged a long and tedious contest in the courts of the Empire they won their case, though not in every particular. During the decade of contention they succeeded in getting financial assistance from their fellows in neighbouring towns, and in persuading the journeymen of those towns to blacklist the Colmar master bakers. There can be, of course, no question of any lineal descent of our modern trade unions, with similar striking proclivities, from the medieval journeymen associations, because in England, where modern trade unions arose, there were probably no independent journeymen associations that survived the Middle Ages, at least none to bridge the gap from the sixteenth to the eighteenth century. Nevertheless the tradition and the example of effort had been set up, and might have passed on from generation to generation. When working-men were once more sorely pressed by industrial changes, notably in the eighteenth century, they again formed secret societies which finally emerged as trade unions, first tolerated then recognized by government and society. On the whole, one cannot make out a very strong case even for a spiritual legacy of medieval trade unionism.

An association quite different from those mentioned, but still found in the Middle Ages, was the cartel. This was an agreement between merchants or others to raise or maintain prices, either directly or through the restriction of output. As is to be expected, but little information would be preserved of such arrangements. But it is known that Florentine and Hanseatic merchants formed cartels, and that salt and alum works were operated by formal agreements of this nature. A more complete investigation might show that such stints and gentlemen's agreements had an unbroken existence from the fifteenth to the twentieth century. It is, indeed, not difficult to discover isolated instances in the intervening period.

The medieval association which constituted the greatest heritage to the modern period was the regulated trading company. This was a society of merchants carrying on one kind of trade or trading in one district. It was highly advantageous for such traders to send their ships in a fleet

G g

for mutual defence against pirates. By combining, they could negotiate for foreign privileges and take measures to maintain them. The association could be responsible for its members who had to submit to common regulations. The Hanseatic League, an association of towns, grew out of regulated companies of merchants. In England the earliest-regulated company seems to have been the Merchant Staplers engaged in exporting wool to the Continent. The Merchant Adventurers, coming later, exported chiefly English cloth. Almost without exception, the English trading companies of the sixteenth century were regulated companies, as were many of those of the seventeenth century. By such companies England won markets in the old world and established colonies in the new. The Middle Ages had forged a potent weapon for the use of the modern period.

The regulation of trade had been the basis of these associations. In fact, it was through such agencies that towns developed their plan of controlling economic activity. In the absence of a large and well-trained municipal civil service there was no other way. Although we cannot say that these associations were created by the town for the purpose of regulation, they certainly became instruments in the hands of town magistrates for the control of business affairs at home and the extension of trade in other districts. At times these servants of the town asserted and established their power and even dominance in urban affairs. And bitter was the rivalry, as one group of associations disputed power with another. On the whole, the gilds and companies probably succeeded in doing what they set out to accomplish : they regulated manufacture and trade in favour of their own members. Of course, any assistance given to producers is filtered through to consumers in some small measure, but excellence of product was apparently not a compensation for the high prices that consumers were requested to pay. However this may be, there were certain trades which the town authorities kept wholly, or in part, under their own direct oversight. The provision of corn and wine, meat and salt, was so important, especially in years of dearth and in time of war, that town councils had at least to legislate for the emergency. Otherwise corn dealers, for instance, would have taken full advantage of the limited supply to reap undue profits by raising prices beyond the capacity of the poor to pay. Almost above all other considerations stood the need to keep the poor fed. Riots and bloodshed within the town walls created just the opportunity that turbulent nobles and feudal lords awaited to turn to their own selfish purposes. On the whole the provision trades, particularly in times of scarcity, were regulated in favour of consumers. Importation was favoured, exports prohibited, fraud checked, and corners in supply prevented. In all essentials the town policy of regulating trade and industry became the policy of the modern state. The earliest form of this state regulation is mercantilism, which, as German scholars have shown, is town regulation writ large. In both towns and states citizens were favoured as against aliens. In both there was great faith in the power of the government to direct, and also the necessity of entrusting most of the supervision to private persons or semi-public bodies. In both, the provision of food had to be given special consideration. Out of both there arose a spirit of revolt, which we may call liberalism and individualism. In town economy it led ambitious individuals to violate municipal ordinances or even to withdraw to the country or to new towns where there was more freedom of action. In national economy it led not only to interloping and rebellion but to the establishment of a rival plan and policy which, under the name of liberalism or *laisser-faire*, has had some vogue here and there for short periods.

Though the medieval town failed to develop, and therefore to bequeath to the modern state, a system of tariff-protection for industry, it did evolve a customs system for revenue purposes, which, for England at least, was probably the model on which the national system was based. English towns had a well-rounded system of tolls or customs on goods sent beyond the walls and on goods brought within the walls for sale. This system was financially impaired by exemptions granted to burgesses or members of the merchant gild. But these very exemptions strengthened the institution in so far as the persons enforcing and maintaining it were profiting, or seemed to be profiting, at the expense of the outsider. In the eleventh and twelfth centuries the kings of England established a national customs system which soon approximated to the local, as persons and even communities gained exemption and as the collection was infeudated or localized. When this national institution had become an obvious failure later kings set up a brand-new system in which the weaknesses of the old one were avoided. Before the appearance of the state, as an economic power, came various local bodies, the town, the village, and the monastery. It was the town, however, and the town only, that had a customs system which could in any way serve as a model for a state system. When we consider the extent to which the English national customs system has in turn been the model for other peoples to follow, we can appreciate the cumulative influence of early English towns.

Besides the local customs system the medieval towns provided weights and measures and coins, as already noted, some of which were adopted as national units, such as the avoirdupois pound of Troyes and the bushel measure of Winchester. These were obvious conveniences of trade, but the town actually engaged in trade itself. Genoa, Basel, and other Continental towns, held a monopoly of the salt trade, and supplied salt to their citizens and to others either directly through officials or indirectly through special associations formed for the purpose. Grain was provided occasionally by Florence for the use of the poor in the fourteenth and fifteenth centuries, and by London also in the fifteenth century. In 1485 the burgesses of Hamburg asked to have a municipal granary established. But it was not until the sixteenth century that public granaries of any significance were set up in England or on the Continent. These and other similar activities are well known, at least in a general way, and can hardly have failed to influence the history of modern states. Indeed, England has from the seventeenth to the twentieth century periodically debated the advisability of maintaining great national granaries.

The provision of foodstuffs was primarily for the poor who could not afford to pay the high prices prevailing in years of dearth. The poor had existed long before the town, but poverty became a problem only in town economy. Physical and mental incapacity had long been a potent force, as had misfortune, in reducing men to the lowest economic levels. But now in town economy to these circumstances was added the partial monopoly of land and capital. Relief before the time of town economy had been provided largely by the family or clan. Within the town it was the monastery, private alms, and craft gilds that came to the assistance of the impoverished and the needy. Gradually, even in the Middle Ages, however, the town itself entered the field of poor relief. By the middle of the fourteenth century there were already traces of communal poor relief in Marburg. But it was not until 1481 that the first secular almshouse was set up. It is to be noted that this was a hundred years before the Reformation reached that city. Early in the fifteenth century Amsterdam had municipal officials for poor relief, who distributed alms and allotted certain available houses to the deserving poor without charge. Of course, these and other such provisions were only small beginnings, but they were clear proof that the secularization of poor relief was practicable. It was the Reformation, the rise in prices, and in England the enclosure movement which precipitated the problem, virtually forcing city or state to take action. Then it was, that is, in the sixteenth century, that townsmen took more careful account of the situation, and drew up elaborate plans of rational treatment, plans which attracted national, and even international, attention.

The accumulation of capital became a characteristic of the flourishing towns. The many wills or testaments of merchants still in existence prove the well-being of a great many traders and handicraftsmen. The large-scale transactions in sale, purchase, and loans of a smaller number indicate considerable concentration of capital. In the very flourishing towns a few gilds of rich business men came to dominate municipal affairs. The Medici of Florence, the Fuggers of Augsburg, and Dick Whittington of London are simply the best known of rich late medieval business men. The German economist, Werner Sombart, has supposed that the capital accumulations of the Middle Ages arose out of urban rents which were later turned into foreign commerce and thereby greatly increased. Sombart is a socialist and was doubtless not displeased to have a base capitalistic system take its root in unearned increment. According to his view the owners of lands situated in growing towns, or in villages developing into towns, had such a large income that they could readily spare considerable sums for investment in foreign trade. And it must be confessed that the participation of Italian nobles in ship partnership, for example in Genoa, lends not a little credence to the general theory. The researches of Heynen, Strieder, and others, however, have cast rather too much doubt on the whole hypothesis to justify its acceptance. It is also quite in keeping with general observation that merchants are more likely to invest in land than landlords in commerce. Especially would that have been the case in the Middle Ages when landlords were noted for their extravagance and consumptive, rather than productive, tendencies. The more plausible, if less striking, theory is that capital accumulated out of the savings of small tradesmen and retail handicraftsmen, and that it further developed in wholesale trade, wholesale handicraft, mining, the management of large landed estates, and loans to princes and governments. But however it originated the capital was accumulated and constituted one of the great legacies of the Middle Ages to the modern period.

How this capital was used to found hospitals and chantries the fifteenth century amply testifies. How it influenced the development of art and learning, the record of the Italian cities at the close of the period clearly demonstrates. The Renaissance may have permeated a large number of persons, but in a peculiar sense it radiated from merchants and princes who were willing to supply the substance and at times the inspiration of artistic production. And out of it all has come the belief, partly based on experiences in the ancient period, that art and learning can have no other pedestal than aristocracy or plutocracy. Maecenas the Roman and the Medici of Florence are replaced, it is true, by the Rothschilds and the Morgans, except that while the former were patrons of artists the latter are patrons of art. It may be that this belief will one day be seen to be a silly superstition : then it may be apparent that it is not so much rank and wealth as education that is the basis of the highest patronage.

The capital accumulations, so advantageous to the art of the medieval period, were indispensable to its larger political enterprises. Popes, princes, and kings could carry on wars only with the help of loans. Only through specialized manufacturers and merchants could sufficient supplies be provided for armies that were to keep the field for any considerable period. Only from the towns could sufficient taxes be collected to maintain the growing state and the costly wars. It was the Government in its ambition for power, and war in its lust for plunder, which were preparing the way for further urban enterprises. The Government, for instance, of Louis XI of France and Henry VII of England, gave the towns law and order; the towns gave these kings the harvests of peace and the sinews of war. The feudal state, based on landed property and personal services, was giving way to the urban state founded on personal property and the exchange of goods. It was not the little commercial town but the growing commercial and industrial centre with its capital accumulations, its peace-loving merchants, and its tax-paying citizens that made the modern centralized state possible. In civic strife he who held London and a few other English towns would soon hold the rest of England. It is, of course, true that the towns did not create the new monarchy, but they made the new monarchy possible by their material assistance.

Capital accumulations may be credited not only with a predominant part in the rise of the new art and the creation of the new monarchy but also with the incoming of the new imperialism based essentially on expansion overseas. Without the large fleets of town ships, the goods to fill the holds, and business knowledge behind the material things, the Atlantic might have been crossed but not spanned, and the Indian Ocean entered but not opened to European trade. Those nations which allowed the owners of wealth to control the colonizing and trading companies had most economic success in the new, as in the old, world. England and the Netherlands left the plantations much more to their merchants than Spain or France did, and reaped a greater material harvest as a result. Of course, the great enterprises of the seventeenth century in the Indies and the Americas grew out of the activities and accumulated wealth of the sixteenth. But the sixteenth century was the fifteenth come to maturity. The later century knew no forms of association and combination, no tricks of trade, no mode of development or exploitation that the earlier century was not already familiar with. Of course, in economic history there is no dividing line at or near 1500. The modern period of economic history, it may be argued with effect, began nearer 1300, when the essentials of the present economic order commenced to unfold themselves in the growing towns. Everything that has happened in the commercial and industrial world since that time is a logical, some may be inclined to say inevitable, outgrowth of that early childhood of economic innovation.

Parallel with the new forms went a new spirit. Not only was capital accumulated but a capitalistic spirit was engendered, not in the whole state but in the towns, especially in those towns which from situation and general favour of location offered the greatest reward to effort. Here and there arose—even in the Middle Ages—a tireless activity, a dignified enterprise, a daring venturesomeness, and a capacity for the almost unlimited use of material goods in display as well as in traffic. Sombart and his followers, delighting in finding origins in the dramatic and the catastrophic, have assigned to the Renaissance and to war a considerable place in the growth of the new spirit of material enterprise. It is much more likely that the new culture was itself a result of the awakening of human activity which first saw its opportunity of sure reward within the walled towns of commerce rather than in the studio or in the *scriptorium*. One may accept the economic interpretation of history thus far without going to the length of denying to the Renaissance a reactionary and reciprocal influence of great moment. The heightening of intellectual endeavour in philosophy and letters created a drive which, in the make-up of some individuals, could find an outlet only in the business world. And it is not to be forgotten that the new art products were objects of commerce as well as of beauty. Not only would art supply trade but, through its direct influence on men, it would engender the demand for its output—in the form of statues, pictures, musical instruments, porcelains, jewellery, and tapestries. The early desire for gain in commerce had doubtless helped to call forth the individualism that carved the figures of Michael Angelo and held the brush of Leonardo da Vinci. But the distinction that came to artists, as to men of learning, in all probability led men who were not artists or scholars to seek success in business.

The same spirit of capitalism, with its restless energy and power to move, broke down the ecclesiastical edifice and cut the theological entanglements of the Middle Ages. The old order was condemned in the medieval period, executed in the modern. But here, as so often, the modern period gets the glory or the opprobrium, as the case may be. Roman Catholicism had grown up as ancient towns were tumbling, and reached its height in the period when village or manorial economy flourished. It was a splendid body of practices and ideals suited to the relatively stagnant condition of rural life. The economic doctrines of the Church grew up in the village market. But the town was rising, and rising to new needs. The economic doctrines of the Church Fathers had to give way to the concessions

of the Schoolmen. These in turn had to be supplemented
by the Canonists' exceptions in favour of town trade.
Each concession to the old doctrines of just price and usury
was a grudging allowance wrung from the Church by its
own necessities as a temporal power and forced on it by
the increase of subterfuges in the towns. During the
Reformation the old shackles on trade were burned with
the martyrs. And in the Post- and Counter-Reformation
period, abandonment of the old economic policy was the
price of ecclesiastical success in Catholic countries. This
is not the first instance in history, nor the last, of a conservative privileged caste being forced to accept reform
from outside. It is true that the glory of leadership had
for the time departed, but there was a real social gain—in the
ultimate spiritual position of the Church and the immediate
rationalization of economic theory.

It is a plausible view that Protestantism was long overdue
—to meet the material needs of the towns, though that
cannot be accepted as the sole explanation of the new
movement, for urban Italy remained Catholic, albeit a
changed Catholic, while rural England became Protestant.
The new economic order of growing capitalism had to face
an old ecclesiastic order of unprogressive ways. Townsmen
were becoming worldly, individualistic, and restlessly
impatient of restraint. In other words, the middle class
of the towns was breaking bounds. The result was manifold.
As we have seen, craft gilds were changed into livery companies ; some ambitious manufacturers forced their journeymen to work at night in violation of the gild regulations,
whilst others left the town for the freer countryside. And
now in the religious field efforts were made to attain
success where Wycliffites and Hussites had failed, success
in snapping the bands that cast aspersion upon the activities
of business men. Feudal landed Catholics would enjoy ;

budding urban Protestants would produce. The Protestant revolution seems, in part, a great social upheaval, the angry protest of an ambitious successful class of individuals who would work, and work hard and ruthlessly, for selfish personal and class interests. It was the same upwelling social force moving against what stood in the road, that first shook the Roman Catholic Church and later even its ally and abettor, the monarchy itself.

The early Middle Ages had nurtured an excessive idealism emotionally suited to the economic conditions of village and manorial existence. The promise of a future life of pleasure had been high hope in a world of village sickness, famine, subordination, and opprobrium. The towns changed this very gradually but very surely. They became oases of endeavour, dignity, and enjoyment. These hardworking capable men could profit from the fruits of their own labour, and, regardless of birth, might even enjoy the results of other people's efforts. The towns grew, while the countryside remained almost stagnant or in some districts indeed even lost in population. Viewed dispassionately, the blow struck by the towns for worldliness, born of opportunity, was both good and bad. Its temporary excesses are clearly enough written into the history of the fifteenth and sixteenth centuries, but its enduring triumphs are being realized more and more as the generations go by.

In mechanism and in spirit the medieval town was progressive, expansive, and full of promise of great things to come. Business organization, capitalistic accumulations, an enterprising attitude, and growing worldliness were strong allies in the making of a new economic order. The medieval town actually took the first steps in the establishment of metropolitan economy. Just as towns had held the neighbouring villages in economic subordination, so did one great commercial centre come to threaten the economic

independence of the towns. In Italy and in Germany we
see this beginning in the Middle Ages, but it did not get
very far. In Florence, for example, we observe the occasional use of political force to bring grain not only from the
immediate countryside (*contado*) but also from the wider
district (*distretto*) made up of other towns with their own
countrysides. There was little or no effort, however, to
make Tuscany look upon Florence as the economic centre
for a very large number of goods and services. The real
interest of the medieval town seems to have been the
development of purely local trade and the most profitable
part of distant or international commerce. The town was
a success in catering for the ordinary needs of its own
citizens and of the countrymen in the neighbouring villages.
It also went far in trading by land and sea in distant parts
of the European world. It went so far as to build up large
business units and prosperous associations to pursue this
profitable commerce. It did not do the same, however, for
a very wide area in its immediate district. The wholesaling
functions were for the more extended and international
exchange of goods. The storage of goods and the business
of banking were on the same basis. In short, there was no
effective large-scale organization of the commerce of a wide
compact area or hinterland. The essence of town economy
was the subordination of villages, not of towns. The growth
of London, Paris, and Berlin, and of Manchester, Liverpool,
Hamburg, and Marseilles, as towering economic centres
for the exploitation of a vast area at home as well as for the
carrying on of commerce in distant parts, is a modern
growth. In the late Middle Ages, as has been indicated,
there was promise of all this, and real preparation for it in
the enlargement and perfection of methods of carrying on
trade with distant parts. The organization of the marketing
system for a wide hinterland was, in fact, a slow and laborious

process until the railroads made transportation both rapid and cheap.

A somewhat similar situation is found in the town's efforts to establish a political unit. Here we find both success and failure. In Italy the town created a fairly wide area of political organization, Genoa in Liguria, Venice in Venetia, and Florence in Tuscany. But the subordinate parts did not accept their lot : Ferrara rose against Venice and Pisa against both Genoa and Florence. And Genoa, Florence, and Venice were individually just strong enough to maintain (intermittently) their own independence. They were unable to form an Italian state, though Machiavelli dreamed of a united state and wrote of it at the close of the medieval period. In Germany the great Hanseatic League of towns was a potent force in the fifteenth century. If it had grown instead of declined it might have formed a state based on urban feudalism with a policy of economic politics—instead of political economics, such as actually has developed. It was no small effort to have brought together between three and four score of towns for a common purpose of trade. But no union formed of rival communities of about the same strength, without the cementing power of force, could make continuous gains or even hold its own indefinitely. The middle class was unable to form a state based upon town economic units. The dominant economic institution was not in a position to forge the political weapon which further economic progress required. And so the way was prepared for another kind of state, either national as in England and France or territorial as in Germany. In such a state both rural nobles and town merchants played a part, as did princely power and proletarian passive resistance. To the new political organization the town contributed its policy and the merchants their wealth. But the new creation was or became national, not urban.

One of the greatest legacies of the medieval towns, indeed of the economic history of the Middle Ages, is the ultimate failure of localism itself. In many forms of organization and in the direction of its intellectual life, the town might have succeeded, but, if it could not expand, it could not hold its own against rival possibilities. On the economic side the possibility was metropolitan economy; on the political side it was the unified state. These two fitted hand and glove. The state gave the most favourably located town an unrestricted area over which to extend its economic dominance. London found no limits put to its economic ambition except distance and insular boundaries. This growing metropolitan economy, in turn, brought to the state a degree of economic unity and concentration that was beyond precedent. Where there was most concentrated material strength there was greatest political stability, both for international struggle and for over-sea expansion. The strength of England for a long time was the strength of London, which was the unrivalled heart of the nation and of the empire.

The medieval town failed to evolve elastic institutions capable of expansion along the marked lines of town economy. It failed to evolve a formulated theory of economics. It failed to do justice to the struggling proletariate which sought to preserve its own health and its own manhood. On the other hand, the solid contributions of town economy, indeed of medieval economic history, are obviously great along the line of capitalism. But it is just at this point that the town's legacy is most boldly challenged in our time. The Christian Church and other critics of our social system have always denounced the legacies of materialism, individualism, and worldliness which capitalism has brought with it. But these tendencies are really marks of social change and are not themselves unchanging or unalterable, but subject to influences which affect them, compelling them to shed their evil repute and show their better possibilities. As they develop under these influences, as scientific study reveals their power for good and explains their meaning, they make fresh conquests for us, promise us new victories in new fields of battle, and so postpone indefinitely any final judgement of their true worth in human affairs.

N. S. B. Gras.

9

ROYAL POWER AND ADMINISTRATION

THE citizen of a modern State, accustomed as he is to regard the constitution under which he lives as a machine for the expression and attainment of the will of the majority, will find, if he studies it in detail, that it has been more or less successfully adapted to a purpose for which it was clearly not designed. Even where, as in the United States or in France, the machine has been remodelled according to modern theories, old forms have a tendency to persist, though sometimes under new names.

> New Presbyter is but old Priest writ large . . .

There is no doubt a vast difference betwixt medieval and modern institutions: but it is due partly to an extension of the functions of government, partly to the increase of the means at its command; such as the facility of communication, the spread of education, and the development of finance. Yet its essential task remains the same. It must keep the peace, at home and abroad, administer justice, and regulate social and economic matters of general concern, such as traffic, weights and measures, and coinage. The material necessities for these objects have to be provided: defences and public offices must be built, soldiers and public servants must be paid. And we shall reasonably expect to find a certain similarity in the devices adopted to meet these ends even where there is no historical connexion.

In most of the States of medieval Europe the constitution was monarchical. But kingship, in its earlier forms, is not widely separated from the loose communal organization of

н h

the tribe. There was probably not much difference politically between a tribe which had a king and one which had not. The king was rather the representative than the lord of the community. In a primitive form of monarchy the royal power is as yet undifferentiated : the king, though no longer the priest of his people, is still their judge, their general, their governor. He is almost as much the head of the family as the chief of the State. His rule is neither absolute nor yet formally limited. And although we can trace, throughout the Middle Ages, a gradual tendency to define and differentiate his power and to impose successive limitations upon it, there remains, through the whole period, a wide scope for the play of individual character. The personal qualities of kings play a far greater part in medieval than in modern history.

The first period of definition lies between the accession of Clovis in 481 and the death of Charlemagne. Under the earlier Merovingians the royal power is growing. The peace is now ' the king's peace ', and the king has moreover the power to grant a special protection to individuals or societies which gives them a privileged position, and renders those unjustly vexing them liable to special penalties. His command or *ban* is enforced by a special penalty bearing the same name. His office is now definitely hereditary, although it does not necessarily descend from father to son, but sometimes to a brother or uncle. This uncertainty of succession persists for a long time in many countries : in some, indeed, as in Poland, the monarchy became entirely elective. And even though it gradually became the rule that the son should succeed to his father, primogeniture, as opposed to partition, did not obtain universally in Europe until the close of the Middle Ages. But the vitality of the hereditary principle is nowhere more clearly shown than in the long period which intervened between the fall of the royal power of the Merovingian kings and the close of their dynasty. For nearly a century their dominions [1] were governed by the powerful Mayors of the Palace who set up and deposed their nominal masters at their pleasure. The powers of the Merovingian kings had already shrunk to nothing; but their persons, distinguished from those of their subjects by their unshorn hair, were still indispensable to sit on the throne, to receive ambassadors, and to pronounce the answers which the Mayors had determined. It was not till A.D. 752 that the last Merovingian, Childeric III, was deposed, and the title of King given to the real holder of the royal power, Pepin, the son of Charles Martel; nor was this done without anxious consultation of the pope, Saint Zacharias.

The royal power was still in theory limited by that of the popular assembly. But two great factors distinguish the Merovingian kingdom from the primitive monarchy with which we began. The Franks had acquired a territory with a Romanized Christian population, and the remains of a Roman provincial organization, and, beginning with the royal house, had accepted Christianity. The king thus became the possessor of all that the Roman Emperor had before him, and had large domains at his disposal, together with what was left of the land—and head-taxes, tolls, customs, and profits of coinage of the Roman province. At the same time he became the official protector, and not far from the official head of the Christian Church in his dominions. Moreover, the monarchy itself acquired a new sacred character. The relation of the subject to his sovereign was sanctioned by the oath of fealty. The king summoned the

---

[1] These were Francia, extending from Brittany to the Rhine basin and divided by a line a little east of Paris into an eastern half called Austrasia, and a western, called Neustria; Aquitaine; Burgundy and Provence. Each province seems to have had its own mayor.

ecclesiastical councils, the proceedings of which coalesced
to some extent with those of the national assemblies of
which we have spoken. The king confirmed the election of
bishops, and frequently appointed them to their sees under
colour of his right of supervision. The power of a Merovingian king had thus no definite limits. In practice, however, the king was not above the law. Thus, for instance,
Charibert, on his accession, promised not to introduce new
laws or customs; and a like moral can be drawn from the
story of the 'vase of Soissons', where a soldier disputed
the claim of Clovis to a particular share of the booty which
had not fallen to him by lot, and seems to have made good
his point, though he lost his life in doing so. Moreover,
the king's power was restricted in three practical ways:
by the alienation of the domain without any corresponding
service, by the creation of Immunities, which took away
both the administration and the profits of justice, and by
the conversion of public offices into hereditary estates. It
was these restrictions which greatly contributed to the fall
of the Merovingian dynasty.

The family of the Carolingians, which had frequently
held the office of Mayor of the Palace in Austrasia, recon-
stituted the Merovingian kingdom by successive victories
over their rivals before venturing to take the name of king.
Charlemagne, extending his dominions over the greater
part of Europe, obtained from the pope in A.D. 800 the
title of Emperor. There is no doubt that the throne of
Constantinople was deemed to be vacant, and that the title
which he assumed implied a claim to be the successor of
Augustus. He did not, however, attempt to obtain possession of the territory of the Eastern Empire, and contented
himself with recognition as Emperor in the West. The
Carolingian Empire was so great (extending as it did from
the Baltic to the Pyrenees and beyond, over most of Italy,

and from the Atlantic to the Vistula) and the Emperor so great a figure, that the influence which its organization has had on the constitutions of European States is almost as great as its share in the legends of the later Middle Ages. Even in lands which never formed part of the Empire, such as England and Scandinavia, imitations may be traced of the great system which overshadowed the rest of Western Europe.

The royal power, reduced to nothing under the previous dynasty, was now re-established and consolidated. The Emperor was not only king in his own dominions, but was regarded as the secular counterpart of the pope, and equally with him bound to the extension of the kingdom of Christ. The victories of Charlemagne over the Saxons, with the consequent wholesale conversion of the vanquished, and the expeditions against the Moors in Spain are examples of the way in which he regarded his office. In ecclesiastical matters the Emperor exercised a supervision over the right of election of bishops and abbots, which in many cases amounted to the right to nominate his own candidates to these offices. He had a special official, one of the most important in the palace, expressly to deal with ecclesiastical business, this was his archchaplain or *Apocrisarius*, who exercised an office corresponding more or less closely to that of the Count Palatine, the chief judge in secular matters. The sacred character which the Merovingian kings had possessed persisted in their successors. The coronation robes of the Emperor resembled those of a bishop, while those of a king were like those of a priest. Both were anointed with holy oil, and as time went on were more and more held to partake of a sacred and inviolable character which could not be removed. The claim of the kings of France and England to touch for the King's Evil is an expression of this doctrine, and in virtue of it the Emperor ranked as a canon of St. Peter's, and the King of Germany as a canon of Aix-la-Chapelle. There is at least a connexion between the appeal of Pepin to Pope Zacharias and the coronation of Charlemagne by Pope Leo in the eighth century and the later doctrine of ' divine right ' or the long alliance of ' Church and King '. Moreover, under the Carolingians the scope of the king's *ban* is extended, and certain definite offences are brought within it, the ' Pleas of the Crown ' of our English law. These were sacrilege, the wronging of widows and orphans, and of poor people powerless to defend themselves, arson, trespass with violence, rape of a free woman, and desertion from the army.

The kingdom was hereditary, but not indivisible, and the king had power to regulate the succession. Thus, not only did Charlemagne divide his dominions in 806 between his three sons, but his youngest son Lewis the Pious who survived his brothers and succeeded to the whole of his father's empire, in like manner divided his realm betwixt Lothar, whom he made joint Emperor with himself, Pepin, who received Aquitaine, and Lewis, who obtained Bavaria and its dependencies. This principle of division persisted throughout the Carolingian period without implying a division of the empire, at all events in theory. The principle that a kingdom is indivisible is of later growth, and is bound up with the conception of nationality, still a very weak and shadowy thing in the ninth century. We may notice something similar in English history, since on the death of William I, Normandy and England devolved upon different sons, nor was any clear rule of primogeniture established before the reign of Henry II. In Germany, in the territories held of the empire, the principles of indivisibility and of primogeniture were of much slower growth. Although the Golden Bull of Charles IV in 1356 forbade the division of the electoral lands, primogeniture was not generally the rule in the territories until the end of the seventeenth century.

The tightening of the bond between the king and the nation or nations which he ruled is the great achievement of Charlemagne. This appears both in military, judicial, and financial affairs, but is particularly expressed in the institution of the oath of allegiance. Every free man, whether or not he had a lord of his own, was bound to swear allegiance to the king on his accession, and the oath was administered from time to time to those who had since come to years of discretion. And though the growth of feudalism weakened this bond, it was long before it ceased to be remembered, even in Germany. Thus in 1028, when Duke Ernest of Swabia rebelled against Conrad II, he reminded his followers of their oath to himself. Two of them, who answered for the rest, replied : ' We do not deny that we promised fealty against all men except him who gave us to you. Had we been the Emperor's slaves, lawfully conveyed to you by him, we could not abandon you. But since we are free men, and the Emperor is the defender of our freedom, if we desert him we lose our freedom, which no good man does, it is said, unless he loses his life with it. We will obey you, therefore, in all that is honourable and right, but if you desire what is not so, we will return freely to him from whom we came upon condition.'

The interpretation given to the oath of allegiance is a ready index of the reality of the royal power. How illusory it might be is shown by the dictum of a thirteenth-century French feudal lawyer, who answers with a confident ' Yes ' the question whether the men of a baron are bound by their oath of fealty to him to serve him against the king. The history of this change of doctrine, and of the gradual reversion in various countries to the earlier conception, is the history of the rise and fall of Feudalism. The failure of the successors of Charlemagne to retain control of the centralized machinery of his empire is the measure of his personal genius. Without a strong head, the system rapidly disintegrated. The king parted with his direct control of his subjects. His officers became hereditary and then independent. A state of anarchy and private war resulted which brought about a new grouping, which is characterized by the predominance of the principle of contract in place of that of public law. For the relation of a feudal superior to his tenant is contractual, and the contract may be denounced by either party. Similarly the public peace was secured so far as might be either by ecclesiastical sanctions, the ' Peace of God ', or by leagues for mutual conciliation, the German ' Landfriede '. The re-establishment of the ' King's Peace ' was the mark, in France as previously in England, of the recovery of the royal power.

We have seen that the Merovingian kings were restricted in their legislative powers, but even in their case there was no formal limitation. The position of Charlemagne was equally undefined, though he was a fertile legislator. He not only codified the laws of the various tribes whom he governed, but added new provisions and issued administrative ordinances sometimes with, and sometimes without the concurrence of the people assembled in the annual Diet. The distinction of ' Statutes ' enacted by the king with the full consent of his subjects, and ' Ordinances ' made by himself with the assistance of his council, is not yet drawn. Carolingian legislation, like that of the Roman Empire, consisted indifferently of laws, edicts, and rescripts. This legislative activity is not kept up in the later Middle Ages, unless perhaps in England. The normal practice was to regard the law as immemorial, like the English ' Common Law ', and to make innovations by way of explanation rather than by enactment. The reception of Roman Law in Germany and in some parts of France had also the effect of discouraging legislation, and limiting it to the sphere of administrative regulations. But although legislation, especially in matters of private law, is less important in the Middle Ages than administration, it is essentially a royal function. It is bound up with the coronation oath, whereby the king binds himself to protect the liberties of his people, and thus the remedies for specific abuses, whether regarded as innovations or as returns to the ancient law, are frequently embodied in the articles of a coronation charter. Thus Henry I, on his accession, not only restores the law of King Edward ' with those amendments with which my father amended it by the advice of his barons ', but makes specific rules as to the taking of reliefs both by himself and by those holding under him. The two elements of the royal will and the popular assent co-exist in legislative matters exactly as they do in the actual appointment of the king, and in both they are differently stressed at different periods. Thus even at the time of the Provisions of Oxford the king's assent could not be formally dispensed with, while on the other hand, in France in the fourteenth century, ordinances made by the king on the advice of his ministers (who are persons of no intrinsic importance) are promulgated as ' by the assent of the prelates and barons '. The meaning to be attached to these formulae is determined by the growth of absolutism and of representative institutions respectively. Charters of Liberties might be granted on other occasions than coronations. Thus just as the aristocratic resistance to the Plantagenet kings is marked by Magna Charta and the Charter of the Forest and their periodical renewals, so in France the rebellion of 1314 against Philip IV led to the grant by his successor Louis X in 1315 of a series of charters to the several provinces as well as to a confirmation of the ordinance of 1303 for the whole of France. But legislation

usually took a less solemn form. Decisions made by the
king with the assent, real or fictitious, of the great council
of the realm were embodied in Assizes or Statutes, ' Ordon-
nances ', ' Reichsabschiede ', and circulated by the Chancery.
In England this practice persists to the present day, except
that circulation through the king's printer has taken the
place of the issue to every county of letters under the
Great Seal. Minor regulations were issued in the form of
proclamations, which were transmitted to the sheriff under
the Great Seal with instructions to have them read aloud
on suitable occasions such as market-days in the principal
towns in his bailiwick. The necessity of publication acted
in France as some restraint on the royal power, since it
became necessary that edicts should be registered in the
' Parlement ', and this afforded an opportunity for the
lawyers who sat there to criticize the proposed order, and
sometimes to procure by their remonstrance its amendment
or withdrawal.

Charlemagne, like his Merovingian predecessors, was the
supreme judge in his dominions. Einhard, his biographer,
tells us that ' while he was putting on his shoes or his cloak,
he not only admitted his friends, but, if the Count Palatine
stated a case which could not be determined without his
order, he bade the litigants be brought in at once, heard
the case, and delivered judgement, just as though he were
sitting in court '. Later kings from time to time observed
the rule of hearing cases in person. Thus Henry III of
England sat in judgement both in the King's Bench and
in the Exchequer. Louis IX heard cases once a week,
sitting under an oak tree at Vincennes. And even Louis XIV
appears to have persuaded himself that he, like his sainted
ancestor, administered justice weekly to all comers. Moreover, Charlemagne resumed that control of justice throughout the realm which the Merovingians had lost. The

owner of an immunity might still, it is true, administer justice to whose who lived in his district, but he was under the strict supervision of the king in the same way as the king's own officers.

It must be remembered that the king, though the supreme judge, is not, in the Middle Ages, the sole fountain of justice. And although few traces remained within the limits of the Empire of the popular tribunals of the barbaric period, the decision of the cases remained in the hands of the free men who composed the court long after the conduct of the trial had become the function of the king's officers. And when offices became hereditary, and supervision ceased, justice was no longer either popular or royal, but seigneurial. The right of appeal was not uncontested nor self-evident. The extension of royal power took various forms: the reception of appeals, the grant of exemptions from the local jurisdiction to particular persons or classes of persons, the reservation of special classes of cases, particularly criminal cases, to the royal courts, and, as in England, the reassertion of the claim to supervise the action of local jurisdictions through royal commissioners, ' Justices in Eyre '. And all these measures were resented by the mesne lords, i.e. those who came between the sovereign and the ultimate subject. Thus, the reception of appeals was not only the constant source of difficulties with France, but provided the occasion of the war of Edward I against the Scots, since the deposition of John Balliol arose out of the reception by Edward of appeal cases from Scotland. Exemptions from jurisdiction, under the name of ' Sauvegarde ', were among the grievances of Edward III in Guienne, as were ' reserved cases '. And one of the principal provisions of Magna Charta is intended to protect the barons from the loss of their courts.

Charlemagne led his own armies into the field, or entrusted them to the great officers of his household, and the king's function as commander in chief has scarcely ceased to be of importance. But in the eighth and ninth centuries war was normal. Spring was the season ' when kings go out to battle '. Every free man was a soldier, bound to equip himself according to his means and to set out, under the severest penalties, at the king's command. This universal obligation has never been cancelled, though its importance is sometimes obscured because the army which it provided was deficient in cavalry. This need was met by the feudal contract, by which the tenant bound himself to assist his suzerain with a definite mounted contingent serving for a limited period. In both cases the personal relation was insisted on. Thus there is a distinction in English law between a ' voyage royal ' and an ordinary military expedition, and in 1297 we find the feudal tenants refusing to go to Gascony unless the king consented to lead them in person. This objection only applied to foreign service, not to national defence. But foreign conquest, in a feudal monarchy, often takes the form of a joint-stock enterprise, like William the Conqueror's expedition to England or that of Henry II to Ireland. In this, as in other matters, the extent to which the king retained a direct relation with his subjects is a measure of his effective power. Thus, in England, scutage, the composition for feudal service, was levied directly upon the land by the king's officer, the sheriff : in France, the extension of the royal power by Philip IV is marked by the calling out of the ' arrière ban '.

The administration of Charlemagne, as it is presented to us by Hincmar, whose picture though clearly too flattering is supported by other evidence, was directly controlled by the king, personally or through his *missi dominici*. As the monarchy declined, these officers assumed a local and hereditary character, like the counts over whom they exercised supervision. The great offices of the household likewise became hereditary, and consequently merely honorific, the work being done by deputies of lower rank. Even when ancient offices remained, the departments under them acquired an independent status and 'went out of court'. A strong king would then entrust the most important duties, military or financial, to officers more immediately under his own control. The overthrow of 'the king's favourites' or 'unworthy ministers', which is so familiar an incident of medieval history, generally represents an effort of the aristocracy to reduce the royal control of the administration. But a better method was needed than the control of the administrative machine by baronial intervention or oligarchical committees. The Middle Ages saw the beginning of a more effective way of holding the balance between absolutism and anarchy by the gradual evolution of representative government.

In the barbaric period representation was unnecessary, since important measures could be submitted to the groans or acclamations of the host of free men assembled for the planning of the annual campaign. And though this method of ascertaining the popular will can only have been illusory in States of the size of the Merovingian or Carolingian dominions, the council of bishops and princes, though not elected by the people, was not for that reason unrepresentative. Holding as they did positions of authority in the various parts of the kingdom, they were able to advise as to the safety or the reverse of any given course of action, exactly as a modern member of parliament may warn the party whips that his constituents will be alienated by some step which the Government proposes to take. Still, the method of obtaining the consent of a nation through its elected delegates, which is what we usually mean when we speak of representative institutions, has no place in the

history of the earlier Middle Ages, though it was familiar
to the Gauls of the Roman province, who had a national
assembly at Lyons. The Saxons also, before their subjuga-
tion by Charlemagne, had an annual assembly of delegates.
These precedents do not seem to have suggested any modification of the formal assembly of the whole people, which,
in consequence of its unwieldy nature, soon disappeared.
The principle of the necessity of the assent of the people
was not, however, lost. In a feudal state, the king, or indeed
any other feudal superior, acted, in matters affecting his
subordinates, by the advice of his court, the free tenants
holding of himself. In the thirteenth century this court
begins to be found insufficient, and means are sought for
giving greater weight to the decisions taken in it. There
are no definite constitutional principles, but it is generally
recognized that the king acts, in more important affairs, by
the advice of his council, and that the full court is required
for the most important matters. A special session of this
kind becomes known as a ' Parliament ' or ' Diet ', and
consists of the full court sitting for judicial, financial, or
deliberative purposes. It is this court which is reinforced
by elected knights and burgesses. The necessity of rein-
forcing the king's ordinary court only gradually appears
and marks a definite stage in national progress. When the
household and territorial officials of the Carolingian council
had become hereditary feudatories, often more powerful
than the king whom they served, it was difficult to secure
their attendance at the regular sessions of the court. Nevertheless, it was a recognized principle that decisions affecting
their rights must be made by their peers, and not by the
officials of lower rank who had succeeded to their duties.
And although all tenants in chief are theoretically ' peers ',
the more powerful succeeded in making themselves into
a special class. Thus we have ' Peers of France ', ' Princes

of the Empire', greater and lesser barons in England. The growth of the royal power at various periods causes them to unite to resist encroachments, and makes them conscious of themselves as an 'Estate'. There was no need of any stimulus in the thirteenth century to awake the self-consciousness of the clergy. The great quarrel over investitures at the end of the eleventh century did not rage so fiercely in England and France as it did in Germany and Italy, but it left an abiding impression all over Europe. And the same struggle between ecclesiastical and civil jurisdiction which led to the martyrdom of Becket marked the clergy in all countries as an estate with interests of its own.

The history of the third [1] estate, the 'commons', is less simple. It is regarded as consisting of all free men who are neither nobles, clerks, nor monks. But even in England, and still more in France and Germany, it owes its character as an estate to the increasing importance of towns. Living close together, and accustomed by the necessities of trade to act together for their common interest, the burgesses purchased from the crown or from their feudal lords special privileges, including various degrees of self-government, and ultimately the right to act together as a single person in law. In France and Germany the 'commons' summoned to the Parliament or the Imperial Diet are the communities of the towns: the rural under-tenants are unrepresented, though they had to contribute to the expenses of the deputies of the clergy and nobles. On the other hand, in England corporate consciousness was awakened in the rural districts by the extension of royal administration with its important machinery of the inquest, by which the verdict

---

[1] The words ' third estate ' are used here as a convenient term ; they are not meant to express any theory of the development of ' estates ' in England.

of the *patria* or venue was taken, by the arrangements for the local assessment and collection of taxes, and by the linking up of the local and central jurisdictions. By a curious paradox every increase in the efficiency of the central government in England, and only in England, produced a corresponding growth of community feeling in the counties; the commons of England are in fact the *communitates comitatuum Anglie*. Again in England the third estate acquired a national character by coalescing with a part of the ' nobility '. The article of Magna Charta which provided for the summons of the lesser tenants in chief to take part in the ' common counsel of the realm ', not by individual summons but through the sheriff, marked a distinction in the nobility which was probably not new. Whether the first ' knights of the shire ' represented this class only, as a strictly legal view of the matter might seem to demand, or, as seems more likely, were elected by the free-holders of the county in full county court, they ceased to deliberate separately after the end of the thirteenth century and combined with the burgesses to form the ' House of Commons '. This coalition did not take place in any other country, probably because the line between ' noble ' and not noble was everywhere more sharply drawn than in England. The result was the development of the Great Council into a representative body, however imperfect, in which the grant of the extraordinary supplies which were constantly necessary could be made dependent on the redress of grievances.

England is thus not a typical case. The division of the nobility into two estates is found in Aragon, but there the inferior nobles had no representatives and appeared in person, nor did they coalesce with the burgesses. In Scotland the right to attend Parliament either in person or by representatives was limited to tenants in chief, and boroughs held of the king. In France, the States-General were never regularly assembled, and lost their connexion with the Parliament of Paris after the fourteenth century. In this earlier period there does not seem to have been any system of representation, although individuals and groups might and did appear by proxy. An effort made in 1483 to secure the joint election of deputies in each district by all three estates was only partly successful, since at Paris the clergy refused to give their proxies to the deputies elected by the nobles and the third estate. Moreover, some of the provinces, like Burgundy, which preserved the relics of their historical independence, elected their deputies in the provincial estates, while in Languedoc, which was part of the king's own dominions separately administered, they were elected locally. This lack of uniformity is the natural consequence of the historical independence of the provinces, just as in the fourteenth century Guienne, being in the hands of the king of England, was not represented by deputies in the States-General, or as, in England, the palatinates of Durham and Chester sent no representatives to Parliament until long after 1485.

The failure of the States-General to secure a permanent footing in the French constitution was due to their association, in the minds of the king and his advisers, with popular disturbance. In France, as in England, it had been a political crisis which induced the Government to call in their support. Philip IV sought the help of the nation in 1302 in his assertion of its independence against the claims of Boniface VIII, just as Edward I had in the previous year, in the parliament of Lincoln, called in the baronage to protest in the name of the nation, whose rights the king had not any power to compromise, against the claim of the same pope to the suzerainty of Scotland. In France, as in England, the needs of the Government under the exhausting pressure of the Hundred Years War, gave the estates their opportunity. Their control of supplies enabled them to obtain reform of the finances, the administration, and the council. But the final effort in 1358 of the clergy and the third estate, unsupported by the nobles, to abolish the provincial estates and thus make it impossible for the Government to obtain supplies by separate negotiation, collapsed with the fall of the leader of the Parisian burgesses, Etienne Marcel, who had turned the reform movement into a revolution. Again, in 1413 the States-General which obtained from the king the famous 'ordonnance Cabochienne' was acting under strong popular pressure, to which an aristocratic reaction succeeded. Still, the States continued to be called at intervals through the fourteenth and fifteenth centuries, as their consent was held to be needed in questions of peace and war and for the imposition of taxes. The recovery of Paris by Charles VII in 1436 strengthened the king's hands, and enabled him to obtain the consent of the States-General held at Poitiers in the same year to the re-establishment of the aids, an unpopular form of indirect taxation ; and this consent he used as a justification for levying these aids yearly on his own authority on the pretext that the convocation of the States was too heavy a burden on the 'poor common people'. The formal right of the king to levy taxes and to make peace and war without consulting the States-General was only secured by Louis XI. A last effort to recover control was made during the minority of Charles VIII in 1484. Thenceforward the control of the army and the taxes remained with the king.

The Imperial Diet, owing to the looser bond and more completely feudal character of the German kingdom, never attained any importance as a representative assembly. The period in which England and France were acquiring political consciousness was the weakest period of the empire. There was thus no struggle to wrest financial control from a strong monarchy, although meetings were held for legislative and other purposes, especially for the pacification of the warring territories. A decree of William of Holland in 1255 specifies the participation of princes, counts, and officials of the empire, and the deputies of the cities of the Rhenish league. In the fifteenth century the diet organized itself in three houses: the electors, clerical, and lay; the other princes and lords; and finally (in 1489) the cities. The concurrence of all three and the sanction of the emperor was necessary to a valid law. Moreover, no estate had the power to bind its absent members. The diet determined the contingents to be provided by the several territories, and voted taxes for extraordinary expenditure from time to time.

A nearer approach to representative institutions will be found in the provincial estates of France and the Territorial Diets of Germany. The French estates, in the fourteenth century, were the States-General in miniature. The rural communes were only represented by the towns in whose circumscription they lay. In the fifteenth, each province is split up into dioceses, or 'assiettes' in each of which the three estates settle the distribution of the burden of the taxes granted by the estates, to which each 'assiette' sends deputies. The Government dealt by preference directly with the provincial estates, whose importance, considerable in the fourteenth century, was much reduced by the successful extension of royal power affected by Charles VII.

The Territorial Diets in Germany, like the French Provincial Estates, appear to derive from the general assemblies held by the Carolingian legates, and after them by the dukes in the provinces under their rule, and to have passed through the same phase of being courts of feudal tenants. In the fourteenth and fifteenth centuries they attained considerable power by the combination of the several classes to resist taxation. The princes had not at first sovereign rights. Their authority was military and judicial, but their financial rights were limited by the feudal contract. They could only levy aids from their own personal vassals, and to extend these to the rest of the population, whose fealty belonged at first exclusively to the emperor, it was necessary to secure their consent. In exchange for this the estates obtained charters establishing their rights, or protecting them from the use of their grants as precedents. In some territories, such as Oldenburg, no diets developed, while in others, like Tyrol and Würtemberg, the peasant class obtained representation. In some there was only one house, in others three or four. The estates very commonly acted selfishly, protecting merely their own interests, but they acquired a large control over legislation and sometimes even administered the territory, or elected their ruler, or restrained him from dividing, pledging, or selling his dominions. In many cases the observance of the charters granted them was guaranteed by a stipulated right of insurrection. The power of the estates was reduced at the end of the fifteenth century by the reform of the German constitution, which by establishing perpetual peace destroyed this guarantee, and at the same time brought about the formal adoption of Roman Law, which greatly augmented the rights of the ruler.

It is usual to regard the Cortes of Castile as the nearest parallel to the English Parliament, and the fact that they retained some control not only on the raising but also on the application of the taxes as late as the sixteenth century gives them a special claim to notice. But this control was exercised only by the towns. The nobles and clergy seem to have been exempt from taxation and were only irregularly represented. Moreover the towns, in Spain as in the rest of Europe, became more and more oligarchical in constitution, and by the end of the fifteenth century only seventeen cities continued to send deputies. The lower nobility and the peasantry were unrepresented. And though Spain was longer than other countries in attaining settled government, the power of the crown became ultimately more absolute there than anywhere else.

We have attempted to sketch the nature and the limitations of the royal power in the Middle Ages without dwelling on the machinery through which it was exercised. Its application to particular cases was determined by two inconsistent principles of which the earlier is the local division of undifferentiated powers, the later the differentiation of functions. The first of these systems rests on territorial divisions, the second on the division of the functions of the king's household among his great officers. But power may be delegated without local or functional limits, either to one person, as to the Merovingian Mayor of the Palace, or to a Regent or Lieutenant of the Realm during the minority or absence of the king, or to a body of men such as a representative assembly or a permanent council.

We have already considered this last body in its origin, and as the basis of representation, but not as a permanent organ of administration. Its composition was arbitrary, since the king might, in theory at least, summon to it whom he would, and, in consequence, aristocratic or popular interference in politics most usually took the form of a demand for the exclusion or inclusion of particular counsellors. Some members of it were always in close attendance on the king. If he were away from his capital, some would be left behind to carry on the government and settle such matters as did not require the king's personal decision. Edward I was accustomed to refer points of detail to the Chancellor and Treasurer and such others as they might think fit to summon, and in the fifteenth century the same two officers

with the keeper of the Privy Seal were competent to act as
the council, though on many occasions much larger numbers
were present. A minority or a weak monarchy tends to
enlarge the council, and to make it a more definitely regulated and better-paid part of the government. As the
functions of the council grow more definite there is a tendency for the business to fall more and more into the hands
of a class of professional councillors, clerks and laymen, who
have the details of the business at their fingers' ends, and
form the link between the council and the administrative
offices. Throughout the Middle Ages the council remains
the repository of the unexhausted power of the crown, and
it is for that reason that it is able to throw off, late in the
fifteenth century, judicial institutions of an equitable kind,
such as the Star Chamber and the Court of Requests in
England, or the ' Grand Conseil ' in France, to meet cases
where, either from the power of litigants, or their lack of
civil status, or the inadequacy of the law,[1] the ordinary
courts were unable to provide a remedy. It is this undifferentiated character of the Council which enabled it to employ
torture in Tudor times, although the inquisitorial procedure
was unknown to the English common law. Moreover the
Council, both in France and England, long retained some
memory of its origin as the standing committee of the
Curia, the King's Court, whether sitting for legislative,
financial, or judicial purposes. The word ' conseil ' was
applied in France to the Parlement, which corresponded
to some extent with the Court of King's Bench, and to the
Chambre des Comptes. In England, as late as the fourteenth
century, we find the Council sitting in the King's Bench,
in the Exchequer, and in the Chancery, to strengthen the
jurisdiction of these courts. In Parliament it was of course
always present. From the fact that the Council exercised

---

[1] The equitable jurisdiction of the Chancellor has another history.

the undifferentiated royal power arose conflicts of jurisdiction, when, as in France, cases were transferred to the Council from the regular courts. For the same reason it became the natural instrument of absolute monarchy, and thus the reaction against the prerogative of the Stuarts took the form of the assertion of the common law against council jurisdiction.

The tribunals which thus found themselves in conflict had nevertheless a common origin, for the Courts of Justice, as well as the Council, trace their pedigree to the court of the king's tenants-in-chief and its Carolingian original. Thus, in England, we see the court divide into the *Curia Regis* or King's Bench, in which the king or his chief justice sits for judicial purposes, and the Exchequer, in which the same persons sit for financial or administrative purposes. From these, or more probably from the latter, is derived the permanent court sitting in a fixed place, and dealing more especially with pleas relating to land, called the Common Pleas. Each of these incarnations of the King's Court gradually acquires its own personnel and defines the limits of its jurisdiction. It is a common principle that each court has jurisdiction over its own officers, at all events in personal actions, since they cannot be spared from their duties to answer in other places the claims which may be brought against them in an age which was, for its civilization, remarkably litigious. Furthermore, by the extension of the jurisdiction of the Exchequer to all cases even remotely affecting the solvency of Crown debtors, and by the importation of the fiction of 'force and arms' into pleas which would otherwise have come before the Common Pleas, it came about that before the end of the Middle Ages these three courts were in active competition with each other and with the equitable jurisdiction of the Chancery for the same class of legal business.

The King's Bench retained some traces of its undifferentiated character, in particular a jurisdiction in Error, but its most important functions as a court of appeal passed to the extraordinary sessions of the King's Court called Parliaments, with which we have already dealt in another connexion. This jurisdiction is still exercised by the House of Lords. It is this judicial function of the Court which is most prominent in France, where the term 'Parlement' means in the first instance a court of law, although the competence of the French court was at first, according to the best authorities, as completely undifferentiated as that of the English *Curia Regis* before the separation of the Exchequer as an independent court. In France, the Parlement of Paris, retaining its nominal character as the court of the Peers of France, early became a body of professional lawyers and officials, clerical and lay, divided into three sections called respectively Parlement, Chambre des Comptes, and Conseil, according as their functions were Judicial, Financial, or Political. These bodies did not forget their common origin, and frequently sat together. Moreover, their personnel was not completely distinct. Thus the same institution which became a somewhat intermittent political assembly in England, early assumed the character in France of a permanent court of law, and in the fifteenth century broke its connexion with the States-General and became purely professional. One consequence of this early regularization was the disappearance of the Peers, who ceased to sit, except for special purposes, just as they had already vanished from the King's Bench and the Exchequer in England. But though the Parlement was essentially a judicial body, it never wholly lost its political character, but gave decisions, either alone or in conjunction with the Chambre des Comptes and Conseil, on matters of national or even international importance.

Passing from the king and his court to the undifferentiated local administration, we find it necessary to go back to a period earlier than that of the highly centralized Carolingian Empire. Of mixed origin, partly Roman and partly Frankish, these local institutions inherited older organizations and combined them into a uniform system. The normal unit of local government is the county, and the officer in charge of it, the king's representative for military, fiscal, and judicial purposes alike, is the count. The county represents sometimes the Gallo-Roman *Civitas*, sometimes the Germanic *Gau*; and the Roman *Comes*, the colleague of the bishop in the administration of his city and district, is equated with the German *Graf*. Thus the county is both the Roman provincial city-district and the German tribal subdivision. The count is distinguished by the right to a third of the profits of justice, and we find the English earl holding the same privilege under the name of the ' third penny of the county '. In the county, the bishop is supreme in spiritual matters and is the chief judge of the clergy, the count of the laity, and in the same way we find the earl and the bishop sitting in the Saxon county court. On a lower level the ancient German division of the *Gau* or *Pagus* into hundreds gave the title of hundredman or *centenarius* to a group of minor officials, whose authority, even if originally popular, was subordinate to that of the count and of the same nature.

Such is the Carolingian model : a simple devolution of powers in three tiers, the king, the count, the hundredman : but it was complicated in two ways; by the impossibility of direct control on so large a scale, and by the grant to religious or even secular persons of a privileged position with respect to the law. The latter of these complexities was an inheritance from the Merovingian period or earlier. If the bishop or an abbot was himself also the count, the scheme was only so far interfered with that the king could not appoint to the office except by virtue of his power to meddle in ecclesiastical affairs. If, however, the bishop or abbot had territory in several counties or hundreds, with jurisdiction over his tenants, a new and often discontinuous area was created which broke up the county organization. The men of this territory did not follow the count's banner to war, or receive justice in the ordinary courts, and enjoyed exemption from the taxes. The lord of the immunity was bound to make arrangements for the military, judicial, and financial administration of his district.

The feudal monarch exercised local administration only in his own demesne. Thus we find that in France, from the reign of Henry I, the local authorities are the Prévôts, or land-stewards of the king, whose ordinary duty is the management of the royal manors. The great feudatories administered their possessions in exactly the same way, though the officers might have different titles, such as Vicomte in Normandy, or Bayle or Viguier (*Vicarius*) in the south. But, in substance, local administration, except in so far as municipalities established themselves, became an appurtenance of real property. And even municipal liberties were conceived in the same way, as a class of property.

The Prévôts were supposed to be guided in their decisions by a council of four ' good men ', and their commands were executed by serjeants (*servientes*). The misdemeanours of these and of their masters led to the appointment in the twelfth century of superior officers, called ' Baillis ', with power to correct abuses and revise decisions. In the south the title was Seneschal. The great feudatories followed the example of the king. These undifferentiated officers persisted throughout the Middle Ages, but their functions were gradually transferred to others. Their judicial powers fell to professional judges of appeal, their financial duties to receivers, their military functions to Captains and Governors.

English local administration was never completely feudalized, except in Cheshire, Durham, and the Welsh Marches, although jurisdiction over the unfree tenants and in civil pleas as to the property in land was attached to landed possessions. The county remains the unit of administration, although the earl, owing to the grouping of counties in the tenth century under ' dukes ', was replaced as president of the shire-moot by the sheriff. The origin of this officer is uncertain, but from the fact that we find him primarily responsible for the farm of the king's manors in the county, it is not unnatural to suppose that he corresponds approximately to the Bailli in France in his capacity of supervisor of the Prévôt. But the Crown retained its direct control of local administration through him, and was always able to remove him for misconduct or incompetence. Like the Bailli the sheriff gradually lost some of his functions, but hardly before the end of the Middle Ages; although during that period new organizations were called into existence to perform new services which would originally have fallen to him. This control of the central government was exercised by the Exchequer, and in judicial matters by the king's courts. Abuses were from time to time remedied by special commissions, such as the Inquest of Sheriffs in 1170, which led to the replacement of most of the sheriffs by new men. While the sheriffdoms very rarely became hereditary, the hundred courts in many cases fell into religious or private possession very early, but this did not materially affect the control of the crown, though it sometimes retarded the operation of the king's writs. Only when the owners of the hundreds had the return of writs and accounted separately at the Exchequer, was the unity of the county disturbed. Besides the bailiffs of the hundreds, the sheriff had a staff of clerks, one of whom acted as receiver, and of serjeants to execute his orders. As the sheriffs remained the effective heads of local administration, though with gradually decreasing importance, it is natural that the control of their appointment should have been, like control of the Council, one of the points most frequently disputed between the crown and the successive reform parties. Election of the sheriffs is one of the claims made by the Provisions of Oxford in 1258, and was temporarily conceded by the crown on more than one subsequent occasion ; and statutes regulating their conduct are frequent in the history of Parliament.

We have followed the undifferentiated power of the king through its local subdivisions, and must now consider the organization which reflects its specific division. Here the framework is provided by the royal household of Charlemagne. It is long before any clear distinction is made between the personal and the official character of the king, and thus the national expenditure is regarded as his private expenditure in the same way that the revenues to which he has a prescriptive right are regarded as his private income. Hence the doctrine, by no means confined to England, that ' the king should live of his own '. First of the household services comes the chapel, under the *Apocrisarius*, whose deputy is the Chancellor. The combination of the duties of chaplain and secretary was due to the lack of lay education, a state of things to which the meaning of the word ' clerk ' in its ordinary acceptation is a sufficient testimony. The official status of the three Rhenish archbishops as chancellors of Germany, Italy, and Burgundy is a relic of this ecclesiastical tradition, and in most countries in Europe the nominal chancellor was often a bishop. In England the minor duties of the Chancery were long performed by the same persons as those of the chapel. The same serjeant looked after the wax for the candles and that for the seal. The Chancellor is the responsible custodian of the king's seal, and determines the form of all instruments to which it is appended. He requires, therefore, an engrossing and recording staff of clerks, and a lay staff of sealers; since it is a principle generally recognized in the Middle Ages that the persons who actually apply the seal shall not be able to read or understand the documents which they seal. Thus, for example, the Pope's leaden Bulls are attached by Cistercian lay-brothers who are *ex officio* illiterate. This division of labour between literate ' clerks ' and illiterate ' serjeants ' or ' knights ' is constantly met with in the medieval Civil Service. The clerical staff of the Chancery soon splits up into two classes, draftsmen and copyists, and a collection of standard formulae is devised, a *Liber Diurnus* or a *Registrum Omnium Brevium*, to meet the needs of everyday administrative and judicial business. The power to vary these standard forms is limited to the highest class of clerks, who are styled ' notaries ' or ' masters ', and they, in default of special instructions from the king or the Chancellor, are governed by precedent. A ' style of the chancery ' is developed, and orders received from the king are made to conform to this style unless they contain special instructions that it shall be disregarded. Hence arises a kind of administrative jurisdiction, since it rests with the Chancery to determine whether the letters which are desired are or are not admissible in form, and whether or not they infringe rights or privileges already granted to third parties. In England in the thirteenth century the Chancery acquired also an equitable jurisdiction, due in all probability to the Chancellor's close association with the Council, of which, in its primitive form, he was the secretary. The provision of new legal or administrative forms to remedy grievances was a duty of the Council, which sat in the Chancery for such a purpose, and in course of time the Chancellor seems to have inherited a share of this jurisdiction. The Chancellor, as custodian of the seal, was originally necessary in all departments where the use of the seal was necessary, and his deputy in the Exchequer is still one of the English ministers of state. But in England, though not in France, this deputy early escaped from the position of dependence and acquired complete control of what was at first a duplicate Great Seal and afterwards developed into the distinct Great Seal of the Exchequer. Again, as the business of the seal increases, it became less and less possible for the Chancellor to be in constant close attendance on the king, and warrants for the use of the Great Seal are sent to the Chancellor authenticated by a smaller seal, or even by the king's signet ring. This smaller or Privy Seal, originally kept by the king or by a member of his immediate household, may in turn go 'out of court', as in England, and become a separate department of state with rules and traditions of its own, its place being taken by a smaller seal or signet. There is a natural tendency for diplomatic and secret correspondence to fall into the hands of the custodian of the seal or signet most nearly attached to the king ; by the thirteenth century we find him called the king's secretary, and his importance rapidly increases towards the end of the Middle Ages ; by the eighteenth century he has become the Secretary of State. But while, in England, each of these smaller seals grows into an independent department, in France all the holders of these seals are grouped together into a college under the control of the chancellor, the seals being appropriated to distinct classes of business, whereas in England they were often merely links in the same process.

The chief lay officer of the Carolingian household is the Count Palatine, who stands in the king's place as judge, and exerts both an equitable jurisdiction and a jurisdiction in appeal from the courts of the local counts. It is probable that a number of these served in rotation, just as we find certain officers doing in the twelfth century in the household of Henry I of England. The Count Palatine of the Empire seems to have disappeared early in the eleventh century though provincial counts palatine remained, and we find the same name for certain judges of the Papal court. But the institution of a chief officer of justice persists. In Germany it attaches itself to the Steward, who was also Count Palatine of the Rhine, and was alone competent to judge the princes of the Empire and even the Emperor himself. In England in the twelfth and thirteenth centuries we find a Justiciar whose powers are almost as extensive as the king's, although subordinate. This office is represented by the Lord Chief Justice and the judges of the High Court. In France there seems to have been no Chief Justice, and the powers of the Count Palatine seem to have been inherited by the Peers of France, and by the corps of professional judges who sat in the Parlement. Aragon had a single justice, Castile a college.

While the extent to which the king's judges can interfere with the local jurisdictions, either by receiving appeals or by direct supervision, depends, as we have already said, on the extent to which the constitution has been feudalized, England is exceptional in the success which attended the efforts of the crown to get the substantial administration of justice into its own hands, by the institution first of the Eyre and afterwards of the Assize system. In the fourteenth century the appointment of local commissions for minor criminal work, under the title of Justices of the Peace and Justices of Labourers, and the establishment of Quarter Sessions, brought the whole of the local administration in public matters directly under the control of the Council, without taking away its local character by imposing an administrator from outside. In Germany, on the other hand, although the Emperor retained a jurisdiction in appeal which developed in 1495 into a national Kammergericht in which both the Emperor and the Estates were represented, the jurisdiction in first instance was completely territorialized. The Emperor was until the fourteenth century the sole source of the right of life and death, and the Count, though appointed by the territorial ruler, had to obtain the 'Blutbann' from him. But his direct administration of justice only survived in the very exceptional institution known as the Westphalian 'Fehmgericht', with its 'Free Counts' and 'Free Schöffen'.

The financial administration of the Carolingian kingdom lies in the department of the Chamberlain, whose function it is to receive the 'gifts' brought to the king at the periods of the national assemblies and to store them in the palace. These gifts formed a considerable portion of the royal revenue, and we find them again in England under Henry II, and possibly in the 'Bede' which the German princes levied on their subjects. The office was regarded as purely domestic, and the Chamberlain was under the orders of the queen and jointly responsible with her for the economy of the household. In the Capetian monarchy the Great Chamberlain is a person of too great dignity to be concerned in actual administration, and is replaced by another officer of lower rank and a slightly different title who performs the duties of Treasurer. This functionary gradually loses his importance and becomes a mere Treasurer of the household, while the treasure is placed in the keeping of the Templars, and is administered by a section of the Parlement, already mentioned as the 'Chambre des Comptes'. After the fall of the Templars, three or four treasurers were appointed under the control of the Chambre des Comptes, but they were exclusively concerned with the receipt and issue of money, not with financial administration.

In England, owing to the fortunate accident that we have a treatise on the Exchequer in the reign of Henry II, the progress of financial development is somewhat less obscure. We can draw a clear line between the Treasury staff, which derives from the Carolingian Chamberlain, and the Court of Exchequer, which approximates to the Chambre des Comptes. The Chamberlains of the Exchequer have already lost any connexion with the Chamberlain of the Household, and have acquired a clerical colleague, the Treasurer. These are jointly responsible for the receipt and issue of money, and for testing its goodness. We gather too that the earliest phase of national finance was based on a primitive system of tribute in kind, derived from the royal manors and gradually exchanged for a money system. The necessity of testing the fineness of the money brings this machinery into close connexion with the supervision of the local moneyers. At a later date, when a central mint is established, we find a close connexion between its operations and those of the treasury, since the king will frequently send to the mint for money or specie, and such expenses must be credited to the keeper of the mint as payments into the treasury, or their equivalent. Even in the twelfth century this treasury organization has lost its connexion with the royal household, in which its place is taken by a privy purse, or *Camera Curie*, in whose coffers are kept not only the king's private store of money, but his jewels, furs, and precious wearing apparel. This also, as we shall see, in time becomes departmentalized: just what happened in the case of the Great and the Privy Seals.

The Exchequer is primarily a special sitting of the King's Court for financial purposes, and while it is sitting, the Treasury staff acts as a part of it, and is known as the Exchequer of Receipt or Lower Exchequer. The Court itself, or Upper Exchequer, consists of the great officers of

K k

state and other barons, and hears the accounts of the sheriffs and other accountants. In process of time the great officers, except the treasurer, only appear by deputy, and the Court assumes a professional character and a continuous existence. Its legal aspect has already been explained. Administratively it supervised the collection of revenue by the sheriffs, and its expenditure by the various spending departments, including the departmentalized 'Wardrobe', which grew up from the *Camera Curie* in the king's household.

The finances of a medieval king were more like those of a private noble than of a modern state. He was himself a great landowner, and in a feudal society it would have been difficult for him to maintain his position without large private estates. The weakness of the German Empire in the fourteenth and fifteenth centuries was largely due to the fact that the imperial domain had been almost entirely alienated. In the early stages of economic development, when money was scarce, and the produce of the royal farms had to be taken in kind, it was almost impossible for the Court to be stationary; and although royal progresses enabled the king to exercise more perfect political and judicial control, it is probable that originally they were due to the necessity of consuming the fruits of the earth near the place which produced them. Thus we find manors in Domesday Book which owed the service of entertaining the king for one or more nights, a service which had been commuted for a money rent, while the Dialogue of the Exchequer tells of a time when these money rents, though estimated in money, were still collected in kind at a fixed rate of commutation. Closely allied with the rent of land were the profits of justice, since the local hundred court tended to be attached to a particular manor and regarded as a part of its profits, and alienable with it. The king, as the principal patron of the Church, could add to his revenue the fruits of ecclesiastical property during the vacancy of sees or abbeys, while to him as feudal superior fell the possessions of tenants in chief dying without heirs. In Germany this latter source of wealth was restricted by a provision enforced by the princes of the empire that such lands must be regranted within a year and a day. He had reliefs on the succession of the heirs, and the custody of wards during their minority. Special officers, called ' escheators ' were appointed in England to administer lands falling into the king's hands in this way. Aids might likewise be demanded of feudal tenants for the ransoming of the king's person, the knighting of his eldest son, and the marriage of his eldest daughter. These feudal rights were not peculiar to the king, but were enjoyed by all lords over their tenants holding by knight-service. Specially royal rights were compositions for military service, for fortification, and for the repair of roads and bridges, and certain tolls, customs, and port dues. The royal rights to gold and silver mines and to salt are less universal, and appear only to have been recognized in Germany in the eleventh and twelfth centuries respectively. In France the salt-tax was no part of the king's ordinary revenue, and we hear little of it in England. Forest-rights also do not seem to be original. The right of coinage was a general and lucrative source of revenue, whether the king established local moneyers on whom he levied dues in exchange for their privilege, or set up a central mint and charged a seigniorage in addition to the cost of coining. The practice of debasement was neither so common nor so lucrative a financial expedient as the charges of the chroniclers would lead us to suppose. The sale of privileges, the profits of the central courts, and the fees of the seal complete the ordinary sources of the royal revenue, within which, in times of peace, the king was expected to live.

For extraordinary needs the king might from time to time levy a tax or tallage on his unfree tenants or on the men of the towns on his domain, or on the Jews, who were in his land on sufferance and regarded as his chattels. Beyond this limit it seems to have been generally held that he could not lawfully go without the consent of his subjects, and the necessity of showing some urgent cause such as the defence of the realm. Taxes thus granted might, and sometimes were, levied by special machinery. They gave rise in France to a special court, the Cour des Aides, which was called into existence by the States-General to regulate the assessment of the taxes and to secure their application to the objects for which they were granted. This precocious development was the result of the misfortunes of the war with England, where the same object was only attained by slow parliamentary pressure long after the close of the Middle Ages, when the French institution had fallen into decay. The taxes granted were of various kinds, tallages or taxes on chattels, land-taxes such as danegeld, hidage, or carucage, and such taxes as export duties, poll-taxes, or temporary monopolies. The growth of absolutism is most clearly indicated by two things which have an intimate connexion : the perpetuation of taxes originally temporary, and the maintenance of a standing army out of the proceeds.

The connexion which subsists between the medieval army and the household offices of the Constable and Marshal does not go back to Carolingian times. The territorial army, of which we have already spoken, was led by the king himself or by a son or trusted servant. Even under the earlier French kings it is the Steward who commands the host. The local contingent was led by the count, who commanded not only the free men of his county but also the men of the immunities in it, though they came to his banner under the conduct of their own lord or his deputy. The cavalry of the Carolingian army was provided by the holders of *beneficia*, whose service with their horses was the price of their life-estates, soon to become hereditary fiefs. In a period of imperfect economic organization the grant of lands was the only means of maintaining a mercenary force of cavalry to meet the danger of Saracens, Normans, or Huns. It is to the predominance of mounted service in the tenth century and later that the Constable and the Marshal, the officers of the royal stable, owe their position as leaders of the feudal host, which is henceforward the mainstay of the army. At the same time there develops a definite military class, supported by landed possessions, and bound to each other by a semi-religious organization which differs little, if at all from a trade guild, and recognizes the same degrees of apprentice or esquire, journeyman or 'bachelor', and master or 'banneret'. Although knighthood in the later Middle Ages seems more a status than a profession, the class was not, at any rate at first, limited to those who were technically free. The feudal host may then be regarded as consisting of little groups of knights serving for forty days at a time under the leadership of the lords from whom they held their lands. Such an army was of little use for protracted operations, since its period of service was so short, and if a knight refused to serve it was difficult in practice to deprive him of his lands. Thus we find the English kings exacting a composition fee equivalent to the wages of a substitute for the obligatory period (Scutage), and a pecuniary fine for the offence of refusing to come without excuse. The mustering of the host is the duty of the Constable and the Marshal, and scutage is levied according to their certificate of attendance. Those who have done their service are entitled to the scutage of their own tenants. The national army, though

existing mainly for defensive purposes, is not superseded.
We find ordinances such as the assize of arms enforcing the
possession by every man of the weapons and armour appropriate to his means. Closely allied to this is the not uncommon rule that all who have land of more than a certain
value must accept knighthood, a regulation which was
enforced in England on several occasions in the thirteenth
and fourteenth centuries. Moreover, the right of the
crown to summon its subjects for national defence is nowhere
completely set aside by the feudal contract. Even in
Germany the Tocsin might be sounded and the whole
population called to arms as the ' Landfolge '; while in
France the king could summon the Arrière-Ban, or in
England bid the sheriff raise the men of his county, or
appoint commissioners of Array to select a proportion of
them. But, in the fourteenth century, both the feudal host
and the national army were found insufficient, and war was
more and more conducted by paid troops, raised by professional captains in accordance with a definite contract,
the beginning of the system under which the modern
regiment is nominally raised and paid by its colonel. The
immediate result of the system was the creation of hordes
of mercenaries, the ' Companies ', whose allegiance to any
particular employer was precarious and who were recruited
very largely by throwing open the prisons. The standing
army of a medieval king, which formed a nucleus for these
temporary troops, consisted of the knights and serjeants of
his household, who were in constant attendance on his
person. These provided officers for the expeditionary force.
In like manner the clerks of his household, who normally
kept its accounts and made its contracts for food and
necessaries, undertook the duties of the commissariat and
the pay-chest. We find the same linking together of clerical
and lay elements which we have already noted in the

Treasury, and which corresponds with the general system of dual control of which we find constant examples. The navy of the Middle Ages was less organized than the army, except in cases such as that of the Knights of St. John, where it was the main weapon of offence. The usual plan was to call upon seaport towns for the loan of one or more ships, or to impress merchant ships found in the various ports for a limited period. Soldiers were shipped on board these vessels for special expeditions. The requisitioning of ships fell, like the commissariat of the army, within the sphere of the king's clerks. When Richard I set out for Palestine he took the exceptional course of purchasing a half-share in each of the ships engaged for the expedition. All ships were armed, and piracy was normal, redress being mainly obtained by reprisals on other ships or merchants of the same nationality. The orthodox method of procedure was for the injured party to obtain ' Letters of Request ' from his ruler addressed to the head of the State to which the offenders belonged, or to the chief officer of their town. If, as usual, no redress was obtained, ' march-law ' was invoked, and any subjects of the State involved might be ' marked ' or subjected to acts of reprisal. The formal issue of ' Letters of Marque ' belongs to the period when international law was becoming generally recognized.

With the remaining offices of the household, those of the Steward and the Butler, the administrative system has little to do. We have alluded to the exercise by the Steward of the functions of Justiciar, and of leader of the host. His place was taken in the household of later times by a person of less dignity, who was the lay head of the actual establishment. Here also, as we have indicated in speaking of the army, we find divided lay and clerical control. The clerical head of the household is its treasurer, and each of the offices has a clerk or clerks to keep its accounts, as well as yeomen to perform the services. The main officers form a household council, in England the 'Board of Green Cloth', and the principal lay officers, the Steward and the Marshal, have jurisdiction over the servants of the household and persons who bring claims against them.

So rapid a survey as this of the functions of the king, with their constitutional limitations, and of the machinery which linked the head of the State with the humblest subject, must necessarily be chiefly remarkable for its omissions. It is bound to appear simpler and more consistent than it ever was in reality. Conditions were not the same in different countries, and even in England, where the monarchy was on the whole strong, justice and police, especially in small matters, were largely in private hands. We have not attempted to indicate in detail how this came about, but have leaned to the theory that these rights were devolutions of royal power, rather than appurtenances of the soil, and we have left unsolved the question to what extent they are to be regarded as survivals of local community jurisdiction. But if such a partial and imperfect survey of one side of medieval society is of little positive service to scientific history, it may perhaps have its value in directing the attention of the student to a field in which there is much to be learned and unending exercise for a mind which delights in comparison and construction.

CHARLES JOHNSON.

10

POLITICAL THOUGHT

NO longer regarded as a philosophical *détour* between Aristotle and Machiavelli, the political thought of the Middle Ages speaks to a steadily widening circle of inquirers. There are the historically-minded who would discover there the principles that guided the Papal monarchy in its assumption of the imperial heritage of Rome ; students of modern diplomacy in search of precedents for international action in the cause of peace; liberal thinkers who see in the medieval demarcation of the spiritual and temporal spheres an early answer to the old question of the limits of State sovereignty over the conscience of the citizen ; jurists and social scientists who, following in the steps of Gierke and Maitland, are pondering in the light of the group-theories of the twelfth to fifteenth centuries the problem of the rights of associations within the State ; and, to speak more generally, many thoughtful persons who reject the view that the State should be all-inclusive and all-absorbing, and would seek in the social process at large the enlightenment and liberation from narrow and selfish interests, the enlargement of personality previously held to be within the sphere of the Great Leviathan. To them the medieval notion of society as a unity and as organic, however decisively they may reject its theological basis, makes on other grounds an appeal which cannot be neglected. Some of these aspects of medieval thought we shall try to consider in these pages.

When at the outset we ask ourselves if the Middle Ages had any conception of the State that approximates to ours, we are met by a difficulty. Theory, especially medieval

theory, studied apart from institutions is not always the
best of guides. If we read only the philosophers, for whom
politics were a branch of theology, we shall probably come
to the conclusion that no conception of the State or of
sovereignty as we know it to-day existed in the Middle
Ages. *Regnum* and *respublica* come nearest to our use
of the former term, yet the notion of public authority
exercised more or less uniformly in the public interest
over a definite territorial area seems lacking. When, for
instance, John of Salisbury in his *Policraticus* (1159–61)
makes the point that *respublica* is a *corpus* or body, we
cannot be quite certain that he does not mean society as
a whole instead of the English kingdom to which he seems
in other passages to be alluding. The terminology which
the medieval theorists use is drawn from the early Christian
Fathers, from Roman Law, or from Latin writers of the
imperial age, that is from contexts and periods of a *ius
commune*, when national monarchies were not thought of.
Furthermore, the writers have deserted the good Aristotelian method of observation and comparative study, are
not in the least concerned with constitutions or systems of
administration, but very frequently are debating the relations between two sets of authorities, the spiritual and
temporal, with arguments so highly metaphorical as to be
almost childish. But the vagueness of their terminology
and the remoteness of their arguments must not lead us to
think that no conception of the State existed in the central
period of the Middle Ages; no more, when we view the
universal prevalence of feudal tenures and feudal notions in
thirteenth-century Europe, should we be wholly justified
in saying that *ex hypothesi* these were different estates, not
different states—that the medieval lines of division were
horizontal rather than vertical. The classical example of
such a generalization is Germany from the ninth to the

thirteenth century. It was stoutly maintained that there, if anywhere, government was largely private property, legislation bore the nature of a private grant; the only ' political ' organizations were the Free Associations (*Genossenschaften*, the guilds and towns), kingship was a patrimonial lordship, public and private law were inextricably confused. Where such conditions existed surely men had no notion of the State. Then came the historian and quietly showed that a distinction between political and feudal elements there did in fact exist and was made by contemporaries : the study of imperial taxation, of the *regalia* and of the system of immunities proved that feudalism was not all-pervading, that the attributes of the State must not be confined to the Free Associations, and that before the fourteenth and fifteenth centuries, the period of separatism, we can legitimately speak of a German State and proclaim the existence of a constitution based on public law administered for the *communis utilitas* or in the public interest.[1] So far can history correct verdicts drawn from theory alone.

Now medieval public law is the ordaining and administration of the king as guardian of the common weal and as purveyor of justice. To medieval thinkers the State is the sphere of the monarch in his dual capacity of protector and magistrate. This, rather than territorial integrity, is its essence. The king is, it is true, the feudal suzerain of his kingdom, first among his tenants-in-chief, perhaps indeed a vassal of some other monarch ; but he is also its political sovereign with rights and duties that lie wholly outside the

---

[1] G. von Below in his remarkable book, *Der Deutsche Staat des Mittelalters*, Bd. I (1925), pp. 1–111, gives a summary of the change in thought wrought by the detailed study of administration and insists on the importance of recognizing the distinction drawn between public and private law in the Middle Ages.

feudal orbit. In the coronation oath English kings make
the threefold promise of peace, justice, and equity to all
their subjects : they are, as the old phrase has it, ' debtors
to all and sundry to do justice,' and, as M. Viollet has said
of the Capetian monarchs, their essential function is that
of judge. That does not mean to imply that there are not
other forms of justice beside the king's, or that the relations
of seignorial courts to the king's court are not a matter of
careful regulation in customary law : for in France it is true,
as Beaumanoir remarked, that every baron is a sovereign
in his barony ; but it does mean that even there in the last
resort, when the common profit of the kingdom is concerned,
royal justice will be put into operation, local immunities
notwithstanding. Royal institutions, Chancery, Exchequer,
and Judicature, though concerned with the king's domanial
and feudal rights and revenues, are yet more than private
institutions : they are expressions of his sovereignty.
Nevertheless that sovereignty has not the uniform extension
and effectiveness of modern public authority. It might
and did vary from year to year with the personal character
of the monarch, the course of his relations with the Church
and with his feudatories, the tenacity and inventiveness of
his administrators, and many other factors. In the Norman
kingdoms that sovereign power is admitted and obeyed.
In the Latin principalities in the near East it scarcely raises
its head at all. We can admit therefore of no further
generalization than that to the medieval Englishman or
Frenchman the state is *rex*, to the medieval German—at
any rate before the fourteenth century—*imperator*. It is
a personal conception, however much men may hold the
king to be under the law or bound not to legislate without
the advice of his Council.

But existing side by side with the king and the sphere of
his personality, the State, is the great international com-

munity that knows neither the anxieties of the royal succession nor the fluctuations of baronial allegiance. The first duty of the monarch is to protect the Church of God : that task specified in the first article of the Great Charter is incumbent on him at all times. Throughout the Middle Ages it would have been hard to find any one who was not convinced that human affairs were divided into two great categories, the spiritual and the temporal—and that society had an other-worldly purpose, a divine end which could only be served if the things belonging to the *regimen animarum*—the guidance of souls—were directed by the society and leader commissioned by the Captain of Salvation. The demarcation of these spheres and in particular the claim of the Church to the guardianship of conscience and morality is an early assertion of the independence of the spiritual life. Its importance for the growth of modern conceptions of liberty is unquestionable. Let us look at this assertion in its primary stages.

As long as the Church in the Roman Empire was an illicit and persecuted body the question of its relation to the imperial authorities could scarcely arise. But when Christianity became the official religion of the Empire and citizenship equivalent to churchmanship, the Church's comprehensiveness and her attitude to the secular authority raised difficult questions. Conversion had been quick : at the beginning of the fifth century the Church contained masses of ignorant people whom, as Mgr. Duchesne has said, ' the water of Baptism had touched, but the spirit of the Gospel had not penetrated '. Should the Church, the holy and immaculate, maintain within herself the worldly, admit them to give or to receive the Sacraments ? And should she rely upon imperial force to coerce doubting and protesting provincials to receive her nominees ? ' Quid Christianis cum regibus ? Aut quid episcopis cum palatio ? '

Petilian had asked. The question raised by the Donatists, who, following the old Christian attitude of the period of persecution, regarded the State as a profane and diabolical institution, struck deep. The problem was to arise, no less disquietingly, in the next three centuries, when the barbarians came crowding into the Empire, and their kings after conversion and baptism used the sole force that made for unity and peace, the Church and churchmen, to aid them in administering their kingdoms. The pessimist and the mystic might evade the issue and seek the cloister; but the secular Church had to mark out its sphere and assert both its connexion with, and its independence of, civil government.

For their answer to the problem in its early form the Fathers turned to the commonplaces of the Roman lawyers and the Stoic philosophy: the freedom and equality of human nature and the contrast between nature and convention. In the primitive and innocent conditions of human life men obeyed the law of nature, principles recognized as universally reasonable and valid, in conditions of brotherhood and equality. The natural was not merely the primitive; it was also the real and the permanent, subsisting beneath change and convention, the ultimately reasonable. The institutions of society were not natural, but conventional; the State with its coercive control of man by man and its institutions of private property and slavery was conventional, conditioned by the Fall and man's loss of innocence, which made necessary a power that would control human appetites and desires. As such it is an institution for remedying and correcting human weakness, not, as Aristotle regarded it, the indispensable means to the good life. Yet given the fact of sin, coercive government is none the less a divinely ordained remedy; justice is the basis, the directing aim of the State, and obedience must be rendered to the powers that be. Gregory the Great would go so far as to maintain that the ruler must not in any circumstances be resisted ; but as a general rule, to quote Dr. A. J. Carlyle's words, ' the Fathers tend to think of the principle of justice as of something which lies outside the power of the civil authority—something which it does not create and to which it is in some measure answerable '. This principle comes by degrees to be regarded as finding expression in the ecclesiastical order ; the Church has its own rules, its own authority independent of the civil power though closely related to it. This attitude is illustrated by the life and the writings of St. Ambrose of Milan († 397). In his letters to the Emperor Theodosius he expresses the view that in religious matters the civil magistrate has no authority over ecclesiastics ; and that, in regard to property, things that are *divina*, consecrated and used by the Church, are not subject to the imperial power. The notion that the Church has an independent position of her own is greatly developed by Pope Gelasius († 496), whose definition of the two spheres became authoritative : in Christian society, he held, the spiritual and temporal powers were entrusted to two authorities, each holding from God, each supreme in its own sphere, each dependent on the other. The division, Gelasius must have known, could not be complete, yet the superiority of the one over the other had not yet been raised. The ninth-century writers Jonas of Orleans († 843) and Hincmar of Rheims († 882) developed the Gelasian view. They maintained that the secular and spiritual powers were both within the Church ; that it was to some extent the duty of the priest to see that the secular ruler did his duty ; and that as in the ceremony of anointing the king the dignity of the consecrator is greater than that of the consecrated, so the dignity of the priest is greater than that of the prince. With the foundation of the Holy Empire it became increasingly difficult to maintain the dualism, in proportion as people saw more and more clearly in daily life the inter-connexion of the two spheres. But till the eleventh century political circumstances which might raise the question of superiority and inferiority in an acute form were still lacking.

Yet the man who did more to accustom Christian thinkers of the West to look beyond the state for justice was a figure belonging almost to classical antiquity—an African with the fierce extremes of the desert in his soul. Politically, St. Augustine stands apart from, yet dominates the patristic age. In the great sea of his thought there are things that stirred Luther and Calvin as well as the most orthodox breasts. The *De Civitate Dei*, profound composite master-piece of varying aims and occasions, the register of never-ceasing religious experience, maintains no one clear doctrine of Church and kingdom : yet its vogue and its importance in later medieval thought cannot be over-estimated ; they were primarily due to two cardinal ideas. First, that justice is not the *ratio*, not the basis of the State. Cicero made Scipio define a republic as *res populi*, and *populus* as ' a body of men united by their agreement about what is just and their participation in what is profitable ' ; Augus-tine defines *populus* as ' a body of rational persons united by harmonious participation in the things it likes '. The State may be permeated by justice, but justice is not of its essence. Secondly, that there are two cities ' confused together in this world, but distinct in the other '—the City of God and the City of men. These two interwoven Societies (for that is what Augustine probably meant) are begotten by two loves, the love of God and the love of self apart from God. Shall we then identify them with Church and State ? Sometimes Augustine will let us, more often he will not. All we can say is that Augustine thought of the *Civitas Dei* as the spiritual association, whether here or in the hereafter, of persons whose minds and lives were directed towards God, a mystic *communio sanctorum*; and of the *Civitas terrena* as the residuum of all who did not acknowledge the predominance of the spiritual motive in their lives, a *communio improborum*. Later generations, who used the great work in apology or polemic, did not hesitate to see in the Church on earth a part of the Divine Society, having its own rules, structure, and catholic organization; and to this view Augustine's own doctrine of the sacraments, his whole construction of the foundations of other Christian dogma, had perhaps already made the greatest contribution. Through him, more than through any other, the Church came to regard herself as a great organized body holding out to man the *scala perfectionis* by which he could ascend from the Babylon of worldly existence to the Heavenly Jerusalem. Augustine's spirit lives in Abelard's famous lines:

> Nostrum est interim mentes erigere,
> Et totis patriam votis appetere,
> Et ad Ierusalem a Babylonia
> Post longa regredi tandem exilia.[1]

The autonomy of the religious life is preserved by the autonomy of the society entrusted with its care. What then if the society, conscious of the predominant importance of the soul's health, claims for its ordained ministers not

[1] Otto of Freising shows in his *Historia de duabus civitatibus* (ed. Hofmeister), p. 9, how deeply St. Augustine's idea had sunk into men's minds: ' Proinde quia temporum mutabilitas stare non potest, ab ea migrare, ut dixi, sapientem ad stantem et permanentem eternitatis civitatem debere quis sani capitis negabit ? . . . Cum enim duae sint civitates, una temporalis, alia eterna, una mundialis, alia caelestis, una diaboli, alia Christi, Babyloniam hanc, Hierusalem illam esse Katholici prodidere scriptores.'

only freedom from contact with the world, but complete
subordination to its primate? Could the relations between
the spiritual and temporal authorities remain the same?
The tendency of the reform inseparably connected with
Hildebrand was to unify, centralize, and withdraw from the
old vague compromise with the State the *clericalis ordo.*
The Church must have her own jurisprudence, her own
jurisdiction that set the Vicar of Christ where the Roman
Emperor had been. The codifying of her canons and
decretals, the strenuous fight for free election and the
chastity and integrity of her officials, the rigid control over
the episcopate were to be the chief weapons of her campaign. However we may estimate Hildebrand's success
it is unquestionable that he aroused a new consciousness of
community throughout the church. But on the other side
national monarchies were steadily realizing themselves in
the eleventh and early twelfth centuries. Law and efficient
systems of royal administration were forging them into
states. The Norman and Capetian monarchs, the Saxon
and Salian emperors had what we may term a secular policy,
developed in their subjects a sense of the common weal and
taught them to look to the dynasty for justice and peace.
Inevitably the early dualist theory of Church and State
had to undergo change. One or other of the authorities
will claim to be the sole source of power : the two swords,
spiritual and temporal, a single hand will attempt to grasp.

The great outburst of pamphleteering in the Investiture-
struggle, in its origin the result of the attempt to apply
reforming ideas to the German system of private churches
and patronage exercised in political interests, does not
provide instances of the claim of either power to sole predominance. It is not the *regnum* but the *rex iniustus* whom
Gregory VII is seeking to suppress. Much has been made
of the depreciation of the State in his famous letter to

Hermann of Metz, in which he expressed the view that kings and rulers took their origin from those who in ' ignorance of God had at the devil's prompting used every kind of malice, perfidy and crime to dominate their fellow men ', and that the power of the humblest exorcist, ' a spiritual emperor for driving out evil spirits', was greater than that given to any lay persons for the sake of temporal rule. Yet these strong expressions and the many instances in which he opposes *iustitia* (for which, as he said, he was dying in exile) to the *superbia* of the Emperor constitute no attempt to assert the theoretical supremacy of *sacerdotium* over *regnum*, nor denial that the temporal power has its coercive task in the world to fulfil. Even the strongest reformer of the period would concede to secular princes a measure of influence in episcopal elections, and imperialist writers admit that lay investiture carried nothing more than the temporalities of the see. The partisans of *regnum* and *sacerdotium* might claim superiority for their respective sides : they did not as yet claim omnicompetence for either of them.

Yet Gregory's conception of ' Justice '—which seems to have meant for him unswerving devotion to the interests of clerical reform—was more far-reaching than he knew. To later generations there could be no mistaking the tendency of its deeper implication, the superiority of divinely directed mind over material force and opportunism, as soon as it was coupled with the notion that the other-worldly end of man must determine the organization by which human society is directed. By the middle of the twelfth century many people were beginning to conclude that theoretically there was one authority alone supreme in Christendom. The metaphor of the two swords was used both by John of Salisbury and Honorius of Augsburg to advance the view that all authority, ecclesiastical or secular, belongs to the spiritual power. John declared that it is from the Church that the prince received the material sword, since both weapons were originally hers. The material sword the prince wields for her use and advantage, and is consequently her minister. Practical considerations—the development of the Canon Law with its emphasis upon the Pope's plenitude of power, the definition of sacramental doctrine, and, not least, the growth of the temporal possessions of the Papacy—indicated the same conclusion. It was crowned by the scholastic philosophy which saw in every particular being in the universal whole the energy of a common transcendental aim to which it was the object of the Church to minister. The Papacy sought to bring under its direction the whole of human activity, learning, and education through the universities which were its organs, trade, and commerce through the enforcement of just prices and the prohibition of interest. The theocracy which it aimed at has been well termed by Dr. Ernest Barker ' a fusion of the actual Church, reformed by papal direction and governed by papal control with actual lay society similarly reformed and similarly governed '. That fusion was to be achieved, not so much (if we may invent two expressions) by de-laicizing the Church—the Hildebrandine policy—as by clericalizing the world. A single mentality was to be engendered, the orientation of every faculty towards God, the complete recognition of a transcendental purpose in life. The greatest of the means to that end was the sacraments, in particular the Mass, the service in which the believer was brought into contact with God by receiving at the hands of the priest His very body and blood. Only the sacrament of penance could secure admission to the supreme festival, and penance was made dependent on periodical confession of sin to a priest. Confession the Lateran Council of 1215 made obligatory upon all the faithful at least once a year. As the complement to this the judgement of sin was both claimed and exercised as a matter of course. 'No one of sane mind is ignorant that it pertains to our office to snatch every Christian from mortal sin; and if he despise correction then to coerce him by ecclesiastical censure' wrote Innocent III to Philip Augustus, and the letter with its famous vindication passed into the Church's law.[1] From that time onwards the Papacy does not look back; astounding to many to-day, yet logically justifiable in the view of Church politicians of his time, came in the end Boniface VIII's declaration that belief in the subjection of every human creature to the supreme Pontiff was necessary to salvation.

The claim was of tremendous consequence. It lies at the root of ultramontane doctrine. At the time it provoked the fierce reaction out of which, as we shall see, later political theory was born. If we are to understand that revolt at all, the presuppositions and the method of argument adopted by medieval thinkers deserve attention: it is here that the powerful influence of the Thomist philosophy described in a previous chapter will be most clearly apparent.

In the first place the universe is regarded as a single whole, mankind as a single society. Every being, whether an individual or a joint-being (i. e. a community), is an integral part, an organic member of the whole; its action is determined by the final cause of the universe; but at the same time it is also a whole in itself, a diminished copy or microcosm of the larger world, the macrocosm. Thus the unified world is not sharply unified; it is a community made

---

[1] *Decretal.*, Gregor. IX, Lib. II, Tit. I, *De Iudiciis*, c. xiii, where also occurs the famous sentence: ' non enim intendimus iudicare de feudo, cuius ad ipsum (regem) spectat iudicium, sed decernere de peccato, cuius ad nos pertinet sine dubitatione censura.'

up of communities, articulated and organized in the most
diverse fashion, each of value to the whole, each essential
to the larger existence. In the second place God is the
monarch of this single realm ; all earthly lordship is, to
quote the words of Gierke, 'a limited representation of the
divine Lordship of the world' : hence the medieval preference for monarchy, both in large and in small units. There
was another reason connected with the idea of representation : the unity in society must find representation in
a governing part, and this can best be realized if the governing element is a unit, and so a single individual. Dante
went farther and deeper in his argument that what unites
bodies politic is will, and that to secure a 'unity in wills'
the governing will of one single person is the best means.
Thirdly, the character of the supreme directing authority of
the whole society depends upon the purpose for which society
exists, and this, it is generally assumed, is the same as the end
of each of its component individuals. Here we meet the point
of division between imperialist and papalist. St. Thomas
Aquinas in his *De Regimine Principum* argues that 'the natural
end of a people formed into a society is to live virtuously ; for
the end of any society is the same as that of the individuals
composing it. But, since the virtuous man is also determined
to a further end, the purpose of society is not merely that
man should live virtuously, but that by virtue he should
come to the enjoyment of God'. If men could attain this
end by natural capacities alone, it would be the duty of the
king to direct them to it : but the fruition of God—that is
union with Him in the Beatific Vision, is not the result of
human direction ; it belongs to Divine Government, the
government of Jesus Christ. 'The administration of this
Kingdom has been committed, not to the Kings of this
world, but to priests, in order that the spiritual should be
distinct from the temporal' ; and so to the Supreme

Pontiff, the representative of Christ, ' to whom all the kings of Christian people should be subject as to our Lord Jesus Christ Himself.' Here the argument is that those who have the care of proximate ends should be governed by the power whose business is to lead men to their ultimate end. Dante, on the other hand, stops short at the immediate end. For him the aim of society is the *vita felice*, the happy life, which is to be attained, as he says, by ' actualizing the potential intellect ' : bringing into play the whole capability of the mind. This can only be accomplished in an atmosphere of peace, whose requisite condition is unity in society, and unity only achieved by the universal empire of a single monarch, who will unite divergent wills of local rulers. That monarch, as the long argument in the *De Monarchia* shows, is the present-day successor of the emperors of Rome.

All truly medieval argument rests upon the premiss of unity. There can be no fundamental change in the method of thought until men have ceased to connect politics with Platonic speculations on the One and the Many, or to hold that a transcendental purpose in life determines the form and extent of political authority. It is when earthly and localized needs are recognized as the determining factors that the great synthesis begins to totter. That recognition began in the protests of secular sovereignty against Papal domination. The publicists like Pierre du Bois, John of Paris, and the author of the *Quaestio in utramque partem* who wrote on behalf of Philip the Fair, good Frenchmen first and foremost, tend to return to the Aristotelian conception of the State unit as the absolute and exclusive concentration of all group-life, and to bring out what Aristotle really meant when he said that the State was by nature ; or, by historical argument to claim that the kingdom of France had never been comprised in the Donation of Constantine, which they bitterly attack. Far more radical was the criticism of the transcendental method in argument found in the *Defensor pacis* (1324), the work of 'two pupils of damnation' Marsiglio of Padua and John of Jandun. Political society, they argue, starts in the recognition of common needs and rests upon the constant will to co-operation in attaining them : but men are continually disposed to act in a way that makes co-operation impossible ; hence arise the notions of morality and justice : the sense of right and wrong in conduct develops because reason recognizes that certain kinds of action are injurious to the community and may even destroy it. Social utility is the criterion here ; and government exists to further this co-operation, to repress injurious activities and to promote *tranquillitas,* the peace and security in which material and intellectual prosperity may flourish. But greater even than the return to Aristotle or the almost Machiavellian doctrine (at the time scarcely heeded) of social utility was the logic of fifteenth-century events, which the upholders of the Papal thesis of unity could not recognize : the discredit into which had fallen both Curial administration, owing to the Papal system of collation to benefices, and imperial sovereignty, owing to its weakness towards the electors ; the rise of mystical and heretical sects, which Rome could neither neutralize nor extirpate ; and the growing secularism, which first demanded the separation of Church and State, and then attacked the property and possessions of the clergy. One attempt was made to restore unity on a basis of self-government. The Conciliar movement aimed at federalism and decentralization in Church : it sought to make the supreme spiritual authority in Christendom a representative assembly ; to give voice and encouragement to the local units which more than two hundred years of ever-increasing Papal absolutism had silenced or overridden. It is to the Conciliar writers in particular that the generalizing of constitutional thought in Europe is due. The idea of representation borrowed from the practice of individual States, when applied to the government of the international Church, received an extension, a publicity unknown before. The conjoined effort to apply to the existing ecclesiastical organization the principle of a mixed constitution or polity, though it broke down at the Council of Basel, popularized and kept alive the idea of checks and balances against absolutism. For the time, however, canonists, Papal administrators, and Concordats made in national interests, combined to strengthen the old ways. Yet before we set it down as a noble dream we may remember that medieval orthodoxy, for all its suppressions and rigidities, stands as a permanent witness to the fact that the life of society is made up of many other activities and interests besides those which can be brought into relation with a political authority; its failure testifies to the difficulty of including the whole complex of human activities within a religious synthesis.

Some of the most far-reaching legacies of the Middle Ages are their contributions to the theory of government. During the epoch of the Reformation and the succeeding period of absolutism two great doctrines underlie the territorial sovereignty of national monarchs and the struggles of religious bodies for toleration and existence: the Divine Right of Kings, and the Right of Resistance based on the claim to enforce some kind of responsibility upon the ruler. The former perished with the collapse of the Dual Monarchy and the expulsion of the Habsburgs; its existence, after the liberal movements of the nineteenth century, had always been precarious. But the latter, in its various forms, has had a powerful and lasting influence upon the formation of

modern conceptions of political liberty. It has been invoked
not merely against the irresponsible sovereign, but against
the Machiavellian conception of the ' reason of state ' as
the basis of all governmental action, and the ' balance of
power ' as the aim of all international diplomacy. These
doctrines of Divine Right and its limitation have their roots
deep in medieval thought and practice.

In the full-blown doctrine of kingship by Divine Right,
as we find it in seventeenth-century works like Filmer's
Patriarcha, are grouped together three separate proposi-
tions : first, that the principle of monarchy is divinely
willed and ultimate, to the exclusion of all other forms of
government ; secondly, that the legitimate sovereign holds
his power in virtue both of hereditary right and also of
religious consecration ; thirdly, that the sovereign is
responsible to no one, is in fact absolute. The first of these
is partly the result of the study of Aristotle (Filmer strongly
emphasizes the *natural* sanction of Monarchy), partly an
inference drawn from the idea of the single divine government of the world strengthened later by the Romanist
idea (which we find later in Hobbes) of the necessity of
having a single impersonator or representative of the
community. The second represents a blending of primitive Teutonic and purely Christian notions. In each
of the early Germanic races a single family, elevated above
the others by a sort of religious or magic virtue, provided
the supply of kings. Within these families, in pagan times
considered to be heroic, that is, descended from gods, the
people chose the worthiest for king. The royal power,
upon this theory, derived its position from being at once
hereditary and elective. Though primogeniture became
during the twelfth century an almost universal rule in
France and England, the idea that the king held his power
as the elected representative of his people maintained itself

throughout the central medieval period, though in practice 'election' might mean very little more than acceptance.[1] The Church on the other hand was monarchist by principle, but not after the Teutonic fashion. She paid little consideration to hereditary right : the true King is the King who governs in conformity with the moral and religious principles of Catholicism, or—which comes to the same—in conformity with clerical interests. In France the Church recognized the successive usurpations of the Carolingian and Capet dynasties : in Germany she succeeded in obscuring the old idea of the legitimate line, until in the thirteenth century it could even be thought 'contrary to justice and reason' that the son of a king should succeed to the imperial throne. With parallels from the Old Testament and Byzantine precedents in her hands she invested kingship with the divine character. By the ceremony of unction in the coronation she lifted the king above the ranks of the laity. He is, as the Carolingian chancery was first to add, *Dei gratia rex*. The phrase was not meaningless ; it appeared, as M. Delisle showed, in Henry II's *diplomata*, after the murder of Thomas Becket—a potent reminder to the penitent king of the source whence his authority was derived. The Anonymous of York (temp. Henry I) who wrote fiercely against the Gregorian depreciators of the royal power, gives a good idea of the influence of the earlier Christian attribution of sanctity to the monarch : ' To him therefore (the king), who is blessed with such great blessings, consecrated and deified with such great sacraments, none other can rightly be preferred, none other is consecrated and deified with more or greater sacraments. Wherefore

[1] On the primitive Germanic custom see H. Brunner, *Deutsche Rechtsgeschichte*, i (1906), 167 : on the blending of hereditary and elective notions of monarchy, F. Kern, *Gottesgnadentum und Widerstandsrecht*, § 2, pp. 14–53, and Appendix I (' Erbrecht und Wahlrecht '), pp. 296–7, for a number of French and English examples.

he is not to be called a layman, since he is the Lord's anointed ' (*quia christus Domini est*).[1] The blending in the popular mind of the two originally distinct notions of legitimism and priestly consecration as the source of the king's divine power comes out very clearly in the royal practice of touching diseased persons. The Church surrounded with her ritual the exercise of the magical healing virtue, inherent in the monarchs of the Capet and Plantagenet families, and the ceremony lasted on into the period of absolutism, till killed in England by a change of dynasty, in France by the mockery of the Enlightenment. The crowds that flocked to Louis XIV and Charles II to be touched for scrofula were paying their testimony to a doubly derived conception of sacerdotal kingship.

Consciousness of a divine nature may lead to irresponsibility. One remembers the famous phrase which a Liège chronicler put into the mouth of the Emperor Henry III. When the Bishop of Liège summoned him to respect the priestly dignity, he replied : ' I too have been anointed with holy oil, and by that have received supreme power.' Against such dangerous pretensions to independence the Church reacted : unction was omitted from among the sacraments, and the publicists of the *Curia* systematically abased the *regnum* before the *Sacerdotium*. But the idea of the divinity of kingship had struck the royal mind too deeply. The arguments advanced by Papal and imperial protagonists to the great struggle of the thirteenth century found their echo at a French court outraged by Boniface VIII. French authors in the time of Philip the Fair assert that the King of France holds his kingdom immediately from God alone. The Papal claim to hold sovereignty by Divine grant is met by the claims of secular sovereigns to a similar

---

[1] M.G.SS. *Libelli de Lite*, iii. 676. On the whole subject of miracle-working kings see M. Bloch, *Les Rois thaumaturges*.

tenure. It is not a far step to Wyclif's argument in the *De Officio Regis* that the king reflects the Godhead of Christ, the priest only his manhood : the king is not subject to positive law : he is *legibus solutus*, his obedience to his own law is voluntary, not compulsory. The logical end of this doctrine is absolutism, the principle which Richard II attempted to put into practice not only by the declaration (which he had borrowed from Boniface VIII) that the laws were in his own mouth and at times within his own breast, but by the whole course of his actions from 1394–9. It is interesting to find secular absolutism, born from the struggle against the international Papacy, in its early stages relying upon the same theological arguments as its opponent. The fundamental medieval notion of the divine origin of all power could cut both ways. In an atmosphere of growing national and territorial consciousness it served as the architect of national monarchy. One further wrench and the State, personified by the monarch, is, in Maitland's brilliant phrase, ' parsonified ' as well : the Erastian régime of the sixteenth century has come into being. James I will declare that kings are justly called gods, ' judges over all their subjects, and in all causes, and yet accountable to none but God only ; that ' to the King is due both the affection of the soul and the service of the body of his subjects '.

The post-Reformation doctrine of Resistance is the outcome of various theoretical restraints and limitations upon monarchy entertained throughout the Middle Ages. The chief of these are the conceptions of an original contract, of the subjection of the ruler to law, human or divine, and of the sovereignty of the Community, whether the people or the group. Each represents in some measure a reaction against the idea of Divine Right, to the formation of which the Middle Ages made, as we have just seen, so considerable a contribution.

The notion that the sovereign is bound by a body of more or less definitely formulated rights which he was bound to observe is a fundamental Teutonic axiom which Roman Law was never able to overcome in this country. In the open struggles between King and nation, personified at first by baronial, later by Parliamentary, elements, it is the assumption that underlies all attempts of the opposition from 1215 to 1688. It is responsible for the idea of 'the reign of law', the supremacy of the constitution, which animates the political systems of the English-speaking peoples. Originally it derives, no doubt, from the restraints of customary codes. If the King commits an act contrary to the 'good customs' of his subjects, their resistance, as the Sachsenspiegel very clearly states, is not to be considered a failure of allegiance. Bracton, while never for a moment denying the royal supremacy, holds that its power should be exercised subject to the law: 'there is no king where arbitrary will, not the law, reigns'; law, the bridle of the royal power, is the ordinance of king and magnates, passed after discussion in the feudal assembly; it is the adjudication and interpretation of already existing custom rather than a work of original creation. The king is like a judge interpreting a system of rights and duties to which he owes his own position and which he is bound to uphold. These were generally received principles in Europe. But in England where the Norman and Angevin kings had created a centralized bureaucracy and a common law, they had from the thirteenth century onwards a peculiar and continuous development. Here there is far smaller sense of a fundamental law, far greater recognition of the binding force of an instrument that is being progressively fashioned by addition, modification, or change. The lawyers blended from year to year new royal justice with the old customary rules, the new royal machinery of government with the old communal institutions, and using the language and technical forms of the civil and canon law created in time a new system which could stand by itself upon a basis neither wholly feudal nor wholly monarchical; and the factor which gave this system its stability and continuity and so perpetuated the doctrine that law should govern the state was the rise of a representative assembly, in intimate alliance with the lawyers, which in course of time was to advance the claim that all legislation must be by the Crown in Parliament.

But there is a higher restraint upon the royal power than the checks of custom and a common law evolved by the lawyers and Parliament. The Romans had identified their *ius gentium*, the law applying generally to cases in which others than Roman citizens were concerned, with the Stoic Law of Nature. The process was carried farther by identifying the Law of Nature with the Law of God. At the head of the *Decretum* of Gratian stands the statement that the Law of Nature is the golden rule, comprised in the Law and the Gospel, supreme over all kinds of law by antiquity and dignity, immutable, prevailing over both custom and express ordinance. It is here that Sir Frederick Pollock has found the origin of the English lawyers' maxim that a custom cannot be good if it is contrary to reason, and of the doctrine current from the sixteenth to the eighteenth century (though not put into effectual practice) that a statute may be held void for being repugnant to reason or ' common right '. Still, the law of nature is not entirely the same as the law of the Church or divine law : it was left to Aquinas to make their relation precise by his definition that natural law is divine law so far as revealed through the medium of natural reason : at all events it could not be in conflict with the divine law, of which it was part. Such law, like the king's equity, could be of practical application when legal texts and authorities on the disputing sides were silent : otherwise it formed throughout the Middle Ages and down to the Renaissance a weapon of controversy used in aid of contending opinions ; most of all, perhaps, it was employed to strengthen the thesis that the commands of the prince who misbehaved towards his subjects were not binding upon them and might be lawfully resisted. It helped the distinction which clericalist writers used to draw between the legitimate prince and the tyrant, with its inevitable conclusion, eagerly snatched at later by the pamphleteers of the *Ligue*, that the overbearing monarch might be put to death. In so far as it stood to perpetuate the old distinction between nature and convention it bequeathed an idea of importance in the political philosophy of the seventeenth and eighteenth centuries. But it is when purged of clericalism and applied to the relations of States with one another that its greatest contribution of the doctrine of Natural Law to the modern age is seen. Grotius in his great work *De Iure Belli et Pacis* accepts the contemporary world of absolute territorial princes : he is not concerned with a theory of resistance or any criticism of the conduct of kings inside their countries : he bases his work on the assumption that men are in a society held together by a natural law which makes certain common duties binding : he held up the notion of a law universal in scope, commanding respect and reverence, that was in effect a sense of international right, which would condemn certain actions of State towards State by attaching to them the stigma of a breach of obligation. Here Grotius—and Gentilis with him—struck at the heart of the Machiavellian total independence of States, their posture as gladiators in the European arena : the service these jurists rendered here, and so ultimately to international law, is that they succeeded in limiting the predominance of the ' reason of state ' as a received rule of international conduct.

The medieval law of nature, stripped of its theological clothing, handed to the opponents of Divine Right and the philosophers of later centuries a doctrine of natural rights and obligations of great significance in the drift towards democratic theory from the Middle Ages to the French Revolution. It was maintained that government derived its authority from a voluntary act by which individuals contracted themselves out of the state of nature ; and that in cases where this authority was abused the contracting parties might rise and take measures against the offender, inasmuch as they retained from that state certain inalienable rights over which no legal obligations could prevail. The contractual theory, as we find it in Protestant and Huguenot publicists, assumes two phases in the compact : an original social compact of man with man made in the state of nature ; and a governmental contract of the community so formed with the individual (or body) who is to rule them. Medieval thinkers, to many of whom the notion of contract was present, do not distinguish very clearly between these stages : if anything, they concentrated upon the latter. The doctrine of resistance to authority they based primarily on the violation of an implicit governmental agreement between lord and subject. ' Since no one ', wrote Manegold of Lutterbach in defence of Gregory VII, ' can create himself Emperor or King, the people elevates a single one person over itself to the end that he may rule and govern it according to the principle of righteous government ; but if in any wise he transgresses the contract of which he is chosen he absolves the people from the obligation of sub-mission, because he has first broken faith with it.' The theory alike here and in post-reformation writers like George Buchanan, Du Plessis Mornay, and Hooker is the outcome of feudalism, whose essence lies in a contractual relation, a reciprocity of protection and service. Lord and vassal were bound by mutual obligations : these unfulfilled, the feudal tie is broken, the oath on either side cannot bind. The king's promise in his Coronation oath could be construed in a similar way. But the reason why it was the governmental rather than the social contract for which the Middle Ages provided its examples and its theories lies perhaps in the fact that the medieval doctrine of popular sovereignty scarcely rested on a contractual basis. It was grounded upon something more primitive, less individualistic ; something which partook more of the nature of a common will and savoured less of the abstract rights of the individual ; something, be it said, that would endure when Hume and Kant had demolished the contractual basis of political obligation.

That foundation was the right of the group or the community taken as a whole. Frequently this view was founded on an exposition of the famous passage in the *Lex Regia*, *Quod principi placuit legis habet vigorem*, which traced the supremacy of the prince to the grant of supreme power made originally by the people. The clearest medieval statement of it was given in a remarkable speech by Philippe Pot, Seneschal of Burgundy, at a meeting of the French States-General in 1484, after the death of the oppressive Louis XI. ' I wish to tell you,' he said, ' as far as my intelligence will allow me, what I have learned from great and wise men on the authority and the liberty of States. It is certain that the royal power is a dignity and not the property (*haereditas*) of the prince. History relates that at the first the sovereign people created Kings by its vote. It is in its own interest that each nation gave itself a master. The whole world repeats that the State is the creation of the people. If it is so, how could the people abandon its charge ? How can flatterers attribute supreme power to the prince who exists only in virtue of the people ? That being so, what is the power in France which has the right of governing when the king is incapable of doing so? Clearly this task reverts neither to a sole prince nor a handful of men, but to all, that is the people, the giver of power. This task it must take up as it were its own, all the more so because it is always the victim, the sole victim of a bad government.' It has been maintained that this right of the group rests in the first instance upon the Germanic idea of a Fellowship, that idea which in the nineteenth century was revived in the revolt against the Romanism which since the Reception had held down the native conceptions of Germanic law. 'Our Germanic Fellowship', wrote Maitland in his famous introduction to Gierke's work on the *Political Theories of the Middle Age*, 'is no fiction, no symbol, no piece of the State's machinery, no collective name for individuals, but a living organism and a real person with a body and members and a will of its own. Itself can will, itself can act; it wills and acts by the men who are its organs as a man wills and acts by brain, mouth, and hand. It is not a fictitious person; it is a *Gesamtperson* and its will is a *Gesamtwille*; it is a group person and its will is a group will.' Yet for all the richness of medieval group life, cities, villages, gilds, ecclesiastical communities and universities, medieval thinkers never succeeded in getting a real expression of this view; they tended to have recourse to Roman Law, and Roman Law would not admit these bodies to be corporate persons in reality, but only by a fiction of the law. Their personality was fictitious, and the fiction theory soon led to the idea that bodies of such character can be created only by the State. The body may indeed behave as a person, act as an entity, yet a corporation so received can only act through specific individuals who are related to it, much as the guardians of a minor are related to their ward; the minor has no will of his own and can only act through them.

To deny real personality to groups, to regard them simply as congeries of men and to fail to realize the sense of corporateness found within them, seemed to Gierke and Maitland the tragedy of modern as well as of medieval thought;[1] and many thinkers of the present, discarding the view that real personality must be predicated of the State alone, have turned back to some federalist idea of the State such as that found in Althusius, who starts not from the individual but from the family, and, in Dr. Figgis's words, ' rises by a series of concentric circles from the family to the town, to the province and the State'; who regards the rights which he allows to families and provinces as anterior to the State, as its foundation, and as subsisting always within it. This federalist, or, more properly speaking, organic idea of the State, raises many difficult questions. To what extent may one kind of group be credited with a corporate character rather than another, and how is group-consciousness to be expressed juridically? Would such expression be, as a friend remarked, ' to substitute a hydra for a single-throated dragon'? Such problems, in themselves of the highest moment to our social and industrial well-being, cannot fall within the scope of a brief historical essay.

The Middle Ages have left two great ideals of political organization. On the one hand they transmitted, though not in a sharply defined way, from the Ancient World the

---

[1] It must at once be added that Maitland showed that in England our acceptance of the fiction theory and the concession theory has been very slight; that the analogy of guardian and ward does not apply to us, since the English guardian is not a representative whose act binds his ward, except within narrow limits; and that the institution of the trust has made possible the growth of bodies with most of the practical advantages of corporations. Cf. also his article ' Trust and Corporation' in *Collected Papers*, iii. 321–404. For a full discussion see, among others, W. M. Geldart, *Legal Personality*, and Raymond Saleilles, *De la Personnalité juridique*.

unitary conception of the State, whether that State be small, as the cities of which Aristotle wrote, or oecumenical, as imperial Rome ; a conception which would unite Canonist, Jesuit, and modern nineteenth-century nationalist in the common desire to concentrate all power at a single centre and to regard every right as a privileged emanation from that central source ; which lays particular stress upon the necessity of a single legal sovereign, ultimate and omnipotent. On the other hand they have given us the more truly characteristic view of the State as a unity in plurality, a community of communities, each of which possesses inherent life and powers, performing work essential to the well-being of the community and performing it in its own way. Neither of these theories in its original form would satisfy the requirements of modern life. To reconcile authority and freedom, direction and spontaneity, civil servant and artist must work hand in hand ; but there is little doubt that it is with the second of these bequests, in some adapted form, that the verdict of the future will reside.

E. F. JACOB.

INDEX